Fodor's 94
Arizona

D1152140

Fodor's Travel Publications, Inc.
New York • Toronto • London • Sydney • Auckland

Fodor's Arizona

Editor: Craig Seligman
Editorial Contributors: Suzanne Carmichael, William Hafford, Mark Hein, Edie Jarolim, Valerie Martone, Marcy Pritchard, Trudy Thompson Rice
Creative Director: Fabrizio LaRocca
Cartographers: David Lindroth, Mapping Specialists
Illustrator: Karl Tanner
Cover Photograph: Peter Guttman

Design: Vignelli Associates

Contents

Maps

Foreword

Many people have assisted in preparing this guide. Special thanks go to Marjorie Magnusson of the Arizona Office of Tourism, whose helpfulness was matched only by her cheerfulness. Thanks also to Frank Miller of the Sedona Chamber of Commerce; L. Greer Price, Information Specialist at Grand Canyon National Park; Roberta Lopez and Sally Hankin of the Tucson Metropolitan Convention & Visitors Bureau; Pat Koester and Robert Reames of the Tombstone Main Street organization; Stan Dupuy of the Bisbee Chamber of Commerce; and, especially, Tim Rodriguez of the Flagstaff Convention and Visitors Bureau, who knows everything there is to know about the area and shared that information generously.

While every care has been taken to ensure the accuracy of the information in this guide, the passage of time will always bring change, and consequently the publisher cannot accept responsibility for errors that may occur.

All prices and opening times quoted here are based on information supplied to us at press time. Hours and admission fees may change, however, and the prudent traveler will avoid inconvenience by calling ahead.

Fodor's wants to hear about your travel experiences, both pleasant and unpleasant. When a hotel or restaurant fails to live up to its billing, let us know and we will investigate the complaint and revise our entries where the facts warrant it.

Send your letters to the editors of Fodor's Travel Publications, 201 E. 50th Street, New York, NY 10022.

Highlights'94 and Fodor's Choice

Highlights '94

The Grand Canyon lures more tourists than any other natural attraction in the nation, and Arizona ranks fifth among the 50 states as a destination for foreign visitors. Now that Arizonans have finally adopted (by popular vote) a **Martin Luther King, Jr., Day,** the state's tourism industry—which had been suffering from embarrassing and highly publicized convention and vacationer boycotts—should boom even bigger.

Sports The King Day vote also restored Arizona to grace with the National Football League; the league has voted to play the 1996 **Super Bowl XXX** in Tempe's Sun Devil Stadium. The **America West Arena,** which opened in 1992, serves as home to the National Basketball Association Phoenix Suns and their superstar Charles Barkley. It's also a venue for rock concerts, and the city is hoping the stadium will help in its bid for a National Hockey League expansion franchise.

Golfers can look forward to two new public courses in the works for 1994. The **Pohlcat Mountain** championship course in Phoenix should open late this year, and Sun City's **Palm Valley,** which unveiled nine holes in 1993, will finish the final nine early this year.

Southwest Heritage The **Tucson Museum of Art** has scheduled its fourth annual **American Women Artists & the West Show and Sale** for February and March. In a similar vein, the **Phoenix Art Musum** will open "Cowboy Artists of America" in late October; the show will concentrate on paintings and bronzes. **"Common Ground/Uncommon Vision: The Michael and Julie Hall Collection of American Folk Art,"** opening in early March, will include paintings, drawings, sculptures, weather vanes, decoys, ceramics, and just about every other kind of object that American folk artists are likely to come up with.

Native American Culture Arizona has more Indian tribes, lands, and populations than any other state. The **Hopi Indians** perform ceremonial dances on weekends throughout the late spring and summer in their villages in the Northeastern part of the state (*see* Chapter 4). Each year Window Rock hosts the five-day **Navajo Nation Fair;** this year's fair, slated for September 7–11, includes horse racing, an intertribal powwow, arts and crafts, traditional cookery, song and dance competitions, and a Navajo Nation parade.

Shopping The **Arizona Center,** a $515 million multiphase development encompassing an eight-block stretch, has become downtown Phoenix's trendiest meeting and people-watching place. More than three acres of restaurants, shops, and entertainment facilities (including a movie theater) are already up and operating; construction is to begin this year on a 600-room hotel, as well as millions of additional square feet of commercial and retail space.

Fodor's Choice

No two people will agree on what makes a perfect vacation, but it's fun and helpful to know what others think. We hope you'll have a chance to experience some of Fodor's Choices yourself in Arizona. For detailed information about each entry, refer to the appropriate chapter.

Activities

A mule ride or hike to the bottom of the Grand Canyon

A raft trip on the Colorado, white water or quiet water, Grand Canyon

The East Rim Tour, along the Grand Canyon's South Rim

Lake Powell excursion to Rainbow Bridge, The Northeast

Picnic in Monument Valley, The Northeast

Hiking tour to Betatakin Ruin, Navajo National Monument, The Northeast

Hiking into Canyon de Chelly National Monument, The Northeast

Looking through the telescope at Lowell Observatory, North-Central Arizona

Hiking along the rim of a volcano at Sunset Crater National Monument, North-Central Arizona

A Jeep ride through the red rocks of Sedona, North-Central Arizona

An early morning walk through the Desert Botanical Gardens, Phoenix

Climbing Squaw Peak at sunset, Phoenix

Casa Grande Ruins National Monument, Central Arizona

San Xavier del Bac Mission, Tucson

Arizona–Sonora Desert Museum, Tucson

The Copper Queen Mine, Bisbee, Southern Arizona

Scenic Drives

The 210-mile drive from the South Rim to the North Rim, Grand Canyon

The dirt-road drive to Point Sublime, North Rim, Grand Canyon

West Rim Drive, South Rim, Grand Canyon

Petrified Forest National Monument—U.S. 163 from
Kayenta to the Goosenecks of the San Juan River, The
Northeast

AZ 264 across the Hopi Mesas, The Northeast

Flagstaff to Sedona via Oak Creek Canyon,
North-Central Arizona

Sedona to Jerome, North-Central Arizona

Phoenix to Prescott and Wickenburg,
Phoenix and Central Arizona

Along I–10 east of Benson through Texas Canyon,
Southern Arizona

Tucson to Kitt Peak, Tucson and Southern Arizona

Shopping

Cameron Trading Post, Grand Canyon

Desert View Trading Post, South Rim, Grand Canyon

Hubbell Trading Post, The Northeast

Navajo Arts and Crafts Enterprises in Cameron
and Window Rock, The Northeast

Coconino Center for the Arts, Flagstaff, North-Central
Arizona

Tlaquepaque Mall, Sedona, North-Central Arizona

The Mercado and Arizona Center,
Phoenix

The Heard Museum gift shop, Phoenix

Main Street, Scottsdale, Central Arizona

Fourth Avenue, Tucson

San Xavier Plaza, Tucson

Tubac, Southern Arizona

Dining

L'Auberge de Sedona, North-Central Arizona (*Very
Expensive*)

Vincent's on Camelback, Phoenix (*Very Expensive*)

El Tovar Dining Room, South Rim, Grand Canyon
(*Expensive–Very Expensive*)

Janos, Tucson (*Expensive–Very Expensive*)

La Hacienda, Scottsdale, Central Arizona
(*Expensive–Very Expensive*)

Compass Room, Phoenix (*Expensive*)

Café Terra Cotta, Tucson (*Moderate*)

Grand Canyon Lodge Dining Room, North Rim, Grand Canyon (*Moderate*)

Heartline Café, Sedona, North-Central Arizona (*Moderate*)

Rustler's Rooste, Phoenix and Central Arizona (*Moderate*)

Rainbow Room at Wahweap Lodge, Lake Powell, Northeast Arizona (*Moderate*)

Adrian's, Phoenix (*Inexpensive*)

Café Poca Cosa, Tucson (*Inexpensive*)

Lodging

The Buttes, Phoenix and Central Arizona (*Expensive–Very Expensive*)

El Tovar Hotel, South Rim, Grand Canyon (*Expensive–Very Expensive*)

The Pointe Hilton on South Mountain, Phoenix (*Expensive–Very Expensive*)

Sheraton Tucson El Conquistador, Tucson (*Expensive–Very Expensive*)

Arizona Inn, Tucson (*Expensive*)

Enchantment Resort, Sedona, North-Central Arizona (*Expensive*)

Thunderbird Lodge at Canyon de Chelly, The Northeast (*Expensive*)

Wahweap Lodge at Lake Powell, The Northeast (*Expensive*)

Best Western Executive Park, Phoenix (*Moderate*)

Casa Tierra Bed & Breakfast, Tucson (*Moderate*)

Grand Canyon Lodge, North Rim, Grand Canyon (*Moderate*)

Little America of Flagstaff, North-Central Arizona (*Moderate*)

Sky Ranch Lodge, Sedona, North-Central Arizona (*Inexpensive–Moderate*)

Hopi Cultural Center Motel at Second Mesa, Northeast Arizona (*Inexpensive*)

Motel 6 Scottsdale, Central Arizona (*Inexpensive*)

Arizona

The United States

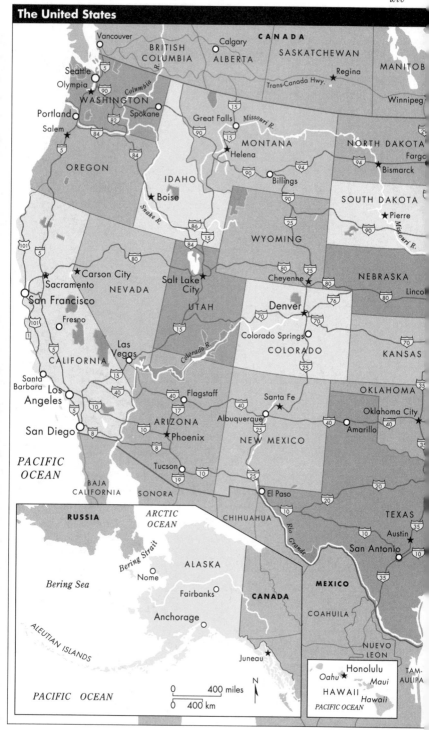

CANADA

BRITISH COLUMBIA — ALBERTA — SASKATCHEWAN — MANITOB

Vancouver • Calgary • Regina ★ Winnipeg

Seattle •
Olympia ★
WASHINGTON
Spokane •
Portland ○
Salem ★
OREGON
Trans-Canada Hwy.
Columbia R.

Great Falls ★
Missouri R.
MONTANA
Helena ★
Billings ○
NORTH DAKOTA
Fargo •
★ Bismarck

IDAHO
★ Boise
Snake R.

SOUTH DAKOTA
★ Pierre
Missouri R.

WYOMING
Cheyenne ★

NEBRASKA
Lincol •

Carson City ★
Sacramento ★
San Francisco ○
Fresno ○
NEVADA
Salt Lake City ★
UTAH
Denver ★
Colorado Springs ○
COLORADO
Colorado R.
KANSAS

CALIFORNIA
Las Vegas ○
Santa Barbara ○
Los Angeles ○
San Diego ○

Flagstaff •
ARIZONA
Phoenix ★
Tucson ○
Santa Fe ★
Albuquerque ○
NEW MEXICO
OKLAHOMA
Oklahoma City ★
Amarillo ○

PACIFIC OCEAN

BAJA CALIFORNIA
SONORA
CHIHUAHUA
El Paso ○
Rio Grande

TEXAS
Austin ★
San Antonio ○

RUSSIA
ARCTIC OCEAN
Bering Strait
Nome ○
Bering Sea
ALASKA
Fairbanks ○
Anchorage ○
CANADA
Juneau ★
ALEUTIAN ISLANDS
PACIFIC OCEAN

MEXICO
COAHUILA
NUEVO LEON
TAM-AULIPA

0 ——— 400 miles
0 ——— 400 km
N

Honolulu ★
Oahu ★ Maui
HAWAII
Hawaii
PACIFIC OCEAN

World Time Zones

MONDAY
SUNDAY

International Date Line

+12 +13

-9

-10

-11

-10

+11

+12

-7

-3

-4

-7

-8

-6

-5 -4

-3:30

-4

-5

-4 -3

-3

Numbers below vertical bands relate each zone to Greenwich Mean Time (0 hrs.).
Local times frequently differ from these general indications,
as indicated by light-face numbers on map.

| +11 | +12 - | -11 | -10 | -9 | -8 | -7 | -6 | -5 | -4 | -3 | -2 |

Algiers, **29**

Anchorage, **3**

Athens, **41**

Auckland, **1**

Baghdad, **46**

Bangkok, **50**

Beijing, **54**

Berlin, **34**

Bogotá, **19**

Budapest, **37**

Buenos Aires, **24**

Caracas, **22**

Chicago, **9**

Copenhagen, **33**

Dallas, **10**

Delhi, **48**

Denver, **8**

Djakarta, **53**

Dublin, **26**

Edmonton, **7**

Hong Kong, **56**

Honolulu, **2**

Istanbul, **40**

Jerusalem, **42**

Johannesburg, **44**

Lima, **20**

Lisbon, **28**

London (Greenwich), **27**

Los Angeles, **6**

Madrid, **38**

Manila, **57**

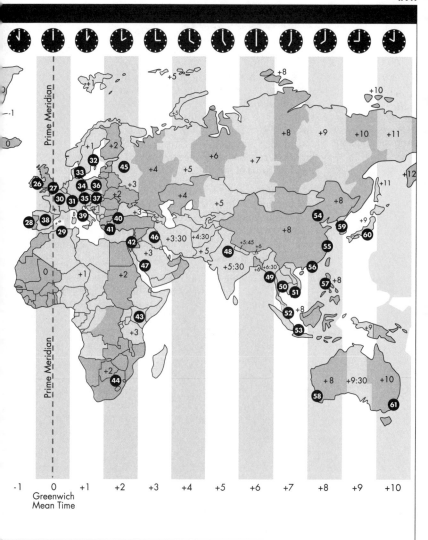

-1   0   +1   +2   +3   +4   +5   +6   +7   +8   +9   +10

Greenwich
Mean Time

Mecca, **47**	Ottawa, **14**	San Francisco, **5**	Toronto, **13**
Mexico City, **12**	Paris, **30**	Santiago, **21**	Vancouver, **4**
Miami, **18**	Perth, **58**	Seoul, **59**	Vienna, **35**
Montréal, **15**	Reykjavík, **25**	Shanghai, **55**	Warsaw, **36**
Moscow, **45**	Rio de Janeiro, **23**	Singapore, **52**	Washington, D.C., **17**
Nairobi, **43**	Rome, **39**	Stockholm, **32**	Yangon, **49**
New Orleans, **11**	Saigon (Ho Chi Minh	Sydney, **61**	Zürich, **31**
New York City, **16**	City), **51**	Tokyo, **60**	

Introduction

By Mark Hein

Mark Hein is an editor and a writer in the features department of the Arizona Republic.

Arizona is an ancient land, etched with the long past of the Earth and of the human race. Aeons of our planet's story are written in the deep, multicolored walls of the Grand Canyon and the cathedral-like stone spires of Monument Valley. Ages of human history echo in the hidden grandeur of Canyon de Chelly, the "sky villages" perched atop Hopi reservation mesas, and the prehistoric ruins of Montezuma Castle and Casa Grande.

At the same time, Arizona is a lively hub of modern life, a quickening center in the emerging web of communications and trade, travel and recreation that links western North America with the Pacific Rim. Phoenix, the state's capital and the Southwest's metropolitan center, is America's ninth-largest and fastest-growing city.

Visitors to Arizona usually wonder about the desert: How hot is it? What should we wear? Is it safe? These are intelligent questions about a land where summer daytime temperatures often exceed 100°F (38°C), major rivers run underground, and the native flora are spiny cactus and thorny scrub.

What few people realize is that Arizona has two deserts. The low desert (roughly the southwestern third of the state) is indeed arid and dotted with tall saguaro cacti, but the high desert—the northeastern tier, with the Grand Canyon and Navajo and Hopi lands—is a savannalike plain, thousands of feet above sea level and mantled in snow all winter. And the middle third of Arizona is not desert at all but rather mountainous terrain, with alpine lakes and the world's largest forest of ponderosa pines.

Even with—and partly because of—its low-desert climate, Arizona draws people almost irresistibly. Long one of the nation's prime tourist destinations, visited annually by millions from around the world, in the past two decades Arizona has been one of America's fastest-growing states, as tens of thousands of immigrants arrive each year.

That growth has transformed Phoenix from a farming town of 60,000 people in 1940 to an urban center of 1 million in 1990; it has also doubled and redoubled the population of Tucson, the "Old Pueblo" in the southern part of the state. Yet Arizona remains a place of boundless vistas, with more than 80% of its land in U.S. and state parks and preserves or Indian reservations. Whether they are in the deserts or the mountains, Arizona's small towns still have vast spaces between them.

Arizona has also retained much of its rich Indian and Hispanic heritage. More Native Americans live here than in any other state, and the Hopi village of Oraibi is the oldest continually inhabited community in North America. Hispanic families arrive daily from Mexico and Central America, many following routes opened by Spanish explorers a century before the Pilgrims landed; numerous Tucson families trace their lineage to Mexican pioneers who arrived in the days of the American Revolution.

Visitors can readily see some of the gifts modern Arizona has received from these ancient cultures: the Indian and Spanish names on most of its mountains and rivers, plants, and animals, even its streets; the pervasive influence of Hopi and Mexican architecture in homes and public buildings. Other aspects of this heritage appear only after some study: the canals that carry Arizona's mountain streams into the low desert, the legal system that gives husband and wife equal shares in their "community property."

One part of Arizona's cultural heritage that almost everyone gets to share is the relaxed pace and style of living: In almost everything, from clothing to art, from home decor to meals, the desert dwellers of each era have learned to prize the unhurried and the informal, to accept the calming lessons of the heat and the majestic landscape. Leave your tie and tails at home and, even if you're on business, plan to take time out: Lean back for a leisurely late lunch during the hottest part of the day; stretch out under a patio awning beside a pool or fountain during the long, cool evenings.

And wherever you take your siesta, cast your eye toward the horizon: You'll see deep skies and luminous, gold-edged sunsets; the towering silhouettes of buttes and mountain ranges, their rugged surfaces subtly alive with shifting shadows and pastel colors; a forest of widely spaced saguaros, standing like many-armed sentinels amid sketchy bushes of creosote and ocotillo, while birds and lizards dart from one spiny haven to the next; the long, green bowl of a mountain meadow, dusted with poppy clusters and blue lupine beds, edged in shimmering aspens. Arizonans and visitors alike never tire of watching the play of sun and shadows on some corner of this magnificent land.

1 Essential Information

Before You Go

Visitor Information

Even if you're not the type to plan your Arizona vacation down to the last cactus, golf ball, or canyon vista, why not do a bit of reading and research anyway? A descriptive passage, a colorful photo, or a historical reference might inspire an unexpected turn or spontaneous twist in your itinerary. With knowledge gleaned and imagination triggered, you'll find even preplanned vacations can take on an aura of adventure.

The **Arizona Office of Tourism** (1100 W. Washington, Phoenix 85007, tel. 602/542–TOUR or 800/842–8257) can send a comprehensive tourist kit as well as a information on the 14 tribal councils, a map of reservations, and a list of addresses and phone numbers.

The **Hopi Tribe Office of Public Relations** (Box 123, Kykotsmovi 86039, tel. 602/734–2441) and the **Navajoland Tourism Department** (Box 663, Window Rock 86515, tel. 602/871–6659 or 871–7371) can inform you of upcoming tribal activities.

Tours and Packages

Should you buy your travel arrangements to Arizona packaged or do it yourself? There are advantages either way. Buying packaged arrangements saves you money, particularly if you can find a program that includes exactly the features you want. You also get a pretty good idea of what your trip will cost from the outset. Generally, you have two options: escorted tours and independent packages. Each has its advantages.

Escorted tours are most often via motorcoach, with a tour director in charge. They're ideal if you don't mind having limited free time and vacationing with strangers. Your baggage is handled, your time rigorously scheduled, and most meals planned. Escorted tours are therefore the most hassle-free way to see a destination, as well as generally the least expensive. Independent packages allow plenty of flexibility. They generally include airline travel and hotels, with certain options available, such as sightseeing, car rental, and excursions. Independent packages are usually more expensive than escorted tours, but your time is your own.

Travel agents are your best source of recommendations for both tours and packages. They will have the largest selection, and the cost to you is the same as buying direct. Whatever program you ultimately choose, be sure to find out exactly what is included: taxes, tips, transfers, meals, baggage handling, ground transportation, entertainment, excursions, sports, or recreation (and rental equipment if necessary). Ask about the level of hotel used, its location, the size of its rooms, the kind of beds, and its amenities, such as pool, room service, or programs for children, if they're important to you. Find out the operator's cancellation penalties. Nearly everyone charges them, and the only way to avoid them is to buy trip-cancellation insurance. Also ask about the single supplement, a surcharge assessed to solo travelers. Some operators do not make you pay it if you agree to be matched up with a roommate of the same sex, even if one is not found by departure time. Remember that a program that has features you won't use, whether for rental sporting equipment or discounted museum admissions, may not be the most cost-wise choice for you. Don't buy a Rolls-Royce, even at a reduced price, if all you want is a Chevy!

Fully Escorted Tours   Escorted tours are usually sold in three categories: deluxe, first-class, and tourist or budget class. The most important differences are the price, of course, and the level of accommodations. Some operators specialize in one category, while others offer a range.

Top operators include **Maupintour** (Box 807, Lawrence, KS 66044, tel. 800/255–4266 or 913/843–1211) and **Tauck Tours** (11 Wilton Rd., Westport, CT 06881, tel. 800/468–2825 or 203/226–6911) in the deluxe category; **Bixler Tours** (Box 37, Hiram, OH 44234, tel 800/325–5087 or 216/569–3222), **Domenico Tours** (751 Broadway, Bayonne, NJ 07002, tel. 800/554–8687 or 201/823–8687), **Gadabout Tours** (700 E. Tahquitz Way, Palm Springs, CA 92262, tel. 800/952–5068 or 619/325–5556), **Globus-Gateway** (95-25 Queens Blvd., Rego Park, NY 11374, tel. 800/221–0090 or 718/268–7000), and **Talmage Tours** (1223 Walnut St., Philadelphia, PA 19107, tel. 800/825–6243 or 215/923–7100 in the first-class range; and Globus' sister operator, **Cosmos** (at the same address) in the budget category.

Most itineraries are jam-packed with sightseeing, so you see a lot in a short amount of time (usually one place per day). To judge just how fast-paced the tour is, review the itinerary carefully. If you are in a different hotel each night, you will be getting up early each day to head out, travel to your next destination, do some sightseeing, have dinner, and go to bed, then you'll start all over again. If you want some free time, make sure it's mentioned in the tour brochure; if you want to be escorted to every meal, confirm that any tour you consider does that. Also, when comparing programs, be sure to find out if the motorcoach is air-conditioned and has a restroom on board. Make your selection based on price and stops on the itinerary.

Independent Packages   Independent packages are offered by airlines, tour operators who may also do escorted programs, and any number of other companies from large, established firms to small, new entrepreneurs.

Airlines offering packages to Arizona include **American Airlines Fly AAway Vacations** (tel. 800/321–2121), **Continental Airlines' Grand Destinations** (tel. 800/634–5555), **Delta Dream Vacations** (tel. 800/872–7786), and **United Airlines' Vacation Planning Center** (tel. 800/328–6877). **Gogo Tours,** which you must book through a travel agent, also offers a variety of packages to the state.

Their programs come in a wide range of prices based on levels of luxury and options—in addition to hotel and airfare, sightseeing, car rental, transfers, admission to local attractions, and other extras. Note that when pricing different packages, it sometimes pays to purchase the same arrangements separately, as when a rock-bottom promotional airfare is being offered, for example. Again, base your choice what's available at your budget for the destinations you want to visit.

Special-interest Travel Special-interest programs may be fully escorted or independent. Some require a certain amount of expertise, but most are for the average traveler with an interest and are usually hosted by experts in the subject matter. When the program is escorted, it enjoys the advantages and disadvantages of all escorted programs; because your fellow travelers are apt to be passionate or knowledgeable about the subject, they can prove as enjoyable a part of your travel experience as the destination itself. The price range is wide, but the cost is usually higher—sometimes a lot higher—than for ordinary escorted tours and packages, because of the expert guiding and special activities.

Biking **Backroads** (1516 5th St., Suite Q333, Berkeley, CA 94710-1740, tel. 800/243–8747 or 510/527–1555) and **Bike Arizona** (7454 E. Broadway #102, Tucson 85710, tel. 602/722–3228) has multiday bike tours that include hotels and meals.

Hiking **Expeditions on Foot** (2925 E. Villa Maria Dr., Phoenix 85032, tel. 602/482–3992) guides hikers and backpackers through desert and mountain landscapes.

Motorcycle Tours **Western States Motorcycle Tours** (543 Wilshire Dr., Phoenix 85003, tel. 602/258–9048) will help you play out all your *Easy Rider* fantasies.

Tips for British Travelers

Tourist Information Contact the **United States Travel and Tourism Administration** (Box 1EN, London W1A 1EN, tel. 071/495–4466).

Passports and Visas British citizens need a valid 10-year passport. A visa is not necessary unless (1) you are planning to stay more than 90 days; (2) your trip is for purposes other than vacation; (3) you have at some time been refused a visa to, or refused admission to, the United States, or have been required to leave by the U.S. Immigration and Naturalization Service; or (4) you do not have a return or onward ticket. You will need to fill out the Visa Waiver Form, 1–94W supplied by the airline.

To apply for a visa or for more information, call the U.S. Embassy's Visa Information Line (tel. 0891/200–290; calls cost 48p per minute or 36p per minute cheap rate). If you qualify for visa-free travel but want a visa anyway, you must apply in writing, enclosing an SAE, to the U.S. Embassy's Visa Branch (5 Upper Grosvenor St., London W1A 2JB), or, for residents of Northern Ireland, to the U.S. Consulate General (Queen's House, Queen St., Belfast BT1 6EO). Submmit a completed Nonimmigrant Visa Application (Form 156), a valid passport, a photograph, and evidence of your intended departure from the United States after a temporary visit. If you require a visa, call 0891/234–224 to schedule an interview.

Customs British visitors aged 21 or over may import the following into the United States: 200 cigarettes or 50 cigars or 2 kilograms of tobacco; one U.S. liter of alcohol; gifts to the value of $100. Restricted items include meat products, seeds, plants, and fruits. Never carry illegal drugs.

Returning to the United Kingdom, you may import duty-free 200 cigarettes, 100 cigarillos, 50 cigars or 250 grams of tobacco; 1 liter of spirits or 2 liters of fortified or sparkling wine; 2 liters of still table wine; 60 milliliters of perfume; 250 milliliters of toilet water; plus £36 worth of other goods, including gifts and souvenirs.

Insurance Most tour operators, travel agents, and insurance agents sell specialized policies covering accident, medical expenses, personal liability, trip cancellation, and loss or theft of personal property. Some policies include coverage for delayed departure and legal expenses, winter sports, accidents, or motoring abroad. You can also purchase an annual travel-insurance policy valid for every trip you make during the year in which it's purchased (usually only trips of less than 90 days). Before you leave, make sure you will be covered if you have a preexisting medical condition or are pregnant; your insurers may not pay for routine or continuing treatment, or may require a note from your doctor certifying your fitness to travel.

The **Association of British Insurers,** a trade association representing 450 insurance companies, advises extra medical coverage for visitors to the United States.

Tour Operators Companies offering packages to Arizona and the Southwest include **Bales Tours Ltd** (Bales House, Junction Rd., Dorking, Surrey RH4 3HB, tel. 0306/76881); **British Airways Holidays** (Atlantic House, Hazelwick Ave., Three Bridges, Crawley, West Sussex RH10 1NP, tel. 0293/611611); Greyhound International Travel (Sussex House, London Rd., East Grinstead, West Sussex RH19 1LD, tel. 0342/317317); **Jetsave Travel Ltd.** (Sussex House, London Rd., East Grinstead, West Sussex RH19 1LD, tel. 0342/

312033); and **Kuoni Travel** (Kuoni House, Dorking, Surrey RH5 4AZ, tel. 0306/742222).

Airlines and Airfares Flying time from London to Phoenix, the major airport for Arizona, is approximately 13½ hours, but varies with the airline and the itinerary.

Car Rentals In the United States you must be 21 to rent a car; rates may be higher for those under 25. Extra costs cover child seats, compulsory for under-5s (about $3 per day); additional drivers (around $1.50 per day); and the all-but-compulsory Collision Damage Waiver. Make the arrangements from home to avoid inconvenience, save money, and guarantee yourself a vehicle. Major firms include **Alamo** (tel. 0800/272–200), **Budget** (tel. 0800/181–181), **EuroDollar** (tel. 0895/233–300), **Europcar** (tel. 081/950–5050), and **Hertz** (tel. 081/679–1799). *See* Car Rentals, *below.*

Travelers with Disabilities Main information sources include the **Royal Association for Disability and Rehabilitation** (RADAR, 25 Mortimer St., London W1N 8AB, tel. 071/637–5400), which publishes travel information for the disabled in Britain, and **Mobility International** (228 Borough High St., London SE1 1JX, tel. 071/403–5688), the headquarters of an international membership organization that serves as a clearinghouse of travel information for people with disabilities.

When to Go

When you travel to Arizona depends on whether you prefer scorching desert or snowy slopes, elbow-to-elbow resorts or wide-open territory. In general, the best seasons are spring and autumn, when the temperatures are milder and the crowds have thinned out.

Winter is prime time in the central and southern parts of the state. The weather is sunny and mild, and the cities bustle with travelers escaping the cold. Conversely, northern Arizona—including the Grand Canyon—can be wintery, with snow, freezing rain, and subzero temperatures; the road to the Grand Canyon's North Rim is closed during this time.

Arizona's desert regions sizzle in summer, and travelers and their vehicles should be adequately prepared. Practically every restaurant and accommodation is air-conditioned, though, and you can get great deals on tony Southern Arizona resorts you might not be able to afford in high season. Summer is also a delightful time to visit northern Arizona's high country, when temperatures are 18°–20°F lower than they are down south.

Climate Phoenix boasts 300 sunny days and an average 7 inches of precipitation annually. Tucson gets all of 11 inches of rain each year, and the high mountains see about 25 inches. The Grand Canyon is usually cool on the rim, about 20°F warmer on the floor. During winter months, approximately 6–12 inches of snow fall on the North Rim, while the South Rim receives half that amount.

The following average daily maximum and minimum temperatures for two major cities in Arizona offer a representative range of temperatures in the state.

Tucson	Jan.	64F 37	18C 3	**May**	89F 57	32C 14	**Sept.**	96F 68	36C 20
	Feb.	68F 39	20C 4	**June**	98F 66	37C 19	**Oct.**	84F 57	29C 14
	Mar.	73F 44	23C 7	**July**	100F 73	38C 23	**Nov.**	73F 44	23C 7
	Apr.	82F 51	28C 11	**Aug.**	96F 71	36C 22	**Dec.**	66F 39	19C 4

Flagstaff	Jan.	41F 14	5C -10	**May**	66F 33	19C 1	**Sept.**	71F 41	22C 5
	Feb.	44F 17	7C - 8	**June**	77F 41	25C 5	**Oct.**	62F 30	17C - 1
	Mar.	48F 23	9C - 5	**July**	80F 50	27C 10	**Nov.**	51F 21	11C - 6
	Apr.	57F 28	14C - 2	**Aug.**	78F 48	26C 9	**Dec.**	42F 15	6C - 9

Information Sources For current weather conditions for cities in the United States and abroad, plus the local time and helpful travel tips, call the **Weather Channel Connection** (tel. 900/WEATHER; 95¢ per minute) from a touch-tone phone.

Time

Arizona sets its clocks to Mountain Standard time—two hours earlier than Eastern Standard, one hour later than Pacific Standard. From April to October, though, when other states switch to daylight savings time, Arizona does *not* change its clocks; during this portion of the year, the Mountain Standard hour in Arizona is the same as the Pacific Daylight hour in California. To complicate matters, the vast Navajo reservation in the northeastern section of the state *does* observe daylight savings time, so that from April to October it's an hour later on the reservation than it is in the rest of the state. Finally, to add to the confusion, the Hopi reservation, whose borders fall within those of the Navajo reservation, stays on the same non-Navajo, non-daylight savings clock as the remainder of the state.

Festivals and Seasonal Events

Arizona's sunny days, sporty lifestyle, fiesta atmosphere, and rich Native American heritage are natural components of a multitude of spirited festivals, musical celebrations, and competitive sporting events. Following is a list of perennial favorites.

January   **Fiesta Bowl Footbowl Classic,** Tempe. This nationally tele-vised New Year's Day event kicks off the year with a match between two of the top college teams.

Phoenix Open Golf Tournament, Scottsdale. Big names both play and attend this PGA tournament at the Tourna-ment Players Club.

Northern Telecom Tucson Open, Tucson. The other top PGA event, this is co-hosted by Tucson National Golf & Conference Resort and Starr Pass Golf Club.

January–February   **Hashknife Pony Express Ride,** Holbrook. Each year a sher-iff's posse transports the U.S. mail from Holbrook to Scottsdale over the Mogollon Rim.

Parada del Sol Rodeo and Parade, Scottsdale. This popular state attraction on Scottsdale Road features lots of dressed-up cowboys and cowgirls, plus horses and floats.

February   **Quartzsite Pow Wow Gem and Mineral Show,** Quartzsite. This gigantic flea market, held the first Wednesday through Sunday in February, attracts more than 100,000 buyers and sellers of rocks, minerals, gems, and related crafts and supplies.

O'odham Tash, Casa Grande. Indian tribes from around the country host parades, native dances, a rodeo, costume dis-plays, and food stands.

Wickenburg Gold Rush Days, Wickenburg. History comes to life when this Old West town puts on a rodeo, dances, gold-panning demonstrations, a mineral show, and other activities.

La Fiesta de los Vaqueros, Tucson. The world's longest "nonmechanized" parade—horses pull the floats and carry the dignitaries—launches this four-day rodeo at the Tuc-son Rodeo Grounds.

Tucson Gem and Mineral Show. Rock hounds–amateur and professional–from all over the world come to buy, sell, and display their geological treasures at this huge downtown event, which includes lectures and competitive exhibits.

March   **LPGA Samaritan Turquoise Classic,** Phoenix. Top women players compete for the prestigious—and lucrative—award.

Pioneer Days, Tucson. Celebrating the era before Arizona became a state, this two-day festival features military re-enactments as well as western crafts displays.

Heard Museum Guild Indian Fair and Market, Phoenix. This prestigious juried show of Native American arts and crafts brings together participants from all over the South-west; visitors can also enjoy Native American foods, music, and dance here.

April   **International Mariachi Conference,** Tucson. The Tucson Convention Center is the setting for four days of mariachi music, plus cultural and educational exhibits, for mariachi music lovers.

Route 66 Fun Run Weekend, Seligman/Topock. The historic road between Chicago and Los Angeles is feted with classic car rallies, hot rod and antique-car shows, and various other events—including a 1950s hop.

Yaqui Easter, Tucson. Visitors are welcome to watch the dances and ceremonies performed by the Yaqui Indians in old Pasqua village on the Saturday nights preceding Palm Sunday and Easter Sunday.

La Vuelta de Bisbee, Bisbee. Arizona's largest bicycle race attracts top racers from around the country.

May   **Justin World Bull Riding Championship,** Scottsdale. Top international bull riders compete for big bucks and titles at this exciting rodeo bash, which also features dances, concerts, food stalls, and shops.

Bill Williams Mountain Men Parade and Rodeo, Williams. The events of the mid-1800s are reenacted by the townspeople, who dress in period costume for the occasion.

May–June   **Trappings of the American West Festival,** Flagstaff. The featured attraction at this two-week festival is cowboy art—everything from painting and sculpture to cowboy poetry readings.

June   **Old West Day/Bucket of Blood Races,** Holbrook. Arts and crafts, western dress, and Native American song and dance are part of the festivities that surround the 10-kilometer fun run and 20-mile bike ride from Petrified Forest National Park to Holbrook.

All Indian Pow-wow and **Native American Arts Fair,** Flagstaff. On the weekend before July 4, tribes from all over the world hold dance performances and competitions, while an international array of crafts is displayed and sold.

July   **Prescott Frontier Days and Rodeo,** Prescott. Billed as the world's oldest rodeo, this event sees big crowds and an equally big party on downtown Whiskey Row.

Loggers Festival, Payson. Loggers from the United States and Canada test their skills and strength.

August   **Payson Rodeo,** Payson. Top cowboys from around the country compete in calf- and steer-roping contests.

Festival in the Pines, Flagstaff. Painters, potters, and other artists from around the United States vie with musicians, carnival rides, and food vendors for the crowd's attention.

September   **Jazz on the Rocks Festival,** Sedona. Six or seven ensembles perform in a striking outdoor setting.

Navajo Nation Annual Tribal Fair, Window Rock. The world's largest Native American fair includes a rodeo, traditional Navajo music and dances, food booths, and an intertribal pow-wow.

October   **Arizona State Fair,** Phoenix. This massive event, at the state fairgrounds, features entertainment, games, rides, exhibits, livestock, art shows, and more.

Tombstone Helldorado Days, Tombstone. The town relives the spirited Wyatt Earp era and the shoot-out at the OK Corral.

London Bridge Days, Lake Havasu City. A triathlon, parade, kinetic-sculpture races, and other contests are part of this week-long event.

November **Heard Museum Native American Art Show,** Phoenix. Exhibits feature fine tribal arts and crafts from across the state.
Havasu Classic Outboard World Championships, Lake Havasu City. Various classes of racing boats compete for prize money and trophies.
Thunderbird Balloon Classic & Airshow, Glendale. One hundred or more balloons participate in a colorful race.

December **Arizona Temple Christmas Lighting,** Tempe. More than 300,000 lights illuminate the walkways, reflection pool, trees, and plants at the Arizona Temple Gardens and Visitors Center.
Festival of Lights Boat Parade, Page. Lake Powell sparkles with the lights of dozens of boats gliding from Wahweap Lodge to Glen Canyon Dam and back.
Old Town Tempe Fall Festival of the Arts, Tempe. The downtown area closes to traffic for three days of art exhibits, food booths, musical performances, and other entertainment.

What to Pack

Clothing Casual clothing and resort wear fit in well with Arizona's climate and attractions. In some of the tonier restaurants in the larger cities, as well as in the dining rooms of the high-class resorts, most men wear jackets and nice slacks; few places require ties, however. Dressy casual wear is also appropriate for women, even in the nicest spots; take along a silky blouse and chunky silver jewelry and you'll fit in almost anywhere.

T-shirts, polo shirts, sundresses, and lightweight shorts, trousers, skirts, and blouses are just right for summer. Cotton fabrics and light colors will help keep you cool. Sun hats, swimsuits, sandals, and sunscreen are mandatory warm-weather items. In winter be sure to include a sweater and a warm jacket, particularly for high-country travel. Jeans and sneakers or sturdy walking shoes are important year-round.

Naturally, bring along the appropriate gear for any sport you plan to pursue. Tennis, golf, ski, and horseback-riding equipment are readily available for rental.

Miscellaneous Pack a camera and film, sunglasses, and an extra pair of prescription glasses or contact lenses. If you have a health problem that may require you to purchase a prescription drug, take enough to last the duration of the trip. And don't forget to pack a list of the addresses of offices that supply refunds for lost or stolen traveler's checks.

Luggage Free baggage allowances on an airline depend on the air-
Regulations line, the route, and the class of your ticket. In general, on

domestic flights and on international flights between the United States and foreign destinations, you are entitled to check two bags—neither exceeding 62 inches, or 158 centimeters (length + width + height), or weighing more than 70 pounds (32 kilograms). A third piece may be brought aboard as a carryon; its total dimensions are generally limited to less than 45 inches (114 centimeters), so it will fit easily under the seat in front of you or in the overhead compartment. There are variations, so ask in advance. The only rule, a Federal Aviation Administration safety regulation that pertains to carry-on baggage on U.S. airlines, requires only that carryons be properly stowed and allows the airline to limit allowances and tailor them to different aircraft and operational conditions. Charges for excess, oversize, or overweight pieces vary, so inquire before you pack.

Safeguarding Your Luggage Before leaving home, itemize your bags' contents and their worth; this list will help you estimate the extent of your loss if your bags go astray. To minimize that risk, tag them inside and out with your name, address, and phone number. (If you use your home address, cover it so that potential thieves can't see it.) At check-in, make sure that the tag attached by baggage handlers bears the correct three-letter code for your destination. If your bags do not arrive with you, or if you detect damage, do not leave the airport until you've filed a written report with the airline.

Insurance In the event of loss, damage, or theft on domestic flights, airlines limit their liability to $1,250 per passenger. Excess-valuation insurance can be bought directly from the airline at check-in but leaves your bags vulnerable on the ground. Your own homeowner's policy may fill the gap; or you may want special luggage insurance. Sources include **The Travelers Companies** (1 Tower Sq., Hartford, CT 06183, tel. 203/277–0111 or 800/243–3174) and **Wallach and Company, Inc.** (107 W. Federal St., Box 480, Middleburg, VA 22117, tel. 703/687–3166 or 800/237–6615), underwritten by Lloyds, London.

Cash Machines

Automated-teller machines (ATMs) are proliferating; many are tied to international networks such as **Cirrus** and **Plus**. You can use your bank card at ATMs away from home to withdraw money from your checking account and get cash advances on a credit-card account (providing your card has been programmed with a personal identification number, or PIN). Check in advance on limits on withdrawals and cash advances within specified periods. Remember that on cash advances you are charged interest from the day you get the money from ATMs as well as from tellers. And note that transaction fees for ATM withdrawals outside your home turf will probably be higher than for withdrawals at home. For specific Cirrus locations in the United States and Canada, call 800/424–7787 (for U.S. Plus locations, 800/

843–7587), and press the area code and first three digits of the number you're calling from (or the calling area where you want an ATM).

Traveling with Cameras, Camcorders, and Laptops

About Film and Cameras If your camera is new or if you haven't used it for a while, shoot and develop a few rolls of film before leaving home. Pack some lens tissue and an extra battery for your built-in light meter, and invest in an inexpensive skylight filter, to both protect your lens and provide some definition in hazy shots. Store film in a cool, dry place—never in the car's glove compartment or on the shelf under the rear window.

Films above ISO 400 are more sensitive to damage from airport security X-rays than others; very high speed films, ISO 1,000 and above, are exceedingly vulnerable. To protect your film, don't put it in checked luggage; carry it with you in a plastic bag and ask for a hand inspection. Such requests are honored at American airports. Don't depend on a lead-lined bag to protect film in checked luggage—the airline may very well turn up the dosage of radiation to see what you've got in there. Airport metal detectors do not harm film, although you'll set off the alarm if you walk through one with a roll in your pocket. Call the Kodak Information Center (tel. 800/242–2424) for details.

About Camcorders Before your trip, put new or long-unused camcorders through their paces, and practice panning and zooming. Invest in a skylight filter to protect the lens, and check the lithium battery that lights up the LCD (liquid crystal display) modes. As for the rechargeable nickel-cadmium batteries that are the camera's power source, take along an extra pair, so while you're using your camcorder you'll have one battery ready and another recharging. Most newer camcorders are equipped with the battery (which generally slides or clicks onto the camera body) and, to recharge it, with what's known as a universal or worldwide AC adapter charger.

About Videotape Unlike still-camera film, videotape is not damaged by X-rays. However, it may well be harmed by the magnetic field of a walk-through metal detector. Airport security personnel may want you to turn the camcorder on to prove that that's what it is, so make sure the battery is charged when you get to the airport.

About Laptops Security X-rays do not harm hard-disk or floppy-disk storage. Most airlines allow you to use your laptop aloft but request that you turn it off during takeoff and landing so as not to interfere with navigation equipment. Make sure the battery is charged when you arrive at the airport, because you may be asked to turn on the computer at security checkpoints to prove that it is what it appears to be. If you're a heavy computer user, consider traveling with a backup battery.

Traveling with Children

Many of the big resorts and dude ranches offer special activities just for children, and many offer baby-sitting services. Children of all ages are enthralled by the Wild West flavor around Tucson and the southeastern part of the state, with Tombstone ranking as a particular favorite. If you're driving some of the long desert stretches, take along plenty of games and snacks.

Publications *A Family Guide to Arizona,* by Catherine Dunes ($6.95,
Local Guides Kids Touring Arizona, 4201 W. Villa Maria Dr., Glendale, AZ 85308, tel. 602/439–2324), contains Arizona-related fun facts, games, puzzles, and palatable educational information.

Newsletter **Family Travel Times,** published 10 times a year by **Travel With Your Children** (TWYCH, 45 W. 18th St., 7th Floor Tower, New York, NY 10011, tel. 212/206–0688; annual subscription $55), covers destinations, types of vacations, and modes of travel.

Books *Great Vacations with Your Kids,* by Dorothy Jordan and Marjorie Cohen ($13; Penguin USA, 120 Woodbine St., Bergenfield, NJ 07621, tel. 800/253–6476) and *Traveling with Children—And Enjoying It,* by Arlene K. Butler ($11.95 plus $3 shipping per book; Globe Pequot Press, Box 833, Old Saybrook, CT 06475, tel. 800/243–0495, or 800/ 962–0973 in CT) both help you plan your trip with children, from toddlers to teens. Also from Globe Pequot is *Recommended Family Resorts in the United States, Canada, and the Caribbean,* by Jane Wilford with Janet Tice ($12.95), which describes 100 resorts at length and includes a "Children's World" section describing activities and facilities as part of each entry.

Getting There On domestic flights, children under 2 not occupying a seat
Air Fares travel free, and older children currently travel on the "lowest applicable" adult fare.

Baggage The adult baggage allowance applies for children paying half or more of the adult fare. Check with the airline for particulars.

Safety Seats The FAA recommends the use of safety seats aloft and details approved models in the free leaflet "**Child/Infant Safety Seats Recommended for Use in Aircraft**" (available from the Federal Aviation Administration, APA–200, 800 Independence Ave. SW, Washington, DC 20591, tel. 202/267–3479). Airline policy varies. U.S. carriers must allow FAA-approved models, but because these seats are strapped into a regular passenger seat, they may require that parents buy a ticket even for an infant under 2 who would otherwise ride free.

Facilities Aloft Airlines do provide other facilities and services for children, such as children's meals and freestanding bassinets (to those sitting in seats on the bulkhead, where there's enough legroom to accommodate them). Make your request when reserving. The annual February/March issue of *Family Travel Times* gives details of the children's services of dozens of airlines (*see above*). "Kids and Teens in Flight" (free from the U.S. Department of Transportation, tel. 202/366-2220) offers tips for children flying alone.

Lodging All **Holiday Inns** (tel. 800/465-4329) allow children age 12 or under to stay free when sharing a room with an adult, and some offer family plans, providing the same privileges for children 18 or under. The **Westin La Paloma Hotel** in Tucson (tel. 800/228-3000) offers year-round, supervised activities for children ages 7-12, as well as junior tennis camps and golf clinics for kids 5 to 18 years old. From Thanksgiving through April, the **Tanque Verde Guest Ranch** (tel. 800/234-3833), also in Tucson, offers activities for children 4-11, including horseback lessons, tennis, and nature walks in the daytime, and arts and crafts and games in the evening. In the Phoenix area, the **Pointe Hilton Resort** (tel. 800/934-1000) runs four-day cowboy camps (Jan.-Apr. and Oct.-Dec.), in which children 8 years and older may participate; in summer, there's a day camp for children 3-12. The **Phoenician Resort** (tel. 602/941-8200, ext. 2572) in Scottsdale has a summer camp, with four week-long sessions for children 5-14; the **Hyatt Regency** (tel. 800/233-1234), also in Scottsdale, offers a full-day recreation and activities program for ages 3-12 on weekends, during spring break, and every day from Memorial Day through Labor Day. All of the above resorts have baby-sitting services, too.

Tour Operators **GrandTravel** (6900 Wisconsin Ave., Suite 706, Chevy Chase, MD 20815, tel. 301/986-0790 or 800/247-7651) offers international and domestic tours for grandparents traveling with their grandchildren. The catalogue, as charmingly written and illustrated as a children's book, positively invites armchair traveling with lap-sitters aboard. **Rascals in Paradise** (650 5th St., Suite 505, San Francisco, CA 94107, tel. 415/978-9800, or 800/872-7225) specializes in programs for families.

Hints for Travelers with Disabilities

Most of the region's national parks and recreation areas have wheelchair-accessible visitor centers, rest rooms, campsites, and trails, and more are being added every year. For information on accessible facilities at specific parks and sites in northeastern Arizona, contact the **National Park Service, Southwest Regional Office** (tel. 505/988-6375); for sites in southwestern Arizona, contact the **Western Regional Office** (tel. 415/744-3929).

Organizations Several organizations provide travel information for people with disabilities, usually for a membership fee, and some publish newsletters and bulletins. Among them are the **In-**

formation Center for Individuals with Disabilities (Fort Point Pl., 27–43 Wormwood St., Boston, MA 02210, tel. 617/727–5540 or 800/462–5015 in MA between 11 and 4, or leave message; TDD/TTY tel. 617/345–9743); Mobility International USA (Box 3551, Eugene, OR 97403, voice and TDD tel. 503/343–1284), the U.S. branch of an international organization based in Britain (*see below*) and present in 30 countries; MossRehab Hospital Travel Information Service (1200 W. Tabor Rd., Philadelphia, PA 19141, tel. 215/456– 9603, TDD tel. 215/456–9602); the Society for the Advancement of Travel for the Handicapped (SATH, 347 5th Ave., Suite 610, New York, NY 10016, tel. 212/447–7284, fax 212/ 725–8253); the Travel Industry and Disabled Exchange (TIDE, 5435 Donna Ave., Tarzana, CA 91356, tel. 818/368– 5648); and Travelin' Talk (Box 3534, Clarksville, TN 37043, tel. 615/552–6670).

Travel Agencies and Tour Operators Group tours for travelers with disabilities are regularly scheduled by the Arizona Recreation Center for the Handicapped (1550 W. Colter St., Phoenix 85015, tel. 602/230– 2226).

Directions Unlimited (720 N. Bedford Rd., Bedford Hills, NY 10507, tel. 914/241–1700), a travel agency, has expertise in tours and cruises for the disabled. Evergreen Travel Service (4114 198th St. SW, Suite 13, Lynnwood, WA 98036, tel. 206/776–1184 or 800/435–2288) operates Wings on Wheels Tours for those in wheelchairs, White Cane Tours for the blind, and tours for the deaf and makes group and independent arrangements for travelers with any disability. Flying Wheels Travel (143 W. Bridge St., Box 382, Owatonna, MN 55060, tel. 800/535–6790 or 800/722–9351 in MN), a tour operator and travel agency, arranges international tours, cruises, and independent travel itineraries for people with mobility disabilities.

Publications Local Guides *Access Arizona: An Atlas & Travel Guide for Disabled & Mature Travelers to Major Outdoor Recreation Areas*, published by the Arizona State Parks Department (800 W. Washington, Suite 415, Phoenix 85007, tel. 602/542–1996), details the accessibility of national and state parks facilities to those with mobility impairments. The Arizona Easter Seal Society (903 N. 2nd St., Phoenix 85004, tel. 602/252– 6061) publishes *Access Valley of the Sun*, covering Phoenix and environs; *Access Tucson & Green Valley*, focusing on the southeastern region; and *Access Northern Arizona*, encompassing Flagstaff and surrounding communities. Also consult the *Arizona Accommodations Directory*, published by the Arizona Hotel and Motel Association (2201 E. Camelback Rd., Suite 125-B, Phoenix 85016, tel. 602/553– 8802).

General Information In addition, several free publications are available from the Consumer Information Center (Pueblo, CO 81009): "New Horizons for the Air Traveler with a Disability," a U.S. Department of Transportation booklet describing changes resulting from the 1986 Air Carrier Access Act and those still to come from the 1990 Americans with Disabilities Act (include Department 608Y in the address), and the Airport Operators Council's *Access Travel: Airports* (Dept. 5804), which describes facilities and services for the disabled at more than 500 airports worldwide.

Twin Peaks Press (Box 129, Vancouver, WA 98666, tel. 206/694–2462 or 800/637–2256) publishes the *Directory of Travel Agencies for the Disabled* ($19.95), listing more than 370 agencies worldwide; *Travel for the Disabled* ($19.95), listing some 500 access guides and accessible places worldwide; the *Directory of Accessible Van Rentals* ($9.95) for campers and RV travelers worldwide; and *Wheelchair Vagabond* ($14.95), a collection of personal travel tips. Add $2 per book for shipping. The Sierra Club publishes *Easy Access to National Parks* ($16 plus $3 shipping; 730 Polk St., San Francisco, CA 94109, tel. 415/776–2211).

Getting Around
By Bus **Greyhound** (tel. 800/752–4841; TDD 800/345–3109) will carry a disabled person and companion for the price of a single fare.

By Train **Amtrak** (National Railroad Passenger Corp., 60 Massachusetts Ave., NE, Washington, DC 20002, tel. 800/USA–RAIL) advises that you request Redcap service, special seats, or wheelchair assistance when you make reservations. Also note that not all stations are equipped to provide these services. All passengers with disabilities are entitled to a 15% discount on the lowest fare, and there are special fares for children with disabilities as well. Contact Amtrak for a free brochure outlining services for the elderly and people with disabilities.

By Car **Avis** (tel. 800/331–1212), **Hertz** (tel. 800/654–3131), and **National** (tel. 800/328–4567) can provide hand controls on some rental cars with advance notice.

Discounts The **National Park Service** (Box 37127, Washington, DC 20013–7127) provides a Golden Access Passport free to those who are medically blind or have a permanent disability; the passport covers the entry fee for the holder and anyone accompanying the holder in the same private vehicle and a 50% discount on camping and some other user fees. Apply for the passport in person at a national recreation facility that charges an entrance fee; proof of disability is required.

Hints for Older Travelers

The state's healthful environment and many retirement communities make it a popular destination for older travelers. As such, Arizona has a multitude of recreational, sports, and entertainment facilities geared especially to senior citizens' needs and interests. In addition, discounts are offered on public transportation, museum entrance fees, fishing and hunting licenses, cinemas, musical and theatrical performances, and a wide variety of other services. The minimum age limit varies between 55 and 65 years. If you fall into this age group, be sure to inquire about discounts before putting your money on the counter; savings can be substantial.

Organizations The **American Association of Retired Persons** (AARP, 601 E St. NW, Washington, DC 20049, tel. 202/434–2277) provides independent travelers the Purchase Privilege Program, which offers discounts on hotels, car rentals, and sightseeing. AARP also arranges group tours, cruises, and apartment living through AARP Travel Experience from American Express (400 Pinnacle Way, Suite 450, Norcross, GA 30071, tel. 800/927–0111); these can be booked through travel agents, except for the cruises, which must be booked directly (tel. 800/745–4567). AARP membership is open to those 50 and over; annual dues are $8 per person or couple.

Two other membership organizations offer discounts on lodgings, car rentals, and other travel products, along with such nontravel perks as magazines and newsletters. The **National Council of Senior Citizens** (1331 F St. NW, Washington, DC 20004, tel. 202/347–8800) is a nonprofit advocacy group with some 5,000 local clubs across the United States; membership costs $12 per person or couple annually. **Mature Outlook** (6001 N. Clark St., Chicago, IL 60660, tel. 800/336–6330), a Sears Roebuck & Co. subsidiary with 800,000 members, charges $9.95 for an annual membership.

Note: When using any senior-citizen identification card for reduced hotel rates, mention it when booking, not when checking out. At restaurants, show your card before you're seated; discounts may be limited to certain menus, days, or hours. If you are renting a car, ask about promotional rates that might improve on your senior-citizen discount.

Educational **Elderhostel** (75 Federal St., 3rd floor, Boston, MA 02110,
Travel tel. 617/426–7788) is a nonprofit organization that has inexpensive study programs for people 60 and older since 1975. Programs take place at more than 1,800 educational institutions in the United States, Canada, and 45 countries overseas, and courses cover everything from marine science to Greek myths and cowboy poetry. Participants generally attend lectures in the morning and spend the afternoon sightseeing or on field trips; they live in dorms on the host campuses. Fees for programs in the United States and Canada, which usually last one week, run about $300, not including transportation. With dozens of Arizona college and university campuses participating, Elderhostel has a particularly extensive program in Arizona. Some scheduled classes include Native American Archaeology, Geology of the Grand Canyon, Flora and Fauna of the Sonoran Desert, Astronomy, and Cowboys and the Old West; one program involves staying on the Hopi reservation and learning about Hopi culture from members of the tribe.

Tour Operators **Saga International Holidays** (222 Berkeley St., Boston, MA 02116, tel. 800/343–0273), which specializes in group travel for people over 60, offers a selection of variously priced tours and cruises. If you want to take your grandchildren, look into **GrandTravel** (*see* Traveling with Children, *above*).

Further Reading

Essays and *Going Back to Bisbee,* by Richard Shelton, *Frog Mountain*
Fiction *Blues,* by Charles Bowden, and *The Mountains Next Day,* by Janice Emily Bowers are all fine personal accounts of life in southern Arizona. The hipster fiction classic *The Monkey Wrench Gang,* by Edward Abbey, details an eco-anarchist plot to blow up Glen Canyon Dam. *Stolen Gods,* a thriller by Jake Page, is set largely in Arizona's Hopi reservation and in Tucson. Three novels by Tucson-based writers skillfully evoke the interplay between Native American culture and contemporary Southwest life: *Animal Dreams,* by Barbara Kingsolver, *Almanac of the Dead,* by Leslie Marmon Silko, and *Yes Is Better Than No,* by Byrd Baylor. Almost any of Zane Grey's Western adventures or Tony Hillerman's mysteries will put you in a Southwest mood.

General History *Arizona Cowboys,* by Dane Coolidge, is an illustrated account of the cowboys, Indians, settlers, and explorers of the early 1900s. Buried-treasure hunters will be inspired by *Lost Mines of the Great Southwest,* by John D. Mitchell, which is just enough of a nibble to start you sketching maps and planning strategy. First printed back in 1891, *Some Strange Corners of Our Country,* by Charles F. Lummis, takes readers on a century-old journey to the Grand Canyon, Montezuma Castle, the Petrified Forest, and other Arizonan "strange corners." *A Roadside History of Arizona,* by Marshall Trimble, is a great book for the person not driving to read aloud while tooling around the state. You can read all about dude ranches, ghost towns, and saloons in *The Best of the Old West, An Indispensable Guide to the Vanishing Legend of the American West,* by Ron Butler.

Native American *The Anasazi: Prehistoric Peoples of the Four Corners Re-*
History *gion,* by J. Richard Ambler, is an intriguing study of this area and its early inhabitants. *Hohokam Indians of the Tucson Basin,* by Linda Gregonis, offers an in-depth look at this prehistoric tribe. In *Hopi,* by Susanne Page and Jake Page, the daily, ceremonial, and spiritual life of the tribe are explored in detail. Study up on the history of Hopi silversmithing techniques in *Hopi Silver,* by Margaret Wright. The beautifully illustrated *Hopi Indian Kachina Dolls,* by Oscar T. Branson, details the different ceremonial roles of the colorful Native American figurines. Navajo homes, ceremonies, crafts, and tribal traditions are kept alive in *The Enduring Navajo,* by Laura Gilpin. Navajo legends and trends from early days to present time are collected in *The Book of the Navajo,* by Raymond F. Locke.

Natural History *A Guide to Exploring Oak Creek and the Sedona Area,* by Stewart Aitchison, provides natural-history driving tours of this very scenic district. In *100 Desert Wildflowers in Natural Color,* by Natt N. Dodge, you'll find a color photo and brief description of each of the flowers included. Also written by Natt N. Dodge, *Poisonous Dwellers of the Desert* gives precise information on both venomous and non-venomous creatures of the Southwest. *Cacti of the Southwest,* by W. Hubert Earle, depicts some of the best-known species of the region with color photos and descriptive material. For comprehensive information on Grand Canyon geology, history, flora and fauna, plus hiking suggestions, pick up *A Field Guide to the Grand Canyon,* by Steve Whitney. *Common Edible and Useful Plants of the West,* by Muriel Sweet, gives the layperson descriptions of medicinal and other plants and shrubs, most of which were first discovered by Native Americans.

Crafts *The Traveler's Guide to American Crafts: West of the Mississippi,* by Suzanne Carmichael, gives browsers and buyers alike a useful overview of Arizona's traditional and contemporary handiwork.

General Interest *Arizona Highways,* a monthly magazine, features exquisite color photography of this versatile state. Useful general travel information, fine pictures, and well-written historical essays all make *Arizona,* by Larry Cheek, a good pretrip resource.

Arriving and Departing

By Plane

Flights are either nonstop, direct, or connecting. A **nonstop** flight requires no change of plane and makes no stops. A **direct** flight stops at least once and can involve a change of plane, although the flight number remains the same; if the first leg is late, the second waits. This is not the case with a **connecting** flight, which involves a different plane and a different flight number.

Most major domestic airlines fly into Phoenix and Tucson from all parts of the United States. Busy Phoenix Sky Harbor International, about 3 miles east of the city center, also serves as the hub for flights to other parts of the state. Tucson International Air Terminal is located about 8½ miles south of the downtown area. Both facilities offer a number of different transportation services into the city, from minivan shuttles to stretch limousines.

Air carriers to Arizona are **Aeromexico** (tel. 800/237–6639), **Alaska** (tel. 800/426–0333), **American** (tel. 800/433–7300), **America West** (tel. 800/247–5692), **Continental** (tel. 800/525–0280), **Delta** (tel. 800/221–1212), **Morris Air** (tel. 800/444–5660), **Northwest** (tel. 800/225–2525), **Southwest** (tel.

800/435–9792), **TWA** (tel. 800/221–2000), **United** (tel. 800/241–6522), and **USAir** (tel. 800/428–4322).

Within the state, **America West** and **Skywest** (tel. 800/453–9417) operate regularly scheduled flights among Phoenix, Tucson, Flagstaff, and Yuma; Skywest also flies to Page/Lake Powell. **Arizona Pacific** (tel. 800/221–7904), based in Prescott, has regularly scheduled routes between that city and the Grand Canyon, Phoenix, and Show Low, Arizona, as well as charter flights.

Cutting Flight Costs The Sunday travel section of most newspapers is a good source of deals. When booking, particularly through an unfamiliar company, call the Better Business Bureau to find out whether any complaints have been registered against the company, pay with a credit card if you can, and consider trip-cancellation and default insurance.

Promotional Airfares All the less expensive fares, called promotional or discount fares, are round-trip and involve restrictions. The exact nature of the restrictions depends on the airline, the route, and the season and on whether travel is domestic or international, but you must usually buy the ticket—commonly called an APEX (advance purchase excursion) when it's for international travel—in advance (seven, 14, or 21 days are usual). You must also respect certain minimum- and maximum-stay requirements (for instance, over a Saturday night or at least seven and no more than 30, 45, or 90 days), and you must be willing to pay penalties for changes. Airlines generally allow some changes for a fee. But the cheaper the fare, the more likely the ticket is nonrefundable; it would take a death in the family for the airline to give you any of your money back if you had to cancel. The cheapest fares are also subject to availability; because only a certain percentage of the plane's total seats will be sold at that price, they may go quickly.

Consolidators Consolidators or bulk-fare operators—also known as bucket shops—buy blocks of seats on scheduled flights that airlines anticipate they won't be able to sell. They pay wholesale prices, add a markup, and resell the seats to travel agents or directly to the public at prices that still undercut the airline's promotional or discount fares. You pay more than on a charter but ordinarily less than for an APEX ticket, and, even when there is not much of a price difference, the ticket usually comes without the advance-purchase restriction. Moreover, although tickets are marked nonrefundable so you can't turn them in to the airline for a full-fare refund, some consolidators sometimes give you your money back. Carefully read the fine print detailing penalties for changes and cancellations. If you doubt the reliability of a company, call the airline once you've made your booking and confirm that you do, indeed, have a reservation on the flight.

The biggest U.S. consolidator, C.L. Thomson Express, sells only to travel agents. Well-established consolidators selling to the public include **UniTravel** (Box 12485, St. Louis, MO 63132, tel. 314/569–0900 or 800/325–2222); **Council Charter** (205 E. 42nd St., New York, NY 10017, tel. 212/661–0311 or 800/800–8222), a division of the Council on International Educational Exchange and a longtime charter operator now functioning more as a consolidator; and **Travac** (989 6th Ave., New York, NY 10018, tel. 212/563–3303 or 800/872–8800), also a former charterer.

Charter Flights Charters usually have the lowest fares and the most restrictions. Departures are limited and seldom on time, and you can lose all or most of your money if you cancel. (Generally, the closer to departure you cancel, the more you lose, although sometimes you will be charged only a small fee if you supply a substitute passenger.) The charterer, on the other hand, may legally cancel the flight for any reason up to 10 days before departure; within 10 days of departure, the flight may be canceled only if it becomes physically impossible to operate it. The charterer may also revise the itinerary or increase the price after you have bought the ticket, but if the new arrangement constitutes a "major change," you have the right to a refund. Before buying a charter ticket, read the fine print for the company's refund policy and details on major changes. Money for charter flights is usually paid into a bank escrow account, the name of which should be on the contract. If you don't pay by credit card, make your check payable to the escrow account (unless you're dealing with a travel agent, in which case, his or her check should be payable to the escrow account). The Department of Transportation's Consumer Affairs Office (I–25, Washington, DC 20590, tel. 202/366–2220) can answer questions on charters and send you its "Plane Talk: Public Charter Flights" information sheet.

Charter operators may offer flights alone or with ground arrangements that constitute a charter package. Well-established charter operators include **Council Charter** (205 E. 42nd St., New York, NY 10017, tel. 212/661–0311 or 800/800–8222), now largely a consolidator, despite its name, and **Travel Charter** (1120 E. Long Lake Rd., Troy, MI 48098, tel. 313/528–3570 or 800/521–5267), with Midwestern departures. **DER Tours** (Box 1606, Des Plains, IL 60017, tel. 800/782–2424), a charterer and consolidator, sells through travel agents.

Discount Travel Travel clubs offer their members unsold space on airplanes,
Clubs cruise ships, and package tours at nearly the last minute and at well below the original cost. Suppliers thus receive some revenue for their "leftovers," and members get a bargain. Membership generally includes a regular bulletin or access to a toll-free telephone hot line giving details of available trips departing anywhere from three or four days to several months in the future. Packages tend to be more

common than flights alone, so if airfares are your only interest, read the literature before joining. Reductions on hotels
are also available. Clubs include **Discount Travel International** (114 Forrest Ave., Suite 203, Narberth, PA 19072,
tel. 215/668–7184; $45 annually, single or family), **Mo-
ment's Notice** (425 Madison Ave., New York, NY 10017, tel.
212/486–0503; $45 annually, single or family), **Travelers Ad-
vantage** (CUC Travel Service, 49 Music Sq. W, Nashville,
TN 37203, tel. 800/548–1116; $49 annually, single or fami-
ly), and **Worldwide Discount Travel Club** (1674 Meridian
Ave., Miami Beach, FL 33139, tel. 305/534–2082; $50 annu-
ally for family, $40 single).

Smoking Since February 1990, smoking has been banned on all domestic flights of less than six hours duration; the ban also
applies to domestic segments of international flights
aboard U.S. and foreign carriers.

By Car

Major approaches from the east and west are I–40, I–10,
I–8, and U.S. 60. Main north–south routes are I–17, I–10,
and U.S. 89. Other artery roads are U.S. 70 and U.S. 64
(U.S. 160 in Arizona) from the east.

Most highways into the state are good to excellent, with
easy access, roadside facilities, rest stops, and scenic
views. The speed limit is 65 miles per hour, but even though
it may be tempting to let the speedometer needle fly in the
wide-open desert, beware—police use sophisticated detec-
tion systems to nab violators.

Hazards to desert drivers include dust storms and flash
floods. Dust storms usually occur mid-July to mid-Septem-
ber (the monsoon months), just before thunderstorms hit,
causing extremely low visibility. If you're on the highway,
pull as far off the road as possible, turn off your headlights,
and wait for the storm to subside. Flash floods strike low-
lying areas during both the monsoon and winter rainy seasons. Dry washes, which fill quickly with running water,
are particularly dangerous and should not be crossed until
you can see the bottom.

Vehicles and passengers should be well equipped for sear-
ing summer heat in the low desert. Always carry plenty of
water, a good spare tire, a jack, and emergency supplies. If
you get stranded, stay with your vehicle and wait for help to
arrive.

At some point you will probably pass through one or more
of the state's 23 Indian reservations. Roads and other areas
within reservation boundaries are under the jurisdiction of
reservation police and governed by separate rules and regulations. Observe all signs and respect residents' privacy.

For more information on the state's highways and byways,
contact the Arizona Department of Transportation (tel.

602/255–7386); for weather conditions, call 602/252-1010, ext. 7623.

Car Rentals

Most major car-rental companies are represented in Arizona, with airport counters and hotel drop-off services, including **Avis** (tel. 800/331–1212, 800/879–2847 in Canada); **Budget** (tel. 800/527–0700); **Dollar** (tel. 800/800–4000); **Hertz** (tel. 800/654–3131, 800/263-0600 in Canada); **National** (tel. 800/227–7368). You will also find **Alamo** (tel. 800/327–9633) and **Thrifty** (tel. 800/367–2277). Prices are not the same throughout the state: At present, for example, rates for a compact with unlimited mileage are slightly lower in Flagstaff (about $140) than in Phoenix (about $150), and much lower than in Page (around $225). This does not include tax, which in Arizona can exceed 14% on car rentals.

Extra Charges Picking up the car in one city and leaving it in another may entail drop-off charges or one-way service fees, which can be substantial. The cost of a collision or loss-damage waiver (*see below*) can be high, also. By prior arrangement, you can also rent four-wheel-drive vehicles, trucks, and or campers.

Cutting Costs If you know you will want a car for more than a day or two, you can save by planning ahead. Major international companies have programs that discount their standard rates by 15%–30% if you make the reservation before departure (anywhere from two to 14 days), rent for a minimum number of days (typically three or four), and prepay the rental. Ask about these advance-purchase schemes when you call for information. More economical rentals are those that come as part of fly/drive or other packages, even those as bare-bones as the rental plus an airline ticket (*see* Tours and Packages, *above*).

One last tip: Remember to fill the tank when you turn in the vehicle, to avoid being charged for refueling at what you'll swear is the most expensive pump in town.

Insurance and Collision Damage Waiver The standard rental contract includes liability coverage (for damage to public property, injury to pedestrians, etc.) and coverage for the car against fire, theft (not included in certain countries), and collision damage with a deductible—most commonly $2,000–$3,000, occasionally more. In the case of an accident, you are responsible for the deductible amount unless you've purchased the collision damage waiver (CDW), which costs an average $12 a day, although this varies depending on what you've rented, where, and from whom.

Because this adds up quickly, you may be inclined to say "no thanks"—and that's certainly your option, although the rental agent may not tell you so. Planning ahead will help you make the right decision. By all means, find out if your own insurance covers damage to a rental car while traveling (not simply a car to drive when yours is in for repairs). And check whether charging car rentals to any of your credit cards will get you a CDW at no charge. Note before you decline that deductibles are occasionally high enough that totaling a car would make you responsible for its full value. In many states, laws mandate that renters be told what the CDW costs, that it's optional, and that their own auto insurance may provide the same protection.

By Train

The *Southwest Chief* operates daily between Los Angeles and Chicago, stopping in Kingman, Flagstaff, and Winslow. The *Sunset Limited* travels three times each week between Los Angeles and Miami, with stops at Yuma, Phoenix, Tempe, Coolidge, Tucson, and Benson. Both services connect with trains to eastern destinations. For details, contact **Amtrak** (tel. 800/USA–RAIL).

By Bus

Greyhound provides service to many Arizona destinations from most parts of the United States. Local offices to call for information include 602/248–4040 in Phoenix, 602/792–0972 in Tucson, 602/774–4573 in Flagstaff, and 602/445–5470 in Prescott.

Staying in Arizona

Shopping

Many tourists come to Arizona for no other reason than to purchase fine **Native American jewelry and crafts.** Collectibles include Navajo rugs and sand paintings, Hopi kachina dolls (intricately carved and colorful representations of Hopi spiritual beings) and pottery, Tohonó O'odham (Papago) basketry, and Apache beadwork, as well as the highly prized silver and turquoise jewelry produced by several different tribes. Many of these items are sold in big-city shops and malls, though going directly to the reservation often gives shoppers additional rewards.

Museums and trading posts on the Navajo and Hopi reservations in the state's northeastern region offer introductions to crafts and their history and have gift shops where you can make purchases. Demonstrations of silversmithing, rug-weaving, and pottery-making techniques are often held on the premises. Roadside stands also offer wares for sale.

You can find exquisite baskets and other crafts of the Tohonó O'odham at the plaza outside the San Xavier Mission on the outskirts of Tucson, as well as at shops in Sells, the tribe's headquarters, about 60 miles southwest of Tucson. Apache beadwork, baskets, wood carvings, and jewelry are sold at reservation trading posts in the eastern part of the state.

Bear in mind that the high quality of Native American arts and crafts is reflected in the prices they fetch. Bargaining is the exception, not the rule. In general, best buys are to be had in the fall, after tourists have gone home.

Highly mineralized Arizona is also a haven for **rock and mineral** collectors. An astounding variety of specimens include agate, jasper, tourmaline, petrified wood, quartz, turquoise, amethyst, precious opal, and fire agate. Buy them at specialty shops or at one of the state's year-round rock and gem shows. The largest shows, held in late January or early February, are at Quartzsite, about 19 miles from the California border, and Tucson.

Sports and the Outdoors

Ballooning Both Phoenix and Tucson have a large number of hot-air balloon operators, whose pilots will take you hovering above metropolitan areas as well as the Sonoran Desert. Some companies offer flights year-round, though most will fly only during the cooler months. Tours last about one hour and are followed by the customary champagne celebration.

Baseball Baseball fans visiting Arizona from late February through early April have a chance to watch major-league teams during spring training. Exhibition games begin in early March, but the eight Cactus League teams start practice at training camps as much as three weeks earlier. The free drills—held in the mornings before the exhibition games— are fun to watch, and there's a good chance you might be able to chat with the players before or after these sessions.

The Phoenix area, where seven of the eight teams practice, is the best place to see Cactus League baseball: The **Chicago Cubs** play at Hohokam Park in Mesa (tel. 602/964–4467), the **Oakland Athletics** at Phoenix Municipal Stadium (tel. 602/392–0217), the **San Francisco Giants** at Scottsdale Stadium (tel. 602/990–7972), the **California Angels** at Diablo Stadium in Tempe (tel. 602/350–5200), and the **Milwaukee Brewers** at the Compadre Stadium in Chandler (tel. 602/ 895–1200). As we were going to press it was announced that in 1994 both the **San Diego Padres** and the **Seattle Mariners** will train in Peoria, another Phoenix suburb, but the exact location has not yet been released. In 1993 the **Colorado Rockies** practiced for their first major league games in Tucson's Hi Corbett field (tel. 602/327–9467).

In some cases, reserved seats sell out the fall before the season, but you can almost always get general admission seats on the day of the games. For current information on all aspects of Cactus League baseball, contact the **Mesa Conven-**

tion and Visitor's Bureau (120 North Center St., Mesa 85201, tel. 602/969–1307).

Bicycling Cyclists can ride on city streets, desert trails, mountain passes, or the open road. Start off with a bike in good repair, a maintenance kit, a sturdy bicycle helmet, and plenty of water. If you're not used to long-distance cycling, don't push yourself. Begin with short jaunts and work up to longer journeys. A lightweight touring bike and extra-low gears for mountain grades will help you along. Most bicycle shops can provide you with tour guides, tips, and, if you decide to go pro, a current racing schedule. Call the county **Parks and Recreation Department** in the area you're visiting for information on nearby bike paths.

Boating and Waterskiing Visitors may be surprised to find so many lakes in this state noted for its desert life. Choices range from secluded, getaway-from-it-all oases to big and boisterous canyon-bound water resorts. The two national recreational areas, Glen Canyon (Lake Powell), in the north-central region, and Lake Mead (including Lake Mohave), in the northwest, offer many facilities, including marinas, launching ramps, and boat and ski rentals. At both lakes you can sign up for a paddle-wheeler tour or take the wheel yourself in a fully equipped houseboat. Lake Havasu, fed by the Colorado River in the western part of the state, is another favored site for boating, waterskiing, and jet-skiing; in the background is the rather surreal vision of London Bridge, which was moved block by block from England and reassembled at this lakeside resort.

Saguaro and Canyon lakes, just east of Scottsdale, offer good boating and waterskiing for those based in the Phoenix area who are looking for a convenient day trip.

Other Water Sports **Swimmers** can take a cool plunge in a mountain lake, dive into an Olympic-size pool, or splash in the acres and acres of water at one of the recreational megaresorts. Virtually every hotel and motel has a swimming pool of some size, and nearly all Arizona cities have at least one public pool; most are heated, and in the northern region many are indoors. You can cavort in the man-made waves at a number of water parks in the Phoenix area, including Water World and Golfland/Sunsplash (in Mesa), and even **surf** the 3- to 5-foot-high waves at Big Surf in Tempe. Bring your own board, or rent one on site. **Tubing** is a popular sport along the Salt River, east of Mesa. Tubes can be rented, and a shuttle bus will pick up or drop off at any of five points, enabling you to choose the length of your float. When the breezes blow, **sailboats** and **Windsurfers** can be seen on Lakes Mead, Powell, and Havasu, as well as a few of the smaller lakes. Check ahead on availability of rental equipment.

Camping *See* Lodging, *below.*

Canoeing Swift currents without rapids make the daylong Topock Gorge trip on the Colorado River a favorite outing. Beginning at Topock, canoeists travel through a wildlife refuge to Castle Rock at the top end of Lake Havasu. Another route, made dramatic by the Black Canyon cliffs, is along the Colorado River below Hoover Dam to Willow Beach. Canoe rentals are available at both locations.

Fishing Fish practically jump out of Arizona's cool mountain streams, major rivers, and man-made lakes and are especially plentiful at the Colorado River resorts. Rainbow, brown, brook, and cutthroat trout, as well as catfish, crappie, bass, pike, and bluegill, are the main species. San Carlos Lake is tops for bass, and the trout are plentiful at Lees Ferry.Fishing licenses are required and can be obtained from the **Arizona Game and Fish Department** (2222 W. Greenway Rd., Phoenix 85027, tel. 602/942–3000).

Golf Your clubs won't gather dust in Arizona. Aside from the big-draw Phoenix and Tucson opens (*see* Festivals and Seasonal Events, *above*), golfers flock to this state to tee off at the myriad top-rank private and municipal courses. The year-round desert courses offer cheaper greens fees during the summer, while those in the northern part of the state usually shut down for winter. Just about every resort has its own course or is affiliated with a private club. For a listing of Arizona's golfing facilities, contact the **Arizona Golf Association** (11801 N. Tatum Blvd., Suite 247, Phoenix 85028, tel. 602/953–5990).

Hiking Hikers can choose from trails that wind through the desert, head over the mountains, delve deep into the forests, or circumnavigate the cities. Whatever your choice of direction, you'll find thousands of miles of marked paths. Protect against sunburn and, if you're hiking in the desert areas, beware of heatstroke. In general, only backcountry hikers need worry about meeting up with poisonous snakes or Gila monsters.

Grand Canyon hikers should be well prepared before starting out. Summer months mean extreme heat, while the winter season can turn alternately snowy, rainy, or sunny. One of the biggest dangers of winter hikes is hypothermia, caused by exposure to cold, wet weather. In summer hikers to the inner Canyon must head out carrying a gallon of water for each day they plan to hike. There is no shade, so a hat and sunglasses are crucial. It is not advisable to hike any remote area alone. **The Backcountry Information Line** (tel. 602/638–7888) provides hikers with trail details, weather conditions, and packing suggestions.

For hikers who prefer to travel with a group, the **Sierra Club** (tel. 602/254–9330) leads a variety of wilderness treks.

Horseback Riding Traveling by horseback through the somewhat wild West or the scenic high country is perhaps the most appropriate way to explore Arizona. Stables offer a selection of mountain- or desert-trail rides lasting a half day, two days, or as long as two weeks. In the northern regions the season is from May through October. If riding is the focus of your Arizona holiday, however, you might consider staying at a dude ranch where you can saddle up every day.

River Rafting Rafting and kayaking trips down the Colorado River and through the Grand Canyon are experiences that keep visitors returning year after year. Trips run from one day to two weeks and operate during the summer season. Other rafting expeditions are offered on the Salt and Verde rivers, through the Sonoran Desert, near Scottsdale. Contact the **Arizona Office of Tourism** (*see* Visitor Information, *above*) for an extensive list of operators.

Rock Hounding Arizona is rock hound heaven, its deserts and mountains laden with a dazzling variety of rocks and minerals. The **Arizona Office of Tourism** (*see* Visitor Information, *above*) produces a free *Arizona Rockhound Guide* that tells you which specimens to look for in each part of the state. Inquire about restrictions before you fill your pockets; taking rocks is illegal on the Navajo and Hopi reservations, for example.

Skiing Cross-country skiing is featured at **Mormon Lake Ski Tour-**
Cross-Country **ing Center** (tel. 602/354–2240), southeast of Flagstaff, and along the miles of crisscrossing trails around **Alpine** (tel. 602/339–4384). Equipment and instruction are readily available, though it's best to make reservations ahead of time for the high season.

Downhill **Apache Sunrise Ski Resort** in McNary (tel. 602/772–SNOW or 800/882–7669 outside AZ), owned and operated by the White Mountain Apache Indians, encompasses three mountain peaks and is the state's largest ski area. Other popular resorts are at **Arizona Snow Bowl,** near Flagstaff (tel. 602/779–1951), and **Mt. Lemmon Ski Valley,** near Tucson (tel. 602/576–1400). Ski resorts cater to all levels, from beginning to expert, and provide instruction and equipment rental.

Tennis Arizona offers a multitude of tennis opportunities, from hard courts on city parks and at university campuses to full-scale programs at ultra-posh tennis-oriented resorts such as **John Gardiner's Tennis Ranch** (5700 E. McDonald Dr., Scottsdale 85253, tel. 602/948–2100), one of the country's best. Most hotels either have their own courts or are affiliated with a private or municipal facility.

National and State Parks and Monuments

National Parks Arizona's two national parks are the granddaddy Grand Canyon National Park (1,218,375 acres) and Petrified Forest National Park (93,533 acres). The **Grand Canyon,** northwest of Flagstaff, has achieved status as one of the Seven Natural Wonders of the World. Travelers come from all parts of the globe to hike, camp, raft, helicopter, or simply ooh and aah at the spectacular views and ever-changing colors, shadows, and light. **Petrified Forest National Park,** east of Flagstaff, features rainbow-colored petrified logs, tree fragments, and chunks of rock—preserved-in-stone remnants of a forest dating from the dinosaur age.

National Monuments **Saguaro National Monument,** which flanks Tucson on its east and west sides, boasts the most specimens in the United States of the towering saguaro cactus, which can live over 200 years. **Organ Pipe National Monument,** in the southwest part of the state, abounds in examples of the saguaro's many-armed cousin. For Native American ruins in scenic settings, visit **Walnut Canyon National Monument** and **Wupatki National Monument** in the Flagstaff area, **Tuzigoot National Monument** south of Sedona, and **Navajo National Monument** near Monument Valley. Little-visited spots of unusual beauty include **Sunset Crater Volcano National Monument,** west of Flagstaff, its black lava flows contrasted against a lush green forest; and **Chiricahua National Monument** in the southeast, where odd rock formations preside over woods that celebrate spring and autumn at the same time.

State Parks Arizona's state parks range from relatively tiny **Slide Rock** (54 acres), near Sedona, to 13,000-acre **Lake Havasu,** comprising three separate units; both feature water-based activities. Boating and water-sports enthusiasts also like to congregate at **Alamo Lake State Park,** north of Wenden, **Roper Lake State Park,** at the foot of Mt. Graham in the southeast, and **Lyman Lake State Park,** in the White Mountains area. **Catalina** and **Picacho Peak state parks,** near Tucson, and **Lost Dutchman State Park,** east of Phoenix, are the best bets for desert activities. **Painted Rocks State Park,** west of Gila Bend, is distinctive for its Indian rock carvings. Those interested in the lively frontier history of this state should enjoy **Riordon Historical State Park** in Flagstaff, **Jerome State Historic Park** in North-Central Arizona, and **Tombstone Courthouse State Historic Park** and **Yuma Territorial Prison State Historic Park,** both in the south. For a complete listing of all state parks and their facilities, contact the **Arizona State Parks Department** (800 W. Washington St., Phoenix 85007, tel. 602/542–4174).

Fragile Life Don't be tempted to pull any of Arizona's century-old saguaro cacti out by the roots. The state flower is protected by law, as are most of the slow-growing desert plants and flowers. Theft or vandalism carries stiff penalties. Similarly, the dry and easily desecrated desert floor takes centuries to overcome human damage. Consequently, it is illegal for four-wheel-drive and all-terrain vehicles and motorcycles to travel off established roadways.

Indian Reservations

Individual tribes own their respective lands. If you venture off main highways that traverse the reservations to do extensive backcountry exploring, you must request permission from the village leader; any local should be able to direct you. Never take photographs without first asking consent and paying a fee, if required. Visitors are occasionally allowed to watch certain tribal ceremonies, but all cameras, tape recorders, and even sketch pads are forbidden. Remember that you are a guest on private property. If you are planning to make extensive visits to the reservations, contact the **Arizona Office of Tourism** (*see* Visitor Information, *above*) for a map of the Arizona reservations and a list of addresses and telephone numbers of the 14 tribal councils in the state.

Dining

Outside the main cities, Arizona cuisine leans mainly toward western-style steaks, barbecued ribs and beans, biscuits with gravy, and chuck wagon–type fare. The Navajo taco (beans, tomatoes, lettuce, and cheese on Indian fry bread) and a few Hopi recipes served on the reservation blend Native American and Mexican food traditions. Mexican food is plentiful everywhere in the state. Phoenix and Tucson offer fine Continental dining, an eclectic mix of ethnic eateries, and, most important, the acclaimed southwestern international–style cuisine, featuring indigenous ingredients prepared in an innovative fashion. Make advance reservations at the better restaurants and don't be misled by the casual lifestyle—ask about dress codes first to avoid being turned away at the door. A few of the tonier establishments, including some at the swank resorts, require men to wear a jacket and tie.

Lodging

Arizona's hotels and motels run the gamut from world-class resorts to budget chains, with historic inns, bed-and-breakfasts, mountain lodges, dude ranches, campgrounds, and RV parks providing even more options. Most nationwide and international companies are represented within the state. Big resorts offer extensive recreational and dining facilities, while modest motels may provide nothing more than a small swimming pool and complimentary coffee. Make reservations well in advance for the high season—winter in the desert south and summer in the high country. Tremendous bargains can be found in the off season, when even the ultraswank spots cut their rates by half.

Bed-and-Breakfasts Many areas of the state offer European-style B&B lodging, in anything from a country ranch to a city mansion. Moderate prices and personalized, homey hospitality are the hallmarks of this type of accommodation. Arizona B&B organizations include **Mi Casa Su Casa** (Box 950, Tempe 85281, tel. 602/990–0682), **Bed and Breakfast in Arizona** (Box 8628, Scottsdale 85252, tel. 800/226–STAY), **Bed and Breakfast Scottsdale** (Box 624, Scottsdale 85252, tel. 602/998–7044), and the **Arizona Association of Bed and Breakfast Inns** (3101 North Central Ave., Suite 560, Phoenix 85712, tel. 602/277–0775). The Arizona Office of Tourism (*see* Vistor Information, *above*) has a statewide list of bed and breakfasts.

Dude Ranches Down-home western lifestyle, cooking, and activities are the focus of guest ranches, situated primarily in Tucson and Wickenburg. Some are resortlike properties where guests are pampered, while the smaller family-run ranches expect *everyone* to join in the chores. Horseback riding and other outdoor recreational activities are emphasized. Most dude ranches are closed during summer months. Contact the Arizona Office of Tourism (*see* Vistor Information, *above*) for the names and addresses of dude ranches throughout the state.

Home Exchange This is obviously an inexpensive solution to the lodging problem, because house-swapping means living rent-free. You find a house, apartment, or other vacation property to exchange for your own by becoming a member of a home-exchange organization, which then sends you its annual directories listing available exchanges and includes your own listing in at least one of them. Arrangements for the actual exchange are made by the two parties to it, not by the organization. Principal clearinghouses include **Intervac U.S./International Home Exchange** (Box 590504, San Francisco, CA 94159, tel. 415/435–3497), the oldest, with thousands of foreign and domestic homes for exchange in its three annual directories; membership is $62, or $72 if you want to receive the directories but remain unlisted. The **Vacation Exchange Club** (Box 650, Key West, FL 33041, tel. 800/638–3841), also with thousands of foreign and domestic listings, publishes four annual directories plus updates; the $50 membership includes your listing in one book. **Loan-a-Home** (2 Park La., Apt. 6E, Mount Vernon, NY 10552, tel. 914/664–7640) specializes in long-term exchanges; there is no charge to list your home, but the directories cost $35 or $45 depending on the number you receive.

Apartment and Villa Rentals If you want a home base that's roomy enough for a family and comes with cooking facilities, a furnished rental may be the solution. It's generally cost-wise, too, although not always—some rentals are luxury properties (economical only when your party is large). Home-exchange directories do list rentals—often second homes owned by prospective house swappers— and there are services that can not only look for a house or apartment for you (even a castle if that's your fancy) but also handle the paperwork. Some send an illustrated catalogue and others send photographs of spe-

cific properties, sometimes at a charge; up-front registra-
tion fees may apply. Among the companies are **Interhome
Inc.** (124 Little Falls Rd., Fairfield, NJ 07004, tel. 201/882–
6864); **Overseas Connection** (31 North Harbor Dr., Sag Harbor, NY 11963, tel. 516/725–9308); **Rent a Home International** (7200 34th Ave. NW, Seattle, WA 98117, tel. 206/
789–9377 or 800/488–7368); and **Vacation Home Rentals
Worldwide** (235 Kensington Ave., Norwood, NJ 07648, tel.
201/767–9393 or 800/633–3284). **Hideaways International**
(767 Islington St., Box 4433, Portsmouth, NH 03802, tel.
603/430–4433 or 800/843–4433), with properties in Europe,
the Caribbean, the United States, Canada, Mexico, and
the South Pacific, functions as a travel club. Membership
($79 yearly per person or family at the same address) in-
cludes two annual guides plus quarterly newsletters; rentals are arranged directly between members, not by the
club staff.

Camping and Campers can choose from a feast of federal, state, Native
Campgrounds American,or private campgrounds in virtually all parts of
the state. Facilities range from deluxe parks with swimming pools and recreation rooms to primitive backcountry
wilderness sites. Most campgrounds provide toilets, drinking water, showers, and hookups. Camping is also permitted in Arizona's seven national forests, but be forewarned
that there are no facilities whatsoever.

Campers should pack according to season, region, and
length of trip. Basic gear should include a sleeping bag, a
tent (optional, and forbidden in some RV parks), a camp
stove, cooking utensils, food and water supplies, a first-aid
kit, insect repellent, sunscreen, a lantern, rubbish disposal
bags, a rope, and a tarp. In case you forget something, almost every camping item is available for sale or rent at one
of Arizona's many sporting-goods shops.

Individual campgrounds should be contacted before travel
for suggestions as to specific equipment to bring, as well as
necessary reservations, advance deposits, and permits.
Most state parks have a 15-day maximum-stay limit. For
further details, contact the **Arizona Office of Tourism** or the
appropriate tribal council (*see* Visitor Information in Before You Go, *above*), **National Park Service** (202 E. Earll
Dr., Suite 115, Phoenix 85012, tel. 602/640–5250), **Bureau
of Land Management** (Box 16563, Phoenix 85011, tel. 602/
640–5547), **Arizona State Parks Department** (*see* State
Parks, *above*), **Apache Sitgreaves National Forest** (Box 640,
Springerville 85938, tel. 602/333–4301), **Coconino National
Forest** (2323 E. Greenlaw La., Flagstaff 86004, tel. 602/
556–7400), **Coronado National Forest** (Federal Bldg., 300
W. Congress St., Tucson 85701, tel. 602/670–4552), **Kaibab
National Forest** (800 S. 6th St., Williams 86046, tel. 602/
635–2681), **Prescott National Forest** (344 S. Cortez, Pres-
cott 86303, tel. 602/445–1762), or **Tonto National Forest**
(Box 5348, Phoenix 85010, tel. 602/225–5200). The **National**

Forest Service hotline (tel. 602/225–5296) gives recorded information and campground updates.

Credit Cards

The following credit card abbreviations have been used: AE, American Express; D, Discover; DC, Diners Club; MC, MasterCard; V, Visa.

2 Portraits of Arizona

The What and the Why of Desert Country

By Joseph Wood
Krutch

On the brightest and warmest days my desert is most itself because sunshine and warmth are the very essence of its character. The air is lambent with light; the caressing warmth envelops everything in its ardent embrace. Even when outlanders complain that the sun is too dazzling and too hot, we desert lovers are prone to reply, "At worst that is only too much of a good thing."

Unfortunately, this is the time when the tourist is least likely to see it. Even the winter visitor who comes for a month or six weeks is mostly likely to choose January or February because he is thinking about what he is escaping at home rather than of what he is coming to here. True, the still warm sun and the usually bright skies make a dramatic contrast with what he has left behind. In the gardens of his hotel or guest ranch, flowers still bloom and some of the more obstreperous birds make cheerful sounds, even though they do not exactly sing at this season. The more enthusiastic visitors talk about "perpetual summer" and sometimes ask if we do not find the lack of seasons monotonous. But this is nonsense. Winter is winter even in the desert.

At Tucson's 2,300 feet it often gets quite cold at night even though shade temperatures during the day may rise to 75° Farenheit or even higher. Most vegetation is pausing, though few animals hibernate. This is a sort of neutral time when the desert environment is least characteristically itself. It is almost like late September or early October, just after the first frost, in southern New England. For those who are thinking of nothing except getting away from something, rather than learning to know a new world, this is all very well. But you can't become acquainted with the desert itself at that time of year.

By April the desert is just beginning to come into its own. The air and the skies are summery without being hot; the roadsides and many of the desert flats are thickly carpeted with a profusion of wildflowers such as only California can rival. The desert is smiling before it begins to laugh, and October or November are much the same. But June is the month for those who want to know what the desert is really like. That is the time to decide once and for all if it is, as for many it turns out to be, "your country."

It so happens that I am writing this not long after the 21st of June and I took especial note of that astronomically significant date. This year summer began at precisely 10 hours and no minutes, Mountain Standard Time. That means that the sun rose higher and stayed longer in the sky than on any other day of the year. In the north there is often a considerable lag in the seasons as the earth warms up, but here, where it is never very cold, the longest day and the hottest are likely to coincide pretty closely. So it was this year. On June 21 the sun rose almost to the zenith so that at noon he cast almost no shadow. And he was showing what he is capable of.

Even in this dry air 109° Fahrenheit in the shade is pretty warm. Under the open sky the sun's rays strike with an almost physical force, pouring down from a blue dome unmarked by the faintest suspicion of even a fleck of cloud. The year has been unusually dry even for the desert. During the four months just past no rain—not even a light shower—has fallen. The surface of the ground is as dry as powder. And yet, when I look out of the window the dominant color of the landscape is incredibly green.

On the low foothills surrounding the steep rocky slopes of the mountains, which are actually 10 to 12 miles away but seem in the clear air much closer at hand, this greenness ends in a curving line following the contour of the mountains' base and inevitably suggesting the waves of a green sea lapping the irregular shore line of some island rising abruptly from the ocean. Between me and that shore line the desert is sprinkled with hundreds, probably thousands, of evenly placed shrubs, varied now and then by a small tree—usually a mesquite or what is called locally a cat's-claw acacia.

More than a month ago all the little annual flowers and weeds which spring up after the winter rains and rush from seed to seed again in six weeks gave up the ghost at the end of their short lives. Their hope of posterity lies now invisible, either upon the surface of the bare ground or just below it. Yet when the summer thunderstorms come in late July or August, they will not make the mistake of germinating. They are triggered to explode into life only when they are both moist and cool—which they will not be until next February or March when their season begins. Neither the shrubs nor the trees seem to know that no rain has fallen during the long months. The leathery, somewhat resinous, leaves of the dominant shrub—the attractive plant unattractively dubbed "creosote bush"—are not at all parched or wilted. Neither are the deciduous leaves of the mesquite.

Not many months ago the creosote was covered with bright yellow pealike flowers; the mesquite with pale yellow catkins. Now the former is heavy with gray seed and on the mesquite are forming long pods which Indians once ate and which cattle now find an unusually rich food.

It looks almost as though the shrubs and trees could live without water. But of course they cannot. Every desert plant has its secret, though it is not always the same one. In the case of the mesquite and the creosote it is that their roots go deep and that, so the ecologists says, there is in the desert no wet or dry season below six feet. What little moisture is there is pretty constant through the seasons of the year and through the dry years as well as the wet. Like the temperature in some caves, it never varies. The mesquite and creosote are not compelled to care whether it has rained for four months or not. And unlike many other plants they flourish whether there has been less rain or more than usual.

Those plants which have substantial root systems but nevertheless do not reach so deep are more exuberant some years than others. Thus the Encelia, or brittlebush, which, in normal years, literally covers many slopes with thousands of yellow, daisylike flowers, demands a normal year. Though I have never seen it fail, I am told that in very dry years it comes into leaf but does not flower, while in really catastrophic droughts it does not come up at all, as the roots lie dormant and hope for better times. Even the creosote bush, which never fails, can, nevertheless, profit from surface water, and when it gets the benefit of a few thunderstorms in late July or August, it will flower and fruit a second time so that the expanse which is now all green will be again sprinkled with yellow. . . .

Obviously the animals and plants who share this country with me take it for granted. To them it is just "the way things are." By now I am beginning to take it for granted myself. But being a man I must ask what they cannot: What *is* a desert and why is it what it is? At latitude 32 one expects the climate to be warm. But the desert is much more than merely warm. It is a consistent world with a special landscape, a special geography, and, to go with them, a special flora and fauna adapted to that geography and that climate.

Nearly every striking feature of this special world, whether it be the shape of the mountains or the habits of its plant and animal inhabitants, goes back ultimately to the grand fact of dryness—the dryness of the ground, of the air, of the whole sum-total. And the most inclusive cause of the dryness is simply that out here it doesn't rain very much.

Some comparisons with regions where it rains more may help us understand what that means. Take, for example, southern New England. By world standards it gets a lot—namely some 40 inches of rain per year. Certain parts of the southern states get even more: about 50 inches for east Tennessee, nearly 60 for New Orleans. Some areas on the West Coast get fantastic amounts, like the 75 inches at Crescent City, California, and the unbelievable 153 inches, or nearly four times what New York City gets, recorded one year in Del Norde County, California.

Nevertheless, New England's 40 is a lot of water, either comparatively or absolutely. The region around Paris, for instance, gets little more than half that amount. Forty inches is, in absolute terms, more than most people imagine. One inch of rain falling on an acre of ground means more than 27,000 gallons of water. No wonder that irrigation in dry regions is quite a formidable task even for modern technology.

In terms of what vegetation can use, 40 inches is ample for the kind of agriculture and natural growth which we tend to think of as "normal." It means luxuriant grass, rapid development of second growth woodland, a veritable jungle of weeds and bushes in midsummer. In inland America the rainfall tends to be less than in the coastal regions. As one moves westward from the Mississippi it declines sharply and begins to drop below 20 inches a year at about the one hundredth meridian or, very roughly, at a line drawn from Columbus, Ohio through Oklahoma City. This means too little water for most broad-leaved trees and explains why the southern Great Plains were as treeless when the white man first saw them as they are today.

Our true deserts—the Great Basin Desert in Utah and Nevada, the Chihuahuan in New Mexico, the Sonoran in Arizona, and the Mohave in California—all lie still further to the west. The four differ among themselves but they are all dry and hot and they all fulfill what is probably the most satisfactory definition of "desert"—namely a region where the ground cover is not continuous; where, that is, the earth remains bare of vegetation between such plants as manage to grow. Over these American deserts the rainfall varies considerably and with it the character and extent of the vegetation. In southern Arizona, for instance, it is about four inches at Yuma, nearly 11 near Tucson. Four inches means sand dunes which look like those pictures of the Sahara which the word "desert" calls to most people's minds. Eleven means that where the soil is suitable, well-separated individuals of such desert plants as the cacti and the paloverde trees will flourish.

But if scanty rainfall makes for deserts, what makes for scanty rainfall? To that there are two important answers. One is simply that most regions other than the mountainous ones tend to be dry if they lie in that belt of permanently high atmospheric pressure which extends some 30 or 35 degrees on each side of the equator where calms are frequent and winds erratic. Old sailors used to call this region "the horse latitudes" though nobody knows why and you can take your choice of three equally unconvincing explanations. One is that it was because horses tended to die when the ships lay long in the hot calms. Another, because the boisterous changeableness of the winds when they do come suggests unruly horses. A third is that they were originally called after the English explorer, Ross, which was mistaken by the Germans for their old word for "horse." In any event, the latitude of Tucson puts it just within the "horse latitudes." Most of the important deserts of the world, including the Sahara and the Gobi, lie within this same belt.

The other important answer to the question, "What makes for scanty rainfall?" is, "Mountains lying across the path of such moist winds as do blow." In our case the Coast Ranges of California lie between us and the Pacific. From my front porch, which looks directly across the desert to some nearer mountains of the southernmost Rockies, I can see, on a small scale, what happens. Many, many times a moisture-laden mass of air reaches as far as these closest mountains. Dark clouds form, sometimes the whole range is blotted out. Torrential rains are falling. But on me not a drop. Either the sky is blue overhead or the high clouds which have blown my way dissolve visibly as the warm air rising from my sun-drenched flats reaches them. I am in what the geographers call a "rain shadow" cast by the mountains. Up at their summit the rainfall is nearly twice as much as it is down here and they are clothed with pines beginning at 6,000 or 7,000 feet and going on up to the 19,000-foot peak. When I do get rain in midwinter and in midsummer, it is usually because winds have brought moisture up from the Gulf of Mexico by an unobstructed southern route, or because in summer a purely local thundershower has been formed out of the hot air rising from the sun-beaten desert floor. Most of the time the sun is hot, even in winter, and the air is usually fantastically dry, the relative humidity being often less than 10.

Naturally the plants and animals living in such a region must be specially adapted to survive under such conditions, but the casual visitor usually notices the strangeness of the landscape before he is aware of the flora or the fauna. And the peculiar features of the landscape are also the result of dryness, even in ways that are not immediately obvious.

The nude mountains reveal their contours, or veil them as lightly as the late Greek sculptors veiled their nudes, because only near the summits of the mountains can anything tall enough to obscure the outlines grow. A little less obvious is the fact that the beautiful "monuments" of northern Arizona and southern Utah owe their unusual forms to the sculpturing of wind-blown sand, or that sheer cliffs often rise from a sloping cone of rocks and boulders because the talus slopes can accumulate in just that way only where there is not enough draining water to distribute them over the whole surrounding plain, as they would be distributed in regions of heavier rainfall. But the most striking example of all is the greatest single scenic wonder of the region, the Grand Canyon itself. This narrow gash, cut a mile deep through successive strata until the river flows at last over some of the oldest rock exposed anywhere on earth, could have been formed only in a very dry climate.

As recently as 200 years ago the best informed observer would have taken it for granted that the river was running between those sheer walls at the bottom of the gorge simply because it had found them out. Today few visitors are not aware that the truth lies the other way around, that the river cut its own course through the rock. But most laymen do not ask the next questions: Why is Grand Canyon unique, or why are such canyons, even on a smaller scale, rare? And the answer to those questions is that a set of very special conditions was necessary.

First there must be a thick series of rock strata slowly rising as a considerable river flows over it. Second, that considerable river must carry an unusual amount of hard sand or stone fragments in suspension so that it will be able to cut downward at least as rapidly as the rock over which it flows is rising. Third, that considerable river must be flowing through very arid country. Otherwise rain, washing over the edges of the cut, will widen it at the top as the cut goes deeper. That is why broad valleys are characteristic of regions with normal rainfall; canyons, large and small, of arid country.

And Grand Canyon is the grandest of all canyons because at that particular place all the necessary conditions were fulfilled more exuberantly than at any other place in the whole world. The Colorado River carries water from a relatively wet country through a dry one, it bears with it a fantastic amount of abrasive material, the rock over which it flows has been slowly rising during several millions of years, and too little rain falls to widen very rapidly the gash which it cuts. Thus in desert country everything from the color of a mouse or the shape of a leaf up to the largest features of the mountains themselves is more likely than not to have the same explanation: dryness.

So far as living things go, all this adds up to what even an ecologist may so far forget himself as to call an "unfavorable environment." But like all such pronouncements this one doesn't mean much unless we ask "unfavorable for what and for whom?" For many plants, for many animals, and for some men it is very favorable indeed. Many of the first two would languish and die, transferred to some region where conditions were "more favorable." It is here, and here only, that they flourish. Many men feel healthier and happier in the bright dry air than they do anywhere else. And since I happen to be one of them, I not unnaturally have a special interest in the plants and animals who share my liking for just these conditions. For five years now I have been amusing myself by inquiring of them directly what habits and what adjustments they have found most satisfactory. Many of them are delightfully ingenious and eminently sensible. . . .

Men of most races have long been accustomed to speak with scorn of the few peoples who happen to live where nature makes things too easy. In the inclemency of their weather, the stoniness of their soil, or the rigors of their winter they find secret virtues so that even the London fog has occasionally found Englishmen to praise it. No doubt part of all this is mere prejudice at worst, making a virtue out of necessity at best. But undoubtedly there is also something in it. We grow strong against the pressure of a difficulty, and ingenious by solving problems. Individuality and character are developed by challenge. We tend to admire trees, as well as men, who bear the stamp of their successful struggles with a certain amount of adversity. People who have not had too easy a time of it develop flavor. And there is no doubt about the fact that desert life has character. Plants and animals are so obviously and visibly what they are because of the problems they have solved. They are part of some whole. They belong. Animals and plants, as well as men, become especially interesting when they do fit their environment, when to some extent they reveal what their response to it has been. And nowhere more than in the desert do they reveal it.

Arizona Crafts

By Suzanne Carmichael

Suzanne Carmichael is the author of The Traveler's Guide to American Crafts: East of the Mississippi *and* West of the Mississippi *and travel and craft articles for such publications as* The New York Times, USA Weekend, *and* Northwest Magazine.

Whether you have $10 or $1,000 to spend, shopping for crafts can make your trip to Arizona memorable, and not only for what you'll take home with you. The pursuit of local wares may take you down desert roads to remote crafts studios, introduce you to snazzy urban galleries and historic trading posts, or involve you in lively crafts festivals. Regional crafts also provide an intimate introduction to an area's history, culture, and peoples, as well as its contemporary interests and trends.

In the Southwest, several cultures have developed strong crafts traditions, some predating European contact by more than 1,000 years. Native American, cowboy, and contemporary crafts—many made from native materials or by capturing local colors, themes, and spirit—are all well developed in this region.

Native American Crafts

Arizona visitors will see Native American crafts everywhere—in specialty shops, airports, motel gift shops, drugstores, and even gas stations. The problem is finding top-notch authentic work. Some so-called Native American crafts are made in Taiwan or Mexico. Others labeled "genuine Indian made" are mass-produced with shoddy material and inferior workmanship.

If you haven't read any books on the subject, study Native American collections at the Heard Museum (Phoenix) or the Museum of Northern Arizona (Flagstaff). These museums also have their own gift shops, which sell good-quality items at reasonable prices. Long-established trading posts, galleries, and Native American dealers are another option. Most first-rate shops will have a range of prices and knowledgeable salespeople who can answer your questions. If everything in a shop is inexpensive, it's probably attributable to the poor quality of the goods rather than to a low overhead. It's a good idea to shop elsewhere.

One way to ensure authenticity and at the same time add an adventurous detour to your trip is to buy directly from craftspeople on the reservations. Look for signs that say "pottery," "rugs," or "baskets" hanging outside homes. Although visiting craftspeople is not a guarantee of quality, it does provide an opportunity to ask questions and learn about the work you are purchasing. And it's fun to watch artisans at work, to see their raw materials being turned into finished pieces.

Reservation gift shops are another option for authentic wares, although quality and prices vary tremendously. And crafts are generally sold at Native American festivals, fairs, and powwows (ceremonial gatherings), which exhibit the work of many artisans and also showcase tribal dancing, story-telling, and food. One recommended event is Flagstaff's annual six-week Festival of Native American Arts held each summer at the Coconino Center for the Arts (2300 N. Valley Rd., U.S. 180, Flagstaff, AZ, tel. 602/779–6921). This juried festival offers high-quality traditional and contemporary tribal arts, including work rarely found elsewhere, such as colorful Pueblo moccasins and miniature pottery. Visitors can also watch jewelry-making, cloth- or basket-weaving demonstrations or participate in various workshops, including one that teaches children how to make Native American masks.

Arizona's Native American crafts legacy includes distinctive tribal arts made by many of the state's 14 tribes. Although the work of the Hopi, Navajo, and Tohonó O'odham (Papago) are best known, equally fine items are produced by the Chemehuevi, Maricopa, Mojave, Paiute, and Pima tribes.

Hopi pottery, baskets, and weaving reflect ancient traditions and techniques, while the tribe's silverwork is of more recent vintage. Artisans of the Hopi tribe live on the reservation's three mesas, each one of which has a craft specialty. First Mesa is home to potters who fashion hand-coiled vessels with pale cream or deep red glazes decorated with stylized birds and figures. Second Mesa's specialty is baskets of thickly coiled yucca joined with colorfully dyed lengths of yucca leaves; wicker baskets decorated with brightly colored designs can be found on Third Mesa. When buying pottery and baskets, look for symmetrical shapes, smooth rims, and neatly painted or evenly woven designs.

Tribal artisans also create kachina dolls, colorfully costumed, masked figures embellished with feathers, textiles, and leather. Modeled after the Hopi religion's kachina ceremonial dancers, the dolls are used to teach children their religious heritage. Hopi weaving, which is done exclusively by men, creates colorful sashes and narrow decorative bands that are used on clothing. Both of these items are woven on belt looms. The vertical threads (warp) on these unusual looms stretch around one rod tied to a tree to another rod held taut by a belt wrapped around the weaver's waist. While making a sash, the weaver leans forward to loosen the warp, backward to tighten it. Although Hopi woven fabric is created primarily for personal use, some pieces are occasionally available through the reservation's crafts cooperative.

Hopi silverwork, a craft that was begun in the late 1890s, reflects a creative collaboration between contemporary silverworking techniques and ancient motifs. Hopi silversmiths use two layers of silver to create some of the Southwest's finest jewelry. Designs, which range from simple sun shapes to those depicting elaborate tribal legends, are carefully cut through the top layer, which is then soldered to the bottom layer. Tiny parallel lines are chiseled inside the design, and the piece is then oxidized to make the motif stand out from the polished silver surrounding it. The best pieces have smoothly cut patterns with neatly stamped, parallel interior lines.

Navajo jewelry traces its origin to the mid-19th century. Tribal craftsmen learned smithing from Mexican artisans, later adding their own styles and designs. Early pieces were made from hammered silver coins and decorated with stamp work. Although turquoise beads date from prehistoric times, Navajos did not combine the stone with silver until the late 1800s. Today, in addition to turquoise, artisans sometimes incorporate coral, lapis, and other semiprecious stones into their designs.

Contemporary Navajo jewelry ranges from simple rings and cast silver bracelets to massive necklaces and concha belts (named for the stamped silver disks strung together on narrow leather strips). Because there are so many variables in the quality of stones and workmanship, you should purchase Navajo jewelry only from reputable dealers. Many Indian traders and jewelry shops throughout the Southwest have one case displaying items of Native American–made jewelry that have been pawned and not retrieved by their owners. Although you can occasionally find older pieces of exquisite quality in these cases, be leery of assertions as to an item's age or caliber.

Navajos are also known for the variety and quality of their woven wool rugs. Sheepherders for centuries, Navajos learned their weaving skills from Pueblo Indians during the 18th century. At first they produced blankets and clothing in natural brown-and-white stripes. During the late 19th century, colors, particularly red, and a wide range of complex designs were added. At this time, most weavers also switched from producing items for personal use to creating rugs for traders. Today Navajo rug patterns range from traditional eye dazzlers with bold zigzag patterns and pictorials featuring animals and other figures to yei rugs that duplicate sand-painting designs and two-faced rugs with different patterns on each surface.

If you purchase a Navajo rug, make sure that it is made entirely of wool (no linen or cotton threads), that the wool is of even thickness throughout the piece, that the design is neatly woven, and that the colors are uniform throughout. A good source of Navajo rugs and other Native American crafts is the Hubbell Trading Post, a National Historic Site in Ganado, on the Navajo reservation 22 miles west of Window Rock. Established in 1878, the post looks exactly as it did in the 19th century when Navajos brought John Lorenzo Hubbell their rugs and jewelry to trade for groceries and other goods. These artisans still bring their crafts for sale or trade, but now they arrive in pickups instead of on horseback.

While Hopi and Navajo crafts are the best-known Arizona Native American arts, other tribes also produce good-quality items that provide an introduction to their cultural history. Among these are traditional Tohonó O'Odham (Papago) baskets. Tohonó O'Odham artisans create coiled, waterproof baskets with intricate designs using techniques and materials that have remained virtually unchanged for more than 11 centuries. Most baskets are broad, slightly sloping vessels with geometric patterns and are made from two Southwest desert plants. Black designs, the most highly prized, are fashioned from black devil's claw, an increasingly rare plant that yields very strong strips of jet-black fiber. Red motifs are woven with the root of banana yucca, a more common plant found in Arizona's higher elevations. One traditional Tohonó O'Odham design is the legendary Man in the Maze, a stylized male figure standing at the top of the basket, about to enter a complex white-and-black labyrinth.

Baskets are also made by the Pima and Paiute. The Pima use coils of cattail stems bound with willow and favor complex zigzag designs. Traditional Paiute baskets have plain, functional shapes, reflecting the fact that they were once used to carry water, harvest or store seeds, and cradle babies. Mojave, Maricopa, and Chemehuevi tribal arts are more difficult to find, but they are worth the effort. Mojave beadwork can be exquisite, especially large, collar-shape necklaces created in traditional network designs resembling intricate lace. Maricopa artisans specialize in cream-colored pottery, decorated with black designs that incorporate both geometric shapes and curvilinear symbols. Finely woven Chemehuevi baskets, another rare but exquisite craft, are made from coiled fiber, sometimes decorated with colorful feathers.

Cowboy Crafts

Even if you don't own horses or cattle, consider buying cowboy crafts: They can add pizzazz to your decor or an unusual flair to your wardrobe and provide an intriguing diversion as you watch them being created by talented artisans.

Arizona ranchers may use computers to keep track of their businesses, but no one has devised the technology to replace cowboys. Although his (and sometimes her) job may include time in a pickup, the daily routine is still dominated by horses, cattle, and traditional equipment rarely influenced by 20th-century innovations. The items cowboys use every day—from saddles and spurs to bridles and hats—form a crafts tradition that spans centuries. Some items originated with Native Americans, while others were adopted from Mexican or California-Spanish traditions.

Arizona cowboy crafts can be found in many shops, and even in department stores, but it's more fun to buy them directly from craftspeople or in tack shops that sell everything a horse and its rider need, from saddles to cowboy hats. Look in telephone books under tack shops, horse furnishings, or specific crafts such as saddlery or hats. For a thorough immersion, attend Flagstaff's annual 5½-week Trappings of the American West Festival, sponsored by the Coconino Center for the Arts; it runs from early May until the second week of June. The festival includes cowboy crafts demonstrations and workshops where you can learn rawhide braiding and bootmaking.

Although cowboy crafts are often decorative, they are first of all functional tools of the trade. Hats protect the wearer from weather, branches, and rocks and double as containers for carrying water and feed. Boots, designed to be pulled off easily and fit comfortably in stirrups, protect feet from mud and brush. Chaps shield the legs from prickly cactus and other hazards. The brush in Arizona is particularly heavy, so cowboys here prefer Arizona bell-bottom chaps made from very heavy leather that is flared at the bottom so they bend with the leg. The best of each? Hats made from beaver-fur felt, custom-made boots, and used chaps with that trail-worn look.

Saddles, which are custom-made to fit horse and rider, are often covered with carved or stamped designs of elaborate floral and leaf motifs. Some cowboys claim that deep carving keeps them from slipping in the saddle. For urban cowpokes, many saddlemakers create stamped or carved leather purses, belts, wallets, and even wastebaskets.

The oldest cowboy craft is leather and horsehair braiding. Conceived by Native Americans, braiding was later adopted by Mexican and American cowboys. Complex patterns decorate braided horse gear, from bridles and reins to other items whose exotic names belie their practicality: bosals and hobbles, romals and quirts. Look also for braided hatbands, belts, and bracelets.

Other cowboy accoutrements include bits and spurs with ornate inlaid designs that are seen only by the cowboy and his horse. Texas cowboys generally favor massive inlaid silver stars and geometric patterns, while California and Arizona cowboys prefer gear embellished with flowers and flourishes. Many smiths also fashion decorative silverwork for saddles, as well as buckles, money clips, and jewelry. Knives, another cowboy necessity, can be found in great variety. Look for those with handles that are made from exotic materials, engraved, or inlaid with precious metal and stones.

Contemporary Crafts

Arizona's contemporary artisans work in every medium, but particularly in ceramics, textiles, and wood. Although the focus of their work varies from abstract to functional, many of the crafts reflect Arizona colors: the splashy hues of a desert sunset, the subtle pastels of cactus flowers, the myriad reds of Sedona's cliffs. There's also a healthy dose of humor in many items: prickly ceramic cactus vases, howling wood dogs, flirty roadrunner sculptures, chairs with coyote armrests. The use of native materials is also common—for example, you may come across cactus-spine baskets or mesquite armoires.

Phoenix, Scottsdale, and Tucson offer a bonanza of contemporary crafts galleries. On a smaller scale, Tubac, an artists' community 35 miles south of Tucson, has numerous crafts studios open to the public. Tubac artisans create everything from avante-garde jewelry and textiles to copper fountains shaped like cacti. To find galleries throughout Arizona, consult *Art Life*, two comprehensive guides (one covers northern Arizona, the other southern Arizona) that describe galleries, provide detailed maps, and include indexes arranged by style, subject, and medium. Available free in many Arizona galleries, the guides can also be ordered by calling Yoakum Publishing (tel. 602/797-1271).

3 Grand Canyon Country and Lake Mead

By William E.
Hafford

Updated by
Edie Jarolim

Although millions of words have been devoted to describing the Grand Canyon, writers have generally conceded that the Earth's greatest gorge is beyond the scope of language. Southwestern author Frank Waters has come closer than most to capturing its power. "It is the sum total," he writes, "of all the aspects of nature combined in one integrated whole. It is at once the smile and frown upon the face of nature. In its heart is the savage, uncontrollable fury of all the inanimate Universe, and at the same time the immeasurable serenity that succeeds it. It is Creation."

To appreciate the Grand Canyon, you must see it. Not even the finest photographs pack a fraction of the impact of a personal glimpse of this vast and beautiful scar on the surface of our planet—277 miles long, 17 miles across at its widest spot, and more than a mile below the rim at its deepest point. Designated one of the Seven Natural Wonders of the World, the Grand Canyon is the quintessence of the high drama of the American western landscape.

More than 65 million years ago, a great wrenching of the earth pushed the land in the region of the canyon up into a domed tableland, today called the Colorado Plateau. Then the Colorado River, racing south through present-day Utah, began chewing at the uplifted region. The river is responsible for much of the erosion, but many side gullies and canyons were formed by melting snow and fierce rainstorms that sent water rushing into the gorge through smaller tributaries. Softer rock formations were washed away by the Colorado and carried to the distant sea; the harder formations remained as great cliffs and buttes.

The twisted and contorted layers of rock reveal a geologic profile of the Earth. The oldest exposed rock on the planet—more than 2 billion years old and formed as part of the Earth's original crust—is the Vishnu Schist at the bottom of the canyon. Today, what remains above the twisting line of river are otherworldly stone monuments with colors that range from muted pastels to deep purples, vibrant yellows, fiery reds, and soft blues. The colors shift with the hours: What you see at midmorning is repainted by the setting sun.

This is also a land of ancient peoples. In some of the deepest and most inaccessible reaches of the Grand Canyon, evidence of early human habitation exists. Stone ruins high in the cliffs reveal the archaeological secrets of a culture more than 4,000 years old. In the higher country above the rims, both north and south, are the ruins of the Anasazi, who remained in the area until about AD 1200. It is believed that they left the region during a period of harsh and sustained drought. Today's Hopi Indians, who live on high rock mesas about 150 miles east of the canyon, may be descendants of that group.

Grand Canyon National Park

KEY

····· Trail

– – – Unpaved Road

PAINTED DESERT

Colorado River

Marble Canyon

Point Imperial

North Rim Entrance Station

KAIBAB NATIONAL FOREST

KAIBAB PLATEAU

67

Bright Angel Point

Cape Royal

Desert View

East Entrance

64

Grandview Point

SOUTH RIM

East Rim Drive

Granite Gorge

Phantom Ranch

Grand Canyon Lodge

NORTH RIM

Point Sublime

Bright Angel Creek

Kaibab Trail

Yaki Point

Grand Canyon Village

South Entrance

180

64

West Rim Drive

Grand Canyon Airport

Hopi Point

Pima Point

Hermit's Rest

Havasupai Point

Inner Gorge

Great Thumb Point

Colorado River

Kanab Canyon

Supai

Havasu Canyon

COCONINO PLATEAU

The Dome

KANAB PLATEAU

N

LAKE MEAD NATIONAL RECREATION AREA

Tuweep

Aubrey Cliffs

0   10 miles

0   15 km

In the year 1540, a small group of Spanish soldiers under the command of Captain García López de Cárdenas became the first white men to look into the canyon. The members of the expedition, dispatched by Francisco Coronado to find an Indian village, were disinclined to stay very long—or to return. Spanish Franciscan missionary and explorer Tomás Garcés visited a Havasupai Indian village in the canyon in 1776, and Lieutenant Joseph Ives went on an official mission for the U.S. government to explore the area in 1857, but no one thought it worth much attention until 1869, when John Wesley Powell, a one-armed adventurer and scholar, put rough-hewn boats into the Colorado and let the swirling white water of the mighty river take him its length.

During the last years of the 19th century, almost all development at or near the canyon was related to mining. In fact, the earliest trails down into the canyon were built by miners searching for precious minerals. Shortly after the beginning of the 20th century, the Santa Fe Railroad completed a line to the South Rim of the canyon, ushering in the era of tourism. In 1903 Theodore Roosevelt visited and drew public interest to the site; it was declared a national park in 1919. Today more than 4 million visitors come each year from around the world to peer into this gorge in amazement.

The Fred Harvey Company opened the world-famous El Tovar Hotel on the rim of the canyon in 1905, heralding the beginning of Grand Canyon Village. Now there are more than 850 motel and hotel rooms in Grand Canyon Village, but the ever-increasing visitor population makes even that number of accommodations insufficient during the summer months. If you can arrange it, try to visit the Grand Canyon in the fall or spring. You might encounter cold weather during those periods, but chances are good that most of the days will be clear and will range from pleasantly cool to warm. In autumn and spring, when the crowds have thinned, reservations are much easier to arrange, and, in some cases, prices drop. Or consider a winter visit. The snow on the ground only enhances the site's sublime beauty.

The North Rim, in the isolated Arizona Strip, draws only about 10% of the Grand Canyon's visitors but is every bit as gorgeous as the South Rim. From southern Arizona, there's only one highway into this area, 210 miles of lonely road to the north and west of Flagstaff. Set in deep forest near the 9,000-foot crest of the Kaibab Plateau, the North Rim is, for many visitors, worth the extra miles. But truth to tell, there's virtually no place along either rim or in the depths of the Grand Canyon that will fail to startle and impress you.

Essential Information

Important Addresses and Numbers

Tourist
Information

Grand Canyon National Park Lodges (Box 699, Grand Canyon 86023, tel. 602/638–2401), for lodging and all other tour and recreational information inside the park at the South Rim.

Grand Canyon National Park (Box 129, Grand Canyon 86023, tel. 602/638–7888), for general information. Write ahead for a complimentary *Trip Planner*, updated regularly by the National Park Service.

North and South Rim camping (MISTIX, Box 85705, San Diego, CA 92138, tel. 800/365–2267 or 619/452–0150 outside the U.S.). When you call this computer-operated system, have the exact dates you'd like to camp on hand.

Grand Canyon Lodge (Box 400, Cedar City, UT 84720, tel. 801/586–7686), for lodging and general information about the North Rim year-round. For information on local services during the season in which the North Rim is open (generally mid-May through late October, depending on the weather), you can phone the lodge directly (tel. 602/638–2611).

Every arriving visitor at the South or North Rim is given a detailed map of the local area. Both rims also publish a free newspaper, *The Guide*, which contains a detailed area map; it is available at the visitor center and many of the lodging facilities and stores.

The park also distributes a free *Accessibility Guide* newsletter, which details the facilities available for those with special needs.

Emergencies **Police, fire, or ambulance** (tel. 911).

Medical
South Rim

Grand Canyon Health Center (Grand Canyon Village, tel. 602/638–2551 or 602/638–2469) offers physician services and receives patients weekdays 8–5:30, Saturday 9–noon. After-hours care and 24-hour emergency services are also available. Dental care (tel. 602/638–2395) is offered by appointment only.

North Rim

The **North Rim Clinic** (Grand Canyon Lodge, tel. 602/638–2611) is staffed by a nurse practitioner. The clinic is generally open weekdays 9–5, but 24-hour emergency service is available.

Pharmacies

At the South Rim there is a well-stocked drugstore at Grand Canyon Village (tel. 602/638–2460), open weekdays 8:30–5:30 year-round, and also Saturday morning in the summer; it's generally closed for an hour at lunchtime during the week. There is no pharmacy at the North Rim.

Road Service At Grand Canyon Village, the **Fred Harvey Public Garage**
South Rim (tel. 602/638–2225) is a fully equipped AAA garage that
provides auto and RV repair and 24-hour emergency service. About ¾ mile down the road, across from the visitor
center, **Fred Harvey Chevron** (tel. 602/638–2631) does oil
and tire changes and minor repairs, and carries propane
and diesel fuel.

North Rim The **Chevron** service station (tel. 602/638–2611), offering
auto repairs, is located inside the park on the access road
leading to the North Rim Campground. No diesel fuel is
available at the North Rim.

Food and **Babbitt's General Store** (tel. 602/638–2262) has three loca-
Camping Supplies tions in the South Rim area: at Grand Canyon Village, in the
South Rim nearby village of Tusayan, and at Desert View near the
east park entrance. The main store, in Grand Canyon Village, is a department store that offers a deli and a full line of
camping, hiking, and backpacking supplies, in addition to
groceries.

North Rim The **North Rim General Store** (tel. 602/638–2611), located
within the park and in the vicinity of the North Rim Campground, carries groceries, some clothing, and travelers'
supplies.

Banks An office of the **Valley National Bank** (tel. 602/638–2437) is
located at the South Rim across from the visitor center in
Grand Canyon Village. Services include a 24-hour teller
machine operating with Valley National Bank, American
Express, Plus (Visa), Star, Arizona Interchange Network,
and Cirrus (MasterCard) access cards. The bank cashes
traveler's checks and exchanges foreign currency, but does
not cash personal checks. Banking hours are weekdays
10–3. No banking facilities are located within Grand Canyon National Park at the North Rim.

Arriving and Departing by Plane

Because most of Arizona's scenic highlights are many miles
apart, an automobile is the most practical mode of transportation for touring the state. However, you won't really need
a car if you're planning to visit only the Grand Canyon's
most popular area, the South Rim. Many people choose to
fly to the Grand Canyon and then hike, catch a shuttle or
taxi, or sign on for bus tours or mule rides in Grand Canyon
Village.

Airports **McCarran International Airport** in Las Vegas (tel. 702/739–
5743) is the primary air hub for flights to **Grand Canyon National Park Airport** (tel. 602/638–2446). You can also make
connections into the Grand Canyon from **Sky Harbor International Airport** in Phoenix (tel. 602/273–3300). Ground
transportation and air-shuttle service (*see* By Air Shuttle
and By Taxi, *below*) are available from the Grand Canyon

Airport either to Grand Canyon Village or to the small tourist community of Tusayan, 6 miles from the South Rim.

Airlines The many carriers that fly to the Grand Canyon from Las Vegas include **Air Nevada** (tel. 800/634–6377), **Grand Airways** (tel. 800/634–6616), **Las Vegas Fliers** (tel. 800/343–2632), and **Scenic Airlines** (tel. 800/634–6801).

Flights depart Monday, Friday, and Sunday from Phoenix to Grand Canyon Airport via **Arizona Pacific Airways** (tel. 800/221–7904). Phoenix Sky Harbor Airport is served by virtually all of the major U.S. commercial airlines (*see* Chapter 6, Phoenix and Central Arizona).

Between the The **Tusayan/Grand Canyon Shuttle** (tel. 602/638–2475 or
Airport and 800/472–6322) operates between Grand Canyon Airport
Grand Canyon and the nearby towns of Tusayan and Grand Canyon Vil-
Village/Tusayan lage; it makes hourly runs daily between 8:15 AM and 5:15
By Air Shuttle PM, with additional trips during the summer months. A day pass for unlimited trips costs $7 for adults and $5 for children under age 12; if you're only going one way, the cost is $4 for adults, $3 for children under 12. Children under age 6 travel free. Those with large families might consider the $20 family pass, which allows unlimited travel back and forth throughout the day; often the company will extend the pass to 48 or even 72 hours for the same rate.

By Taxi **Fred Harvey Transportation Company** (tel. 602/638–2822 or 602/638–2631) offers 24-hour taxi service at Grand Canyon Airport, Grand Canyon Village, and the nearby village of Tusayan; taxis also make trips to other destinations in and around Grand Canyon National Park.

Transportation During the summer, transportation services desks are
Services maintained at **Bright Angel Lodge, Maswik Lodge,** and **Yavapai Lodge** in Grand Canyon Village; in winter only the desk at Bright Angel Lodge is open. The desks provide information and handle bookings for taxi and bus service, mule and horseback rides, Phantom Ranch (at the bottom of the Grand Canyon), and sightseeing tours. These are geared primarily to in-person visits, but you can call (tel. 602/638–2631) for additional information.

Arriving and Departing by Train or Bus

By Train **Amtrak** (tel. 800/USA–RAIL) provides daily service into Arizona from both the east and west, with its most convenient stop (for Grand Canyon access) at Flagstaff. From Flagstaff, bus connections can be made for the final leg of the trip to the South Rim through **Nava-Hopi Tours** (tel. 602/774–5003).

An alternative way to complete your journey is a scenic rail trip: Travel to Williams by train and bus, then continue to the Grand Canyon on an old but beautifully restored steam train on the Grand Canyon Railway (*see* Guided Tours, *be-*

low). The part of the trip from Flagstaff to Williams is by bus and is included in the price of the Amtrak train ticket.

By Bus **Greyhound/Trailways Lines** provides bus service from all points in the United States to Flagstaff or Williams, both considered gateway communities to the Grand Canyon. To obtain Greyhound/Trailways travel information, use the number provided under the Greyhound/Trailways listing in your local yellow pages. This will connect you with the firm's national information center in Omaha, Nebraska.

From either Flagstaff or Williams, bus service to the South Rim of the Grand Canyon is offered by **Nava-Hopi Tours** (tel. 602/774–5003 or 800/892–8687).

Getting Around

By Car If you are traveling into Arizona by car from the east, or coming up from the southern part of the state, your best access to the Grand Canyon is from Flagstaff. You can take U.S. 180 northwest (81 miles) to Grand Canyon Village on the South Rim. Or, for a scenic route with stopping points along the canyon rim, drive north on U.S. 89 from Flagstaff, then turn left at the junction of AZ 64 (52 miles north of Flagstaff) and proceed west for an additional 57 miles.

To visit the North Rim of the canyon, proceed north from Flagstaff on U.S. 89 to Bitter Springs, then take U.S. 89A to the junction of AZ 67, which leads to the North Rim, a distance of approximately 210 miles from Flagstaff.

If you are crossing Arizona on I–40 from the west, your most direct route to the South Rim is on AZ 64 (U.S. 180), which runs north from Williams for 58 miles to Grand Canyon Village.

Keep in mind that summer traffic leading to the South Rim can be quite heavy and, at times, congested in the vicinity of Grand Canyon Village and the various parking areas along the rim. If you visit from October through April, you should experience only light to moderate traffic in the vicinity of the canyon. The more remote North Rim, which reaches elevations of more than 7,000 feet, has no services available from late October through mid-May; the road is open for day use only until the first heavy snowfall of the year (generally in November or December), at which point the roads close until spring. The South Rim stays open to auto traffic all year, though access to the West Rim is restricted during the summer because of overcrowded roads.

Rental Cars It's imperative to make reservations in advance for the busy summer months; for the rest of the year, you'll avoid disappointment if you book a car well ahead of time. Be sure to ask about weekly rates and unlimited mileage opportunities.

Major companies serving Phoenix and Flagstaff include **Avis** (tel. 800/331–1212), **Budget** (tel. 800/527–0700), **Dollar** (tel. 800/800–4000), **Hertz** (tel. 800/654–3131), and **National** (tel. 800/227–7368). Budget and Dollar are located at Grand Canyon Airport.

By Shuttle Bus In summer free shuttle service offered by the **National Park Service** (tel. 602/638–7888) runs from Grand Canyon Village to Hermits Rest and Yaki Point, popular viewing areas on the South Rim. Generally, this service, which runs approximately every 15 minutes from 6:30 AM to 6:45 PM, is available late May through September. Also under the aegis of the National Park Service, CTS runs a year-round shuttle that takes hikers from the Backcountry Reservations Office (across from the Visitors Center), Maswik Lodge, and Bright Angel Lodge to South Kaibab Trailhead at Yaki Point; the price is $3, and there are two departures every morning. Check for times upon arrival. From May 15 through the end of October, **Trans Canyon Van Service** (tel. 602/638–2820), a South Rim to North Rim shuttle, leaves from Bright Angel Lodge at 1:30 PM and arrives at the North Rim at about 6 PM; the return from Grand Canyon Lodge is at 7 AM, with arrival at the South Rim at about 11:30 AM. The fare is $60 each way ($100 round-trip), and a 50% deposit is required two weeks in advance.

Guided Tours

By Train The Grand Canyon Railway began running from Williams to the South Rim of the Grand Canyon in 1989, offering a modern version of a route that was first established in 1901. The railroad had been out of operation since 1968, but an $85 million restoration put the old steam engines and Pullman cars back in business. The ride from the renovated station in Williams, which takes about 2½ hours each way, features refreshments, commentary, and corny but fun onboard entertainment. Even if you don't take the train, stop by the Williams Depot, built in 1908. Attractions here include the locomotive and passenger car of a turn-of-the-century steam train; a small but interesting railroad museum (admission free); and a gift shop where you can find such kitschy souvenirs as a tie that plays "I've Been Working on the Railroad." *518 E. Bill Williams Ave., Williams 86046, tel. 800/THE–TRAIN. Fare: Round-trip, $54.81 adults, $29.40 ages 17–19, $25.40 ages 13–16, $15.67 ages 12 and under; one-way, $45.08 adults, $24.54 ages 17–19, $20.54 ages 13–16, $12.43 ages 12 and under; for children and teens traveling with adults on the family plan, children pay half regular child fare and teens (13–19) pay approximately half adult fare. Departure from Williams June–Sept., daily 9:30 AM, return 5:30 PM; Wed.–Sun. Mar.–May and Oct.; Fri.–Sun. Nov.–Feb.*

By Plane Flights over the Grand Canyon by airplane or helicopter are offered by a number of companies operating either from

Grand Canyon Airport or from heliports in Tusayan. **Air Grand Canyon** (tel. 602/638–2618 or 800/247–4726), **Grand Canyon Airlines** (tel. 800/528–2413), and **Windrock Aviation** (tel. 602/638–9591 or 800/247–6259) fly small planes, while **Air Star Helicopters** (tel. 602/638–2622 or 800/962–3869), **Grand Canyon Helicopters** (tel. 602/638–2419 or 800/528–2418 outside AZ), and **Kenai Helicopters** (tel. 602/638–2412 or 800/541–4537) operate whirlybirds. Prices and length of flights vary greatly with tours, but start at about $50 for short flights originating from Grand Canyon Airport. Inquiries and reservations can be made at any Grand Canyon lodge transportation desk (*see* Transportation Services, *above*).

By Bus From Memorial Day weekend to October 1, a free **shuttle bus service** is offered by the National Park Service (*see* By Shuttle Bus in Getting Around, *above*) in the South Rim area. This does not provide a guided tour, but you can get a good feel for the region by taking advantage of trips through Grand Canyon Village, Yavapai Museum, and Hermits Rest on the West Rim. In addition, the **Fred Harvey Transportation Company** (tel. 602/638–2822 or 602/638–2631) in Grand Canyon Village provides a veritable menu of daily motorcoach sightseeing trips along the South Rim and to destinations as far away as Monument Valley on the Navajo reservation. Prices range from $11 for the short trips to $70 for all-day tours. Children's half-price fares apply to those under 16 for in-park tours, under 12 on the longer out-of-park tours. For schedules, call the South Rim reservations number (tel. 602/638–2401) or inquire at any transportation desk (*see* Transportation Services, *above*).

By Mule Mule trips down the precipitous trails to the Inner Gorge of the Grand Canyon are nearly as well known as the canyon itself. But, especially for the summer season, it's very hard to get reservations unless you make them months in advance; write Reservations Department (Box 699, Grand Canyon 86023, tel. 602/638–2401). These trips have been conducted since the early 1900s, and no one has ever been killed by a mule falling off a cliff. Nevertheless, the treks are not for the faint of heart or people in questionable health. Riders must be at least 4 feet 7 inches tall, weigh less than 200 pounds, and understand English; they cannot be visibly pregnant. The all-day ride to Plateau Point costs $87 (lunch included). An overnight with a stay at Phantom Ranch at the bottom of the canyon is $259 ($464 for two) for one night, $359 ($608 for two) for two nights; meals are included in these prices.

Weather

Weather information and road conditions for both the North and South rims can be obtained by calling 602/638–7888.

In general the South Rim, with an elevation of 7,000 feet, has summer temperatures ranging from lows in the 50s to highs in the upper 80s. There are frequent afternoon thunderstorms. Winter temperatures have average lows of around 20°F and average highs near 50°F, with the mercury occasionally dropping below zero. In spring and fall, temperatures generally stay above 32°F and often climb into the 70s. The North Rim, accessed through country that ranges in altitude from 8,000 to 9,000 feet, gets heavy winter snows and thus is open to the public only from mid-May through October. Temperatures during this open season go from lows in the 30s to highs in the 70s. It frequently rains in the afternoon; in May and October, it occasionally snows as well. As you proceed down either rim into the canyon toward the Inner Gorge, temperatures rise. In the summer along the Colorado River at an elevation of about 2,400 feet, temperatures range from lows in the 70s to highs above 100°F. Winter sees lows in the 30s, highs around 50. It rarely snows at the bottom of the Grand Canyon, even in winter; the snow on the rims usually turns to rain as it falls into the Inner Gorge.

Telephones

It's often hard to get through to the Grand Canyon: The trunk lines into the area are limited and often overloaded with people calling this most popular of Arizona's attractions. You'll get a fast busy signal if this is the case. In addition, when you do get through to the National Park Service or South Rim Reservations numbers—which handle many of the services listed in this chapter—you'll have to punch a lot of numbers on a computer-voice system before you reach the service you want. Be patient; it's possible to get through to a human being eventually. Writing ahead for the information-packed *Trip Planner (see* Tourist Information, *above)* is likely to save you a phone call. Remember, too, that the park does not accept reservations for backcountry permits by phone; they must be made in writing.

Safety Tips

Be careful when you or your children are near the edge of the canyon or walking any of the trails that descend into it. Guard rails exist only on portions of the rims. Infrequently, but tragically, visitors have been killed in falls from viewing points. Before engaging in any strenuous exercise, be aware that the canyon rims are more than 7,000 feet in altitude. Being at this height can cause some people to get dizzy or faint. Before hiking down into the canyon, assess the distance of the proposed hike against your physical condition. Descending into the canyon is not especially difficult, but going back up can be very strenuous. Be sure to take water and food on hikes into the canyon. During summer months, temperatures in the Inner Gorge can climb above 105°F.

Entrance Fees

The fees levied by the National Park Service vary depending on your method of entering Grand Canyon National Park. If you arrive by automobile, the fee is $10, regardless of the number of passengers. Individuals arriving by public conveyance (bus, taxi, or train) pay $4. The entrance gates are open 24 hours a day but are generally supervised from about 7 AM until 6 PM. If you arrive when there's no one at the gate, you may enter legally without paying.

Exploring the Grand Canyon

Both the South Rim and the North Rim areas of the Grand Canyon were established as recreational and sightseeing enclaves under the direction of the National Park Service. Unfortunately, most of Grand Canyon Village at the South Rim was laid out before the Park Service existed, so the area is not well prepared to accommodate the large crowds that converge on the area every summer (and, increasingly, throughout the spring and fall as well). Still, there are routes for escape everywhere, and the most trafficked spots are popular for good reason: You'll quickly forget that there's anyone nearby as you turn your gaze toward the vast abyss.

There are two ways to discover the canyon: walking or driving along the rim (Tours 1–6) and hiking down into its depths (*see* Hiking in Sports and Outdoor Activities, *below*). The first view of the canyon will stay with you a lifetime. But the truth is, after a half-dozen lookouts, one's sense of wonder begins to diminish. The problem is that it's impossible to establish a personal relationship with so much grandeur. Traveling along the rim, the visitor easily tires of putting his or her nose up against this beauty and safely, almost antiseptically, peering in. By all means stop along the rim, but we can't encourage you strongly enough to take a walk, however brief, into the canyon itself. Bright Angel Trail is easier, the South Kaibab Trail steeper but more spectacular. A 20-minute walk into the maw of this abyss will open up a totally new perspective, and permit you to develop a personal relationship with the canyon that is unattainable at the rim.

Highlights for First-time Visitors

South Rim Country   **Bright Angel or Kaibab Trails** (*see* Tours 2 and 3)
Desert View and The Watchtower (*see* Tour 2)
El Tovar Hotel (*see* Tour 3)

Hermits Rest Overlook (*see* Tour 4)
Lookout Studio (*see* Tour 3)
Powell Memorial (*see* Tour 4)
Visitor Center (*see* Tour 1)
Yavapai Museum (*see* Tour 2)

North Rim Country   **Cape Royal** (*see* Tour 6)
Grand Canyon Lodge and Bright Angel Point (*see* Tour 6)
Marble Canyon (*see* Tour 5)
Vermilion Cliffs (*see* Tour 5)

Tour 1: Approaching the South Rim

Numbers in the margin correspond to points of interest on the South Rim: Tours 1 and 2 map.

Because the approach to the South Rim of the Grand Canyon is across the relatively level surface of the 7,000-foot Coconino Plateau, you won't see the great gorge until you're practically at its edge. **Mather Point** gives you your first glimpse of the canyon from one of the most impressive and accessible vista points on the rim; it's easily reached from Grand Canyon National Park's east entrance (on AZ 64) or from the south entrance (on AZ 180). If you're arriving from the east, you might be tempted to stop at Desert View, just inside the park, but we suggest that you save this and other vista points on the eastern approach for a later East Rim tour (*see* Tour 2, *below*).

❶ Located on the outskirts of Grand Canyon Village, **Mather Point** is approximately 24 miles from the east entrance and 4 miles from the south entrance. Whether you enter the park from the east or south, you'll arrive at the junction of AZ 64 and AZ 180. Proceed in the direction of Grand Canyon Village for less than a mile, and you'll see a large parking area with a sign for Mather Point.

This overlook of the canyon, named for the National Park Service's first director, Stephen Mather, affords an extraordinary view of the Inner Gorge of the canyon and of numerous buttes that rise out of the eroded chasm: Wotan's Throne, Brahma Temple, Zoroaster Temple, and many others. The Grand Canyon Lodge, on the North Rim, is almost directly north from Mather Point and only 10 miles away—yet you have to drive nearly 210 miles to get from one spot to the other.

After your first view of the canyon, proceed into Grand ❷ Canyon Village, and stop in at the **National Park Service's visitor center,** which has something for even the most independent traveler. Not only does the center orient you to many facets of the site (history, geology, and sightseeing), but it's also an excellent place for gathering information, whether about escapist hikes or group tours. At the visitor center, you'll get an intriguing profile of the area's natural and human history. The region's first inhabitants were

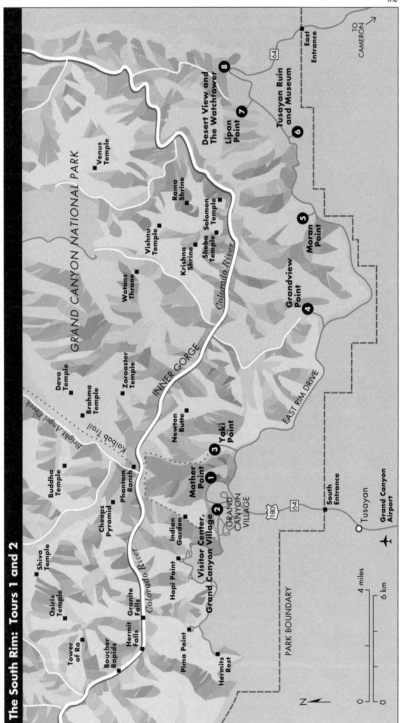

The South Rim: Tours 1 and 2

GRAND CANYON NATIONAL PARK

Colorado River

INNER GORGE

Bright Angel Creek

Kaibob Trail

Venus Temple

Rama Shrine

Sheba Solomon
Temple Temple

Krishna Shrine

Vishnu Temple

Wotans Throne

Deva Temple

Brahma Temple

Zoroaster Temple

Buddha Temple

Cheops Pyramid

Phantom Ranch

Shiva Temple

Osiris Temple

Tower of Ra

Boucher Rapids

Hermit Falls

Granite Falls

Indian Garden

Hopi Point

Pima Point

Hermits Rest

Newton Butte

Mather Point ❶

Yaki Point ❸

❷ Visitor Center, Grand Canyon Village

GRAND CANYON VILLAGE

Grandview Point ❹

Moran Point ❺

EAST RIM DRIVE

Lipan Point ❼

Desert View and The Watchtower ❽

Tusayan Ruin and Museum ❻

East Entrance

64

TO CAMERON

South Entrance

64

180

Tusayan

Grand Canyon Airport

PARK BOUNDARY

N

0   4 miles
0   6 km

probably Paleo Indians, who lived here more than 11,000 years ago. Artifacts from the Archaic culture, which followed, are on display here: perfectly preserved figurines of animals, made more than 4,000 years ago from willow twigs and found in caves deep in the canyon. Sometime after AD 1, the Anasazi culture flourished, but it disappeared about AD 1200. Exhibits give glimpses of some of the more than 2,000 Anasazi sites that have been discovered in the Grand Canyon area, including many deep within the canyon. The museum also traces the arrival of the early Spanish explorers, including Captain García López de Cárdenas, leader of the first expedition of white men to see the Grand Canyon (1540), and of John Wesley Powell, an American who was the first person to travel through the canyon by boat. The various crafts that have navigated the white-water rapids of the Colorado River are on display.

The visitor center also presents short movies and slide shows on the canyon, and its bookstore carries a wide variety of printed matter, videotapes, and slides. Park rangers are on hand to answer questions and aid in planning Grand Canyon excursions. The center also has a schedule for ranger-guided walks along the South Rim. *East side of Grand Canyon Village, about 1 mi east of El Tovar Hotel, tel. 602/ 638–7888. Admission free. Open Memorial Day–Labor Day, daily 8 AM–6 PM; the rest of the year, daily 8–5.*

Tour 2: East Rim

This breathtaking drive on the East Rim proceeds east for about 25 miles along the South Rim from Grand Canyon Village to Desert View. Before beginning the drive, consider stopping to see the exhibits and attend the free mini-lectures offered by park naturalists at Yavapai Museum, three-quarters of a mile east of the visitor center. There are four signed picnic areas along the route, and rest rooms at Tusayan Museum and Desert View.

❸ To get to **Yaki Point,** the first stop on the tour, from the village, head east to the junction of AZ 180 and AZ 64. Turn onto AZ 64 and continue east. From this vantage point, look to the northeast for an exceptional view of Wotan's Throne, a majestic flat-topped butte named by François Matthes, a U.S. Geological Survey scientist who developed the first topographical map of the Grand Canyon. Due north is Buddha Temple, capped by limestone; Newton Butte, with its flat top of red sandstone, lies to the east. At Yaki Point the popular Kaibab Trail starts the canyon descent to the Inner Gorge, crosses the Colorado over a steel suspension bridge, and wends its way to rustic Phantom Ranch, the only lodging facility at the bottom of the Grand Canyon. You might take this opportunity to hike a short distance down the Kaibab Trail, just to get a feel for a descent into the canyon. If you plan to go more than a mile, carry water with you (*see* Hiking in Sports and the Outdoors, *below*). If you encounter a mule train, be aware that the animals have the right-of-way. Move to the inside of the trail and wait as they pass.

4 About 7 miles east of Yaki Point, **Grandview Point,** at an altitude of 7,496 feet, supports large stands of ponderosa pine, piñon pine, oak, and juniper. The view from here is one of the finest in the canyon. To the northeast is a group of dominant buttes, including Krishna Shrine, Vishnu Temple, Rama Shrine, and Shiva Temple. A short stretch of the Colorado River is also visible. Directly below the point and accessed by the Grandview Trail is Horseshoe Mesa, where you can see ruins of the Last Chance Copper Mine. Grandview Point was also the site of the Grandview Hotel, constructed in the 1890s but closed in 1908; logs salvaged from the hotel were used for the roof of the Desert View Watchtower (*see below*).

5 The next overlook is about 5 miles east at **Moran Point,** named for American landscape artist Thomas Moran, who painted Grand Canyon scenes from many points on the rim but was especially fond of the play of light and shadows from this location; he first visited the canyon with John Wesley Powell in 1873. Moran's vivid canvases helped convince Congress to create a national park at the Grand Canyon. This is also a favorite spot for photographers.

6 Three miles east of Moran Point on the south side of the highway is the entrance to **Tusayan Ruin and Museum,** which offer evidence of early habitation in the Grand Canyon and information about the lifestyles of the Anasazi people (circa AD 1–1200). The partially intact rock dwellings here were occupied for perhaps 20 years by a group of about 30 Indian hunters, farmers, and gatherers. They left suddenly, driven to a new location, archaeologists believe, by a severe drought. The museum and bookstore feature artifacts, models of the Anasazi dwellings, and exhibits on more modern tribes of the region. *Tel. 602/638–2305. Admission free. Open daily 8–5; closed Thanksgiving and Christmas.*

7 **Lipan Point,** 1 mile east of Tusayan Ruin, is the canyon's widest point. From here you can get an astonishing visual profile of the gorge's geologic history, with a view of every eroded layer of the canyon.

8 **Desert View and The Watchtower** offer a climactic final stop. At 7,500 feet, Desert View is the highest point along the tour, and the vista is spectacular. If you climb to the top of the 70-foot stone-and-mortar Watchtower, built in 1932 by the Fred Harvey Company in the style of Southwest Indian structures, you can see the muted pastel hues of the distant Painted Desert to the east and the 3,000-foot-high Vermilion Cliffs rising from a high plateau near the Utah border. You also get an extraordinary glimpse of the upper reaches of the canyon as it angles away to the north toward Marble Canyon, and at this point an impressive stretch of the Colorado River reveals itself. The Watchtower houses a glass-enclosed observatory with powerful telescopes, as well as galleries decorated with reproductions of ancient Indian pictographs, and a curio shop where paintings by contemporary Indian artists are sold. *Watchtower tel. 602/638-2736, trading post tel. 602/638-2360. Admission free, but there is a 25¢ charge to climb The Watchtower. Trading post open Memorial Day–Labor Day daily 8–8; rest of year daily 8–6. Watchtower closes ½ hour before trading post.*

Tour 3: The Village Rim

Numbers in the margin correspond to points of interest on the South Rim: Tours 3 and 4 map.

This is a fairly short walking tour (about 1 mile round-trip) over level ground via a paved pathway that runs along the rim. The **Hopi House** is a good place to begin (if you're driving, leave your car at the nearby El Tovar parking lot). This multistoried structure of rock and mortar was modeled after buildings found in the Hopi village of Oraibi, Arizona, the oldest continually inhabited community in the United States. Part of an attempt by the Fred Harvey Company to encourage Southwest Indian crafts at the turn of the century, Hopi House was established as one of the first curio stores in the Grand Canyon. It has the air of a museum, with some artifacts too priceless to sell today, but it remains one of the best-stocked gift shops in the vicinity (*see* Shopping, *below*).

A few yards to the west of Hopi House is the most renowned hotel in the nation's National Park System, the historic **El Tovar Hotel.** Built in 1905 to resemble the great hunting lodges of Europe, this massive log structure underwent a major renovation in 1991, but it retains the ambience of its early days. If the weather is cool, stop in front of the massive stone fireplace to warm your hands. The rustic lobby, with its numerous stuffed and mounted animal heads, is a great place for people watching.

From El Tovar, return to the rim and pick up the trail heading west toward **Lookout Studio.** Built in 1914 as a lookout point, the Pueblo–style building was later used as a photography studio. Today it's a combination lookout point, museum, and gift shop, featuring an extensive collection of geologic samples from around the world as well as many fossil specimens. An upstairs loft provides another excellent overlook into the mighty gorge below.

Not many yards to the west of Lookout Studio is **Bright Angel trailhead,** the starting point for perhaps the best-known of all the trails that descend to the bottom of the canyon. It was originally a bighorn sheep path and was later used by the Havasupai Indians; in 1890–91 it was widened for prospectors trying to reach mining claims in the canyon. Today Bright Angel Trail is a well-maintained avenue for mule

The South Rim: Tours 3 and 4

Kaibob Trail

Bright Angel Creek

Phantom Ranch

INNER GORGE

Colorado River

GRAND CANYON NATIONAL PARK

INNER GORGE

Yaki Point

Mather Point

Yavapai Geologic Museum

Visitor Center

Camper Services

Hopi House

Lookout Studio

9

El Tovar Hotel

10

13

Bright Angel Lodge

11

Bright Angel Trailhead

12

GRAND CANYON VILLAGE

Camper Services

EAST RIM DRIVE

TO CAMERON

64

TO SOUTH ENTRANCE

180

64

TO GRAND CANYON AIRPORT

Powell Memorial

15

Maricopa Point

14

Trailview Overlook

16

17

Hopi Point

18

Mohave Point

The Abyss

19

WEST RIM DRIVE

West Rim Drive closed to private vehicles in summer.

Pima Point

20

Hermits Rest

21

1200 yards

1200 meters

0

N

and foot traffic. If you intend to go very far—the trail descends 4,460 feet to the Colorado River—you should be prepared with proper shoes, clothing, equipment, and water (*see* Hiking in Sports and the Outdoors, *below*); discuss your intentions with the park service representatives at the visitor center before you go.

Bright Angel Trail is the turnaround point on this short walking tour. If you'd like to go farther west, *see* Tour 4: West Rim Drive *below*. From Bright Angel Trail, walk directly east rather than returning to the rim trail. You'll pass the barn that houses some of the tour mules; it's worth a brief stop, especially if children are along. Continue east ⓭ to **Bright Angel Lodge,** which was built in 1935 of logs and native stone, with rustic cabins set away from the main building. It's another good place to people watch, especially in the area of the "geologic" fireplace, made of regional rocks arranged in the order in which they are layered in the Grand Canyon. A history room displays memorabilia from early years at the South Rim.

Time Out For light snacks—sandwiches, ice-cream dishes, and soft drinks—try the **Soda Fountain** in the Bright Angel Lodge. *Tel. 602/638–2631. Open May–Sept., daily 11–9.*

From Bright Angel Lodge, take the village road back to your parking spot near El Tovar.

Tour 4: West Rim Drive

This tour cannot be made by car in the summer months; at that time the West Rim Road is closed to auto traffic because of congestion. From Memorial Day weekend to October 1, a free shuttle bus makes most of the stops on the described itinerary (*see* By Shuttle Bus section in Getting Around, *above*).

Originally called the Hermit Rim Road, the **West Rim Drive** was constructed by the Santa Fe Company in 1912 as a scenic tour route. Cars were banned on the road because they frightened horses pulling the open-topped touring stages. West Rim Drive today offers 10 scenic overlooks spread out over 8 miles (one-way). Consider covering half on the first leg of the trip and the others on the way back; there's easy access to the lookout points from both sides of the road.

Start out at **Bright Angel Lodge** and head west for about a ⓮ mile until you come to **Trailview Overlook.** If you turn and look away from the canyon toward the south, you'll have a wonderful, unobstructed view of the distant San Francisco Peaks, Arizona's highest mountains (the tallest is 12,633 feet), as well as of Bill Williams Mountain (on the horizon) and Red Butte (about 15 miles south of the canyon rim). As its name suggests, this overlook also affords a dramatic view of the Bright Angel and Plateau Point trails as they zigzag down the canyon. In the deep gorge to the north flows Bright Angel Creek, one of the few permanent tributary streams of the Colorado River in the region.

⑮ **Maricopa Point,** about seven-tenths of a mile from Trailview, merits a stop not only for the arresting scenery, which features a clear view of the Colorado River below, but also for its towering headframe of an early Grand Canyon mining operation. On the rim to your left, as you face the canyon, are the Orphan Mine and, in the canyon below, a mine shaft and cable lines leading up to the rim. The copper ore in the mine, which started operations in 1893, was of excellent quality, but the cost of removing it from the canyon finally brought the venture to a halt.

About a half-mile beyond Maricopa Point, the large granite
⑯ **Powell Memorial** stands as a tribute to the first man to ride the wild rapids of the Colorado River through the canyon in 1869. John Wesley Powell, a one-armed Civil War hero and explorer, measured, charted, and named many of the canyons and creeks of the river. It was here that the dedication ceremony for Grand Canyon National Park took place on April 3, 1920.

⑰ From **Hopi Point** (elevation 7,071 feet), a half-mile down the road, you can see a large section of the Colorado River; although it appears as a thin line from here, the river is nearly 350 feet wide below this overlook. Across the canyon to the north is Shiva Temple, which, until 1937, remained an isolated section of the Kaibab Plateau. In that year, Harold Anthony of the American Museum of Natural History led an expedition to the rock formation in the belief that it supported life that had been cut off from the rest of the canyon. Imagine the expedition members' surprise when they found an empty Kodak film box on top of the temple.

⑱ Four-fifths of a mile to the west, **Mohave Point** also affords spectacular views of the Colorado River. In addition, Granite and Salt Creek rapids can be seen from this point.

⑲ **The Abyss,** 1 mile farther, is one of the most awesome stops on this tour, revealing a sheer canyon drop of 3,000 feet to the Tonto Plateau in the gorge below. From this spot, you'll also see several impressive isolated sandstone columns, the largest of which is called The Monument.

⑳ **Pima Point,** 3 miles away, provides a bird's-eye view of the Tonto Platform and the Tonto Trail, which wends its way through the canyon for more than 70 miles. If you look down on the plateau toward the west, you may be able to see the foundations of an old tourist camp built in the first decade of the century and used until 1930. Also to the west, two dark, cone-shaped mountains—Mt. Trumbull and Mt. Logan— are visible on clear days. They rise in stark contrast to the surrounding flat-topped mesas and buttes.

㉑ **Hermits Rest,** the westernmost viewpoint, and the Boucher Trail that descends from it (*see* Hiking in Sports and the Outdoors, *below*) were named for the "hermit" Louis Boucher, a 19th-century prospector who had a number of mining claims and a roughly built home down in the canyon. Canyon views from here include Hermit Rapids and the towering cliffs of the Supai and Redwall formations. The stone building at Hermits Rest sells curios and refreshments and provides the only rest rooms on the West Rim tour.

Tour 5: The Drive to North Rim

Numbers in the margin correspond to points of interest on the North Rim: Tours 5 and 6 map.

This tour is not an option during the winter, when heavy snows close highway access to, and facilities in, the North Rim.

This long excursion—about 210 miles, whether you start out from Grand Canyon Village on the South Rim of the canyon or from Flagstaff—is the best way to get to the North Rim and offers plenty to see along the way. It begins at the

㉒ **Cameron Trading Post,** on U.S. 89, 1 mile north of the junction with AZ 64 (which you will be on if you're coming from Grand Canyon Village) and 53 miles north of Flagstaff. Founded in 1916, this historic trading post, one of the few remaining in the Southwest, has an extensive stock of Native American jewelry, rugs, baskets, and pottery. Most of the items sold here are made by nearby Navajo and Hopi artisans, but some are created by New Mexico's Zuni and Pueblo Indians.

Time Out At the **Cameron Trading Post** restaurant (tel. 602/679–2231) you can enjoy American food that ranges from light snacks to complete dinners; if you're a hearty eater, order the huge Navajo tacos, Indian fry bread heaped with cheese, chopped meat, guacamole, and salad. You can get a sandwich and soft drink for under $6, complete meals for under $12.

The route north on U.S. 89 affords a wide and unobstructed

㉓ view of the **Painted Desert** off to the right. The desert, which covers thousands of square miles and extends far to the south and east, is a vision of harsh beauty, with windswept plains and mesas, isolated buttes, and barren valleys in delicate patterns of soft pastels. In the few places in which there is vegetation, it is mostly desert scrub, which provides sustenance for only the hardiest wildlife. Most of the undulating hills belong to the Chinle formation, deposited more than 200 million years ago and containing countless fossil records of ancient plants and animals.

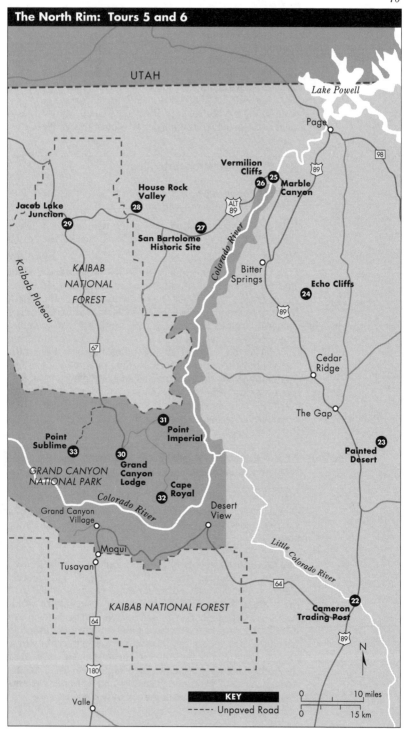

The North Rim: Tours 5 and 6

UTAH

Lake Powell

Page

Vermilion Cliffs 26 **25** **Marble Canyon**

House Rock Valley 28

ALT 89

98

89

27

San Bartolome Historic Site

Jacob Lake Junction 29

Bitter Springs

Echo Cliffs 24

KAIBAB NATIONAL FOREST

Kaibab Plateau

67

89

Cedar Ridge

The Gap

Point Sublime 33

31 **Point Imperial**

Painted Desert 23

GRAND CANYON NATIONAL PARK

30 **Grand Canyon Lodge**

Colorado River

32 **Cape Royal**

Grand Canyon Village

Desert View

Moqui

Tusayan

Little Colorado River

KAIBAB NATIONAL FOREST

64

64

180

Cameron Trading Post 22

89

N

Valle

KEY

0 ——— 10 miles
0 ——— 15 km

--- Unpaved Road

About 40 miles north of the Cameron Trading Post, the Painted Desert country gives way to soaring sandstone cliffs that run for many miles off to the right. Brilliantly hued, and ranging in color from light pink to deep orange, **(24)** the **Echo Cliffs** rise to well over 1,000 feet in many places. They are also essentially devoid of vegetation, but in a few isolated places high up, you'll spot thick patches of tall cottonwood and poplar trees, nurtured by springs and water seepage from the rock escarpments.

At Bitter Springs, 60 miles north of Cameron, leave U.S. 89 and take U.S. 89A north. Fourteen miles out of Bitter **(25)** Springs, **Marble Canyon,** actually the beginning of the Grand Canyon, comes into view. Like the rest of the Grand Canyon, Marble Canyon has been carved by the force of the Colorado River. Navajo Bridge, the old steel bridge across the gorge, is sturdy, but many first-time visitors approach it with trepidation because of the structure's antique appearance and because it spans a chasm that's more than 500 feet deep. A visitor parking area on the north side of the bridge is a good place to stop for photographs. There's a turnoff nearby for Lees Ferry, 3 miles away, where most of the Grand Canyon river rafts put into the water. Huge trout also lurk in the river near Lees Ferry, but be sure you have an Arizona fishing license before casting a line. After crossing the Navajo Bridge, you'll be in Arizona Strip country (*see* Off the Beaten Track, *below*).

Heading west, you'll be treated to views of some of the world's most spectacular geologic formations. Rising to the **(26)** right of the highway are the sheer **Vermilion Cliffs,** in many places more than 3,000 feet high.

As you continue the journey to the North Rim, the immense blue-green bulk of the Kaibab Plateau stretches out before you. About 18 miles past Marble Canyon, a sign directs you **(27)** to the **San Bartolome Historic Site,** commemorating the Dominguez-Escalante expedition of 1776. The members of the expedition, the first non-Indians to enter the Arizona Strip area, nearly lost their lives trying to cross this harsh and forbidding land, which does not have a single permanent lake or stream. The group was saved when it found a place, farther to the east, to wade across the Colorado. The Crossing of the Fathers, as the location was later called, provided the only safe passage across the river for more than a half-century.

(28) Proceeding about 2 miles west, you'll enter **House Rock Valley,** where a large sign on the road announces the House Rock Buffalo Ranch. A 23-mile dirt road leads to the home of one of the largest herds of American bison in the Southwest. You may drive out to the ranch, but be aware that you may not see any buffalo: The expanse of their range is so great that they frequently cannot be spotted from a passenger car.

About 25 miles west of Marble Canyon on U.S. 89A, you'll start climbing to the top of the Kaibab Plateau, heavily forested, rife with animals and birds, and more than 9,000 feet at its highest point. The rapid change from barren desert to lush forest is dramatic. At an elevation of 7,900 feet, the **❷❾ Jacob Lake junction** is a good place to stop for groceries and gas. Turn left (south) from the junction to access AZ 67. From here to the North Rim, a distance of 44 miles, you'll be driving through one of the thickest stands of ponderosa pine in the United States. Watch for wildlife along the way. Visitors frequently see mule deer and, once in a while, catch a glimpse of rare Kaibab squirrels; you can recognize them by their all-white tails and ears with long tufts of white hair.

Tour 6: Bright Angel Point, Point Imperial, Cape Royal, Point Sublime

❸⓿ When you arrive at the historic **Grand Canyon Lodge,** you are, literally, at the end of the road; there are no meandering streets as there are at South Rim. A massive stone structure built in 1928 by the Union Pacific Railroad, the lodge is today listed in the National Register of Historic Places. Inside, the huge lounge area with hardwood floors and high, beamed ceilings affords a marvelous view of the canyon through massive plate-glass windows. On warm days, visitors sit in the sun and drink in the surrounding beauty at an equally spacious outdoor viewing deck.

The trail to Bright Angel Point, one of the most awe-inspiring overlooks on either rim, starts on the grounds of the Grand Canyon Lodge and proceeds along the crest of a point of rocks that juts out into the canyon for several hundred yards. The walk is only 1 mile round-trip, but the trek is exciting because there are sheer drops just a few feet away on each side of the rail. At places where the route gets extremely narrow, metal railings along the path ensure visitors' safety. The trail is quite safe, but visitors have been known to clamber out to precarious perches to have their picture taken. Be very careful: There have been tragic falls at the Grand Canyon.

If you'd like to take another walk, this time through the deep forest, head for the beginning of the Transept Trail near the corner of the lodge's east patio. This 3-mile (round-trip) trail stays near the rim for part of the distance, then plunges into the forest, ending at the North Rim Campground and General Store, 1½ miles from the lodge.

Time Out Lunch, dinner, or a snack in the huge, high-ceilinged, rock-and-log dining room of the **Grand Canyon Lodge** (tel. 602/638–2611) is an integral part of the North Rim experience. The menu, which changes every season, is surprisingly sophisticated for the rustic locale: You might find marinated pork kebabs, grilled swordfish, or linguine with cilantro and pesto among the entrées. Prices are moderate, dress is casual.

To get to the North Rim's most popular lookouts—Point Imperial and Cape Royal—drive north from Grand Canyon Lodge and veer right at the signed fork in the road. **Point Imperial,** 11 miles from the lodge, is the highest vista point (elevation 8,803 feet) on either rim, offering magnificent views of both the canyon and the distant country for many miles around: the Vermilion Cliffs to the north, the 10,000-foot Navajo Mountain to the northeast in Utah, the Painted Desert to the east, and the Little Colorado River canyon to the southeast.

Return west to the signed junction and turn left (south) to reach **Cape Royal,** about 23 miles from your starting point at the lodge. From the parking lot at the road's end, it's a short, scenic walk on a paved road to this southernmost viewpoint on the North Rim. In addition to another large slice of the Grand Canyon, Angel's Window, a giant, erosion-formed hole, can be seen through the projecting ridge of Cape Royal. If you would like to experience a very pleasant walk in this area of the rim, drive north about ⅛ mile to Angel's Window Overlook. At this point, Cliff Springs Trail starts its 1-mile route (round-trip) through a forested ravine. The easily navigated trail passes an Anasazi ruin, winds beneath a limestone overhang, and terminates at Cliff Springs, where the forest opens on another impressive view of the canyon walls.

An excellent option for those who want to get off the beaten path, the trip to **Point Sublime** is intended only for visitors driving vehicles with high-road clearance (pickups and four-wheel drive). It is also necessary to be properly equipped for wilderness road travel: Check with a park ranger or at the information desk at Grand Canyon Lodge before taking this journey. Drive north from the lodge about 2⁷⁄₁₀ miles to the North Rim Campground and turn left on a dirt road that winds for 17 miles through gorgeous high country to Point Sublime, an overlook that lives up to its name. You may camp here, but only after obtaining a permit from the Backcountry Reservations Office at the park ranger station (*see* Hiking in Sports and the Outdoors, *below*).

What to See and Do with Children

The Grand Canyon is family vacation country, and the children will enjoy essentially the same things as the adults. However, many activities at both North and South rims will appeal especially to them. It's worth checking the extensive menu of free daily programs offered by the National Park Service. The activities calendar changes seasonally, but an updated version can be found in the free Grand Canyon newspaper, *The Guide,* available to all arriving visitors at both rims. Some typical offerings are nature walks, geology talks, natural-history discussions—suitable for adults as well as children.

Animal Rides   Extremely gentle horses can be rented at the **Moqui Lodge** (tel. 602/638–2424) in the village of Tusayan, South Rim. The cost is $20 an hour, $34 for two hours. A four-hour East Rim ride goes for $55, a campfire horse- and haywagon ride for $25 ($7.50 if you ride in the wagon rather than on your own horse). The rides operate daily.

Short mule rides suitable for children are offered on the easier trails along the North Rim. A one-hour ride, available to those 6 years of age and older, runs about $10. Half-day trips on the rim or into the canyon (minimum age 8) cost $30; full-day trips (minimum age 12), which include lunch, go for $70. These excursions are very popular, so try to make reservations in advance at the mule rides desk at **Grand Canyon Lodge** (tel. 602/638–2292 or, preseason, 801/679–8665). Rides are available on a daily basis from May 15 to the end of October.

Films of   An enjoyable documentary, *Grand Canyon, Hidden Se-*
the Canyon   *crets*, is shown on the world's largest screen (60 feet by 80 feet) at the Imax Theater. The script is informative, and some of the shots—especially those of boats running the rapids—are positively dizzying. *Tusayan, tel. 602/638–2203. Admission: $7 adults, $4 children age 3–11. Open Mar. 1–Oct. 31, daily 8:30–8:30; Nov. 1–Feb. 28, daily 10:30–6:30; shows every hour starting on the half-hour.*

The computer-controlled *Over the Edge* multimedia show tells the Grand Canyon story in words and song—with the help of 12 projectors and strobe effects. The photography is often stunning. *Community Building, Grand Canyon Village, tel. 602/638–2229. Admission: $4 adults, $3.50 senior citizens 55 and older, $2 children 8–15, children 7 and under free. Open Mar.–Oct., daily 9–9; Nov.–Feb., daily 10–6; shows every 30 min.*

Off the Beaten Track

Arizona Strip   The **Arizona Strip** is the 12,000-square-mile northwestern portion of the state, cut off from the rest of Arizona by the giant scar created by the Colorado River as it comes out of Utah and winds its way through the Grand Canyon to the western border of the state. The only highway access to this area from southern Arizona is across an old steel bridge at Marble Canyon on U.S. 89A. Sometimes called the American Tibet because it's so isolated, the area boasts only two small towns, the farming and lumbering community of Fredonia and, near the Utah border, the polygamous Mormon town of Colorado City. Their combined population is less than 7,000, and fewer than 700 permanent residents—including 150 members of the Kaibab-Paiute tribe—live in the rest of the strip. An information center for this area, a good one- or two-day side trip from the Grand Canyon's North Rim, is open at Jacob Lake (tel. 602/643–7298) from May 1 through the end of November.

The first of the two main destinations in the area is **Pipe Spring National Monument,** 90 miles from the North Rim. Head north from the rim on AZ 67, and at Jacob Lake take AZ 89A to Fredonia; continue 14 miles beyond Fredonia on the same highway (now called AZ 389). Located at Pipe Spring, one of the few reliable sources of water in the Arizona Strip, the park features a restored rock fort and ranch, with exhibits of southwestern frontier life; in the summer there are living-history demonstrations, such as ranching operations or weaving. Completed in 1871 to fend off Indian attacks (which never came because a peace treaty was signed before it was finished), the fort was originally built as a ranch for the managers sent to oversee the Mormon church's tithed herds. It ended up functioning mainly as headquarters for a dairy operation, and in 1871 became the first telegraph station in the Arizona territory. Also on the site are a well-stocked bookstore, a coffee shop, and exhibits in the visitor center. About a half-mile north of the monument is a campground and picnic area run by the Kaibab-Paiute tribe. *HC 65, Box 5, Fredonia 86022, tel. 602/643–7105. Admission: $2 adults, children under 17 and senior citizens over 62 free. Historic structures open daily 8–4; visitor center/museum open daily 8–4:30; closed Thanksgiving, Christmas, and New Year's Day.*

After touring the old fort, backtrack on AZ 389 for 6 miles, then take a right turn on the dirt road to **Toroweap Overlook,** a distance of approximately 60 miles. You'll be riding through starkly beautiful, uninhabited country. Toroweap, a lonely and awesome overlook of the Grand Canyon, is the narrowest stretch of the canyon (less than 1 mile across) and also the point with the deepest sheer cliff (more than 3,000 feet straight down). From this vantage point, you can see upstream to sedimentary ledges, cliffs, and talus slopes. Looking downstream, you can see miles of lava flow that forms steep deltas, some of which look like black waterfalls frozen on the cliff.

Be sure you have plenty of gas, drinking water, good tires, and a reliable car; a high-clearance vehicle (one that sits high up off the ground, like a pickup truck) is best for this trip. Don't try to go in wet weather, when the dirt road is likely to be washed out. There's a ranger station near the rim as well as a primitive campground. If you plan on returning the same day, you should make motel reservations in advance at one of the Arizona Strip motels (*see* Lodging, *below*).

Havasu Canyon, South Rim For those who want to get away from the crowds, Havasu Canyon, south of the middle part of the national park, exhibits a Shangri-la-like beauty. It is the home of some 500 Havasupai, a tribe that has populated this beautiful, isolated country for centuries. Spectacular waterfalls (one drops 200 feet) cascade over the red cliffs, spilling blue-green water into immense travertine pools surrounded by thick foliage and sheltering trees.

From Grand Canyon Village, head south on U.S. 180 (AZ 64) for 57 miles to Williams, then take I–40 west 44 miles to Seligman. From there, go 34 miles west on AZ 66 until you come to Indian Rte. 18. A drive 60 miles north will take you to the head of the 8-mile-long Hualapai Trail. You can hike into the canyon or ride a horse or mule down for about $70; the trail twists along the edges of rock walls that go straight down for hundreds of feet. The hurried—or faint of heart—can take a helicopter; **Grand Canyon Helicopters** (tel. 800/528–2418) offers round-trips for $392 per person. If you are hiking or riding, you'll want to stay overnight (*see* Lodging, *below*). All visitors are charged a $12 fee to enter the Havasupai tribal lands. For additional information, contact Havasupai Tourist Enterprise (Supai 86435, tel. 602/448–2121 [tourist office], or 602/448–2111 [lodging]).

Lake Havasu City In case you haven't heard, London Bridge isn't in London anymore. In 1968, the historic span was dismantled stone by stone and shipped to a barren stretch of desert near Arizona's Lake Havasu, 172 miles southwest of the South Rim of the Grand Canyon. Envisioned by developer Robert McCulloch as the centerpiece for the community he had planned on the shores of the lake, the venerable structure, precisely reassembled (all 10,000 tons of it) to span a narrow arm of the lake, is indeed a focal point in a rapidly growing community of more than 32,000.

In addition to the bridge, Havasu City is known for sunshine, water sports, and fishing. The weather is wonderful in spring, fall, and winter, but summers often see temperatures that exceed 100°F. Recreational opportunities abound on and around 45-mile-long Lake Havasu: houseboat, ski-boat, jet-ski, fishing, and sailboat rentals; marinas, RV parks, and campgrounds; golf, tennis, guided fishing expeditions, and more. The area has more than 20 lodging establishments—from inexpensive roadside motels to posh resorts—and more than 40 eating places, from fast-food emporiums to fancy restaurants. To reach Lake Havasu City from Grand Canyon Village, take U.S. 180 (AZ 64) south 57 miles to Williams, then I–40 west 116 miles to Kingman; go another 35 miles to the intersection with AZ 95, and drive south for 19 miles. For more information on Lake Havasu City and its many attractions, contact the Lake Havasu Chamber of Commerce (1930 Mesquite Ave., Lake Havasu City 86403, tel. 602/453–3444 or 800/242–8278).

Shopping

At the South Rim, nearly every lodging facility and retail store offers Native American artifacts and Grand Canyon souvenirs. In truth, you'll find that after visiting a few of the curio and jewelry shops, all the merchandise begins to look alike. However, the items at most of the lodges and at major gift shops are authentic. The following are among the most interesting places for browsing or buying.

Desert View Trading Post offers a mix of traditional southwestern souvenirs and authentic Native American pottery and jewelry, plus sundries. *East Rim Dr. near The Watchtower at Desert View, tel. 602/638–2360. Open Memorial Day–Labor Day, daily 8–8; Labor Day–Memorial Day, daily 8–6.*

The historic locale of the **El Tovar Hotel Gift Shop** provides a nice atmosphere for shopping for Native American jewelry, rather expensive casual wear, and souvenir gifts. *Near the rim in Grand Canyon Village, tel. 602/638–2631. Open daily 7 AM–10 PM.*

Hopi House, opened in 1905, still offers one of the widest varieties of Native American artifacts—some of museum quality and not for sale—in the vicinity of the Grand Canyon. Many are very pricey, but there are some excellent, affordable items to be found here. *East of El Tovar Hotel, tel. 602/638–2631. Open May–Sept., daily 8–8; Oct.–Apr., daily 9–5.*

Established on the Navajo reservation in 1916, the huge **Cameron Trading Post**—doubled in size in 1993—stocks crafts of the Navajo, Hopi, Zuni, and New Mexico Pueblo peoples. The vast array of goods and prices will satisfy everyone's taste and purse, but it helps to come armed with knowledge of Native American artisanship if you're looking at high-ticket items. A new art gallery highlights the works of Indian artists. Located near the junction of U.S. 89 and AZ 64, it's accessible to visitors coming or going to the South Rim through the east entrance and to those heading toward the North Rim. *On U.S. 89 1 mi north of junction with AZ 64, tel. 602/679–2231. Open Apr.–Oct., daily 6 AM–10 PM; Nov.–May, daily 7 AM–9 PM.*

Sports and the Outdoors

Participant Sports

Bicycling A few visitors to the Grand Canyon arrive on bicycles, but these are all highly conditioned and experienced long-distance cyclists. It's 80 miles from Flagstaff to the South Rim, 210 miles to the North Rim—both routes offering only limited water stops. If you wish to cycle inside the park, where there are miles of scenic paved thoroughfares, bring your own bike; there are no rentals available in the canyon area. Be aware that the park roads have narrow shoulders and are heavily trafficked; use extreme caution. Bicycles are not permitted on any of the trails in Grand Canyon National Park.

Camping   Camping inside Grand Canyon National Park is permitted only in designated areas. (For information about campgrounds in and around the park, *see* Lodging, *below*.)

Fishing   The high-plateau country of northwestern Arizona is a land of little rain and quick runoffs. Consequently, fishing opportunities are limited. However, the Colorado River in the vicinity of Lees Ferry, just across Marble Canyon Bridge on U.S. 89 (the route to the North Rim), is known for its huge trout. Before trying your luck, be sure to get an Arizona fishing license, available at most marinas and sporting-goods stores in the state. Licenses are obtainable at Babbitt's General Store at the South Rim and at Marble Canyon Lodge, near Lees Ferry, but you won't be able to get them at the North Rim. They can also be obtained in advance from the **Arizona Game and Fish Department** (2221 W. Greenway Rd., Phoenix, AZ 85023, tel. 602/942–3000). For details on fishing regulations, check with the Backcountry Reservations Office (*see* Hiking, *below*).

Hiking   Hiking trails are numerous and the scenery always spectacular in Grand Canyon country. Opportunities range from leisurely walks on well-defined paths through level or easy-rolling country to arduous treks to the bottom of the canyon—even all the way across it to the other rim. Easy hikes can be found in the Exploring section (*see* Tour 3 and Tour 6, *above*). In addition to some of the most popular trails outlined below, national park rangers or visitor center personnel will gladly provide you with hiking information and local maps of trails featuring varying degrees of difficulty.

Note: Overnight hikes require a permit that can be obtained by written request only to the **Backcountry Reservations Office** (Box 129, Grand Canyon, AZ 86023). Permits are limited, so it's wise to make a reservation in advance. If you arrive without one, go to the Backcountry Reservations Office at either rim: South Rim near the entrance to Mather Campground, North Rim at the ranger station.

Bright Angel Trail, South Rim   One of the most popular and scenic hiking paths from the South Rim to the bottom of the canyon (9 miles), the well-maintained Bright Angel Trail was used in the late 1800s as a route to mining claims. There are rest houses for hikers at the 1½-mile and 3-mile points and at Indian Garden. Plateau Point, 1½ miles below Indian Garden, is a good turnaround point for a day hike. As the climb out is an ascent of 4,460 feet, the trip should be attempted only by those in good physical condition and is not recommended during the summer.

Hermit Trail, South Rim
This 9-mile trail, which starts at Hermits Rest, 8 miles west of Grand Canyon Village, is unmaintained, steep, and suitable only for experienced long-distance hikers; a particularly tricky area is a ⅛-mile section of rock slides. No water is available along the way. The route, leading to the Colorado River, offers some inspiring views of Hermit Gorge and the Redwall and Supai formations. It's 6 miles from the head of the trail to now-abandoned Hermit Camp, operated as a tourist resort by the Santa Fe Railroad after 1912.

South and North Kaibab Trails, South and North Rims
South Kaibab Trail, which begins near Yaki Point on East Rim Drive near Grand Canyon Village, connects at the bottom of the canyon (after the Kaibab Bridge across the Colorado) with the North Kaibab Trail, the only maintained trail into the canyon on the North Rim. Plan on three days if you want to hike the gorge from rim to rim. South Kaibab Trail is steep, descending 4,800 feet in just 7 miles, with no campgrounds or water and very little shade; if you're going back up to the South Rim, ascend via the Bright Angel Trail. Accommodations for hikers along the way include the campgrounds at Indian Garden and Bright Angel or Phantom Ranch (*see* Lodging, *below*).

Safety Tips
Water must be carried for hikes into the Inner Gorge—at least 1–1½ gallons per day. To avoid dehydration, it is important to drink frequently, about every 10 minutes, especially during summer months. To avoid fatigue, take food—preferably energy snacks such as trail mix, bananas, and fig bars. Wear hiking boots or running shoes that have been broken in and proven on previous hikes. In case of a medical emergency, stay with the distressed person and ask the next hiker to go for help. Do not attempt to make the round-trip to the Colorado River in one day. The trek down is deceptively easy, the route back up very fatiguing.

Mule Trips
Almost everyone who knows anything about the Grand Canyon has heard of the mule rides to the bottom of the canyon. Since they are conducted under the auspices of an experienced trail guide, these rides are profiled in the Guided Tours section, *above*.

Rafting
Many people who have made the white-water trip down the Colorado River through the Grand Canyon say it is the adventure highlight of a lifetime. White-water trips embark from Lees Ferry, below Glen Canyon Dam near Page, Arizona. Trips that run the length of the canyon (a distance of over 200 miles) can last from three days to three weeks. Shorter trips, also starting at Lees Ferry, let passengers off at Phantom Ranch at the bottom of Grand Canyon (a distance of about 100 miles); these pass through a great amount of white water, including Lava Falls rapids (on the longer trips), considered the wildest navigable rapids in North America. For those who would like a more tranquil turn on the Colorado, there are also one-day, quiet-water raft cruises just below Glen Canyon Dam near Page. Although more than 25 companies currently offer these excur-

sions, reservations for raft trips (excluding the smooth-water, one-day cruises) often must be made more than six months in advance. For a complete list of river-raft companies, call 602/638–7888 from a touchtone phone and press 1-3-71, or write to the River Permits Office, Grand Canyon National Park, Box 129, Grand Canyon, AZ 86023. Whitewater companies include **Canyoneers, Inc.** (tel. 602/526–0924 or, outside AZ, 800/525–0925), **Diamond River Adventures** (tel. 602/645–8866 or 800/343–3121), **Expeditions Inc.** (tel. 602/774–8176), and **Wilderness River Adventures** (tel. 602/645–3296 or 800/992–8022). Smooth-water, one-day-trip companies include **Fred Harvey Transportation Company** (tel. 602/638–2822) and **Wilderness River Adventures** (tel. 602/645–3279 or 800/343–3121). Prices for river-raft trips vary greatly, depending on type and length. Day trips on smooth water run as low as $39 per person; trips that negotiate the entire length of the canyon and take as long as 14 days can cost well over $1,000.

Skiing Though you can't schuss down into the Grand Canyon, you can hit the slopes at the nearby **Williams Ski Area** (Box 953, Williams 86046, tel. 602/635–9330), open when there's snow in the region; take South 4th Street for 2 miles, then turn right at the sign and go another 1½ miles. This is not the major Williams resort that's being planned, but it offers four groomed runs (including one for beginners) and a variety of trails for downhill skiers and areas suitable for cross-country enthusiasts. Lift tickets range from $7.50 to $18 depending on your age and level of expertise; lessons are available on a group ($15 per person) and individual ($25) basis. *See* Chapter 5, North-Central Arizona, for information on skiing Flagstaff's Arizona Snowbowl.

Dining and Lodging

Dining Throughout Grand Canyon country and the vast areas of northwestern Arizona, restaurants cater to tourists who generally move from one place to another at a good clip. Therefore, most establishments offer standard American fare, prepared quickly and offered at reasonable prices. However, there are a few dining opportunities, noted below, that merit mention. In addition, for a quick meal at reasonable prices, there are cafeterias on the South Rim in Grand Canyon Village at **Yavapai Lodge** and **Maswik Lodge** (tel. 602/638–2401 for both) or at **Desert View Trading Post** (AZ 64, 23 mi east of Grand Canyon Village, tel. 602/638–2360). On the North Rim, the cafeteria is located in **Grand Canyon Lodge** (tel. 602/638–2611). Restaurants are open daily unless otherwise noted. Highly recommended restaurants are indicated by a star ★.

Category	Cost*
Very Expensive	over $25
Expensive	$17–$25
Moderate	$10–$17
Inexpensive	under $10

*per person, excluding drinks, service, and 5% sales tax

Lodging When it comes to lodging in Grand Canyon country, there is one thing to be aware of above all else. The popular South Rim is very crowded during the summer. The North Rim is less crowded, but that area has limited lodging facilities. You would be well advised to make reservations as soon as your itinerary has been decided, even as early as six months in advance. If you're unable to find accommodations in the immediate area of the South Rim, you might find rooms in the nearby communities of Williams (*see below*), Flagstaff (*see* Chapter 5, North-Central Arizona), or—a bit farther afield—Tuba City (*see* Chapter 4, The Northeast). For those going to the North Rim, we list three small roadside motels in the sparsely populated Arizona Strip country on the approach to the North Rim on U.S. 89A. Prices at many of the hotels and motels in Grand Canyon country are lower in spring, fall, and winter.

Highly recommended lodgings are indicated by a star ★.

Category	Cost*
Very Expensive	over $100
Expensive	$75–$100
Moderate	$50–$75
Inexpensive	under $50

*All prices are for a standard double room, excluding 5.5%–6.7% tax and service charges.

South Rim **El Tovar Hotel.** Built in 1905 of native stone and heavy pine
Dining and logs, El Tovar is reminiscent of a grand European hunting
Lodging lodge. Maintaining its tradition of excellent service and lux-
★ ury, the hotel is, as when first built, operated by the Fred Harvey Company. Some rooms have a canyon view. For decades the hotel's world-class restaurant has enjoyed a reputation for fine food served in a classic 19th-century room of hand-hewn logs and beamed ceilings. The Continental menu changes seasonally but includes a daily vegetarian special along with innovatively prepared fish, poultry, and meat dishes; free-range chicken breast with lemon wasabi sauce or crab cakes Creole style might be among your dinner options. *Box 699, Grand Canyon 86023, tel. 602/638-2401 (reservations) or 602/638-2631 (switchboard). 65 rooms and 10 suites with bath. Facilities: cocktail lounge,*

gift shop, dining room, air-conditioning, phones, TV, room service. AE, D, DC, MC, V. Very Expensive.

★ **Bright Angel Lodge.** Designed by Mary Jane Colter for the Fred Harvey Company in 1935, this log-and-native-stone structure sits within a few yards of the canyon rim and offers rooms in the main lodge or quaint cabins (some with fireplaces) scattered among the pines. Don't come for luxury but for a historic structure that blends superbly with the spectacular natural environment in which the lodge is set. Bright Angel Restaurant is a memorable but informal spot for breakfast, lunch, or dinner. *Box 699, Grand Canyon 86023, tel. 602/638–2401 (reservations) or 602/638–2631 (switchboard). 11 rooms with bath, 13 rooms with semi-bath (sink and toilet but no bathtub or shower), 6 rooms without bath, 42 cabins with bath. Facilities: dining room, cocktail lounge, soda fountain, gift shop, TV, phones. AE, D, DC, MC, V. Moderate–Expensive.*

Dining **The Steak House.** This is a warmly appointed, typical southwestern steak house, right down to the black-and-white-cowhide–pattern tablecloths, massive brick fireplace, displays of Native American and western art, and traditional country music on the jukebox. The John Wayne bar is lined with memorabilia of the actor. The food is well prepared, and there's plenty of it, with the menu consisting almost entirely of mesquite-grilled steaks and barbecued chicken entrées; a Mexican plate is always on offer, as are specials for senior citizens and a children's menu. *Junction of U.S. 180 and AZ 64, 2 mi south of Grand Canyon entrance, directly north of the Imax Theater, tel. 602/638–2780. Reservations accepted only for parties of 8 or more. Dress: casual. AE, MC, V. Open Mar. 1–Dec. 15, daily 6:30 AM–2 PM and 5–10 PM. Inexpensive–Moderate.*

Lodging **Best Western Squire Inn Grand Canyon.** Located 1 mile from the national park entrance, this motel lacks some of the charm of the older lodges at the canyon rim, but it offers a longer list of amenities. The rooms feature standard American roadside design and decor, but all are clean and comfortable. Ask for a room with a woodside view; others face the highway. *Box 130, Tusayan 86023, tel. 602/638–2681 or 800/528–1234. 250 rooms with bath. Facilities: dining room, coffee shop, heated pool, wading pool, tennis courts, sauna, indoor whirlpool, air-conditioning, phones, TV. AE, D, DC, MC, V. Expensive–Very Expensive.*

Quality Inn. The design and interior of this facility in Tusayan, 6 miles south of the South Rim on U.S. 180, are typical of Quality Inns elsewhere—unpretentious, but offering a satisfactory comfort level in a land where motel vacancies are often difficult to find in the busy summer season. Rooms are done in soothing shades of light blue, peach, or tan. In contrast to many other chain hotels, individual service is emphasized here. *Box 520, Tusayan 86023, tel. 602/638–2673 or 800/221–2222. 137 rooms with bath. Facilities: dining room, gift shop, pool, Jacuzzi, air-*

conditioning, TV, phones. AE, D, DC, MC, V. Very Expensive.

Fred Harvey Motels. The Fred Harvey Company has seven lodges on the South Rim. Of them, El Tovar and Bright Angel (*see above*) are outstanding, but in an area where tourist traffic is heavy and lodgings are limited, it's good to have options. Maswik Lodge, Yavapai Lodge, Moqui Lodge, Kachina Lodge, and Thunderbird Lodge do not have the antique charm of Bright Angel and El Tovar, but they are all comfortable and nicely appointed. Moqui is located on U.S. 180, just outside the national park. The others are in Grand Canyon Village. With the exception of Maswik Lodge, which has rooms in the Moderate range, accommodations in all the motels fall into the Expensive price category. *Box 699, Grand Canyon 86023, tel. 602/638–2401 (reservations) or 602/638–2631 (switchboard), fax 602/638–9247. (The box, telephone, and fax nos. are the same for all Fred Harvey accommodations on the South Rim.) 855 rooms with private bath. Facilities: phones, TV, restaurant on site or close by. AE, D, DC, MC, V. Moderate–Expensive.*

Camping Camping inside Grand Canyon National Park is permitted only in designated areas. Campgrounds at the South Rim are listed below.

Mather Campground in Grand Canyon Village has 97 RV and 190 tent sites (no hookups), flush toilets, water, showers, and a laundromat; the cost is $10 per site. *Reservations through MISTIX (Box 85705, San Diego, CA 92138, tel. 800/365–2267 or 619/452–0150 outside the U.S. Open all year; no reservations taken from Dec. 1–Mar. 1.*

Desert View Campground, 23 miles east of Grand Canyon Village off AZ 64, offers RV and tent sites, flush toilets, and water but no hookups. The cost is $10 per site, with no reservations. *Box 129, Grand Canyon 86023, tel. 602/638–7888. Open May–Oct.*

Trailer Village, in Grand Canyon Village, has 78 RV sites with full hookups for $17 per site. *Box 699, Grand Canyon 86023, tel. 602/638–2401. Open all year.*

Commercial and Forest Service campgrounds outside the park include:

Flintstone Bedrock City, 30 miles south of the park, offers 28 tent and 32 partial RV hookups. Basic rates are $12 per site for two people; add $2 for electricity hookup, $2 for water hookup, and $1.50 for each additional person. *Grand Canyon Hwy., HCR 34, Box A, Williams 86046, tel. 602/635–2600. Open Apr.–Oct.*

Grand Canyon Camper Village in Tusayan, 6 miles south of the rim, has 250 RV hookups, some partial, some full ($20 for two people, plus $1 for each additional person over the age of 6) and 100 tent sites ($13 for two people). *Box 490, Grand Canyon 86023, tel. 602/638–2887.*

Ten X Campground is run by the Forest Service about 9 miles south of the park. It offers 70 family sites plus a group site (available for groups of up to 100 people), water, and pit toilets for $10 per day but no hookups. No reservations are accepted (except for the group site). *Kaibab National Forest, Tusayan Ranger District, Box 3088, Grand Canyon 86023, tel. 602/638–2443. Open May 1–Sept. 30.*

Bottom of the Canyon
Dining and Lodging

Phantom Ranch. Built on the site of an earlier hunting camp in 1932, this group of wood-and-stone buildings is set among a grove of cottonwood trees at the bottom of the canyon. For hikers (who need a backcountry permit to come down here), dormitory accommodations—20 beds for men and 20 for women—are available, as are two cabins (one sleeping four people, the other 10). There are also seven cabins reserved exclusively for mule riders; lodging, meals, and mule rides are offered as a package (*see* Guided Tours in Essential Information, *above*). The restaurant at Phantom Ranch, probably the most remote eating establishment in the United States, has a limited menu. All meals are served family style, with breakfast, dinner (including a selection for vegetarians), and box lunches available. Arrangements—and payment—for both food and lodging should be made 9 to 11 months in advance. *Box 699, Grand Canyon 86023, tel. 602/638–2401 (reservations) or 602/638–2631, ext. 6015 (switchboard). 4 dormitories for hikers with shared bath, 11 cabins for mule riders with shower outside. Facilities: dining room. AE, D, DC, MC, V. Inexpensive.*

Camping

There are two free campgrounds en route to Phantom Ranch: **Indian Garden,** about halfway down the canyon, and **Bright Angel,** closer to the bottom. Both offer toilet facilities and running water (no showers). A backcountry permit is required. For information, contact Backcountry Reservations Office (Box 129, Grand Canyon 86023, tel. 602/638–7888).

Havasu Canyon
Dining and Lodging

Havasupai Lodge The lodge and restaurant at the bottom of Havasu Canyon, operated by the Havasupai tribe, offers clean, comfortable rooms at about $80 for a double (this rate is in addition to the $12 per person fee to enter the Havasupai tribal lands). The restaurant serves three meals a day, generally sandwiches and fast-food–type fare, and a special daily meal; dinner prices are around $8–$10. For information about camping in the canyon, call the Havasupai Tourist Enterprise (tel. 602/448–2121). *Supai 86435, tel. 602/448–2111 (lodge), or 602/448–2981 (restaurant). 24 rooms. No credit cards accepted at any facilities; personal checks accepted for deposit, traveler's checks or cash required upon arrival. Expensive.*

En Route to the North Rim/ Arizona Strip
Dining and Lodging
★

Cameron Trading Post. In 1993 the 1930s-era inn abutting the historic trading post was razed and replaced by a two-building motel complex. Rooms are still southwestern-style, with hand-carved wooden furniture, but now have contemporary amenities, such as remote-control TVs, as well as balconies overlooking the Colorado. The original native stone landscaping—including fossilized dinosaur tracks—was retained, as was the small, well-kept garden with lilacs, roses, and crab apple trees. A new cafeteria, designed to serve the tour bus trade, is unusually elegant, with an antique backbar and light fixtures; the older dining room, with its original tinwork ceilings, kiva fireplace, and beautiful oak sideboards, offers hearty meals at good prices. Boozers note: The trading post is on the Navajo reservation, so no alcohol is served here. *Box 339, Cameron 86020, tel. 602/679-2231 or 800/338-7385. 65 rooms with bath, 3 suites. Facilities: market, restaurant, cafeteria, gift shop, art gallery. AE, D, MC, V. Expensive.*

Cliff Dwellers Lodge. One of three modest motels in the Vermilion Cliffs/Marble Canyon area of the Arizona Strip, Cliff Dwellers recently expanded its motel and dining facilities. You can buy waterproof river-rafting gear here. *HC 67-30, Marble Canyon 86036, tel. 602/355-2228. 20 rooms with bath. Facilities: restaurant, convenience store, gas station. D, MC, V. Moderate.*

Jacob Lake Inn. This modest but clean motel, on five acres in Kaibab National Forest (at the junction of U.S. 89A and AZ 67, 45 miles north of the North Rim), is a good option for lodging in the area. Both basic cabins and standard motel-type units are available. All rooms are rustic, with simple wood furnishings; most overlook the highways. The hotel's restaurant serves American food at moderate prices. *Jacob Lake 86022, tel. 602/643-7232. 11 motel units, 3 family units, 22 cabins. Facilities: gas station, gift shop, grocery, café, restaurant. AE, D, DC, MC, V. Moderate.*

Marble Canyon Lodge. Also close to Lees Ferry and historic Navajo Bridge, this motel offers ordinary rooms with extraordinary views of the Vermilion Cliffs and the desert. The newer accommodations building adjoins the original 1920s native stone lodge, now used for meetings. *Marble Canyon 86036, tel. 602/355-2225. 60 rooms with bath. Facilities: restaurant, gift shop, gas station, laundry, coin-op showers. MC, V. Moderate.*

Lees Ferry Lodge. Geared toward the Lees Ferry trout-fishing trade, this lodge will outfit you, guide you, and freeze or cold-store your catch. At the end of the day you can sit out on one of the garden patios of this rustic building, constructed of native stone and rough-hewn beams in 1929. The hotel's Vermilion Cliffs Bar and Grill is a popular gathering spot for the men and women who pilot and guide the river rafts through the Grand Canyon, and it serves surprisingly good American fare—especially the steaks and seafood—in an authentic western setting. *HC67, Box 1, Marble Canyon 86036, tel. 602/355-2231. 8 rooms with bath, 5-person trailer with bath. Facilities: restaurant, fly/curio shop, boat for rent. MC, V. Inexpensive.*

Camping **Jacob Lake Campground,** at the junction of U.S. 89A and AZ 67, 45 miles north of the North Rim, has family and group RV and tent sites, but no hookups, for $10 per vehicle per day. In summer rangers give interpretative evening programs. No reservations accepted. *Kaibab National Forest, North Kaibab Ranger District, Box 248, Fredonia 86022, tel. 602/643–7395. Open May–Oct.*

North Rim **Grand Canyon Lodge.** This historic property offers com-
Dining and fortable if not luxurious accommodations in a setting of ex-
Lodging traordinary beauty; it's the premier lodging facility in the
★ remote and sparsely populated North Rim area. The main
building was constructed in the 1920s and exhibits massive
limestone walls and timbered ceilings. Room choices include small, very rustic cabins, newer and larger cabins
(some with a canyon view and some with two bedrooms),
and traditional motel rooms. The hotel's huge, high-ceilinged dining room is an excellent spot for breakfast, lunch,
or dinner. *TW Recreational Services, Cedar City, UT
84721, tel. 801/586–7686 (reservations) or 602/638–2611
(switchboard). 40 rooms with bath, 54 Western cabins (for
up to 5 people), 82 Frontier cabins (up to 3 people), 21 Pioneer cabins (4 or 5 people), 4 handicapped-accessible cabins. Facilities: dining room, cafeteria, cocktail lounge, gift
shop, visitor center, talks and programs. D, MC, V. Moderate.*

Camping On the North Rim there is only one designated campground
inside Grand Canyon National Park. **North Rim Campground,** located 3 miles north of the rim, has a total of 83 RV
and tent sites, but no hookups, for $10 per day. *Reserva-
tions through MISTIX (Box 85705, San Diego, CA 92138,
tel. 800/365–2267 or 619/452–0150 outside the U.S). Open
May 15–Oct 26.*

Forest Service campgrounds outside the park include
Demotte Campground, 16 miles north of the rim, with 22
single-unit RV and tent sites, but no hookups, for $8 per
day. There are campfire interpretative programs in the
summer. No reservations accepted. *Kaibab National Forest, North Kaibab Ranger District, Box 248, Fredonia
86022, tel. 602/643–7395. Open June–Oct.*

Williams **Mountain Side Inn & Resort.** The most upscale lodging in a
Dining and down-home town, this pleasant motel wouldn't be called a
Lodging resort anywhere else, but its rooms are comfortable and
tastefully decorated in contemporary style. On summer
nights, live country-and-western bands play in the recently
opened Miss Kitty's Steakhouse. The waitresses at the Dining Car restaurant will make sure you get through the copious breakfast buffet in time to catch the Grand Canyon
Railroad. *642 E. Bill Williams Ave., Williams 86046, tel.
602/635–4431 or 800/462–9381. 96 rooms with bath. Facilities: 2 restaurants, cocktail lounge, pool, spa, gift shop.
AE, D, DC, MC, V. Expensive.*

Lodging **Norris Motel.** This no-frills motel offers clean, comfortable
rooms at good rates. You can distinguish it from the many
others on the town's main drag by the British flag flown by
the genial English owner. *1001 W. Bill Williams Ave., tel.*

602/635–2202 or 800/341–8000. 33 rooms with bath. Facilities: spa, cable TV, air-conditioning, refrigerators in most rooms. AE, D, MC, V. Moderate.

Nightlife

Unless you head for nearby Williams or Flagstaff after dark, nightlife in this part of the Southwest consists of watching a full moon above the soaring buttes of the Grand Canyon, roasting marshmallows over a crackling fire, crawling into your bedroll beside some lonely canyon trail, or attending a free evening program on the history of the Grand Canyon. Dinner at **El Tovar Restaurant** (it has an excellent wine list) would be a memorable evening. In addition, the following Grand Canyon properties have cocktail lounges: **El Tovar Hotel** (piano bar), **Bright Angel Lodge** (live entertainment), **Maswik Lodge** (sports bar), **Yavapai Lodge** (dancing), and **Moqui Lodge** (live entertainment). Call 602/638–2401 for reservations and further information.

Excursion to Lake Mead and Hoover Dam

From the most popular viewing points on both the North and South rims, the Grand Canyon charts an erratic path for more than 200 miles to the west, where the wild-running Colorado River fills the dark, eroded canyons of the Black Mountains to form the largest man-made body of water in the United States, Lake Mead.

Lake Mead, whose surface covers 229 square miles and whose irregular shoreline extends for 550 miles, was formed when **Hoover Dam** was built in 1935 to hold back the Colorado River. The dam, which required 4.4 million cubic yards of concrete poured into place by a crew of 5,000 men working in shifts around the clock, is so impressive that it has drawn nearly 30 million visitors since it was completed.

Sightseeing is the number one visitor pastime in the Lake Mead area, but boating, water sports, swimming, camping, and fishing are extremely popular, too. The weather in this desert region is pleasant during winter months, ideal in spring and fall (50s to 80s), and hot in the summer (over 100°F). Primarily a recreation area for Nevadans or visitors wanting a break from dropping money at the Las Vegas casinos, Lake Mead is less impressive than Lake Powell, the other man-made lake in the Grand Canyon area (*see* Chapter 4, The Northeast), and has fewer facilities. As a result, though, it's also less crowded.

Tourist Information

The best place for finding out about the Lake Mead region is the **Alan Bible Visitor Center** (601 Nevada Hwy., Boulder City, NV 89005, tel. 702/293–8906). You can also contact the **Boulder City Chamber of Commerce** (1497 Nevada Hwy., Boulder City, NV 89005, tel. 702/293–2034) for information about the area.

Getting There

To reach Lake Mead from Grand Canyon National Park, take U.S. 180 (AZ 64) south to Williams. Then proceed west on I–40 to Kingman, where you will veer northwest on U.S. 93 to Hoover Dam and Lake Mead. It's 184 miles from Williams to Hoover Dam.

The Lake Mead National Recreation Area and Hoover Dam can also be accessed by flying into Las Vegas's **McCarran International Airport** (tel. 702/739–5743) or by **Greyhound/ Trailways** bus (see your local yellow pages for information).

Getting Around

The only practical way to explore the vast land areas of Lake Mead is by car. Naturally, the almost endless waterways of the lake require a boat. If you aren't pulling your own, there are plenty for rent at the marinas along the shore (*see* Boating and Water Sports, *below*).

Guided Tours

By Boat A 1½-hour cruise of the Hoover Dam area on a 250-passenger stern-wheeler is available daily through Lake Mead Cruises (Lake Mead Marina, near Boulder Beach, tel. 702/ 293–6180); rates are $12 adults ($16.50 on Sunday), $5 children under 12 ($8 on Sunday); sunset dinner cruises cost $32.50. A motorized raft trip on the Colorado from the base of Hoover Dam down Black Canyon to Willow Beach, a distance of about 15 miles, is offered daily by Gray Line Tours (tel. 702/384–1234). Prices run about $70 per person and include lunch and transportation back.

Exploring

Numbers in the margin correspond to points of interest on the Lake Mead map.

The visual impact of the incredible mass and height of
❶ Hoover Dam nearly compels the visitor to make this the first stop on a visit to the area. Created for flood control and the generation of electricity, the dam is 727 feet high (the equivalent of a 70-story building) and 660 feet thick (more than the length of two football fields). Its construction required 4.4 million cubic yards of concrete, enough to build a

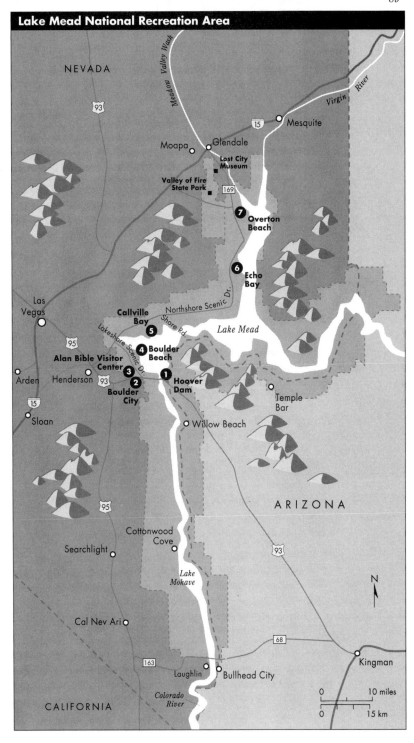

Lake Mead National Recreation Area

NEVADA

Meadow Valley Wash

Virgin River

93

15 Mesquite

Moapa

Glendale

Lost City Museum

Valley of Fire State Park

169

7 Overton Beach

6 Echo Bay

Las Vegas

Northshore Scenic Dr.

Callville Bay

5

Shore Rd.

Lake Mead

Lakeshore Scenic Dr.

95

4 Boulder Beach

Alan Bible Visitor Center 3

Arden

Henderson 93 **2**

1 Hoover Dam

Boulder City

15

Sloan

Temple Bar

○ Willow Beach

A R I Z O N A

Cottonwood Cove

Searchlight

93

Lake Mohave

N

Cal Nev Ari

68

Kingman

163

Laughlin ○ Bullhead City

Colorado River

0		10 miles
0		15 km

CALIFORNIA

two-lane highway from San Francisco to New York. Every
year more than 600,000 people take one of the Bureau of
Reclamation's guided tours, which lead visitors deep inside
the structure for a look at its inner workings. The tours
leave every few minutes from the exhibit building at the top
of the dam. A huge new visitor center, scheduled to open on
the Nevada side on Memorial Day 1994, will feature three
revolving theaters, an exhibition gallery, an observation
tower with views of Lake Mead, and a much-needed five-
story parking garage. *Tel. 702/293-8367. Admission free.*
Guided tours: $2 adults, $1 seniors over 62 with Golden Age
Pass, children under 12 free. Open Memorial Day–Labor
Day, daily 8–7:15; Labor Day–Memorial Day, daily
9–4:15; closed Christmas.

② About 8 miles west of Hoover Dam on U.S. 93, **Boulder City**
is a small, pleasant town with a movie theater, numerous
gift shops and eateries, and a small hotel. Developed in the
early 1930s to deter workers on the Hoover Dam project
from spending their hard-earned dollars on wine, women,
and Las Vegas, Boulder City is to this day the only community in Nevada where gambling is illegal. Originally, 4,000
workers lived here; when the dam was completed, the city
served as a center for the management and maintenance of
the site.

Just northeast of Boulder City, at the intersection of U.S.
93 (also called Nevada Highway) and Lakeshore Scenic
③ Drive (NV 166), you'll come to the **Alan Bible Visitor Center,** named for Alan Bible, a former Nevada senator. The
best place to become acquainted with the area, the center
offers films on Lake Mead and Hoover Dam, a botanical garden featuring local plant life, and a wildlife exhibit. A complete auto tour guide to the area costs 50¢ here, and free
brochures provide information on recreational opportunities. *601 Nevada Hwy., Boulder City, NV 89005, tel. 702/*
293-8906. Admission free. Open daily 8:30–4:30 (summer
until 5), closed Thanksgiving, Christmas, and New Year's
Day.

Turn left outside the parking lot of the Alan Bible Visitor
Center, and go down the hill to pick up Lakeshore Scenic
Drive (NV 166). This route, wending its way along the
shore of Lake Mead in a northwesterly direction for 9 miles,
④ also provides access to **Boulder Beach,** a favorite swimming
area.

If you wish to extend your auto tour of the Lake Mead area,
Lakeshore Scenic Drive intersects NV 167 (Northshore
Scenic Drive) about 7 miles north of Boulder Beach. You can
⑤ ⑥ take 167 northeast along the Nevada shoreline to **Callville**
⑦ **Bay** (12 miles), **Echo Bay** (37 miles), or **Overton Beach** (47
miles). Marinas and campgrounds are available at all three
sites, and there is a motel at Echo Bay.

Sports and the Outdoors

Boating and   If you have your own boat, find a marina or boat launch and
Water Sports   put it in the water. If not, you'll have the option of choosing
from a long list of rental opportunities. We suggest that you
pick up a free list of all marinas at the **Alan Bible Visitor
Center** (*see* Tourist Information, *above*). Houseboat rentals
are available at **Callville Bay Resort and Marina** (Callville
Bay, tel. 702/565–7340) or at **Echo Bay Resort** (Echo Bay,
tel. 702/394–4066). Prices for a boat that sleeps 10 range
from about $650 (three days in low season) to $1650 (a week
in high season); the most expensive time of year is summer,
and a minimum rental of three nights is required. Small
boats, including patio boats, fishing boats, and ski boats,
are offered at these locations and at **Lake Mead Resort**
(Boulder Beach, tel. 702/293–3484), as well as at other Lake
Mead locations. Prices vary greatly depending on type and
size of boat. Typical price ranges for one-day rentals would
be about $100 for a 16-foot skiff, $200 for a 19-foot power-
boat.

Fishing   Sports fishermen from far and wide travel to Lake Mead,
where it's open season on all species year-round. Largemouth bass and striped bass grow to impressive sizes, the
latter sometimes to more than 50 pounds. The lake has also
been planted with rainbow and cutthroat trout and offers
bluegill, black crappie (sometimes 5 to 6 pounds), and channel catfish. The north shore of Lake Mead is in Nevada, the
south shore in Arizona. To fish from shore you must have
the proper state license. From a boat, you need a license
from one state and a stamp from the other. Licenses are
available at most marinas and sporting-goods stores in the
state. Permits can also be obtained in advance from the **Arizona Game and Fish Department** (2221 W. Greenway Rd.,
Phoenix 85023, tel. 602/942–3000).

Hiking   You may hike anywhere within the vast Lake Mead National Recreational Area. However, most hiking is of the cross-
country variety, since there are few maintained trails. For
short treks, pick a place that suits you at a stopping point
along the shore. But stay in sight of landmarks—this is
rough, lonely, and very dry country. For longer hikes, consult with park rangers and obtain topographic maps. Taking along at least one gallon of water per day is advised for
hikers. Use extreme caution in summer months. For information on trails, contact the Alan Bible Visitor Center (*see*
Tourist Information, *above*).

Dining and Lodging

The resorts listed below—both owned by the same company—are the main lodging options in this area. Except for
the **Temple Bar Resort** (Temple Bar, AZ 86443, tel. 602/
767–3211 or 800/752–9669), about 39 miles south and east of
Hoover Dam, there are no other lodging facilities on the

lake. The closest Arizona motels are in Kingman, 73 miles south on U.S. 93. However, there are about 15 motels and numerous eating establishments (from fast-food outlets to formal restaurants) in Boulder City, Nevada, 8 miles west of Hoover Dam on U.S. 93. For information, contact the Boulder City Chamber of Commerce (tel. 702/293–2034).

Echo Bay Resort. Looking rather like a concrete bunker with nautical touches, the main building of this resort houses reasonably attractive rooms done in southwestern patterns and shades of turquoise; all but four have patios. But you don't come to this remote (some might say desolate) spot to stay indoors. The draw here is water sports: There's a full slate of lakeside recreational activities on offer, including ski-, patio-, and fishing-boat rentals as well as houseboat rentals, RV sites, a convenience store, a marine fueling station, and moorage. An attractive sea-themed, plant-filled restaurant serves competent American fare. *Echo Bay, Overton, NV 89040, tel. 702/394–4000 or 800/752–9669. 52 rooms with bath. Facilities: restaurant, lounge, TV, air-conditioning. MC, V. Moderate–Expensive.*

Lake Mead Resort. Located near popular Boulder Beach, this rustic, tile-roofed lodge with a magnificent view of the lake provides comfortable rooms with a hint of southwestern decor. The resort's floating Tail o' the Whale restaurant and Pelican Perch lounge serve breakfast, lunch, and dinner; dishes are primarily American, with some Italian specialties. At the resort's marina, a mile down the road, there are many recreational facilities, including ski-, fishing-, and patio-boat rentals; a convenience store; and a marine fueling station. *322 Lakeshore Rd., Boulder City, NV 89005, tel. 702/293–2074 or 800/752–9669. 42 rooms with bath. Facilities: pool, walking trails, TV, air-conditioning; pets allowed with $25 deposit. MC, V. Moderate.*

4 The Northeast

*Petrified Forest,
Hopi and Navajo Country,
Lake Powell*

By William E.
Hafford

Updated by Edie
Jarolim

If you like wide-open spaces, you'll want to visit northeastern Arizona, a vast and lonely land of shifting red dunes and soaring buttes, where horizons capped by pure blue skies are almost always a hundred miles or more away. Covering more than 30,000 square miles, most of the northeast belongs to the Navajo and Hopi peoples, who have held on to their ancient cultural traditions—based on strong spiritual values and an affinity for nature—to the present day. Excellent Native Americans arts and crafts can be found in shops, galleries, and trading posts throughout the region. Visiting here is like crossing into a foreign country—one that is, sadly, less prosperous than much of the rest of the United States. In some respects, life on the Hopi Mesas does not seem very different from what it must have been in the last century, and it's not uncommon to hear the Navajo language spoken in towns such as Tuba City and Window Rock.

The sprawling Navajo reservation (known to its people as the Navajo Nation) incorporates about 25,000 square miles of the entire northeastern corner of Arizona; in its approximate center lie the 4,000 square miles of Hopi reservation, a series of stone and adobe villages built on high mesas that overlook agricultural land. Within the stunning landscape of Navajo National Monument and Canyon de Chelly rest the mysterious ruins of the ancient Anasazi Indian tribes, who first wandered here thousands of years ago.

Outside the borders of the Navajo Nation, you'll find two of the most popular attractions in the area. Just below the southeastern boundary of the reservation, straddling I–40, is Petrified Forest National Park, an intriguing geological open book of the Earth's distant past. The park includes a large portion of the famed Painted Desert, with its stratified bands of multicolored hills in which ancient life-forms and huge fallen tree trunks have petrified over hundreds of millions of years. Above the far northwestern corner of the Navajo reservation on U.S. 89 lies Glen Canyon Dam—and behind it, more than 120 miles of Lake Powell's emerald waters held in precipitous canyons of erosion-carved stone. Many find Lake Powell one of the most serene and beautiful spots in the world.

Most of Indian country is arid land, with soil and rock formations ranging in color from delicate salmon pink to rusty orange—and sometimes nearly red. Driving for long distances, you'll generally see immense vistas of mesas, rock spires, canyons, and cliffs, but you'll also pass some impressive mountain ranges. The Chuska Mountains to the north and east of Canyon de Chelly are covered with striking stands of ponderosa pine, and Navajo Mountain to the north and west in Utah soars above 10,000 feet.

Essential Information

Important Addresses and Numbers

Tourist Information For more information regarding Indian country, contact the **Navajoland Tourism Department** (Box 663, Window Rock 86515, tel. 602/871–6659 or 871–7371) and the **Hopi Tribe Office of Public Relations** (Box 123, Kykotsmovi 86039, tel. 602/734–2441); both publish tourist-oriented newspapers. The **Page/Lake Powell Chamber of Commerce** (Box 727, Page 86040, tel. 602/645–2741) and the **National Park Service/Glen Canyon Recreation Area** (Box 1507, Page 86040, tel. 602/645-2511) are both excellent sources for Lake Powell vacation information and prices.

Emergencies **Navajo tribal police: Chinle** (tel. 602/674–5291), **Tuba City**
Police (tel. 602/283–5242, **Window Rock** (tel. 602/871–6113 or 871–6116); **Hopi tribal police: Hopi Mesas** (tel. 602/738–2233).

Hospitals/ Medical Clinics Medical care in Indian country is not as easily accessible as in heavily populated urban areas. People with chronic medical conditions or those in frail health may wish to avoid a trip into Arizona's sparsely populated northeast. Hospital emergency care is generally not more than 60 minutes' driving time from any location on a paved highway.

Sage Memorial Hospital (tel. 602/755–3411), a public hospital located in Ganado, on the Navajo reservation, offers medical and dental services. **Monument Valley Hospital** (tel. 801/727–3241) in Utah (near Goulding's Trading Post off U.S. 163 at the Arizona–Utah border) has medical and dental services. Emergency care through the U.S. Public Health Service Indian Hospitals is available in the reservation communities of Fort Defiance (tel. 602/729-5741), Chinle (tel. 602/674-5281), Tuba City (tel. 602/283-6211), and Keams Canyon (tel. 602/738-2211). Another option in a medical emergency is to contact the Navajo or Hopi tribal police (*see* Police, *above*).

Pharmacies There are no pharmacies on the Navajo or Hopi reservation; for emergency medical supplies, go to the private or public hospitals noted in the Hospital/Medical Clinics section, above.

Road Service **Fed Mart Automotive** (AZ 264 near Window Rock, tel. 602/871–4764), **Tuba City Motors** (corner of Birch and Oak Sts., Tuba City, tel. 602/283–5330 during the day, 602/283-5300 at night), **Kayenta Discount Auto Parts** (Kayenta on Hwy. 160, tel. 602/697-3200), **Onsae Auto Repair** (Second Mesa, across from the Hopi Cultural Center, Hopi Mesas, tel. 602/734–2211).

Arriving and Departing by Plane

No major airlines fly directly to Indian country. To get closer to the northeastern part of the state, travelers will need to make flight connections in Phoenix to travel either on to Flagstaff, located on I–40 near the southwestern corner of the Navajo reservation, or the community of Page, on U.S. 89 near Lake Powell and the northern border of Arizona. At the end of your flight, you'll need to rent a car for the rest of the journey (*see* Rental Cars, *below*).

Airports and Airlines **Sky Harbor International Airport** (tel. 602/273–3300) in Phoenix is the primary hub for air travel coming into Arizona from points out of state. **Flagstaff Pulliam Municipal Airport** (tel. 602/774–1422) or **Page Municipal Airport** (tel. 602/645-2494) are both small but modern. **Sky West** (tel. 800/453-9417) has daily flights from Phoenix and Flagstaff into Page. (*See* Chapter 6, Phoenix and Central Arizona, and Chapter 5, North-Central Arizona, for information on airlines servicing those cities.)

Arriving and Departing by Train or Bus

By Train **Amtrak** (tel. 800/USA–RAIL) provides daily service into Arizona from both the east and the west. It makes scheduled stops in Flagstaff, which is a good jumping-off point for a car trip into Indian country. No passenger train enters the interior of the Navajo or Hopi reservation.

By Bus **Greyhound** (Phoenix, tel. 602/248–4040; Flagstaff, tel. 602/774–4573) has numerous Arizona destinations, but there is no service into Indian country. If you're coming from out of state and wish to tour northeastern Arizona, you can take a bus to Phoenix or Flagstaff and then rent a car to visit Indian country.

Getting Around

By Car If you are arriving from southern California or southern Arizona, Flagstaff is the most likely entry point into northeastern Arizona. If you are coming from the north or northwest, you might choose to come in from Utah via U.S. 89, starting your tour at Page, Arizona. For those driving south from Colorado, a logical entry point would be west from Farmington, New Mexico, via U.S. 64. Gallup, New Mexico, or Flagstaff, Arizona, both located on I–40, are convenient jumping-off points for those arriving from most eastern locations.

Road Maps Because a tour of Indian country involves driving long distances among widely scattered communities, a detailed, recently published road map is absolutely essential. A wrong turn in this lonely country could send you many miles out of your way. Gas stations carry adequate state maps, but two other maps are especially recommended: the Automobile

Association of America's guide to Indian Country or the excellent map of the northeastern region prepared by the **Navajoland Tourism Department** (*see* Important Addresses and Numbers, *above*).

Road Service and Weather It isn't easy to find a place to service your car in sparsely populated Indian country. We recommend that you make sure your car was recently inspected and serviced prior to your trip. Also, seek weather information if you see ominous rain clouds in summer or signs of snow in winter. Never drive into dips or low-lying road areas during a heavy rainstorm; they could be flooded. (For road service locations and emergency and weather information, *see* Important Addresses and Numbers, *above*, and Weather, *below*.) If you heed these simple precautions, car travel through Indian country will be as safe as travel anywhere else. Paved highways in the interior are well maintained and patrolled by trained and courteous tribal police officers.

Rental Cars Rental cars in heavily touristed Arizona are plentiful and usually available, but it's still smart to reserve a car in advance of your arrival. Major companies serving Phoenix and Flagstaff include **Avis** (tel. 800/331–1212), **Budget** (tel. 800/527–0700), **Hertz** (tel. 800/654–3131), and **National** (tel. 800/227–7368). Avis and Budget also offer rentals in Page. Weekly rates for a compact with unlimited mileage are most reasonable in Flagstaff (about $140 without any discounts), slightly higher in Phoenix (about $150), and much higher in Page (around $225).

By Bus The **Navajo Transit System** (Drawer 1330, Window Rock 86515, tel. 602/729–5449, 729–5457 or, at Navajo Nation Inn, tel. 602/871–4108) offers regularly scheduled service on fixed routes throughout the Navajo reservation as well as charter service; write ahead for schedules. The buses are modern, in good condition, and generally on time. However, this method of travel, across vast areas of Indian country where towns and bus stops are many miles apart, may be too slow for most visitors.

Guided Tours

Except during winter months, the **Navajo Transit System** (*see above*) offers tours of Indian country departing from Window Rock, the tribal capital. Destinations include Canyon de Chelly, the Painted Desert, and the Petrified Forest. **Nava-Hopi Tours, Inc.** (tel. 602/774–5003 or 800/892–8687), an affiliate of Gray Line, schedules tours into Indian country from Flagstaff. **Crawley's Monument Valley Tours** (tel. 602/697–3463) is located on the Navajo reservation, with tours embarking from the small town of Kayenta. Half-day and full-day truck and Jeep tours into Canyon de Chelly on the Navajo reservation depart from nearby **Thunderbird Lodge** (tel. 602/674–5841); the half-day tours leave twice daily (when there is a minimum of six passengers) throughout the year, while full-day tours are available only from April to October. The newspaper published by the Navajoland Tourism Department (*see* Important Addresses and Numbers, *above*) has a listing of operators offering jeep and horseback tours on the Navajo reservation.

Weather

With elevations generally between 4,500 and 6,000 feet, the region's summer temperatures average about 87°F but can climb beyond 100°F. Winter daytime temperatures range from the 30s to the 70s but can drop to zero or below. While the area gets less than 10 inches of rainfall in an average year, fierce summer thunderstorms can quickly fill the arroyos and turn them into raging torrents. Sometimes during the winter months, heavy snows virtually stop all traffic on the dirt back roads.

KTNN radio, located at AM 660, provides periodic weather information. This station serves the Hopi and Navajo reservations from studios in Window Rock. Some of the programming is in Navajo, but there are news and weather reports in English. You might also telephone the Canyon de Chelley (tel. 602/674-5500) or the Navajo or Hopi tribal police (*see* Emergencies, *above*) for weather updates.

Time

Unlike the rest of Arizona (including the Hopi reservation), the Navajo reservation observes daylight saving time. Thus for half the year—April to October—it's an hour later on the Navajo reservation than everywhere else in the state.

Banks

Citibank has branch offices in Window Rock and Tuba City on the Navajo reservation, but there are no automated teller machines at these locations. The Arizona communities of Flagstaff, Page, Winslow, and Holbrook, all adjacent to the reservation, have banks and automated teller machines.

The Hopi and the Navajo

No one knows where the ancestors of today's Hopi Indians came from, and archaeologists cannot pinpoint exactly when they arrived. However, the Hopi consider themselves to be the first people to arrive in the Americas, and their oral history has it that these ancestors came by sea, crossing on boats or rafts from one "stepping-stone" to the next. They may have island-hopped across the Pacific rather than crossed the frozen land of the Bering Straits. Many anthropologists think the Hopi are descended from the Anasazi people. Hopi stories suggest that they probably migrated widely for a very long time before being spiritually guided to the mesas that are their present home. It is believed that Oraibi, the earliest village, was established in about AD 1150. Over the years the Hopi have been an extremely peaceful people, taking a warlike posture only when Spanish priests came to the area around 1630, hoping to convert them to Christianity. In 1680, they joined the Indians of the New Mexico pueblos in a revolt that destroyed the Spanish missions and drove the intruders away.

The Navajo, a more warlike tribe believed to be related to the Athabascans of northeastern Canada, arrived in the Southwest sometime after the Hopi, probably around AD 1300. Thanks to the Pueblo Indians already established in the area, they learned the skills of pottery and weaving, and they also raised livestock and became expert horsemen after the arrival of the Spanish in the 17th century; the Navajo have continued farming and creating arts and crafts to this day. In the years 1863 and 1864, the U.S. Army descended on the Navajo and forced them to make the infamous Long Walk to a virtual concentration camp in eastern New Mexico, releasing them four years later. In 1868 the U.S. government established the Navajo Indian reservation, today the largest in the country, occupying not only the entire northwestern portion of Arizona but also spilling over into Utah and New Mexico. The much smaller Hopi territory, smack in the middle of the Navajo holdings, was ceded to the tribe by the federal government in 1882. Border disputes between the two tribes continue, negotiated in court and before Congress. Differences are evident in their way of life, too: The Hopi tend to live together in villages, whereas the Navajo dwellings are usually dispersed.

Although the Navajo and Hopi peoples fall under certain federal laws, they are essentially self-governing. In earlier days, the Navajo were ruled largely by a complex clan system, but in 1923, they established a tribal government that consists of an elected tribal president, vice president, and more than 80 council members representing the various chapters throughout the Navajo Nation. In 1868, when the reservation was established, there were fewer than 8,000 Navajo, but now this democratically governed Native American entity has more than 185,000 people.

The Hopi live in 12 villages on their three primary mesas, with a population of about 10,000. Their government, like that of the Navajo, is solidly based on democratic principles. Although both the Navajo and Hopi peoples rely on their own tribal governments and adhere tenaciously to ancestral cultures, they are patriotic Americans as well; large numbers of Hopi and Navajo have served in the U.S. military with distinction.

Courtesy in Indian Country

Both the Hopi and Navajo peoples are friendly to tourists. However, their privacy, customs, and laws should be respected.

Do not wander across residential areas or disturb property. Always ask permission before taking photographs of the locals; you may have to pay to take the picture.

Littering is not allowed.

No open fires are allowed; fires are permitted only in grills and fireplaces. Bring your own wood or charcoal.

Observe quiet hours from 11 PM until 6 AM at all camping areas.

Animals, plants, rocks, or artifacts must not be disturbed or removed. They are protected by Tribal Antiquity and federal laws, which are strictly enforced.

The possession and consumption of alcoholic beverages or drugs is illegal.

No off-trail hiking or rock climbing is allowed.

A permit is required for fishing in lakes or streams or hunting for game; the use of firearms is otherwise prohibited.

Off-road travel by four-wheel-drive vehicles, dune buggies, Jeeps, and motorcycles is not allowed.

Bikinis or similar scanty clothing should not be worn in public.

Pets should be kept on a leash or in a confined area.

On the Hopi reservation making videos, tape recordings, and sketches of villages and ceremonies is strictly prohibited. At all sacred events, neat attire and respectful etiquette are requested. Camping is permitted for a maximum of two nights, but only in designated areas. All Hopi villages have separate rules about visitors; check with the individual village Community Development Offices (*see* Tour 2: The Hopi Mesas, *below*), or call the **Hopi Tribe Office of Public Relations** (tel. 602/734–2441) in advance for information.

Hopi Ceremonies

The Hopi are well known for their colorful ceremonial dances, many of which are supplications for rain, fertile crops, and harmony with nature. Most of these ceremonies take place in village plazas and kivas (underground ceremonial chambers) and last two days or longer; outsiders are permitted to watch only certain segments and are never allowed into the kivas. The dances may involve masks, beaded costumes, drums, and chanting. The best-known is the snake dance, in which participants carry live snakes, including poisonous rattlers, but this ceremony has not been open to the public in recent years. The seasonal kachina dances have also been restricted: Now only those in Moenkopi, Old Oraibi, and Kykotsmovi may be observed by those who are not Native American.

The dances that visitors are allowed to watch usually take place on weekends, extending through the day until dusk. Each of the tribal clans has its own sacred rituals, and starting times and dates are determined by tribal elders. Visitors should show the proper respect while observing the dances. For more information, contact the **Hopi Tribe Office of Public Relations** (tel. 602/734–2441).

Exploring the Northeast

Excursions into northeastern Arizona can range from a brief, one-day tour to an extended sojourn of seven days or more. The tours that follow all begin at Flagstaff, the city from which most travelers set out. If you choose one of the other entry points (*see* Getting Around, *above*), you'll need to adjust the recommended tours accordingly.

Tour 1 of the Petrified Forest National Park and the Painted Desert may be included as part of Tour 3 of the southern Indian country if time permits. Tour 2 of the Hopi Mesas may be incorporated into both Tour 3 and Tour 4 of the northern Indian country.

Highlights for First-time Visitors

Canyon de Chelly (*see* Tour 3)

The Hopi Mesas (*see* Tour 2)

Lake Powell and Rainbow Bridge (*see* Tour 5)

Monument Valley (*see* Tour 4)

Navajo National Monument (*see* Tour 4)

Petrified Forest National Park and the Painted Desert (*see* Tour 1)

Tour 1: Petrified Forest National Park and the Painted Desert

Numbers in the margin correspond to points of interest on the Northeastern Arizona map.

❶
❷ From **Flagstaff,** drive east on I–40 for 115 miles to the north entrance (25 miles east of Holbrook) of **Petrified Forest National Park,** a geological trip back in time. In 1984 the fossil remains of one of the oldest dinosaurs ever unearthed— more than 225 million years old, dating back to the Triassic period of the Mesozoic era—were discovered here; other plant and animal fossils in the park go back to the same period. Remnants of ancient human beings and their artifacts, dating back some 8,000 years, have been recovered at more

Goosenecks 21

Gouling's Trading Post 22

UTAH

Four Corners 160

COLORADO

ARIZONA

San Juan River

Monument Valley Navajo Tribal Park 20

Mexican Water

Teec Nos Pos

64

163

Dennehotso

191

TO FARMINGTON →

160

Kayenta 19

160

160

CHUSKA MOUNTAINS

Red Rock

Black Mesa 18

Chilchinbito

Round Rock

12

NAVAJO INDIAN RESERVATION

59

Navajo Community College

NAVAJO INDIAN RESERVATION

Many Farms

Tsaile

12

Chinle

Canyon de Chelly 13

Cottonwood

First Mesa 4

alpi

Keams Canyon Trading Post

264 Polacca 3

Steamboat Rock 15

Kinlichee Ruins Navajo Tribal Park

N E W   M E X I C O

cond sa

Hubbell Trading Post National Historic Site

14 Ganado 12

264

Window Rock 11

Gallup

191

12

Seba Dalkai

Greasewood

NAVAJO INDIAN RESERVATION

Lupton

ARIZONA

40

Indian Wells

77

Chambers

N

Petrified Forest National Park 2

KEY

Sun Valley

40

Holbrook

180

0   30 miles

0   45 km

Indian Highway

Reservation boundary

Unpaved roads

than 500 sites in this national park. The park derives its
name from the fact that the grounds are also strewed with
tree trunks whose wood cells were replaced over centuries
by brightly hued mineral deposits—including silica, iron
oxide, manganese, aluminum, copper, lithium, and car-
bon—and fossilized; in many places, the petrified logs scattered about the landscape resemble giant jackstraws. Most
of the park's 94,000 acres include portions of the vast,
lunarlike landscape known as the Painted Desert. In the
northern area of the park, this colorful but essentially barren and waterless series of windswept plains, hills, and
mesas is considered by geologists to be part of the Chinle
formation, deposited at an early stage of the Triassic period. The most dramatic colors occur at dawn and sunset,
when the oblique light causes shadows to deepen and makes
the smaller chasms glow bright red.

If your schedule permits, you can easily spend most of a day
in the park, which has 28 miles of paved roads with walking
trails, parking areas, and spur roads. Along the way you
can see some spectacular desert scenery and visit several
petrified-wood sites. During the early years of this century, looters hauled away pieces of wood in large quantities.
In 1906, President Theodore Roosevelt created a national
monument in the area, and to this day, it is illegal to remove
even a small sliver of petrified wood from the park (there
are plenty of pieces on sale at the visitor center gift shop if
you want a souvenir).

The **Rainbow Forest Museum and visitor center,** located at
the south entrance (off U.S. 180), features three skeletons
from the Triassic period, including that of the ferocious
phytosaur, a crocodilelike carnivore. The museum has numerous exhibits relating to the world of cycads (tropical
plants), ferns, fish, and other early life, as well as artifacts
and tools of ancient humans. The self-guided **Giant Logs
Trail** starts at the Rainbow Forest Museum and visitor center and loops through a half-mile of huge fallen trees. The
base of one specimen stands taller than 6 feet.

A movie entitled *The Stone Forest,* which traces the natural
history of the area, is shown at regular periods each day in
the **Painted Desert visitor center,** located at the north entrance of the park (off I–40). Within the park's boundaries,
visitors also have access to gift shops, a restaurant, a soda
fountain, and a service station.

Picnicking is allowed inside the park, but there are no overnight accommodations. You may hike into the nearby wilderness areas, but you must first obtain a park permit for
an overnight stay. Free permits are issued at both visitor
centers (*see above*).

*North entrance: off I–40, 25 mi east of Holbrook. South en-
trance: off U.S. 180, 19 mi southeast of Holbrook. Tel. 602/
524–6228. Admission: $5 per vehicle, free with Golden Ea-*

*gle, Golden Age, or Golden Access pass. Open daily 8–5
(budget permitting, 1994 summer hours may be extended;
call ahead to inquire). Park closed Christmas and New
Year's Day.*

Tour 2: The Hopi Mesas

From Flagstaff, drive east on I–40. AZ 99, 87, and 77 all go
north into the Hopi reservation, but the best of these highways is AZ 87, the turnoff for which is 62 miles east of Flagstaff (4 miles past Winslow). From here, head north 58
miles to the Hopi's Second Mesa, where you will intersect
AZ 264.

Drive 21 miles east on AZ 264 to start your tour at the
❸ **Keams Canyon Trading Post,** established by Thomas Keam
in 1875. Originally, it served only the Indians of the area,
but today the trading post also includes a modest motel,
restaurant, and shopping center (*see* Shopping, *below*), and
a primitive campground (*see* Dining and Lodging, *below*).
An administrative center for the Bureau of Indian Affairs,
Keams Canyon also hosts a number of government buildings. The first 3 miles of the canyon running toward the
northeast can be seen by car. At Inscription Rock, about 2
miles down the road, early frontiersman Kit Carson engraved his name in stone. Though there are several picnic
spots in the wooded canyon, the main attraction here is the
trading post, offering authentic Indian arts and crafts.
Don't expect anything on the scale of the historic Cameron
or Hubbell trading posts (*see below*) on the Navajo reservation, though.

From Keams Canyon, head west on AZ 264 for a tour of the
Hopi villages, most of which are situated on the top of or at
the base of a trio of mesas: First Mesa, Second Mesa, and
Third Mesa. You'll need permission beforehand to visit the
Hopi villages. For information, call the **Hopi Tribe Office of
Public Relations** (tel. 602/734–2441), which also provides
phone numbers for village leaders or village community de-
velopment offices.

❹ On **First Mesa,** 15 miles west of Keams Canyon, you will initially approach **Polacca;** the older and more impressive villages of **Hano, Sichomovi,** and **Walpi** are situated at the top
of the mesa. From Polacca, a paved road (off AZ 264) angles
up to a parking lot near the village of Sichomovi. For permission to visit Hano, Sichomovi, and Walpi, or to gain information regarding the guided walking tours of these
villages, call the **First Mesa Visitor's Center at Ponsli Hall**
(tel. 602/737–2262). Guided tours can be arranged between
9 AM and 4 PM daily, except when ceremonies are being held;
they are free, but a contribution is suggested.

All the older Hopi villages have structures built of rock and
adobe mortar in a simple architectural style. **Hano** actually
belongs to the Tewa, a Pueblo tribe that fled from the Span-

ish in 1696 and secured permission from the Hopi to build a new home on First Mesa. **Sichomovi** is built so close to Hano that only the residents know the actual boundary line. Constructed in the mid-1600s, this village is believed to have been built to ease overcrowding at Walpi, the highest point on the mesa.

For most outsiders, **Walpi** is usually the most impressive stop on the Hopi reservation, but it can be visited only if you are accompanied by a Hopi guide. Built on solid rock and surrounded by steep cliffs, Walpi stands against an immense expanse of distant earth and sky. At its narrowest point, the mesa measures only 15 feet across. Inhabited for more than 300 years, Walpi's cliff-edge houses seem to be an extension of the nearby terrain. Today, only about 30 residents occupy this settlement, which has neither electricity nor running water. Important ceremonial dances frequently take place here. You can purchase kachina dolls made by the local men and authentic Hopi pottery created by the local women.

❺ Second Mesa, accessed by AZ 264, is 10 miles west of Polacca. The small villages of **Sipaulovi** and **Mishongnovi** are situated off a paved road that goes north from 264, about ⅛ mile east of the Hopi Cultural Center. Both communities lie on a projection of the Second Mesa; Mishongnovi, the easternmost settlement, was built in the late 1600s. If you'd like to visit Sipaulovi, the most recently established village, call the Sipaulovi Village Community Center (tel. 602/737–2570).

Shungopavi, the largest and oldest village on Second Mesa, may be reached by a paved road angling south off AZ 264 between the junction of AZ 87 and the Hopi Cultural Center. The famous Hopi snake dances (now closed to the public) are held here in August during even-numbered years. For permission to visit Shungopavi, call the village's **Community Development Office** (tel. 602/734–2262).

One of the livelier spots on Second Mesa is the **Hopi Cultural Center,** on the north side of AZ 264, west of the junction at AZ 87. In addition to its shops and pueblo-style museum, the center features a good restaurant serving American and native dishes and an immaculate motel (*see* Dining and Lodging, *below*). The cultural center is not only an excellent spot for an overnight stop, but it is also one of the best places on the reservation from which to obtain information. *Tel. 602/734-2401 (restaurant and motel), tel. 602/734–6650 (museum). Museum admission: $3 adults, $1 children under 13. Open mid-May–Oct., weekdays 8–5, weekends 9–4; Nov.–mid-May, weekdays 8–5, closed weekends.*

If you drive 8 miles to the west of the Hopi Cultural Center on AZ 264, you'll approach **Kykotsmovi** at the eastern base **❻** of **Third Mesa.** Indians from Oraibi (*see below*) descended from the mesa and built this village in a canyon with a perennial spring; the community is known for its greenery and peach orchards. The town also serves as the home of the **Hopi Tribal Headquarters** and the **Office of Public Relations** (tel. 602/734–2441), another good source of information regarding ceremonies and dances.

Oraibi, a few miles west and on top of Third Mesa, is widely believed to be the oldest continually inhabited community in the United States, dating from around AD 1150. It was also the site of a rare, bloodless conflict between two groups of the Hopi people; in 1906, a dispute, settled uniquely by a "pushing contest," sent the losers off to establish Hotevilla (*see below*). Oraibi is a dusty spot, and as an act of courtesy, tourists are asked to park their cars outside and approach the village on foot.

As you continue to drive west on AZ 264, you'll pass more crafts shops and art galleries. The Third Mesa villages are known for their baskets, kachina dolls, weaving, and jewelry.

Hotevilla and **Bacavi** are about 4 miles west of Oraibi, and their inhabitants are descended from the former residents of that village. The men of Hotevilla continue to plant crops along the mesa slopes, and in warmer months these gardens on the cliffs are lovely to behold.

Beyond Hotevilla, AZ 264 descends from Third Mesa, and you will soon exit the Hopi reservation and cross Navajo **❼** land. About 30 miles west of Hotevilla, you'll pass **Coal Canyon,** where Indians have long mined coal from the dark seam just below the rim. This canyon of colorful mudstone, dark lines of coal, and bleached white formations has an eerie, ghostlike appearance, especially by the light of the moon.

Another 20 miles to the west is **Moenkopi,** the last Hopi outpost, just before Tuba City at the junction of AZ 264 and U.S. 160. Established as a farming community, it was also settled by the descendents of former Oraibi residents. **❽** Across U.S. 160, **Tuba City** is the administrative center for the western portion of the Navajo Nation, with about 5,000 permanent residents. In addition to a motel, a hostel, and a few restaurants, this small town has a hospital, a bank, and a historic trading post. Founded in the early 1880s and recently restored, the octagonal **Tuba City Trading Post** (Main St., tel. 602/283–5441) carries authentic Indian rugs, pottery, baskets, and jewelry; it also sells groceries.

From Tuba City, take U.S. 160 west. About 5½ miles from the city, between mileposts 316 and 317, you'll see a small **❾** sign for **Dinosaur Tracks.** More than 200 million years ago, carnivorous bipedal reptiles over 10 feet tall left their imprints in soft mud that subsequently turned to sandstone. There's no charge for a look.

Four miles west of the Dinosaur Tracks on U.S. 160, turn left on U.S. 89; 16 miles south, you will arrive at the ⑩ **Cameron Trading Post** (tel. 602/679–2231). Established in 1916, this is one of the few remaining authentic trading posts in the Southwest. *See* Chapter 3, Grand Canyon Country and Lake Mead, for details.

From the Cameron Trading Post, it's another 52 miles back to Flagstaff. In order to see the Hopi Mesas at a reasonable pace, it's a good idea to take at least one overnight on this tour, either at the Hopi Cultural Center on Second Mesa or, if you're planning to head north into Navajo country, at a hotel in Tuba City (*see* Dining and Lodging, *below*).

Tour 3: Indian Country—Southern Tour

To take the complete tour, allow at least three days and two nights. Begin your drive at **Petrified Forest National Park** and the **Painted Desert** (*see* Tour 1, *above*), if you haven't stopped here before.

From the Petrified Forest, continue east on I–40 to Lupton; turn north on Indian Highway 12, which will take you to ⑪ **Window Rock;** the total distance is 82 miles. Named for an immense hole in a massive sandstone ridge nearby, Window Rock is the capital of the Navajo Nation. With a population of less than 5,000, this small community serves as the shopping, business, and social center for countless Navajo families from the surrounding rural areas. It is also the home of the **Navajo Nation Council Chambers** (turn east off Indian Highway 12, about ½ mile from AZ 264), a handsome structure that resembles a large hogan—the traditional six-sided Navajo house with a domed roof. Visitors can observe sessions of the council, where 88 delegates representing 100 reservation communities meet on the third Monday of January, April, July, and October. The sessions are conducted mostly in the Navajo language. When the council is not being held, you can walk around the chamber, where colorful murals decorate the circular walls. Near the Council Chambers lies Window Rock Navajo Tribal Park, a pleasant picnic area with juniper trees that provides a close-up view of the huge rock with a circular opening that gives the town its name.

A short drive south of Tribal Park is the **Navajo Tribal Museum,** a small space devoted to the art and culture of the region and the history of the Navajo people; there's an excellent selection of books on the Navajo Nation here. The adjoining **Navajo Arts and Crafts Enterprise** has local creative works on view, including pottery, jewelry, and blankets. *On AZ 264, next to Navajo Nation Inn, tel. 602/871–4090 or 602/871–4095 (Arts and Crafts Enterprise), 602/871–6673 (museum). Admission free. Museum and Crafts Enterprise open Apr.–Oct., Mon.–Sat. 8–6; Nov.–Mar.,* *weekdays 8–5 (often later during the busy season from Thanksgiving to New Year's Day).*

If you're curious about wildlife in northeastern Arizona, make a stop at the **Navajo Nation Zoological Park,** just east of the Navajo Tribal Museum. The small zoo—set amid sandstone monoliths—features golden eagles, hawks, elk, wolves, cougars, coyotes, and many other birds, reptiles, and mammals from the area. *East of Navajo Nation Inn and north of AZ 264, tel. 602/871–6573. Admission free. Open daily 8–5.*

Window Rock is a good place to stop for lunch, supplies, and gas. The local restaurants carry standard American fare, Navajo dishes, and fast food. Near the center of downtown is the **Navajo Tribal Fairgrounds,** the site of many all-Indian rodeos (in the Navajo Nation, many Indians are cowboys). The community hosts the annual July 4 Powwow, with a major rodeo, ceremonial dances, and a parade, and the Navajo Nation Tribal Fair (much like a traditional state fair, with a Navajo accent) in early September; for more information about both events, call the Navajo Nation Fair Office (tel. 602/871–6478).

12 **Kinlichee Ruins Navajo Tribal Park** lies 22 miles west of Window Rock on AZ 264; a marked turnoff leads to this 640-acre park. A complex of ruins here dates from the early Anasazi, a culture of prehistoric Native Americans who mysteriously abandoned their Southwest dwelling places prior to AD 1300. The park, which is always open, has a self-guided trail that takes you past the ruins and trailside exhibits (you are not permitted to descend into the pit, where the kiva is); it also offers picnic areas and a primitive campground. A camping fee of $1 per person may be collected.

Next, drive 6 miles west on AZ 264, passing through the community of **Ganado,** and continue for another 5 miles until you reach the intersection of U.S. 191 north; turn right and drive 30 miles to Chinle, a good place for an overnight stop before a visit to Canyon de Chelly. In the vicinity, you'll find three motels, several restaurants, and a campground. Especially during the summer months, you should call ahead for motel reservations.

13 The nearly 84,000-acre **Canyon de Chelly** (pronounced deh-SHAY) near Chinle is one of the most spectacular national monuments in the Southwest. Its main gorges—the 26-mile-long **Canyon de Chelly** and the adjoining 35-mile-long **Canyon del Muerto**—have sheer, heavily eroded sandstone walls that reach up to 1,000 feet; ancient pictographs decorate some of the cliffs. Gigantic stone formations rise hundreds of feet above small streams, hogans, tilled fields, peach orchards, and grazing lands.

The first inhabitants in the canyons, the Anasazi people, arrived more than 2,000 years ago and built stone cliff dwellings between AD 300 and AD 1300. After the Anasazi disappeared around 1300, Hopi farmers settled here, followed by the Navajo, beginning around 1700. Centuries-old traditions have been passed down to the Navajo families now living here, who farm and raise sheep. Although the monument is administered by the National Park Service, the land itself belongs to the Navajo.

Canyon de Chelly and Canyon del Muerto each have a paved rim drive that offers marvelous views of the massive canyons, with prehistoric ruins that sometimes lie near the base of cliffs and at other times perch on high sheltering ledges. Occasionally you will also see the modern dwellings and cultivated fields of the present-day Navajo in the flatlands between the cliffs. Each canyon drive takes about two hours.

The **South Rim Drive** of Canyon de Chelly starts at the visitor center and ends at **Spider Rock Overlook,** where the cliffs drop 1,000 feet. Here you'll have a view of two pinnacles, Speaking Rock and Spider Rock; the latter rises about 800 feet from the canyon floor. Other highlights on the South Rim Drive are **Junction Overlook,** where Canyon del Muerto joins Canyon de Chelly; **White House Overlook,** which allows access to the canyon floor (*see below*); and **Sliding House Overlook,** where you can see ruins on a narrow, sloped ledge across the canyon.

The **North Rim Drive** of Canyon del Muerto also begins at the visitor center and continues northeast on Indian Highway 64 toward Tsaile, the site of Navajo Community College. Major stops on this drive include **Antelope House Overlook,** the site of a large ruin named for the animals painted on an adjacent cliff; the **Mummy Cave Overlook,** with the monument's largest cliff dwelling well preserved in two caves; and **Massacre Cave Overlook,** the last stop on the drive, which marks the spot where 115 Navajo were killed by the Spanish in 1805.

Within the monument, only one hike—the **White House Ruin Trail,** on the South Rim Drive—can be done without an authorized guide. The trail is easy to negotiate and starts near White House Overlook along the South Rim Drive of Canyon de Chelly, where sheer walls drop about 550 feet. The trail leads to the White House Ruin, with dwelling remains of nearly 60 rooms and several kivas. Bring your own water for this 2½-mile hike (round-trip).

Visitors can explore the area of Canyon de Chelly National Monument by taking truck and Jeep tours (*see* Guided Tours in Essential Information, *above*), or by hiking with rangers and paid guides. (*see* Hiking in Sports and the Outdoors, *below*). The **visitor center** features exhibits on the history of the Anasazi cliff dwellers and provides information on scheduled hikes, tours, and other programs within the national monument; it also has a good selection of books on the area and on Navajo culture. *Box 588, Chinle 86503,* *tel. 602/674–5436. Admission free. Open May–Sept., daily 8–6; Oct.–Apr., daily 8–5.*

Retrace your steps after you depart Canyon de Chelly: head back south again for about 30 miles on U.S. 191, then turn east onto AZ 264 and continue on for several miles to ⑭ **Hubbell Trading Post National Historic Site.** This trading post was established in 1878 by John Lorenzo Hubbell, a native of the Southwest who was born in Pajarito, New Mexico. To the Navajo, Hubbell was not only a merchant but a good friend and teacher who translated letters, settled family quarrels, explained government policy, and helped the sick. During the 1886 smallpox epidemic in the area, he turned his home into a hospital and personally ministered to the sick and dying. Hubbell died in 1930 and is buried not far from the trading post.

Today the Hubbell Trading Post operates much as it did more than a century ago. At the visitor center, National Park Service exhibits illustrate the post's history, and Navajo men and women frequently demonstrate the crafts of making jewelry and rugs. You may also take a guided tour of Hubbell's house, which contains one of the finest personal collections of Native American artistry anywhere, including rugs and paintings; six tours are given daily in summer, four in winter. The affiliated shop, run by the Southwest Parks and Monuments Association, specializes in Navajo rugs (*see* Shopping, *below*). *On AZ 264, 1 mi west of Ganado, tel. 602/755–3475. Admission free. Open June–Sept., daily 8–6; Oct.–May, daily 8–5. Closed Thanksgiving, Christmas, and New Year's Day.*

About 20 miles west of the trading post on the north side of ⑮ AZ 264 is **Steamboat Rock,** an immense, jutting peninsula of stone that resembles an early-day steamboat, complete with a geologically formed waterline.

At Steamboat Rock, you are only 5 miles from the eastern boundary line of the Hopi reservation, where you can visit the **Hopi Mesas** (*see* Tour 2, *above*). After driving through the mesas on AZ 264, you can join Tour 4 (*see below*) at Tuba City, 50 miles west of the Hopi village of Hotevilla.

Tour 4: Indian Country—Northern Tour

Twenty-two miles northeast of Tuba City on U.S. 160 is the ⑯ tiny community of **Red Lake.** Off to the left of the highway is a geological phenomenon known as **Elephant Feet.** These massive eroded sandstone buttes make a good photo stop.

If time permits, you might enjoy a short side trip to real ⑰ Navajo backcountry and a look at **White Mesa Natural Bridge,** about 17 miles north of Red Lake on Indian Highway 21, a graded dirt road. The payoff is a view of a massive arch of white sandstone that extends from the edge of White Mesa. Return by the same route to Red Lake.

About 30 miles north of Red Lake on U.S. 160, you'll come to the turnoff for Navajo National Monument (*see below*).

⑱ Continue north from this turnoff and take note of the plateau to the right, the long **Black Mesa,** which will remain in view for about the next 15 miles. Above the prominent escarpments of this land formation, mining operations—a major source of revenue for the Navajo Nation—are busy delving into the more than 20 billion tons of coal deposited there.

⑲ Turn more directly north from U.S. 160 onto AZ 163; you'll soon approach **Kayenta,** a small town with a few grocery stores, a motel, and a hospital. Kayenta is near the magnificent **Monument Valley,** which stretches to the northeast into Utah. At an altitude of approximately 5,500 feet, this sprawling expanse was originally populated by the ancient Anasazi and has also been home to generations of Navajo who have farmed and herded livestock in this arid country. With its soaring red buttes, eroded mesas, deep canyons, and naturally sculpted rock formations, Monument Valley is best enjoyed by simply driving through and pausing from time to time at roadside stops. Many westerns, including *Stagecoach, She Wore a Yellow Ribbon,* and *How the West Was Won,* have been filmed here.

⑳ Within this vast area lies the 30,000-acre **Monument Valley Navajo Tribal Park,** located 3½ miles off U.S. 163 and about 24 miles north of Kayenta. The park offers a scenic 17-mile self-guided tour, but the road is unpaved and rutted; if you don't want to wear out the shocks on your car, you might consider taking one of the many guided tours offered by operators in and around the visitor center; most take visitors around in enclosed vans and charge about $15 for 2½ hours. Also at the visitor center are an Indian crafts shop and exhibits devoted to both ancient and modern Indian history within the area. The park features a 100-site campground, which closes from early October through April. *Visitor center, tel. 801/727–3287. Park entrance fee: $2.50 adults, $1 senior citizens 60 and older, children under 5 free. Visitor center open May–Sept., daily 7–7; Oct.–Apr., daily 8–5. Closed Christmas and New Year's Day; open Thanksgiving 8–noon.*

㉑ Monument Valley's scenic route, U.S. 163, continues from Arizona into Utah, where the land is crossed, east to west, by a stretch of the San Juan River known as the **Goosenecks**—so named for the type of twists and curves it takes at the bottom of a wildly carved canyon. Set in a lonely, untrafficked domain, this barren, erosion-blasted gorge has a stark beauty that is nearly as awesome as that of the Grand Canyon. The scenic overlook for the Goosenecks is reached by turning west from U.S. 163 onto UT 261, 4 miles north of the small community of **Mexican Hat** (named for the sombrero-like rock formation you'll see on the hills to your right as you drive north), then proceeding on UT 261 for 1 mile to a directional sign and a 4-mile side road to the vista-point parking lot.

After a stop at the viewpoint for Goosenecks, retrace your route down U.S. 163 and then take Indian Highway 42 a half-mile west to **Goulding's Trading Post.** Established in 1924 by Harry Goulding and his wife, this remote outlet was used as a headquarters by director John Ford when he was filming the western classic *Stagecoach.* Because of the numerous westerns that have been shot in the area, the trading post, motel, and restaurant have gained a measure of international fame. In the old trading post building, a museum showcases prehistoric and modern Indian artifacts as well as memorabilia of the Goulding family. The lodge here is an ideal place to stay overnight, but call in advance for reservations. Alternatively, you can overnight in or near Kayenta, where there are three motels (*see* Dining and Lodging, *below*).

Take Indian Highway 42 back to the junction with U.S. 163, and proceed south until you reach U.S. 160; continue south, making a right turn on AZ 564 and traveling 9 miles to **Navajo National Monument.** Here two unoccupied 13th-century cliff pueblos, **Keet Seel** and **Betatakin,** stand under the overhang of soaring orange and ocher cliffs. The largest Indian ruins in Arizona, these pueblos were built by the Anasazi people, whose reasons for abandoning the pueblos prior to AD 1300 are still disputed by scholars. The two large stone-and-mortar complexes were obviously built for permanent occupancy, yet the Anasazi had lived in them for only about three decades when they disappeared. Betatakin (Navajo for "ledge house") consists of a well-preserved, 135-room ruin situated in a large alcove. Keet Seel (Navajo for "broken pottery") is also in good condition, with 160 rooms and five kivas in a serene setting.

For an impressive view of Betatakin, walk to the rim overlook about a half-mile from the visitor center. You can also hike to Betatakin (5 miles round-trip from the visitor center), but only on tours with ranger guides, offered between May 1 and September 30. The trips, held once a day in early May and most of September, twice a day from Memorial Day to Labor Day (weather permitting), are limited to groups of 24. No reservations are accepted; tours are on a first-come, first-served basis.

Explorations of Keet Seel, which lies 16 miles from the visitor center (round-trip) at an elevation of 7,000 feet, are even more restricted: Only 20 people are allowed to visit per day, and only between Memorial Day and Labor Day, when a ranger is present at the site. A permit—which also allows campers to stay overnight near Keet Seel ruin—is required. Those interested in horseback trips can arrange through the visitor center to rent horses and guides from a Navajo family. Trips to Keet Seel are very popular, and reservations are taken up to (but not beyond) two months in advance; call 602/672–2367 to reserve a visitor's permit (and, if you like, a horse) as soon you know the date you're coming.

The visitor center houses a small museum, exhibits of prehistoric pottery, and a crafts shop. Free campground and picnic areas are nearby, and rangers sometimes present campfire programs in the summer. No food, gasoline, or lodging is available at the monument. *Navajo National Monument, HC71 Box 3, Tonalea 86044, tel. 602/672–2366. Admission free. Open daily 8–5. Closed Thanksgiving, Christmas, and New Year's Day.*

This tour may be followed by a visit to Page, Lake Powell, Glen Canyon Dam, and Rainbow Bridge (*see* Tour 5, *below*). To reach Page from the Navajo National Monument, return to U.S. 160 and travel south for 12 miles, then take AZ 98 for 66 miles. If, on the other hand, you'd like to follow this tour with a visit to Canyon de Chelly (*see* Tour 3, *above*), stop at Navajo National Monument before you go on to Monument Valley. Then, from Kayenta, take U.S. 160 east for 41 miles and, just before Mexican Water, pick up U.S. 191; it's another 62 miles south to Chinle.

Tour 5: Lake Powell and Rainbow Bridge

From Flagstaff, take U.S. 89 on a route almost directly north and drive 136 miles to Page and nearby Glen Canyon Dam and Lake Powell. For many miles of this trip, you'll pass an impressive stretch of the Painted Desert off to the right of the highway, with a multihued geography almost identical to that of the Painted Desert contained within the boundaries of Petrified Forest National Park (*see* Tour 1, *above*). Farther north, this landscape gives way to the immense Echo Cliffs, orange sandstone formations that rise well over 1,000 feet above the highway in some places. At Bitter Springs, the highway ascends the cliffs and provides a spectacular view of the 9,000-square-mile expanse of the Arizona Strip to the west and the sheer, 3,000-foot Vermilion Cliffs to the northwest.

㉔ Prior to 1957, the broad mesa on which the community of **Page** is situated was essentially barren land, but when construction of Glen Canyon Dam commenced that year, Page was born. Initially a construction camp, after the completion of the dam and the formation of Lake Powell, Page became a tourist stop and gradually grew to its present population of about 7,000—the largest community in far northern Arizona.

Page has two museums that are worth visiting. The **John Wesley Powell Memorial Museum** downtown honors the work of explorer John Wesley Powell, who, between 1869 and 1872, led the first expeditions down the Green River and the rapids-choked Colorado through the Grand Canyon. The one-armed Civil War hero mapped, explored, and kept detailed records of his trips, naming the Grand Canyon and many other geographic points of interest in northern Arizona.

Exhibits include expedition drawings and photographs, as well as fossils and minerals that cast light on the geological past of the Colorado River and the massive canyons it helped form across a span of millions of years. Others trace the cultural patterns of the Indians of the Southwest with examples of pottery, baskets, tools, and weapons. The museum also serves as an information center for river and lake trips and scenic flights. *6 N. Lake Powell Blvd. (corner N. Navajo Dr.), tel. 602/645–9496. Requested donation: $1 adults, 50¢ children. Open May–Sept., Mon.–Sat. 8–6, Sun. 10–6; Oct., Mon.–Sat. 8–6; Nov., Mar.–Apr., weekdays 9–5. Closed Dec.–Feb.*

If you drive 2 miles east of Page on AZ 98, you'll reach the **Big Lake Trading Post and Dinebekah Museum and Gallery,** which was funded by actor Chris Robinson of TV's *General Hospital.* Robinson has collected an array of modern and prehistoric Indian artifacts, with the newer pieces available for purchase. Besides crafts, groceries and fishing supplies are on offer, along with service for your car. *Tel. 602/645–2404. Admission free. Shop open weekdays 5:30 AM–midnight, weekends 6 AM–midnight; museum open daily 8–8.*

Drive northwest on Lake Powell Boulevard, which becomes U.S. 89 business route. Once you leave the Page business district, the **Glen Canyon Dam** and Lake Powell behind it immediately become visible. Completed in September 1963, the construction of this concrete-arch dam and its power plant was an engineering feat rivaling the building of Hoover Dam. Nearly 5 million cubic feet of concrete were required. The dam's crest is 1,560 feet across and rises 710 feet from bedrock and 583 feet above the waters of the Colorado River. Lake Powell is 560 feet deep at the dam at full pool elevation.

Just off the highway at the north end of the bridge is the **Carl Hayden Visitor Center,** a museumlike facility dedicated to telling the story of the creation of Glen Canyon Dam and Lake Powell. Among the several exhibits is a giant, three-dimensional topographic map of Lake Powell country. The center's huge reception and observation room, with floor-to-ceiling glass, provides panoramic views of the dam, the wildly sculpted cliffs that border Lake Powell, and the immense sandstone buttes that protrude, islandlike, from the lake's emerald waters. Visitors also have the opportunity to take a 40-minute self-guided tour through the dam complex. *Glen Canyon Dam, tel. 602/645–2511. Admission free. Open daily 7 AM–7 PM Memorial Day–Labor Day, daily 8–5 the rest of the year. Closed Christmas and New Year's Day.*

Lake Powell, with more than 1,900 miles of shoreline, is the heart of the huge (1,255,400-acre) Glen Canyon National Recreation Area. Created by the barrier of Glen Canyon Dam and fed by the mighty Colorado River, the jade-green lake extends through eroded canyon country that is nearly devoid of vegetation and so rugged that it was the last major area of the United States to be mapped. The waters of Lake Powell are confined by immense red cliffs that twist off from the main body of the lake into 96 major canyons and countless inlets and coves—so many, in fact, that no single person claims to have explored all of them. In a number of places, huge sandstone buttes jut from the water. Seeing the stark and stunning geography of Lake Powell often makes tourists feel they are visiting another planet.

The most popular destination on the lake, which stretches 120 miles through northern Arizona and southern Utah, is **㉖ Wahweap,** a vacation village 5 miles north of the Glen Canyon Dam on U.S. 89. Most of the recreational activity in the region takes place around here, where everything needed for a water-oriented holiday is available. Visitors can easily rent boats and a wide variety of water-sports equipment (*see* Sports and the Outdoors, *below*). Stop at **Wahweap Lodge** (*see* Dining and Lodging, *below*) for an excellent view of the lake area.

Summer is a busy time in the Lake Powell area, and advance reservations are essential. Travelers seeking a quieter vacation should plan a visit during late October through early May, when there are fewer people and lower prices. Skies in the Lake Powell area are blue nearly all year, and only about 8 inches of rain falls annually. Summer temperatures range from the 60s to the 90s (sometimes more than 100°F). Many fall and spring days are balmy, with daytime temperatures often in the 70s and 80s, but it is possible for chilly weather to set in. In winter the risk of a cold spell increases, but all-weather houseboats and tour boats make year-round cruising possible.

The best way to appreciate the beauty of Lake Powell is by boat. If you don't have access to one, the half-day excursion **㉗** cruise to **Rainbow Bridge National Monument** is the way to go. Along the 50-mile route (one-way from Wahweap Marina), you're treated to ever-changing, beautiful and bizarre scenery, including huge monoliths that look like people turned into stone and a butte that resembles a dinosaur. You might also see eagles perched on ragged outcrops of rock. Finally, after gliding through a deep and twisting canyon waterway, the boat docks near Rainbow Bridge, the massive 290-foot red sandstone arch that straddles a cove of the lake. The world's largest natural stone bridge, it can be reached only by water or by an arduous hike from a remote point on the Navajo reservation (*see* Sports and the Outdoors, *below*).

The excursion boats, which leave Wahweap daily, are two-tiered craft with sun decks, upstairs and interior seating with windows downstairs. Experienced pilots provide commentary throughout the trip. Pack a lunch or take snacks; no food is sold on the boats, though coffee and water are provided for passengers. And be sure to bring your camera.

Other cruises are offered at the Wahweap Marina, including an all-day trip that stops at Rainbow Bridge and then proceeds farther into the Utah portion of the lake. (*See* Boating and Cruises in Sports and the Outdoors, *below*, for information on prices and reservations.)

Off the Beaten Track

Most of the 25,000 square miles of the Navajo reservation and other areas of northeastern Arizona are actually off the beaten track. Many visitors to the northeast generally stay on the paved roads, but this vast, sparsely populated region is crisscrossed with dirt roads. If you don't have the equipment for wilderness travel—including a four-wheel-drive vehicle, water, food, tools, and bedrolls—and do not have backcountry experience, we recommend that you stay off the dirt roads unless they are signed and graded, and the skies are clear.

Chuska Mountains. These impressive mountains in Navajo high country are covered with huge stands of ponderosa pine. To explore this part of the reservation, take Indian Highway 64 from the Canyon de Chelly visitor center to the community of Tsaile (23 miles). Here Navajo medicine men worked in conjunction with architects to design Tsaile's **Navajo Community College** (tel. 602/724–3311). Because all important Navajo activities traditionally take place in a circle (a hogan is essentially circular), the campus was laid out in the round with all of the buildings within its perimeter. The college's **Hatathli Museum** is devoted to Native American culture. *Tel. 602/724–3311. Donations accepted. Open weekdays 8–5; groups by appointment.*

Two miles northeast of Tsaile, turn left on Indian Highway 12 and continue 26 miles to Round Rock, where Indian Highway 12 meets U.S. 191. During your drive, the high country will rise off to the right. Dirt roads traverse the mountains, but they are often unsuitable for passenger cars. At U.S. 191, turn left and head back south to Chinle if you are following Tour 3, *above*.

Four Corners Monument. A simple concrete slab inlaid into the ground marks the only point in the United States where four states meet: Arizona, New Mexico, Colorado, and Utah. Most visitors—in summer, nearly 2,000 a day—stay only a few minutes to record the spot on film; you'll see many people posed awkwardly, with an arm or a leg in each state. *Off U.S. 160, 7 mi northwest of the U.S. 160–U.S. 164* *junction (near Teec Nos Pos). The monument is a 75-mi drive from Kayenta, near Monument Valley.*

What to See and Do with Children

Although northeastern Arizona is an extremely popular area for families on vacation, the region has no attractions designed specifically for children. However, many youngsters will be fascinated by the area's scenic beauty and Indian culture. They will particularly enjoy the Navajo Nation Zoological Park in Window Rock (*see* Tour 3, *above*); and at the Petrified Forest (*see* Tour 1, *above*), Canyon de Chelly (*see* Tour 3, *above*), and Navajo National Monument (*see* Tour 4, *above*), they'll have plenty of space for running around and exploring. In the Lake Powell region (*see* Tour 5, *above*), many motels have swimming pools, and there are numerous water-related recreational activities for children.

Younger children may get restless during some of the long and lonely stretches on the Indian reservations, so it's a good idea to bring along lots of toys and books for the car.

Shopping

Groceries, over-the-counter medicines, gasoline, and other supplies can be purchased in all of the major communities and trading posts on the Navajo and Hopi reservations, including Page, Window Rock, Fort Defiance, Ganado, Chinle, Hopi Second Mesa, Keams Canyon, Tuba City, Kayenta, Goulding's Trading Post, and Cameron Trading Post. Some of the smaller communities offer limited supplies; in general, don't count on a wide selection. Plan your gas stops for the locations cited.

Beyond the necessities for travel, most visitors to Indian country are looking for pottery, turquoise and sterling-silver jewelry, handwoven baskets, beautiful and often expensive Navajo wool rugs, and other examples of Native American crafts. In addition to the work of Hopi and Navajo artisans, many of the trading posts also carry the work of New Mexico's tribes, including exquisite Zuni jewelry and the world-acclaimed pottery of the Pueblo Indians. Many vendors have roadside stands that resemble Navajo shade arbors. Most products offered on the Hopi and Navajo reservations are authentic, but the possibility of imitations still exists. The trading posts are usually reliable.

Telephone lines—and thus connections with credit card verification sources—are often iffy at the Hopi Mesas. It's a good idea to carry cash or traveler's checks in order to make purchases here or anywhere else outside of the trading posts.

Outlets of **Navajo Arts and Crafts Enterprises,** in Window Rock (off AZ 264, next to Navajo Nation Inn, tel. 602/871–4090 or 602/871–4095) and Cameron (on U.S. 89 at the junction with AZ 64, tel. 602/679–2244), stock fine authentic Navajo products. The nearby **Cameron Trading Post** has a large selection of goods from a variety of tribes; *see* Chapter 3, Grand Canyon Country and Lake Mead, for details. The **Hopi Cultural Center** (off AZ 264, Hopi Second Mesa, tel. 602/734–2463) has a collection of shops featuring the work of local artists and artisans. **Keams Canyon Arts and Crafts** (Keams Canyon, tel. 602/738–2295) also sells Hopi wares. The gift shop at **Navajo National Monument** (tel. 602/672–2404) has an excellent selection of jewelry. **Hubbell Trading Post** (off AZ 264, 1 mi west of Ganado, tel. 602/755–3254) is famous for its "Ganado red" Navajo rugs; the quality is outstanding but prices are accordingly high. Be forewarned, though: It's hard to resist these beautiful designs and colors. But it's also possible to find exactly what you want, at a good price, at a reservation roadside vendor. If you would like some tips on quality, the **Navajoland Tourism Office** (*see* Important Addresses and Numbers in Essential Information, *above*) has printed material on the subject.

Sports and the Outdoors

Bicycling For biking enthusiasts, the news is good and bad. If you carry a bike on your car, as many cyclists do these days, you will find endless miles of paved roads, and most of the time, traffic is very light. The bad news is that the mostly two-lane highways do not have paved shoulders, and local motorists and tourists alike are not accustomed to encountering cyclists. As a result, you should practice extreme caution when riding. For safe bike rides, the roads at Canyon de Chelly National Monument, Navajo National Monument, Monument Valley Navajo Tribal Park, and Kinlichee Navajo Tribal Park are your best bets. There are no bicycle rental companies in Indian country.

Boating **Lake Powell, Wahweap Marina.** The boating opportunities on Lake Powell are almost limitless. If you have your own boat, docks and launching ramps are available at State Line Marina, 1½ miles north of Wahweap Lodge. Rental boats, excursion boats, and water-sports equipment, including ski packages, water sleds, and motorized wave cutters, are available near Wahweap Lodge, 5 miles north of Page on U.S. 89. Houseboats range widely in size and price; one that sleeps six (in three double beds) costs $675 for three nights. Houseboats should be reserved well in advance. Small boats, too, vary in size and price. An 18-foot powerboat for eight passengers runs about $185 per day. Most of these prices drop after the summer months. For further information about Wahweap Marina, call 800/528–6154 (outside of Phoenix) or 602/278–8888.

Camping and RV Parks Although Indian country stretches thousands of square miles across an open and sparsely populated region, most visitors will want to camp in authorized areas. Most campgrounds are primitive, in many cases nothing more than open, level areas where sleeping bags can be laid out or RVs can be parked; only Monument Valley has developed camping facilities. If you plan to stay in national monument and park areas, camping permission can be obtained on-site; for other camping situations, contact the **Navajo Parks and Recreation Department** (Box 308, Window Rock, 86515, tel. 602/871–6647) to find out whether you need a permit. (*See* Dining and Lodging, *below*, for some of the recommended campsites in the area.)

Cruises **Lake Powell to Rainbow Bridge.** Both half- and full-day cruises leave from the dock at Wahweap Lodge to Rainbow Bridge National Monument. The 290-foot arch spans an isolated cove 50 miles from Wahweap. Experienced guides pilot the modern, double-decker scenic cruisers. *For advance reservations and information, call 800/528–6154. Half-day cruise, summer season: $51.30 adults, $27.50 children; full-day: $64.65 adults, $34.50 children. Prices are lower Oct.–Apr.*

Lake Powell Sunset Dinner Cruise. *See* the Page/Lake Powell section in Dining and Lodging, below.

Wilderness River Adventures. These guided and piloted 4½-hour rafting excursions cover a portion of the Colorado River that is relatively calm, with no white-water rapids. The scenery through Glen Canyon Dam is spectacular as the rafts glide beneath multicolored sandstone cliffs that are frequently adorned with Indian petroglyphs (rock drawings). Transportation is furnished from Wahweap Lodge to Page, the point of departure, and back from Lees Ferry, where the raft trip ends. *For advance reservations and information, call 800/528–6154. Cost: $38.70 adults, $31 children under 12. Prices are lower Oct.–Apr.*

Fishing Indian country has scattered lakes, most of them remote and small, that contain game fish. Two of the more popular and accessible lakes are located in the eastern portion of the Navajo reservation in the vicinity of Canyon de Chelly: **Wheatfields Lake,** on Indian Highway 12 about 11 miles south of the community of Tsaile, and **Many Farms Lake,** near the community of Many Farms, on U.S. 191. Permits are always required for fishing on the reservation. Contact **Navajo Fish and Wildlife Office** (Box 1480, Window Rock 86515, tel. 602/871–6451 or 602/871–6452).

Lake Powell and the area below Glen Canyon Dam are excellent fishing sites. Lake Powell features largemouth and striped bass, black crappie, catfish, bluegill, and walleye. The Colorado River below Glen Canyon Dam is known for its large trout. Keep in mind that Lake Powell stretches through both Arizona and Utah, and the appropriate permit is required depending on where you fish. (*See* Chapter 1, Essential Information, for more information on fishing permits.)

Hiking There are many excellent places to hike at the national monuments, tribal parks, and other points of interest in Indian Country, but the following merit special mention.

In **Canyon de Chelly,** some of the best hiking is up the streambed between the soaring orange sandstone cliffs, with the ruins of the old Anasazi communities frequently in view. Guides, required for all but the White Horse Ruin Trail, currently charge about $10 per hour for groups of up to four people for day hikes. For overnights, there's a $20 surcharge for the guide and usually a $30 charge for permission to stay on private land in the area to which the guide will take you; groups of up to 15 people can be accommodated. From Memorial Day through Labor Day, free three-hour ranger-led hikes leave from the visitor center at 9 AM (*see* Tour 3, *above*). Also during the summer, four-hour hikes costing $10 per person leave from the visitor center in the morning and afternoon; rates for two-hour evening hikes are $5 per person. Some of the hikes are a bit strenuous and precepitious, without clearly defined or gently graded trails. Visitors with health problems or a fear of heights should question the guide about the difficulty of the hike they're considering.

In addition to casual hikes along the rim areas where the ruins of Betatakin can be viewed, in the spring and summer **Navajo National Monument** offers a guided 5-mile hike (round-trip) to Betatakin once a day (twice a day from Memorial Day through Labor Day); visitors may also obtain permits to hike 16 miles (round-trip) on their own to the Keet Seel ruins during that period. *See* Tour 4, *above*, for details.

Seasoned hikers in good physical condition might want to try either of the two trails leading to **Rainbow Bridge,** the 290-foot sandstone arch in a remote cove on Lake Powell; each runs about 26–28 miles round-trip. Take Indian Highway 16 north toward the Utah state border. When you come to a fork in the road, go down either "prong" for about 5 miles and you'll come to a trailhead leading to Rainbow Bridge. Excursion boats pull in at the dock at the arch, but no supplies are sold there. For a backcountry hiking permit, contact the **Navajo Parks and Recreation Department** (Box 308, Window Rock 86515, tel. 602/871–6647). Note, too, that the trails are often poorly marked and ill maintained in this wilderness area. The **Glen Canyon Natural History Association** (Box 581, Page 86040, tel. 602/645–3532) sells good topographical maps of the region as well as useful publications on hiking here.

Horseback Riding **Justin's Horse Rental** (Box 881, Chinle 86503, tel. 602/674–5678), near the South Rim Drive entrance of Canyon de

Chelly, offers trips into the canyon for $8 per hour for each horse plus $8 per hour for a guide.

Native American guides conduct horseback tours to Keet Seel at Navajo National Monument daily from Memorial Day weekend through Labor Day weekend; rates are approximately $50 per day. Reservations should be made two months in advance; there's often a waiting list. Contact Virginia Austin (c/o Navajo National Monument, HC-71 Box 3, Tonalea, AZ 86044, tel. 602/672–2366 or 602/672–2367) for details.

If you've always wanted to ride off into the sunset at Monument Valley, get in touch with **Ed Black's Horseback Riding Tours** (Box 155, Mexican Hat, Utah 84531, tel. 800/551–4039). Prices for trail rides, which can be as short as 1½ hours or as long as five days, range from $20 to $65 (per overnight); rides leave from the corral, a half-mile north of the Monument Valley visitor center.

Rainbow Trails & Tours (Box 7218, Shonto, AZ 86054, tel. 602/672–2397) runs pack trips in Lake Powell country from May through September. Tailored to individual interests and skills, Navajo-guided rides include a day trip to Rainbow Bridge and an overnight with tepee accommodations at Desha Canyon near Navajo Mountain. Rates are $75 per person per day, including meals.

Dining and Lodging

Dining Northeastern Arizona offers no fancy restaurants for fine dining. Dress is casual, seating is on a first-come, first-served basis, and prices are reasonable. Only in the Page/Lake Powell area at the height of the summer season is it advisable to make reservations.

Because northeastern Arizona is a vast area and few communities offer eating establishments, visitors should keep in mind the following major locations that have restaurants and fast-food service: Page, Window Rock, Fort Defiance, Ganado, Chinle, Hopi Second Mesa, Keams Canyon, Tuba City, Kayenta, Goulding's Trading Post/Monument Valley, and Cameron. Most serve standard American fare, and some also feature Mexican and Native American dishes. In some of the smaller reservation communities, only fast food may be available.

Restaurants are open daily unless otherwise noted. Highly recommended restaurants are indicated by a star ★.

Category	Cost*
Very Expensive	over $25
Expensive	$15–$25

| Moderate | $10–$15 |
| Inexpensive | under $10 |

per person, excluding drinks, service, and sales tax (6.7%),except on the Hopi and Navajo reservations, where no tax is charged

Lodging Northeastern Arizona is a big land with few people and long distances between communities, and a top priority for travelers here is simply making sure that you have a place to lay your head at the end of the day. Half the battle is knowing in which of the scattered communities motels are located. During summer months, it is especially wise to make reservations in advance. Fortunately, most of the motels in Indian country are clean and comfortable, and the majority of the dozen motel and hotel locations in Page and at Lake Powell are also well maintained.

Unless otherwise indicated, all the establishments listed have air-conditioning, private baths, telephones, and TVs in their rooms. Highly recommended establishments are indicated by a star ★.

Category	Cost*
Expensive	over $80
Moderate	$50–$80
Inexpensive	under $50

All prices are for a standard double room, summer rates (rates may be lower at other times), excluding service charges and hotel tax: 8½% in the Page area, 5% on the Navajo reservation. No hotel tax is charged on the Hopi reservation.

Cameron

Dining and Lodging **Cameron Trading Post and Motel.** This is a good place for stop if you're driving from the Hopi Mesas to the Grand Canyon. (*See* Dining and Lodging in Chapter 3, Grand Canyon Country and Lake Mead, for details.)

Camping **Cameron RV Park** (on U.S. 89, 26 mi southwest of Tuba City, tel. 602/679–2231 or 800/338–7385) is adjacent to the Cameron Trading Post, with its restaurant, grocery store, and post office. The fee with hookup is $14 per day. The park is open all year.

Canyon de Chelly/Chinle/Tsaile

Dining and Lodging **Coyote Pass Hospitality.** You're not like to encounter a more unusual place to stay than this roving bed and breakfast run by the Coyote Pass clan of the Navajo Nation. It's not for everyone: You sleep on a mattress on the dirt floor of a hogan (its location depends on the season, but most are near Canyon de Chelly), use an outhouse, and eat a traditional

Navajo breakfast prepared on a wood-burning stove. But if you don't mind roughing it a bit, this is a rare opportunity to immerse yourself in Native American culture in beautiful surroundings. Guided hikes, nature programs, and other meals are optional extras. *Contact Will Tsosie, Jr., Box 91, Tsaile 86556, tel. 602/724–3383 or 602/674–9655. Rates per night: $75 1 person, $10 each additional person; phone for tour and additional meal rates).*

Holiday Inn Canyon de Chelly. The newest (1992) lodging near Canyon de Chelly is less generic than you might expect: This territorial-style, Navajo-staffed complex stands on the site of a former trading post and incorporates part of the historic structure. Rooms, on the other hand, are predictably pastel and contemporary. The lobby restaurant, low-key by most standards, is the most upscale place to eat in town, serving well-prepared Native American dishes, fish and vegetarian entrées, and steaks and burgers. *BIA Rte. 7, Box 1889, Chinle 86503, tel. 602/674–5000 or 800/23–HOTEL, fax 602/674–8264. 108 rooms. Facilities: restaurant, pool, gift shop, Native American music and dance evenings in season. AE, D, DC, MC, V. Expensive.*

Thunderbird Lodge. Set in an ideal spot at the mouth of Canyon de Chelly, this pleasant establishment has stone and adobe units that match the architecture of the site's original 1896 trading post. Inviting rooms feature roughly hewn beamed ceilings, rustic wood furniture, and Navajo decor. You'll find the staff friendly and knowledgeable about the locale. The manicured lawns and large, sheltering cottonwood trees help create a resortlike atmosphere. A traditional cafeteria offers an inexpensive American menu that ranges from soup, salads, and sandwiches to complete meals, including charbroiled steaks, prepared by an all-Navajo staff. *Box 548 (½ mi south of Canyon de Chelly visitor center), Chinle 86503, tel. 602/674–5841. 72 rooms. Facilities: cafeteria, gift shop, Jeep tours. AE, D, DC, MC, V. Expensive.*

Lodging **Canyon de Chelly Motel.** This two-story, western-style motel, about a mile from Canyon de Chelly, has modern, cheerful rooms with light oak furnishings and American Indian-print bedspreads and drapes. *Box 295 (on Rte. 7, ¼ mi east of U.S. 191), Chinle 86503, tel. 602/674–5875, 602/674–5288, or 800/327–0354. 102 rooms. Facilities: restaurant, indoor pool, gift shop. AE, D, DC, MC, V. Expensive.*

Camping **Cottonwood Campground** (Canyon de Chelly National Monument, near visitor center, Chinle, tel. 602/674–5436) has about 94 sites (including RV spaces but no hookups), available on a first-come, first-served basis, on grounds with cottonwood trees and a picnic area. Camping is free, and the campground is open all year, with water available April–September.

Hopi Reservation—Second Mesa

Dining **Tunosvongya Restaurant.** Also known as the Hopi Cultural Center Restaurant, this clean, comfortable establishment operated by Native Americans provides the opportunity to sample traditional dishes, including Indian tacos, Hopi blue-corn pancakes, fry bread, and a lamb stew that goes by the Hopi name *nok qui vi. On AZ 264 on Second Mesa, tel. 602/734–2401. DC, MC, V. Inexpensive.*

Lodging **Hopi Cultural Center Motel.** This pleasant pueblo-style
★ lodging set high atop a Hopi mesa offers immaculate rooms with mauve and white walls and charming Native American decor, including interesting artwork. *Box 67 (on AZ 264, at Hopi Cultural Center), Second Mesa 86043, tel. 602/734–2401. 33 units. Facilities: restaurant, museum, gift shop. DC, MC, V. Moderate.*

Kayenta

Dining and **Anasazi Inn at Tsegi.** This unpretentious roadside motel,
Lodging convenient to both Navajo National Monument and Monu-
★ ment Valley, offers clean, comfortable accommodations and striking views of Tsegi Canyon from its rear-facing rooms. Its restaurant, which features tasty Navajo fry-bread sandwiches and tacos, is among the best in the area. *Box 1543 (on U.S. 160, 10 mi west of Kayenta), Kayenta 86033, tel. 602/697–3793. 56 units. Facilities: restaurant. AE, D, DC, MC, V. Moderate.*

Lodging **Holiday Inn.** Except for the contemporary southwestern-style decor, this accommodation about a half-mile from Monument Valley provides what you would expect from the Holiday Inn chain. It's clean and comfortable, and has one of the few swimming pools in the western section of Indian country. *Box 307 (south of junction of U.S. 160 and U.S. 163), Kayenta 86033, tel. 602/697–3221 or 800/465–4329. 160 rooms. Facilities: restaurant, gift shop, swimming pool, Monument Valley tours. AE, D, DC, MC, V. Expensive.*

Wetherill Inn Motel. Named for John Wetherill, a frontier rancher, trader, and explorer who discovered many of the major prehistoric Native American ruins in Arizona, this clean and cheerful two-story motel without frills has orange-and-brown room decor and a well-stocked gift shop. *Box 175 (on U.S. 163), Kayenta 86033, tel. 602/697–3231. 54 rooms. Facilities: gift shop, nearby café. AE, D, DC, MC, V. Moderate.*

Keams Canyon

Dining **Keams Canyon Restaurant.** At this typical rural roadside dining spot, furnished functionally with Formica tabletops, you can choose from American dishes and a few Native American items, including Navajo tacos, made with Indian fry bread (not unlike a soft pizza crust) heaped with ground beef, chili, beans, lettuce, and grated cheese. *Keams Canyon Shopping Center (near AZ 264), tel. 602/738–2296. MC, V. Open weekdays 7 AM–8 PM, weekends until 6 PM. Inexpensive.*

Lodging **Keams Canyon Motel.** This motel in a rustic trading-post setting is conveniently located near the Hopi Mesas. The rooms are basic, with a hint of Native American decor, and some units have kitchenettes. *Box 188 (off AZ 264, adjacent to Keams Canyon Shopping Center), Keams Canyon 86034, tel. 602/738–2297. 20 units. Facilities: restaurant, grocery store, service station, post office all nearby. MC, V. Inexpensive.*

Camping **Keams Canyon Campground** (near Keams Canyon Trading Post on AZ 264, tel. 602/738–2297) offers free camping at two sites; there's no water or other facilities.

Monument Valley

Dining **Stagecoach Restaurant.** Set deep in Monument Valley, this
★ establishment is a part of the Goulding's Trading Post and motel complex. The restaurant stands in the lee of a massive red butte; large windows and the elevated vista provide a splendid view across the valley. The interior's southwestern decor features memorabilia from movies shot in the area. The mostly standard American dishes are well prepared, and the service is excellent. *2 mi west of U.S. 163, just north of Utah border, tel. 801/727–3231 or 800/ 874–0902. AE, D, DC, MC, V. Moderate.*

Lodging **Goulding's Lodge.** Built near the base of an immense red
★ sandstone butte with spectacular views of Monument Valley from all the rooms, this comfortable motel often serves as headquarters for the location crews of filmmakers. The lodge has handsome pueblo-style buildings stuccoed in a deep reddish brown that makes them appear to be a part of the surrounding red-rock formations. The cozy rooms are furnished in contemporary style, with southwestern colors and Navajo-design bedspreads. *Box 1 (2 mi west of U.S. 163, just north of Utah border), Monument Valley, UT 84536, tel. 801/727–3231 or 800/874–0902. 62 rooms. Facilities: museum, heated pool (both closed Nov. 15–Mar. 15), restaurant, Monument Valley tours. AE, D, DC, MC, V. Expensive.*

Camping **Goulding's Good Sam Campground** (off U.S. 163, near Goulding's Trading Post, 27 mi north of Kayenta, tel. 801/ 727–3235 [campground], 801/727–3231 [reservations when campground is closed]) has tents and RV sites. The fee is $14 with no hookups, $20 with hookups. *Open Mar. 15–Oct. 15.*

Mitten View Campground (Monument Valley Navajo Tribal Park, near visitor center, off U.S. 163, 25 mi north of

Kayenta, tel. 801/727–3287) has sites with a table, a grill, and a deck. Water is available; the fee is $10 per site; hot showers are extra. *Open Mar.–Oct.*

Navajo National Monument

Camping   **Navajo National Monument** (reached by turnoff on U.S. 160, 21 mi south of Kayenta, tel. 602/672–2366) has two campgrounds with RV and tent sites, water, and rest rooms, but no hookups. Camping here is free and is available May–October.

Page/Lake Powell

Dining   *Canyon King Paddlewheeler.* Visitors embark on this 95-
★ foot boat, designed as an 1800s riverboat, for a 2½-hour sunset dinner cruise. Presented buffet style on the fully glassed lower deck, dinner includes one entrée—prime rib with fresh garden vegetables and a baked potato—and a salad and dessert. Cocktails are available at an extra charge. The cost of the dinner cruise is $41.20 for both children and adults; adults who wish to take the cruise without eating pay $19.65, and it's $13.10 for children. *Board at Wahweap Lodge (off U.S. 89, 5 mi north of Page), tel. 602/ 645–2433 or 800/528–6154. Departure times vary seasonally, and the cruise has a 10-passenger minimum. AE, D, DC, MC, V. Very Expensive.*

Rainbow Room in Wahweap Lodge. You can't beat the beautiful setting of this attractive semicircular restaurant with panoramic views of Lake Powell and a colony of houseboats bobbing offshore. The dining room connects to a cocktail lounge, and live entertainment is offered during the summer months. An extensive menu features southwestern, standard American, and some Continental fare, accompanied by a good wine selection. Specialties include Southwest chicken breast, marinated in a sauce of honey and green jalapeño peppers, and coho salmon, panfried with a Dijon-mustard cream sauce. In season, there is a nightly salad-and-soup bar and a breakfast buffet. *Wahweap Lodge (on U.S. 89, 5 mi north of Page), tel. 602/645–2433 or 800/528–6154. AE, D, DC, MC, V. Moderate.*

Lodging   **Wahweap Lodge.** On a promontory above Lake Powell, Wah-
★ weap Lodge serves as the center for recreational activities in the area. This attractively landscaped property offers accommodations with oak furnishings and balconies or patios; many of the rooms have a lake view (rates are a bit higher for these). The brightly colored, southwestern-style suites in the newest building are very attractive. Guests can enjoy two pools, a cocktail lounge, a marina, and the Rainbow Room (*see above*) for dining. *Box 1597 (on U.S. 89, 5 mi north of Page), Page 86040, tel. 602/645–2433 or 800/528–6154. 350 rooms. Facilities: 2 gift shops, rental*

boats, cruises, fishing and water-skiing equipment, river-rafting excursions, houseboats. AE, D, DC, MC, V. Expensive.

Inn at Lake Powell. Situated on a high bluff in the small community of Page, this motel has service and amenities you would expect from a good hotel. A number of the large rooms, with queen-size beds and southwestern-print bedspreads, provide fine views of Glen Canyon Dam and Lake Powell at a slightly higher rate. *Box C (716 Rim View Dr.), Page 86040, tel. 602/645–2466 or 800/826–2718. 103 rooms. Facilities: restaurant, cocktail lounge, conference rooms, pool, hot tub. AE, D, DC, MC, V. Moderate–Expensive.*

Lake Powell Motel. Operated by Wahweap Lodge, this no-frills motel offers clean rooms with great views of Lake Powell and the surrounding countryside at reasonable rates. Guests can use the facilities at Wahweap, 3 miles down the road. *Box 1597 (on U.S. 89, 4 mi north of Glen Canyon Dam), Page 86040, tel. 602/645–2477 or 800/528–6154. 22 rooms. AE, D, DC, MC, V. Moderate.*

Camping   **Wahweap Campground** (5 mi north of Page on U.S. 89 near shore of Lake Powell, tel. 602/645–2511) has 180 sites, some near the marina. The adjacent RV park, also operated by Wahweap Lodge (tel. 602/645–1004 or 800/528–6154) and offering 120 full-service sites, has coin showers and a laundromat that campers may use. The fee with hookup is $20.20, and the fee for campsites with drinking water is $11; the RV park accepts reservations, but the campground operates on a first-come, first-served basis.

Tuba City

Dining   **Pancho's Family Restaurant.** The main fare here is Mexican, but the menu also features American and Navajo dishes. Mexican entrées are copious and traditionally prepared, with chicken enchiladas and beef tamales as good as any you'll find south of the border. The large dining room looks like a western coffee shop but has beamed wood ceilings and incorporates such Native American touches as handmade pottery chandeliers and Navajo rugs on the walls. *Main St., adjacent to Tuba City Motel and Trading Post, tel. 602/283-5260. AE, D, DC, MC, V. Inexpensive.*

Lodging   **Tuba City Motel.** In the largest community in the western part of Indian country, this property is conveniently situated near Pancho's Family Restaurant (*see* Dining, *above*), a trading post, and shops for essentials, gifts, and souvenirs. The well-maintained rooms are adequate for an overnight stopover before or after a visit to the Hopi Mesas. *Box 247 (at AZ 264–U.S. 160 junction), Tuba City 86045, tel. 602/283-4545. 80 rooms. Facilities: gift shop, nearby restaurants, post office, trading post. AE, D, DC, MC, V. Moderate.*

Grey Hills Inn. Students at Grey Hills High School run this unusual lodging, a former dorm offering large, clean accommodations at excellent rates. The queen-size beds are comfortable, and pastel Native American print bedspreads and kitschy paintings add character to the otherwise plain rooms. Bathrooms and showers are down the hall, and it's hard to find your way to the inn's entrance in the large high-school complex at night, but you can't beat the prices: $10 for members of American Youth Hostel; $31.50 for singles, $40.95 for doubles for nonmembers. *Box 160 (off U.S. 160, ½ mi north of junction with AZ 264), Tuba City 86045, tel. 602/283–6271 or 602/283–6273 (on weekends or after school hours). 32 rooms. No credit cards. Inexpensive.*

Window Rock

Dining and Lodging

Navajo Nation Inn. Indian officials in town on government business frequently stay in this motel in the Navajo Nation's tribal capital. The exterior is typical of contemporary roadside motels, but the rooms have been pleasantly decorated with Spanish Colonial furniture and Navajo art. The inexpensive restaurant serves standard American as well as Navajo entrées; the mutton stew is hearty, and the tasty fry-bread taco could easily feed two. *Box 2340 (on north side of AZ 264), Window Rock 86515, tel. 602/871–4108 or 800/662–6189 (reservations only). 56 units. Facilities: restaurant, conference rooms, nearby shopping and services. AE, DC, MC, V. Moderate.*

Camping

Summit Campground (off AZ 264, 9 mi west of Window Rock, tel. 602/871–6645) has picnic tables but no water. A fee of $1 per person may be charged. *Open year-round.*

Tse Bonito Tribal Park (near AZ 264, Window Rock, tel. 602/871–6645), set among sandstone monoliths, is a historically significant site: The Navajo camped here before being forced on the Long Walk to Fort Summer. The campground has shaded picnic tables and nearby rest rooms but no water. A fee of $2 per person may be charged. *Open year-round except Christmas and New Year's Day.*

Nightlife

Aside from sitting by a campfire, nightlife in northeastern Arizona is minimal. The Page/Lake Powell area offers the most options. The cocktail lounge at Wahweap Lodge (on U.S. 89, 5 mi north of Page, tel. 602/645–2433) on the shore of Lake Powell and the sunset dinner cruise that departs from the dock at Wahweap Lodge (*see* Dining and Lodging, *above*) are two possibilities. Page also has a movie house (Mesa Theater, 42 S. Lake Powell Blvd., tel. 602/645–9565), a combination bowling alley/off-track betting parlor/comedy club (Canyon Bowl, 24 N. Lake Powell Blvd. tel. 602/645–9020), and a country-western music and dancing spot (Ken's Old West, 718 Vista Rd., tel. 602/645–5160). In addition, there's an inexpensive first-run movie theater in Tuba City.

Keep in mind that no alcoholic beverages are sold on the Navajo and Hopi reservations, and possession or consumption of alcohol is against the law in these areas.

5 North-Central Arizona

Sedona and Flagstaff

*By Trudy
Thompson Rice
and Edie Jarolim*

Rich in history and natural attractions, north-central Arizona draws visitors to the striking red-rock formations of Sedona, the volcanic fields around Sunset Crater, the rolling, forested hills of Jerome, and Arizona's highest peaks, just north of Flagstaff. Several national and state parks hold well-preserved evidence of the architectural accomplishments of the many early Native American settlers who made their homes in this area.

Sedona sits at the southern end of Oak Creek Canyon, 125 miles north of Phoenix, where the Colorado Plateau meets the Sonora Desert to the south. Since about 1985, Sedona has developed a reputation as a center for New Age believers, who consider it one of the Earth's 11 most powerful energy centers. The city's full-time population of about 15,000 swells during the summer, when Arizona desert dwellers as well as out-of-state tourists come here to escape the heat. Throughout the year, travelers going to Flagstaff and on to the Grand Canyon choose scenic U.S. 89A, which traverses the town and Oak Creek Canyon. Just south of Sedona, funky old Jerome, a boomtown gone bust that has now been reclaimed by a few of the state's artsier residents, is also worth a visit. The forested mountain scenery is striking, and the drive is an adventure, with its many climbs, narrow curves, and switchbacks. Flagstaff, the largest city in north-central Arizona, is largely considered a jumping-off point for tours of the region, but it has many of its own lures, especially for those interested in Arizona history, astronomy, and Native American culture and crafts.

Essential Information

Important Addresses and Numbers

**Tourist
Information**

One of the busiest tourist information offices in the country, the **Flagstaff Visitors Center** (101 W. Rte. 66, tel. 602/774–9541 or 800/842–7293) is open every day of the year, including Christmas: Monday–Saturday 8 AM–9 PM, Sunday 8 AM–5 PM. The building, which the center shares with the **Flagstaff Chamber of Commerce** (Flagstaff 86001, tel. 602/774–4505), stands adjacent to the railroad tracks at the intersection of Route 66 and Beaver Avenue, close to the Amtrak station.

For hiking maps and camping tips, contact the **U.S. Forest Service** (2323 E. Greenlaw La., tel. 602/527–7400).

The **Sedona–Oak Creek Canyon Chamber of Commerce,** at the corner of North U.S. 89A and Forest Road (Box 478, Sedona 86339, tel. 602/282–7722 or 800/288–7336), is staffed with knowledgeable residents who can help guide you to points of special interest; it's open Monday–Saturday 9–5, Sunday 9–3.

Emergencies Call 911 to reach the **fire department, police,** and **emergency medical services.**

Hospitals and Doctors At an altitude of nearly 7,000 feet, Flagstaff has "thin" air; heart and respiratory patients may experience difficulty here, particularly upon exertion.

Flagstaff Medical Center, a full-service hospital, has a 24-hour emergency room downtown (1200 N. Beaver St., tel. 602/779–3366), about nine blocks north of Route 66. The facility also provides referrals to local doctors and dentists.

The **Sedona Medical Center** has a doctor on call 24 hours. *75 Kallof Pl., tel. 602/282–1285. Walk-in hours weekdays 8–6, weekends 10–4.*

Late-Night Pharmacies The pharmacy at the **Flagstaff Medical Center** (*see above*) is open 24 hours. **Walgreen's** (1500 E. Cedar St., tel. 602/773–1011), a few blocks north of downtown off 4th Street, is open Monday–Saturday 9 AM–10 PM, Sunday 9 AM–8 PM; the pharmacy at **Smith's Food and Drug** (201 Switzer Canyon Rd., corner Route 66, tel. 602/774–2719) is open Monday–Saturday 9 AM–9 PM, Sunday 10 AM–4 PM.

In Sedona **Walgreen's** (180 Coffee Pot Dr., tel. 602/282–2528) stays open until 9 during the week, until 6 on weekends; **Payless** (2350 W. U.S. 89A, tel. 602/282–9577) closes at 9 every day except Sunday, when it closes at 7.

Arriving and Departing by Plane

Flagstaff Air travelers arrive in Flagstaff at **Flagstaff Pullium Airport** (tel. 602/774–1422), 4 miles south of town off I–17 at Exit 337.

Both **America West** (tel. 800/247–5692) and **Sky West** (tel. 800/453–9417), a division of Delta Airlines, have frequent daily flights into Flagstaff from Phoenix; Sky West also offers direct flights from Page, Arizona.

If you plan to rent a car, the most cost-effective plan might be to fly into Phoenix, which has more flight options, and rent a car there. The drive from Phoenix to Flagstaff is a pretty one, climbing almost 5,000 feet in 134 miles.

Sedona The tiny **Sedona Airport** (tel. 602/282–4487) has a very scenic location up on Airport Mesa; from West Sedona, take U.S. 89A to the top of Airport Road.

Arizona Air Sedona (1225 Airport Rd., Suite 3, Sedona, tel. 602/282–7935 or 800/535–4448) has five daily round-trips between Phoenix and Sedona year-round; the cost is $90 round-trip.

Between the Airport and Downtown Flagstaff *By Taxi* A taxi ride from the airport to the downtown area should cost about $10. Cabs are not regulated; some, but not all, have meters. It's wise to agree on a rate before you contract with a driver to take you to your destination. **Alpine Taxi Cab** (tel. 602/527–2400) and **Flagstaff Taxi & Limousine**

(tel. 602/774–1374) are both known to be reliable and fair in their pricing.

By Bus There is no public bus from the airport to downtown. Some hotels offer a shuttle service; inquire when making reservations.

By Rental Car Rental-car agencies represented at the airport include **Budget** (tel. 800/527–0700) and **Hertz** (tel. 800/654–3131). Ask about a rate that allows you unlimited mileage, as you're likely to drive several hundred miles while you're in this part of the state.

To reach downtown from the airport, follow the signs out of the airport to I–17 (the airport is just off the highway). Turn right (north) on I–17, then exit at the downtown turnoff, less than 5 miles away.

Between the There are no cabs waiting at the airport, but if you call
Airport and **Bob's Taxi** (tel. 602/282–1234), a car will show up in about
Downtown Sedona five minutes. A ride to town should run about $8.
By Taxi

By Rental Car **Budget Rent-A-Car** (tel. 602/282–4602) has an office at the Sedona Airport.

Arriving and Departing by Car, Train, and Bus

By Car **Flagstaff** lies at the crossroads of I–40 (running east–west) and I–17 (running south from Flagstaff). It's 134 miles from Phoenix via I–17 (also known in Phoenix as Black Canyon Freeway) north. The road is a four-lane divided highway the entire way; there are several steep climbs and descents (you'll see a number of runaway-truck ramps—emergency stopping places for truckers who have lost their brakes on the steep declines). In summertime make the trip with extra water for humans, pets, and radiators. In the winter, snowstorms can occasionally restrict travel to vehicles with snow chains.

To get to **Sedona** from Phoenix, take I–17 north for 113 miles, then drive another 15 miles on AZ 179; the trip should take about 2½ hours. From Flagstaff, it's a scenic 27-mile drive on U.S. 89A through Oak Creek Canyon.

By Train Flagstaff is a railroad town: The tracks that gave rise to the city's growth still run through the town today. **Amtrak** (tel. 602/774–8679 or 800/872–7245) comes into the downtown station at 1 Route 66 twice daily.

There is no rail service into Sedona.

By Bus In **Flagstaff,** the **Greyhound/Trailways** station is downtown at 399 South Malpais Lane (tel. 602/774–4573). There are daily connections to Phoenix, but none to Sedona. Buses also serve travelers to San Francisco, Los Angeles, Las Vegas, and other cities. **Nava-Hopi** buses also depart daily to the Grand Canyon and offer sightseeing trips to Sedona (*see* Special-Interest Tours, *below*).

The **Sedona/Phoenix Shuttle Service** (Box 3342, West Sedona 86340, tel. 602/282–2066 or 800/448–7988 in Arizona) makes three trips daily between those cities; the fare is $30 one-way, $50 round-trip. You can catch the bus at three terminals of Sky Harbor International Airport in Phoenix.

Getting Around

Flagstaff is a compact town, much of it situated along the railroad tracks. Just north of, and roughly parallel to, the tracks is the busy street that was called Santa Fe Avenue for many years; in 1992 it officially resumed its famous original name, Route 66. Not all the signs in town have been changed yet, however, and many maps—and most locals— still refer to Santa Fe Avenue, so the change will likely cause confusion for some time. I–40 lies to the south of the tracks and also runs east–west; the main north–south thoroughfare is I–17, which turns into Milton Road, Humphreys Street, and then U.S. 180 as you drive north through town. Fast-food restaurants and motels line all these major roads.

Because Flagstaff is the gateway to the Grand Canyon, most people on the road here are from out of town; keep that in mind when you ask for directions!

Sedona is even more compact than Flagstaff, with U.S. 89A, which runs roughly east–west through town, as the main thoroughfare. U.S. 89A is bisected by AZ 179. The more commercial section of U.S. 89A east of AZ 179 is known as Uptown; locals tend to frequent the shops on the other side, called West Sedona. To the south of U.S. 89A, AZ 179 is lined with upscale retailers for a couple of miles. There is no public transportation in Sedona; if you don't have your own wheels, you'll need to rent a car or jeep (*see* By Car and By Jeep, *below*) or take a taxi (*see* Between the Airport and Downtown Sedona, *above*).

By Bus and Trolley The local bus company, **Pine Country Transit** (2323 N. Walgreen St., Suite 103, tel. 602/779–6624), offers clean and reliable service throughout the city of Flagstaff for 75¢. Senior citizens age 60 and older, disabled riders, and children 7–17 pay only 60¢ a ride; children age 6 and under ride free. Three bus lines run weekdays 6:15 AM–6:30 PM; only one bus line, on a more limited schedule, operates Saturday and holidays, and there is no service on Sunday. Disabled passengers should check with the office to find out which buses are outfitted to accommodate wheelchairs.

By Car It makes sense to rent a car at the airport if you fly into Flagstaff or Sedona (*see* Between the Airport and Downtown sections, *above*). In downtown Sedona **Super Star Rent A Car** (2730 W. U.S. 89A, tel. 602/282–2897) offers reliable service.

By Jeep If you want to explore the back roads of Sedona's red rocks on your own, you can rent a four-wheel-drive vehicle from **Sedona Jeep Rentals** (La Pasada Plaza, tel. 602/282–2227).

Opening and Closing Times

Flagstaff is a traveler's and student's town, so restaurants tend to stay open late, some of them 24 hours. Sedona, on the other hand, is a resort that caters to many retirees, so restaurants tend to close earlier, many of them by 10 PM. In both places banking can be done at odd hours by way of automated teller machines (ATMs) located all over town. Some banks stay open until 6 PM on Friday. During the summer, shops and attractions are open longer: 9–9 during the week, 9–6 on Saturday, and noon–5 on Sunday.

Guided Tours

Orientation For self-guided tour maps of Flagstaff itself, stop at the **Flagstaff Visitors Center** (*see* Tourist Information, *above*); if you're going to spend any time in town, it's well worth taking the route outlined in the "Historic Downtown Walking Tour" pamphlet. If you're interested in a look at the **Northern Arizona University** campus (tel. 602/523–2491), from September through May tours are conducted Monday–Saturday at varying times. From June through August, tours are conducted weekdays at 11 AM.

Special-Interest The Gray Line of Flagstaff, operated by **Nava-Hopi Tours**
Tours (114 W. Route 66 [Box 339], Flagstaff 86002, tel. 602/774–
Flagstaff 5003 or 800/892–8687), runs bus trips from its downtown bus station to the **Grand Canyon** ($36 round-trip, including park entry fee). A tour of **Sedona** costs $34 per person; there are no drop-offs—that is, all passengers must return to Flagstaff on the same bus that evening. The company also offers a variety of package tours, such as the one to the **Hopi Indian Reservation** ($62 round-trip, including lunch). All require reservations, which are taken until two hours before departure. Free hotel and motel pickups are included in the price.

The Ventures program, run by the education department of the **Museum of Northern Arizona** (3001 N. Valley Rd. [Box 720], Flagstaff 86001, tel. 602/774–5211), offers tours of the area led by local scientists, artists, and historians. Trips might include rafting excursions down the San Juan and lower Verde rivers, hikes into the Grand Canyon or Arizona Strip Country, or bus tours into Albuquerque or Santa Fe. Prices start at $300 and go up to $1,300, with most tours in the $300 to $600 range.

Alpine Air Service (Box 252, Flagstaff 86002, tel. 602/779–5178) plane tours of the area's attractions leave from Flagstaff Pullium Airport. The cost for the pilot and plane, which carries three passengers, is $90 an hour plus tax.

FAA regulations prevent tour companies, including this one, from flying over the Grand Canyon.

Sedona In the Sedona area, an option to consider is a **Jeep tour;** there are several operators headquartered along Sedona's main drag who offer a variety of excursions, some focusing on geology, some on vegetation, some on vortices, and some on all three. Some trips end with a western-style shoot-out; others are designed for more serious adventurers who like to head off the beaten track. **Pink Jeep Tours** (Box 1447, Sedona 86339, tel. 602/282–5000 or 800/8–SEDONA), **Sedona Red Rock Jeeps Tours** (Box 10305, Sedona 86339, tel. 602/282–6826 or 800/848–7728), and **Time Expeditions** (Box 2936, Sedona 86339, tel. 602/282–2137 or 800/999–2137) are the only operators with permission from the government to go out on U.S. Forest Service trails. Prices start at about $18 per person for one hour, $25 per person for two hours. Car seats are available for youngsters; if you need one, check with your operator before you buy. Although all the excursions are safe, those who dislike heights should choose one that's easy on the nerves.

A **hot-air-balloon tour** of Sedona provides a unique perspective of the magnificent red-rock landscape. Prices generally start at $135 per person for a one- to two-hour tour. Plan to spend about three or four hours on this venture, including driving time to launch sites—most companies pick up their passengers at their hotels in Sedona and transport them in vans to the outskirts of town—inflating and deflating the balloon and, in some cases, offering a picnic along the way. Balloon companies here are very safety minded, flying only in clear, still weather and generally departing at sunrise, when winds are at their calmest. Children under the age of 4 aren't allowed. It can be chilly up in the air, even in the summertime, and downright cold in the winter, so dress warmly. Recommended companies include **Northern Light Balloon Expeditions** (Box 1695, Sedona 86339, tel. 602/282–2274) and **Red Rock Balloon Adventures** (Box 2759, Sedona 86339, tel. 602/284–0040).

It's the rare visitor who won't snap a roll or two of film in beautiful Sedona; those who need some guidance in their picture taking may want to call Sue Winters at **Photo Tours** (tel. 602/282–4320). She'll take you to all the prime spots and help you take your best shot. Rates are $25 per hour for one person; $28 for two hours or $38 for three hours for two people.

Those interested in the photographs of others—and in art in general—might consider a tour of some of the galleries in town; contact **Sedona Art Tours** (Box 10578, Sedona 86339, tel. 602/282–7686) for information.

Exploring North-Central Arizona

Highlights for First-time Visitors

Arizona Snowbowl (*see* Flagstaff and Environs)

Jerome (*see* Sedona and Environs)

Lowell Observatory (*see* Flagstaff and Environs)

Museum of Northern Arizona (*see* Flagstaff and Environs)

Oak Creek Canyon (*see* Sedona and Environs)

The red rocks of Sedona (*see* Sedona and Environs)

Riordan Mansion (*see* Flagstaff and Environs)

Sunset Crater Volcano National Monument (*see* Flagstaff and Environs)

Walnut Canyon National Monument (*see* Flagstaff and Environs)

Wupatki National Monument (*see* Flagstaff and Environs)

Sedona and Environs

Numbers in the margin correspond to points of interest on the North-Central Arizona map.

● **Sedona,** 125 miles north of downtown Phoenix and 27 miles south of Flagstaff, is perhaps the most attractive stopover en route north to the Grand Canyon. With its numerous galleries, shops, resorts, and restaurants, as well as a splendid setting in the midst of red-rock country, Sedona also makes a fine weekend destination in its own right.

The former artists colony is now home to some 15,000 residents, many retired, and many (alas) more interested in making money than in creating beauty. Expansion during the past 10 years has been rapid, and the lack of planning has taken its toll in increased traffic and congestion, especially on weekends and during the busy summer months, when Phoenix residents, overcome by heat, flee north to higher elevations.

That said, it's easy to see what draws so many visitors to Sedona. The deep-red rocks poke holes in what is almost always a clear blue sky—which seems even bluer above the dark green of the forests. The wilderness—canyons, creeks, Indian ruins, and always a dreamscape of twisted red rock—is readily accessible on foot or on any number of Jeep tours. The rugged landscape once attracted filmmakers, who shot more than 80 westerns in the area in the 1940s and '50s. These days, Sedona—which seems likely to become the next Santa Fe—draws enterprising restaura-

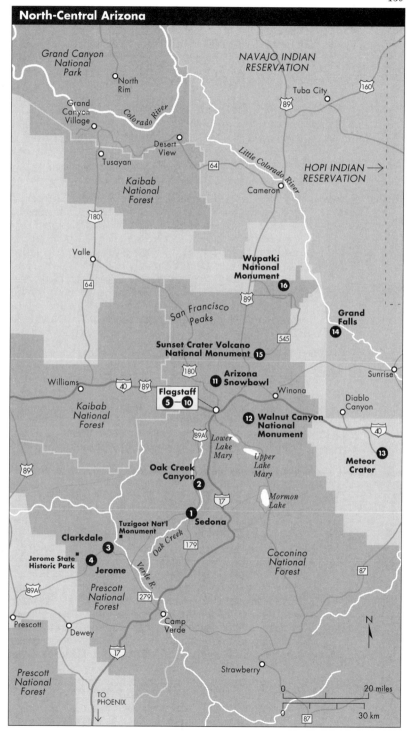

North-Central Arizona

Grand Canyon National Park

NAVAJO INDIAN RESERVATION

North Rim

Tuba City

[160]

Grand Canyon Village

Colorado River

[89]

Desert View

Tusayan

[64]

Kaibab National Forest

HOPI INDIAN RESERVATION →

Little Colorado River

Cameron

[180]

Valle

[64]

Wupatki National Monument ⑯

[89]

Grand Falls ⑭

San Francisco Peaks

[545]

Sunset Crater Volcano National Monument ⑮

Williams

[40] [89]

[180]

Arizona Snowbowl ⑪

Sunrise

Kaibab National Forest

Flagstaff ⑤—⑩

Winona

Diablo Canyon

[89]

[89A]

Walnut Canyon National Monument ⑫

[40]

Lower Lake Mary

Upper Lake Mary

Meteor Crater ⑬

Oak Creek Canyon ②

[17]

Mormon Lake

①

Sedona

Tuzigoot Nat'l Monument

Clarkdale ③

Oak Creek

[179]

Coconino National Forest

Jerome State Historic Park

Jerome ④

[87]

[89]

Prescott National Forest

Verde R.

[279]

Prescott

Dewey

Camp Verde

N

[17]

Strawberry

0   20 miles

Prescott National Forest

TO PHOENIX ↓

0   30 km

[87]

teurs and gallery owners from the East and West coasts. The town has also become a center of interest to New Age followers, who believe that the area contains some of the more important vortices of the Earth. Each vortex is said to give out energy that heightens creativity; thus the town has become something of a haven for artists, the tofu set, and others in between. In the mid-1980s Sedona was one of a handful of towns to host the Harmonic Convergence, celebrated to mark an unusual alignment of the planets that was believed to herald the dawn of a new, more peaceful age. Several entrepreneurs have set up crystal shops or New Age bookshops here, catering to the curious as well as to true devotees.

Exploring Sedona   Visitors have a choice of Jeep tours (*see* Special-Interest Tours in Essential Information, *above*) and of a number of attractive hikes among the red rocks; the entire region is crisscrossed with trails. For free detailed maps and advice, speak to the rangers at the **Sedona Ranger District** office (250 Brewer Rd., tel. 602/282–4119), which is open Monday–Friday 7:30–4:30. Ask here or at your hotel for directions to trailheads for Devil's Kitchen, Long Canyon, or the Indian ruins in Boynton Canyon. Nearby Red Rock State Park and Slide Rock State Park (*see below*), both within 10 miles of Sedona, also provide many trekking opportunities.

Those who don't have the time or the inclination to get out of their cars for long won't lack for photo opportunities either. The drive out to the Enchantment Resort, in Boynton Canyon, is stunning; even if you're not staying there, consider stopping in for a scenic lunch or a late-afternoon drink. The views from the Chapel of the Holy Cross (*see below*) are also outstanding. Weather permitting, the Schnebly Hill Scenic Drive is another ooh-and-ah–inspiring option, and the vistas of the town from Airport Mesa at sunset can't be beat.

Although it's set in an area that was inhabited by Native Americans for centuries, the town of Sedona itself is very new—it wasn't incorporated until 1988—so there are few historical sights for visitors to peruse. The main activity here is shopping, mostly for southwestern-style paintings, rugs, jewelry, and Native American artifacts. During the warmer months it makes sense to visit the air-conditioned shops midday and save the hiking and Jeep tours for very early morning or late afternoon, when the light is softer and the heat less oppressive. The so-called **Uptown shopping area** is cut in half by U.S. 89A; many locals are upset by what they call the rubber-tomahawk quality of the shops here, which cater primarily to the tour-bus trade.

Time Out   Chairs are molded plastic at the **Sedona Coffee House and Bakery** (293 N. U.S. 89A, tel. 602/282–2241), and everything comes in Styrofoam or paper, but for healthy sandwiches this is your best bet Uptown. A short walk away, on

the north side of U.S. 89A, is the **Sedona Fudge Company**
(257 N. U.S. 89A, tel. 602/282–1044). Some maintain that
the mere act of watching the candy makers pour the fudge
from giant copper kettles onto marble slabs can add bulk to
your hips—so you may as well go all the way and indulge.

For more upscale shopping, drive less than a minute south
to the attractive **Tlaquepaque** development (AZ 179, tel.
602/282–4838), where more than 100 artists, most of them
painters and sculptors, sell their works. Prices tend to be
high here; when asked how to pronounce the name of this
shopping complex, locals joke that it's "to-lock-your-pock-
et." **Isadora** (tel. 602/282–6232) features contemporary silver and turquoise jewelry, and **Carusetta** (tel. 602/282–
7793) showcases the more unusual combination of gold and
turquoise. Some good bets for southwestern art are
Wolfwalker Galleries (tel. 602/282–1480), **El Prado Galleries** (tel. 602/282–7390), **Estaban's** (tel. 602/282–4686), and
Aguajito del Sol (in the belltower, tel. 602/282–5258).

A half-mile south of Tlaquepaque (take a right out of the
parking lot), at the junction of U.S. 179 and Schnebly Hill
Road, a small strip of shops includes **Garland's Navajo Rugs**
(tel. 602/282–4070), with its huge collection of new and antique carpets, as well as Native American kachina dolls,
pottery, and baskets. Next door to Garland's, **Sedona Pottery** (tel. 602/282–1192) features unusual pottery, including
life-size ceramic statues by shop owner Mary Margaret.

Drive another minute or two south on AZ 179 and you'll
come to the **Hillside Courtyard & Marketplace** (671 AZ 179,
tel. 602/282–4500). Among the 23 shops and galleries,
Chula (tel. 602/282–3899) carries a good selection of folk art
from all over the world. Across the street from Hillside,
Ratliff-Williams Gallery (556 AZ 179, tel. 602/282–1404)
has two floors of southwestern art, much of it by not-yet-
established artists; well-heeled buyers can find lots of fun,
functional pieces.

You don't have to be religious to be inspired by the setting
and the architecture of the **Chapel of the Holy Cross** (tel.
602/282–4069; look for the Chapel Rd. turnoff on AZ 179
about 2 mi south of the Hillside mall, then drive another
mile to the top of the road). Built by Marguerite Brunwige
Staude, a disciple of Frank Lloyd Wright, this striking
modern structure, with a huge cross on the facade, rises between two red-rock peaks; the vistas of the town and the
surrounding area are spectacular. There are no regular services, but visitors are welcome to come in daily 9–5 (9–6 in
summer) for quiet meditation. A small gift shop sells religious articles and books.

Inveterate bargain hunters will want to continue south on
AZ 179 for another 2 miles to the Village of Oak Creek; at
the **Oak Creek Factory Stores** (6657 S. AZ 179, tel. 602/284–

2150), Corning/Revere, Mikasa, Anne Klein, Van Heusen, and many other manufacturers have factory outlets.

Two miles west of Sedona on U.S. 89A, you'll come to the turnoff for the 286-acre **Red Rock State Park;** drive another 3 miles to enter the newest state park in Arizona (opened in October 1991), and one of the most beautiful. An ideal place to enjoy both the red rock formations of the Sedona area as well as lovely Oak Creek, it's also a less crowded alternative to the popular Slide Rock State Park (*see below*). The five park trails (all fairly easy and short—the longest is 1.9 miles) are well marked and provide beautiful vistas. One trail leads to the House of Apache Fire, an unfinished residence started in 1946 by the former owners of the land, Jack and Helen Fry. (He was president of TWA.) You can enter the house only on ranger-led tours, offered daily; birdwatching tours and nature walks are also given every day, weather permitting. *Box 3864, West Sedona 86340, tel. 602/ 282–6907. Admission: $3 per car Oct.–Mar., $5 per car Apr.–Sept. Open daily 8–5.*

Other Area Attractions ❷ Whether you want to swim, hike, picnic, or enjoy beautiful scenery framed through a car window, head north on U.S. 89A through the wooded **Oak Creek Canyon.** This is the most attractive route to Flagstaff and the Grand Canyon. Although the forest is primarily evergreen, there are enough changing colors in the fall to make the view especially glorious then. The road winds through a steep-walled canyon, and visitors crane their necks for views of the dramatic rock formations above. Oak Creek, which runs along the bottom of the canyon, is lined with tent campgrounds, fishing camps, cabins, motels, and restaurants.

Look for **Slide Rock State Park** on your left, 7 miles north of Sedona. It's a good place for a picnic and a hike back into the forest. On a hot day, you can plunge down a natural rock slide into a swimming hole—a delightful experience. (Bring an extra pair of jeans to wear on the slide.) About 3 miles farther north is the popular West Fork Trail, which follows a creek where you can cool off in summer. The only downside to this trip is the traffic and crowds, particularly on summer weekends. *Box 10358, Sedona 86339, tel. 602/ 282–3034. Admission: $3 per car Oct.–Mar., $5 per car Apr.–Sept. Open daily 8–5.*

South of Sedona, just east of Clarkdale, **Tuzigoot National Monument** is an impressive complex of ruins of the Sinagua Indians, who lived on this land overlooking the Verde Valley from about AD 1125 through 1400. Items used for food preparation, as well as jewelry, weapons, and farming tools excavated from the site, are displayed in the visitor center, where there is also a reconstructed room from the pueblo. *Box 68, Clarkdale 86324, tel. 602/634–5564. Admission: $2 adults, children under 17 and senior citizens free. Open Memorial Day–Labor Day, daily 8–7; Labor Day–Feb., daily 8–5; Mar.–May, daily 8–6 (call ahead in Apr. and*

May to check; the schedule is affected by the Easter holidays).

❸ **Clarkdale** draws train buffs who catch the **Verde River Canyon Excursion Train** just east of the business district, for a 22-mile ride that ends up in Perkinsville. There's food and beverage service on board. A highlight of the trip is a 680-foot-long stone tunnel barely 1 foot wider than the train itself. For an additional fee you can ride the comfy, living-room–like club car, snacks included. Every Saturday, musical entertainment along the banks of the Verde River is part of the ride. *Arizona Central Railroad, Box 103, Clarkdale 86324, tel. 602/639–0010. Round-trip rides: $32.95 adults, $29.95 senior citizens, $17.95 children under 12. Club car: $49.95. Trains depart June–Mar., Wed.– Sun.; Apr.–May, Wed.–Mon. Call for times.*

❹ From Clarkdale, continue on U.S. 89A to **Jerome,** once known as the Billion Dollar Copper Camp. After the last mines closed in 1953, a booming population of 15,000 dwindled to a low of 50 determined souls. The town saw a slight revival during the mid-1960s, when hippies moved in and turned it into a funky art colony of sorts. Today some 450 people reside here full-time, but the tourists keep the place alive. Worth a visit for its historic interest as well as for its scenery, Jerome is literally built into the side of Cleopatra Hill, and from here you can see Sedona's red rocks, Flagstaff's San Francisco Peaks, and even eastern Arizona's Mogollon Rim country (*see* Chapter 6).

Jerome sits about a mile above sea level, but structures within town vary in elevation by up to 1,500 feet, depending on whether they're perched on Cleopatra Hill or at its foot. Blasting at the mines regularly shook buildings off their foundations, and the town's jail slid across a road and down a hillside, where it can still be seen today. That's not all that was unsteady about Jerome. In 1903, a reporter from a New York newspaper called Jerome "the wickedest town in America" because of its abundance of drinking and gaming establishments; 1880 town records list 24 saloons. Whether due to divine retribution or drunken accidents, the town was burned down several times—some historians say five, others two or three.

Of the three mining museums in town, the most comprehensive is at **Jerome State Historic Park;** just south of town, signs on U.S. 89A will direct you to the turnoff for the park. The museum occupies the mansion of Jerome's mining king, Dr. James "Rawhide Jimmy" Douglas, Jr., who purchased Little Daisy Mine in 1912; the house was built in 1917 at the height of Little Daisy's success. On the grounds you'll see some of the tools and heavy equipment used to grind ore. A video details the history of Jerome; the bawdy parts have been left out, but you can read between the lines for some sense of the town's wild mining days. Views from the picnic grounds around the mansion are spectacular. *State Park*

Rd., tel. 602/634–5381. Admission: $2 adults, $1 children 12–17, under 12 free. Open daily 8–5.

The other worthwhile mining museum, **The Mine Museum,** is downtown. Staffed by the Jerome Historical Society, the museum's collection of mining stock certificates alone is worth the (small) price of admission—the amount of money that changed hands in this town 100 years ago boggles the mind. *Main St., tel. 602/634–5477. Admission: 50¢. Open daily 9–4:30.*

Jerome, like Sedona on a smaller scale, is a scenic shopper's haven. Chic, artsy boutiques and galleries carrying local and imported goods line the streets in the tiny downtown area (*see* Shopping, *below*).

For those who plan to continue from Jerome to Prescott (*see* Chapter 6), the 34-mile drive southwest down a mountainous section of U.S. 89A is gorgeous (if somewhat harrowing in bad weather), filled with twists and turns through the Prescott National Forest.

Flagstaff and Environs

Few visitors slow down long enough to explore Flagstaff, a town of 42,000, known locally as "Flag"; most stop only to spend the night at one of the town's many motels before making the last leg of the trip to the Grand Canyon, 80 miles north. But the city, set against a lovely backdrop of pine forests and the snowcapped San Francisco Peaks, retains a frontier flavor downtown and is home to several attractions, including the excellent Museum of Northern Arizona, the Riordan mansion, and the Lowell Observatory. Festivals celebrating the summer season often fill Flagstaff's streets with parades and its sidewalks with Native American art exhibits and crafts sales.

Flagstaff has more fast-food outlets per permanent resident than most cities do, no doubt because of the incredible demand for it: Two major interstate highways crisscross the town; thousands of tourists drive through on the way to the Grand Canyon; thousands of students attending Northern Arizona University reside here; and many Native Americans come from nearby reservations. The city is also packed with motels, although there are no major hotels or resorts. Traffic to the Grand Canyon is heavy all year, but in the summertime it skyrockets, increasing the number of overnight visitors. During that time of year, the streets are filled with Phoenix residents seeking relief from the desert heat.

Phoenicians also come to Flagstaff in winter to ski at the Arizona Snowbowl, a small ski resort about 15 miles northeast of town among the San Francisco Peaks. At any time of the year, temperatures in Flagstaff are approximately 20°F cooler than in Phoenix. It's wise to reserve a room ahead of time in Flagstaff, and during the summer months, it's essential.

Central Flagstaff *Numbers in the margin correspond to points of interest on the Flagstaff map.*

Though it's now somewhat seedy, the **downtown historic district** offers a glimpse of Flagstaff in its prime, with some excellent examples of late Victorian and early Art Deco architecture. A walking-tour map of the area, prepared by ❺ the Arizona Historical Society, is available at the **Visitors Center** (*see* Important Addresses and Numbers, *above*), which is an excellent place to begin the tour. Highlights include the adjacent Tudor Revival–style Santa Fe Depot, the Monte Vista Hotel (*see* Lodging, *below*), and the gabled-roof Orpheum Theatre. You may notice a lot of structures that bear the name Babbitt, after one of Flagstaff's wealthiest founding families. Former Arizona governor and current Secretary of the Interior Bruce Babbitt is just the latest member of the family to wield power and influence.

❻ To reach **Lowell Observatory,** less than 2 miles from downtown, drive west on Route 66 (which resumes its former name, Santa Fe Avenue, before it merges into Mars Hill Road). This scientific institution was founded in 1894 by Boston businessman, author, and scientist Percival Lowell, who studied the planet Mars from here. His predictions of the existence of a ninth planet led to the discovery of Pluto at Lowell in 1930 by Clyde Tombaugh. V. M. Slipher's observations here between 1912 and 1920 led to the theory of the expanding universe.

Facilities for visitors are currently limited (there are no public rest rooms, for example), but they are in the process of being expanded. During the day, the staff welcomes guests and offers slide lectures and tours, including a look at the 24-inch Clark telescope. Hours change every month, so call when you're in town, or when you know on what date you plan to visit. There are several interactive exhibits (simple, but interesting) for children, who will especially enjoy the Pluto Walk, a scaled-down version of our solar system that is designed for exploring.

On different evenings each month except January, weather permitting, the public is invited to peer through the telescope. The greatest number of viewings are offered from June through August; again, call ahead for a schedule. The observatory dome is open and unheated—any change in temperature would affect the telescope lens—so dress for an outdoor rather than an indoor activity. *1400 W. Mars Hill Rd., tel. 602/774–2096. Admission: suggested donations $1 per individual, $3 per family. Hours vary, so call ahead.*

A unique artifact of Flagstaff's logging heyday, the ❼ **Riordan mansion,** near Northern Arizona University, is a must-see. Built in 1904 for Michael and Timothy Riordan,

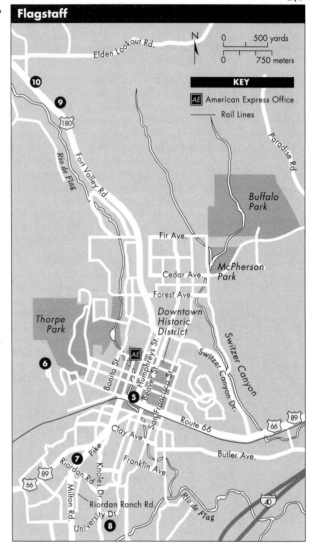

lumber baron brothers who married two sisters, the 13,300-square-foot, 40-room log-and-stone structure was designed by Charles Whittlesley, who was also responsible for the El Tovar Hotel at the Grand Canyon. The house contains a good deal of furniture by Gustav Stickley, father of the American Arts and Crafts design movement. Fascinating interior details abound; windows in the game room, for example, are transparent photo plates of the Grand Canyon. Everything on display—from books to family photos and clothes—is original to the house, half of which was occupied by members of the family until 1986. Now the centerpiece of Riordan Historical State Park, the mansion may be explored only on a guided tour. Family tales of a resident ghost make the special evening tours during Halloween week very popular; they're limited to groups of 20, so book at least a month in advance if you want to be spooked. *1300 Riordan Ranch Rd., tel. 602/779–4395. Admission: $3 adults, $2 children 12–17, 11 and under free. Park open mid-May–mid-Sept. daily 8–5, with house tours at 9, 10, 11, 2, 3, and 4; mid-Sept.–mid-May daily 12:30–5, with tours at 1, 2, 3, and 4.*

8 Riordan State Park lies near **Northern Arizona University.** Go two blocks south on Milton Road, then make a left onto University Drive. After about a half-mile, turn right on San Francisco Street and continue to the university's **observatory.** The observatory and 24-inch telescope were built in 1952 by Dr. Arthur Adel, who had been a scientist at Lowell Observatory until he joined the college faculty as a professor of mathematics. His work on infrared astronomy pioneered research into molecules that absorb light passing through Earth's atmosphere. Today's studies of our planet's shrinking ozone layer rely on some of Dr. Adel's early work. Visitors to the observatory—which houses one of the largest telescopes that the public is allowed to move and manipulate—are usually hosted by friendly students and faculty members of the university's Department of Physics and Astronomy.

Public viewings take place every clear Thursday night from 7:30 PM to 10 PM. Tours for individuals and small groups can be arranged any day except Thursday by calling at least 24 hours in advance. The staff requests a minimum of a week's notice for large tours. *Northern Arizona Campus Observatory, c/o Dept. of Physics and Astronomy, S. San Francisco St., tel. 602/523–7170. Admission free.*

Flagstaff Museums and the Arizona Snowbowl In a wooded residential section at the northwest end of town, the Pioneer Historical Museum, Coconino Center for the Arts, and the Museum of Northern Arizona give visitors an introduction to the natural and cultural history of the area. They're all on the way to the Arizona Snowbowl, which is worth visiting even in the summertime, when a ski lift to the top of the San Francisco Peaks affords marvelous views of the area.

From downtown, drive north on Humphreys Street, which turns into U.S. 180 after veering a block to the left. Once you're on U.S. 180, you'll soon see a large brown sign on the right-hand side of the road for the Pioneer Historical Museum and the Coconino Center for the Arts.

The first building as you enter the Fort Valley Park complex **9** is the **Pioneer Historical Museum,** operated by the Arizona Historical Society in a volcanic rock building constructed in 1908—Coconino's County's first hospital for the poor. You can still see one of the (depressingly small) patients' rooms, an old iron lung, and a reconstructed doctor's office, but most of the displays touch on more cheerful aspects of Flagstaff history—for example, road signs and children's toys. The museum hosts a folk-crafts festival on the Fourth of July, where you can watch traditional tradespeople, such as blacksmiths, weavers, spinners, quilters, and candle makers, at work. Their crafts, and those of other local artisans, are sold in the museum's gift shop, a tiny space filled with teddy bears, dolls, hand-dipped candles, and hand-stitched quilts. *2340 N. Fort Valley Rd., tel. 602/774–6272. Suggested donation: $1 per individual, $3 per family. Open Mon.–Sat. 9–5.*

Walk a few hundred feet up a gentle hill to reach the **Coconino Center for the Arts,** a nonprofit community center that puts on two major annual arts and crafts festivals (*see* the Arts and Nightlife, *below*) and hosts exhibits, performing arts events, and educational programs throughout the year. A gallery features the work of local artists, from photographers to sculptors and lithographers, on a rotating basis; write or phone for a calendar of events. Warning: The gift shop, filled with handcrafted jewelry, pottery, and posters by featured artists, can be detrimental to your pocketbook. All proceeds go to the center, though, so you're shopping for a worthy cause—and there's no tax on your purchases. *2300 N. Fort Valley Rd., Box 296, Flagstaff 86002, tel. 602/779–6921. Admission free. Open Apr.–Oct., Tues.–Sun. 10–5; Nov.–Mar., Tues.–Sat. 10–5. Closed Easter, Thanksgiving, and Dec. 24–Jan. 6.*

When you leave the complex, turn right out of the parking lot and drive 1 mile northwest on U.S. 180; on your left you'll see the **Museum of Northern Arizona,** a large stone building shaded with trees. Founded in 1928, the museum is now respected worldwide for its research and for its collections centering on the natural and cultural history of the Colorado Plateau; only 1% of its vast holdings on the archaeology, ethnology, geology, biology, and fine arts of the region is on display at any given time. Among the permanent exhibitions are an extensive collection of Navajo rugs as well as an authentic Hopi kiva (men's ceremonial chamber). Every summer, the museum hosts exhibits and sales by Native American artists, whose wares are also sold in the museum gift shop (*see* The Arts in Arts and Nightlife, *below*). Two interesting outdoor features are a life-zone exhibit, which shows the changing vegetation in the area from the bottom of the Grand Canyon to the highest peak in Flagstaff (the equivalent of a trip from Mexico to Canada), and a nature trail that heads down across a small stream into a canyon and up into an aspen grove.

Two new galleries—one devoted to the biology and the other to the geology of the area—opened in 1992. The latter includes a cast of the dilophosaurus; this medium-size carnivorous dinosaur, unique to northern Arizona, roamed the area back when much of it was swampland.

The museum is not particularly child-oriented, but both of the new galleries include some hands-on displays. Docent-led tours are available for individuals or groups, but appointments must be made at least two weeks in advance. In addition, the museum's education department sponsors excellent tours of the area and some as far away as New Mexico and California (*see* Guided Tours *in* Essential Information, *above*). *3001 N. Valley Rd., tel. 602/774–5211. Admission: $4 adults, $3 senior citizens over 55, $2 children and students under 21. Open daily 9–5. Closed Thanksgiving, Christmas, and New Year's Day.*

Five miles farther along the same road is the turnoff for the **Arizona Snowbowl.** The Fort Valley Lodge to the right is a good place to stop for groceries and clean rest rooms, as well as for information about skiing and other recreational opportunities at the Snowbowl; it's open in the daytime only. If there's a crowd visiting the ski area or a recent heavy snow that makes travel difficult, park here and ride the shuttle to the top; it runs continuously and costs $3 per person round-trip.

After you leave U.S. 180, it's another 7 paved miles on Snowbowl Road to the **Arizona Snowbowl Skyride** (tel. 602/779–1951), which takes you through the Coconino National Forest to a height of 11,500 feet. From this vantage point, you can see up to 70 miles; views include the North Rim of the Grand Canyon. The Hart Prairie and Agassiz lodges closer to the lifts offer parking, food, and rest rooms year-round. *Skyride tickets: $7 adults, $5 senior citizens age 65 and older, $3.50 children 6–12, free for children 5 and under. Group discounts are available. The ride, which takes 25 minutes each way, operates Memorial Day weekend–mid-October, weekends and holidays 10–4. Operating hours and prices may change, so call before you go.*

There is plenty of **hiking** here in Arizona's alpine tundra, where more than 80 species of plants grow on the upper elevations of the San Francisco Peaks. The habitat is fragile, so hikers are asked to stay on established trails (and there are lots of them). The Humphreys Peak Trail is 9 miles round-trip, with a vertical climb of 3,133 feet to the summit of Arizona's highest mountain (12,633 feet). Those who don't want a long hike will be well rewarded if they do just the first mile of the 8-mile-long Kachina Trail; completely flat, this route is surrounded by huge stands of aspen and offers fantastic vistas. It's particularly worthwhile in fall, when the changing leaves paint the landscape shades of yellow, russet, and amber. All trails are well marked and maintained by the **Coconino National Forest** (tel. 602/556–7400). The altitude here will make even the hardiest hikers breathe a little harder, so individuals with cardiac or respiratory problems should be cautious of overexertion.

In winter the Arizona Snowbowl offers an average of 250 inches of snow and 35 trails of varying difficulty (8 novice,

17 intermediate, and 10 advanced) for **skiing.** Enthusiasts who favor the challenging slopes of Colorado's Rockies might find the Snowbowl a bit disappointing, but it's just fine for skiers of beginning or moderate ability. Senior citizens age 65 years and older pay only $5, and children 7 and younger ski for free; all-day lift tickets for adults run $29. Half-day discounts are available, and group-lesson packages (including two hours of instruction, an all-day lift ticket, and equipment rental) are a good buy at $42. Many Flagstaff motels offer ski packages, including transportation to the Snowbowl. Write or call the Arizona Snowbowl Ski Area (Box 2430, Flagstaff 86003, tel. 602/779–1951) for more information. For the current snow report, phone 602/779–4577.

East of Flagstaff   *Numbers in the margin correspond to points of interest on the North-Central Arizona map.*

The area east of Flagstaff is often overlooked by visitors to the region because there's little, regardless of beauty or historical significance, that can compete with the Grand Canyon, west of Flagstaff. But if you have any extra time, traveling east has its unique rewards, including Walnut Canyon, once home to thousands of Sinagua Indians; Grand Falls, a part-time waterfall that flows only during the spring; and the 4,100-foot-wide Meteor Crater, created more than 49,000 years ago. If you don't have enough time to do everything, opt for taking the quick drive to Walnut Canyon—only about 15 minutes out of town—and staying in this lovely spot for as long as you can; for many, Meteor Crater is worth neither the extra hour or so (round-trip) spent crossing a desolate landscape nor the high entrance fee.

⓬ **Walnut Canyon National Monument** is 7½ miles east of Flagstaff (exit 204 off I–40), then 3 miles south. Towering Douglas firs, piñon pines, and alligator juniper trees keep the area green—hundreds of shades of green—year-round; the canyon is especially beautiful on a snowy winter day.

The Sinagua Indians (possibly ancestors of today's Pueblo Indians) lived and farmed the area starting in approximately AD 800. They vanished around 1250; archaeologists have speculated that they left because of a drought—the name Sinagua means "without water"—or because invaders chased them out. The canyon was unoccupied until 1883, when more than 300 cliff dwellings abandoned by the Sinagua were discovered by Mormon settlers from Utah, who regarded the ruins as curiosities but nothing more.

A national monument, maintained by the National Park Service, was established here in 1915. Today an informative visitor center is staffed by guides who conduct tours daily during the summer and on weekends in the winter. You can see many of the cliff dwellings at close range—a number of them in near-perfect condition—by descending 185 feet by way of the mile-long stepped Island Trail, which starts at the visitor center. The dwellings are in such good condition because visitors are restricted from entering them; they were also carefully constructed under the protection of overhanging cliffs, and the weather here is dry and temperate. The Island Trail, which closes one hour before the park closes, takes about an hour to complete. Those with health problems should opt for the easier Rim Trail (a half-mile route that most people can complete in about a half-hour), which takes visitors past several overlooks from which the dwellings can be viewed, as well as an excavated and reconstructed pit house.

No food or drinks are sold here (there are water fountains and rest rooms), but attractive picnic areas dot the grounds and line the road leading to the park. Although no fires are permitted, gas stoves are allowed in picnic areas. A store at the visitor center carries a nice range of books about the region's history and natural attractions. *Walnut Canyon Rd., tel. 602/526–3367. Admission: $2 per person entering by bus or bicycle, $4 per car. Open Labor Day–Memorial Day, daily 7–6; off-season, daily 8–5.*

⓭ To reach **Meteor Crater** from Walnut Canyon, drive about 33 miles farther east on I–40, get off at Exit 233, then go 6 miles south on Meteor Crater Road. This natural phenomenon, set in a privately owned and run park, is impressive if for no other reason than its sheer size. A hole in the ground 600 feet deep, nearly a mile across, and more than 3 miles in circumference, Meteor Crater is large enough to accommodate the Washington Monument or 20 football fields. It was created when a meteorite came hurtling through space at a speed of 43,000 miles per hour and crashed here some 49,000 years ago. The area looks so much like the surface of the moon that NASA made it one of the official training sites for the *Apollo* astronauts.

Visitors can't descend into the crater because of the efforts of its owners to maintain its present excellent condition—scientists consider this to be the best-preserved crater on Earth—but a 3-mile rim trail gives visitors a bird's-eye view of the hole. Two short, rather corny films, which play every half-hour, detail the history of the crater and of astronaut training here. A small snack bar sells soft drinks, coffee, and sandwiches. Rock hounds will enjoy the Lapidary Shop, filled with raw specimens from the area as well as with jewelry made from native stones. *Meteor Crater Rd., 40 mi east of Flagstaff, tel. 602/289–2362. For information, write or call administrative offices, 603 N. Beaver St., Suite C, Flagstaff 86001, tel. 602/774–8350. Admission: $7 adults, $6 senior citizens 65 and over, $4 students, $2 children 13–17, $1 children 6–12, children 5 and under free. Open May 16–Sept. 14, daily 6–6; Sept. 15–May 15, daily 8–5.*

⑭ If you're touring this area in March or April, **Grand Falls** is a worthwhile detour on your way back to Flagstaff. Head toward town on I–40 and take the Winona exit (number 211), which leads to Camp Townsend–Winona Road. Turn right and drive 2 miles, then turn right again onto Leupp Road. Signs will direct you to Grand Falls (you'll turn left onto 10 miles of dirt road). You're on Navajo land here, so tribal laws apply. For example, if you have an accident or hit any of the many free-roaming livestock, you'll be tried in a tribal court. Consuming or even possessing alcohol on Indian territory is prohibited. (*See* Chapter 1, Essential Information, and Chapter 4, The Northeast, for details on reservation regulations.)

The muddy 180-foot waterfall generally slows to a drip during the rest of the year, but in springtime, when the snow melts, there is often a raging cascade, impressive for its sheer power. The falls were created about 100,000 years ago by a lava flow from Merriam Crater, 10 miles southwest; today they plunge over a cliff into the Little Colorado River below. At peak strength, the roar of the rushing water greets you before you actually see the torrent. This is not a well-touristed site; no food or drinks are sold here. Dogs must be kept on a leash to prevent them from disturbing the area's livestock.

To return to Flagstaff, drive back to I–40, which is about 7 miles east of town.

San Francisco Volcanic Field North of Flagstaff, the San Francisco Volcanic Field encompasses 2,000 square miles of fascinating geological phenomena—the San Francisco Peaks themselves, some of which soar to almost 13,000 feet; ancient volcanoes; cinder cones; and valleys carved by water and ice—as well as some of the most extensive Indian ruins in the Southwest. If you have any time at all, don't miss Sunset Crater and Wupatki; these national monuments are not only extremely interesting but can be explored in relative solitude during a large part of the year. The area is short on services, so fill up on gas and consider bringing along a picnic; there are plenty of lovely spots for lunch along the way. A good source for hiking and camping information in this area is the Peaks Ranger Station (5075 N. U.S. 89, tel. 602/526–0866).

⑮ To get to **Sunset Crater Volcano National Monument,** so designated in 1930, take Santa Fe Avenue east of town to U.S. 89, and drive north for about 20 miles. Turn right onto the road marked Sunset Crater—it's another 2 miles from here to the visitor center.

Sunset Crater, a cinder cone that rises some 1,000 feet into the air, was an active volcano 900 years ago. The final eruption contained iron and sulfur, which gives the rim of the crater its glow and thus its name, Sunset. You can walk around the base, but you can't descend into the huge but fragile cone. If you take the Lava Flow Trail, a half-hour, mile-long self-guided walk, you'll have a good view of the evidence of the volcano's fiery power: lava formations and holes in the rock where volcanic gases vented to the surface. Three smaller cones to the southeast were formed at the same time, and along the same fissure, as Sunset Crater.

If you're interested in hiking a volcano, head to **Lenox Crater,** about a mile east of the Sunset Crater visitor center. It's 280 feet to the top of the cinder cone. Wear closed, sturdy shoes if you plan to do this; the cinder is soft and crumbly, without vegetation.

From **O'Leary Peak,** 5 miles from the visitor center on Forest Route 545A (an unpaved but decent road), there are some great views of the San Francisco Peaks, the Painted Desert, and beyond.

The Sunset Crater visitor center is staffed by rangers who are knowledgeable about the area, as well as about volcanoes and geology in general. Films of Hawaii's active Kilauea volcano help visitors imagine the former fury of this site. Sunset Crater is open daily 8–5, and entry fees are $4 per car, which includes admission into Wupatki National Monument (*see below*). For more information, write or call the National Park Service business office (2717 N. Steves Blvd., Suite 3, Flagstaff 86004, tel. 602/556–7042).

Drive 20 miles north of the Sunset Crater visitor center
16 along AZ 545 to get to the entrance of **Wupatki National Monument.** En route, parts of the Painted Desert are visible in the distance; the immediately surrounding landscape is starkly beautiful, without much vegetation. Exhibits at the site's visitor center show how the area's earliest inhabitants lived—including examples of their pottery, baskets, and farm implements—and how the community evolved. During the summer months, rangers give interpretive lectures on the history of the region.

Some 2,700 identified sites contain archaeological evidence of Native American settlement in this area. Families from the Sinagua, Anasazi, and perhaps other cultures are believed to have lived together in harmony here, farming and trading with one another and with others who passed through their "city." The eruption of Sunset Crater, 20 miles away, may have caused migration to this area—and may have disrupted the settlement more than once around 1064. The earliest inhabitants are believed to have settled here around AD 600, and some anthropologists think the last of them had abandoned the land by about AD 1300 because of a drought; others conjecture that poor soil conservation or social unrest may have led to the desertion of the pueblo.

The site for which the national monument was named, the **Wupatki,** originally three stories high, was built above a system of unexplored natural caves. The structure had almost 100 rooms and a large, open ball court, which was probably the site of religious ceremonies. Next to the ball court is a blowhole, a geologic phenomenon in which air is forced upward by underground pressure; scientists speculate that early inhabitants may have attached some spiritual significance to the many blowholes found in the region.

Although there are extensive, easily viewed remnants of Native American settlements at Wupatki National Monument, most of them are closed to the casual visitor. Many are being studied by professional archaeologists (the park service can provide information on these research projects). Permits are available from the park service for limited access beyond the open areas, but rules regarding entering closed sites are strictly enforced.

If you are interested in an in-depth tour of the area, consider taking a ranger-led overnight hike to the **Crack-in-the-Rock Ruin.** The 14-mile trek (round-trip) covers areas marked by ancient petroglyphs and dotted with well-preserved ruins. The cost is $10; anyone who is interested should contact the rangers at the Wupatki National Monument (HC 33, Box 444A, Flagstaff 86004, tel. 602/556–7040) for details. There are a limited number of trips, conducted in April and October; it's best to call in February and August if you'd like to take part in the lottery for one of the 100 available places on these hikes.

The visitor center is open daily 8–5; entry fee to the monument is $4 per car, $2 to enter on foot or by nonmotorized vehicle. As noted earlier, one admission price gets you into both Wupatki and Sunset Crater. For more information, contact the business office at the National Park Service (*see* Sunset Crater, *above*).

The archaeological site in the park closest to U.S. 89 (the most direct route back to Flagstaff) is the **Citadel Ruin,** a pueblo that sits on a knoll above a limestone sink. It's 9 miles northwest of the visitor center on the main loop road. Between the Wupatki and Citadel ruins, the **Doney cinder hole** affords 360° views of the Painted Desert and the San Francisco Volcanic Fields. It's a perfect spot for a sunset picnic.

What to See and Do with Children

Small children should enjoy the **Grand Canyon Deer Farm,** 25 miles west of Flagstaff on I–40, at Exit 171 (8 miles east of Williams). Visitors can pet and feed the deer, including the tiny fawns born every June and July. There are also pygmy goats, llamas, and other animals to pet. *100 Deer Farm Rd., Williams 86046, tel. 602/635–4073. Admission: $4.95 adults, $3.50 senior citizens over 62, $2.75 children 3–13, children under 3 free. Open Mar.–May, daily 9 AM–dusk; June–Aug., daily 8 AM–dusk; Sept.–Oct., daily 9 AM–dusk; Nov.–Feb., daily 10–5 if the weather is good.*

Anglers young and old will enjoy the sure catch at the **Rainbow Trout Farm.** For $1 you'll get a cane pole with a hook and bait. There's a charge for every fish you catch: $3 for anything under 10 inches, $3.50 for 10–13-inchers, and another 50¢ an inch for everything bigger. The real bargain is that the staff will clean your fish for 50¢ each and pack them in ice for you. *3 mi north of Sedona on U.S. 89A, tel. 602/ 282–3379. Open weekdays 9–5, weekends 8–6; summer, daily 8–7, weather permitting.*

Youngsters will love the plunge down the **natural rock slide** into the water at Slide Rock State Park in Oak Creek Canyon (*see* Sedona and Environs, *above*).

School-age children will be impressed by **Meteor Crater** (*see* Flagstaff and Environs, *above*). All ages enjoy **Jeep tours** in Sedona (*see* Special-Interest Tours in Essential Information, *above*). The **train from Clarkdale** (*see* Sedona and Environs, *above*) also keeps children entertained.

Shopping

Flagstaff

There aren't as many interesting shops in Flagstaff as there are in Sedona, but a few places are worth a browse, especially if you like antiques and vintage clothing. **The Carriage House** (413 N. San Francisco St., tel. 602/774–1337) is a collection of 19 antiques shops featuring old clothes, furniture, fine china, and jewelry. The **Old Highway Trading Post** (698 E. Rte. 66, tel. 602/774–0035) also brings together a number of purveyors of advertising art, jewelry, clothing, and other collectibles. Rhoda Vihel's **Pine Country Quilts** (1 W. Riordan Rd., tel. 602/779–2194) is packed with fabrics, notions, and antique quilts, and there is likely to be a lesson going on in the shop when you visit.

Old Town Gallery (2 W. Rte. 66, tel. 602/774–7770), owned by anthropologist Bruce Hudgens, features fine art and Native American jewelry. **Crystal Magic** (5 N. San Francisco St., tel. 602/779–2528) carries New Age books, records, tapes, and crystals. The **Coconino Arts Center** gift shop (*see* Flagstaff Museums and the Arizona Snowbowl, *above*) carries high-quality art posters and crafts.

Most shops are downtown; the **Flagstaff Mall** (4650 N. U.S. 89, tel. 602/526–4827) is just east of town off Exit 201 of I–40. Small by most standards, this mall has the most department and specialty stores in the area, including Dillards, Sears, and J C Penney. It's a good place for travelers who need camping gear, car-repair items, or warm clothing to cope with the area's cool nights.

Jerome

Shoppers in Jerome will find a variety of boutiques in houses perched precariously on the side of Cleopatra Hill. The town has its share of art galleries, but they're likely to be a bit more on the funky side than the ones you'll find in Sedona. An exception is the **Anderson-Mandette Art Studios** (Old Mingus High School, Bldg. C, tel. 602/634-3438). Robin Anderson and Margo Mandette made the building their workplace in 1978; at almost 20,000 square feet, it is considered by many to be the largest private art studio and gallery in the United States. The gallery is open daily 11–6; guided tours are available on request.

Shopping is easy in Jerome; all you need to do is stroll up and down Main Street. Your eyes may begin to glaze over after browsing one boutique after another with tasteful—and generally pricey—southwestern goods. At the bottom of Main, **Aurum** (tel. 602/634-3330) carries lovely imported and locally made jewelry, much of it silver. Next door, you'll be drawn in by the bright patterns and attractively styled women's clothing of **Designs on You** (tel. 602/634-7879). Farther up the hill, **Sky Fire** (tel. 602/634-8081) has two floors of items to adorn your person and your house, ranging from wrapping paper and confetti to a $1,000 fabric bench in the shape of an iguana. **Nellie Bly** (tel. 602/634-0255) offers a wide range of walking sticks in addition to a good selection of jewelry. Around the corner, the **Gift Shop of Jerome** (Jerome Ave., tel. 602/634-5105) is a good source for moccasins, hats, pottery, minerals, and other Jerome souvenirs ranging from tacky (plastic-encased scorpion or tarantula paperweights) to collectible.

Sedona

See Exploring Sedona, *above.*

Sports and the Outdoors

Camping   There are more than 50 campgrounds in the Flagstaff, Sedona, and Jerome areas. The best way to learn about them is to consult the *Arizona Camping and Campgrounds Guide*, available from the **Arizona Office of Tourism** (*see* Chapter 1, Essential Information).

In **Coconino National Forest** near Flagstaff (ranger's tel. 602/556-7400), the campgrounds near Mormon Lake and Lake Mary—including Pinegrove, Lakeview, Forked Pine, Double Springs, and Dairy Springs—are popular to the point of overcrowding in summer.

Campgrounds close to **Sedona** often fill up in the summertime, especially those along Oak Creek in Oak Creek Canyon; two good places to try are Manzanita and Banjo Bill (ranger's tel. 602/282-4119).

Jerome's campgrounds are generally less crowded. Try Jerome State Historic Park (tel. 602/624–5381) or Mingus Mountain and Potato Patch (tel. 602/634–8851).

If you're camping in the wintertime, remember that this area gets quite cold, with frequent snowstorms. In summertime, night temperatures can dip to the 40s, while daytime temperatures can reach 90°F.

Golf   In addition to the many private clubs in the Flagstaff–Sedona area, golfers will find semiprivate courses, which accept a limited number of nonmembers, as well as public courses. Among the recommended ones in the **Flagstaff** vicinity are the Fairfield Flagstaff resort's **Elden Hills Golf Club** (2380 N. Oakmont Dr., Flagstaff, 602/527–7999), a public course, and **Pinewood Country Club** (Box 584, Munds Park, tel. 602/286–1110), which is semiprivate. In the **Sedona** area, the **Oak Creek Country Club** (690 Bell Rock Blvd., Sedona, tel. 602/284–1660) is a good semiprivate option. Contact the **Arizona Golf Association** (11801 N. Tatum Blvd., Phoenix 85028, tel. 602/953–5990) for more information.

Hiking   Hikers will find an abundance of trails all across the region. In **Sedona,** contact the **Sedona Ranger District** office (250 Brewer Rd., tel. 602/282–4119) for detailed hiking maps. Just **north of Flagstaff,** but still in town, the **Peaks Ranger Station** (5075 N. U.S. 89, tel. 602/526–0866) also has excellent hiking and recreational guides. Around Mormon Lake, **south of Flagstaff,** the **Happy Jack Ranger Station** (Forest Hwy. 3, Happy Jack, tel. 602/527–7371) provides information about treks in the area. The **Verde Ranger District** office of the **Prescott National Forest** (General Crook Trail, Camp Verde, tel. 602/567–4121) is a good resource for places to hike—as well as to fish and boat—along the Verde River. The **Coconino National Forest** north and east of Camp Verde is mapped by the **Beaver Creek Ranger District** (Forest Service Rd. 618, Rimrock, tel. 602/567–4501). (*See* Red Rock State Park and the Arizona Snowbowl in Exploring, *above,* for other hiking options.)

Horseback Riding   Spring, summer, and fall are the best times of the year to ride in this area. In **Flagstaff,** the wranglers at **Hitchin' Post Stables** (448 Lake Mary Rd., tel. 602/774–1719 or 602/774–7131) lead rides into Walnut Canyon as well as horseback or horsedrawn wagon rides with sunset barbecues. In **Sedona, Kachina Riding Stable** (5 J La., Lower Red Rock Loop Rd., West Sedona, tel. 602/282–7252) offers a package that includes an Oak Creek swim and picnic lunch. Weight limit for riders is 225 pounds.

Skiing   The ski season usually starts in mid-November and ends in mid-April. A good option for downhill skiers is the nearby **Arizona Snowbowl** (*see* Flagstaff and Environs in Exploring, *above*). Cross-country skiers can find well-groomed trails in several places around Flagstaff, among them **Flag-**

staff **Nordic Center** (15 mi northwest of town, tel. 602/774–6216); drive U.S. 180 to milepost 232, where you'll see the center. All-day trail passes cost $12 for adults; children 12 and under ski free. **Mormon Lake Ski Center** (21 mi southeast of Flagstaff by way of Lake Mary Rd., Mormon Lake, tel. 602/354–2240) also offers cross-country skiing, as does **Montezuma Nordic Ski Center** (just north of Mormon Lake, tel. 602/354–2220.

Dining and Lodging

Dining Highly recommended restaurants are indicated by a star ★.

Category	Cost*
Very Expensive	over $35
Expensive	$25–$35
Moderate	$15–$25
Inexpensive	under $15

per person, excluding drinks, service, and sales tax (6% in Flagstaff, 7% in Sedona)

Lodging Highly recommended lodgings are indicated by a star ★.

Category	Cost*
Very Expensive	over $125
Expensive	$90–$125
Moderate	$50–$90
Inexpensive	under $50

All prices are for a standard double room in high (summer) season, excluding room tax (8% in Flagstaff, 10½% in Sedona).

Flagstaff

Dining **Chez Marc Bistro.** In late 1991, the Cannes-born head chef of L'Auberge de Sedona resort headed north to set up his own restaurant in a restored mansion, built in 1911 by the influential Babbit family. In three lovely French country–style dining rooms one can enjoy such entrées as blackened ahi tuna atop pink and green lentils or roast quail with elephant garlic and lobster mushrooms. Don't expect the sophisticated service or attention to culinary detail you'd find in a major city; the salad dressing can be heavy and the French bread not very crusty. A light ski dinner ($10.95) is served between 3:30 and 5:30. *503 Humphreys St., tel. 602/774–1343. Reservations advised. Dress: casual but neat. MC, V. Closed Mon. lunch and Sun. Moderate–Expensive.*
Black Bart's Steakhouse Saloon & Old West Theater. Fans of

the Old West—or a sanitized facsimile thereof—will enjoy the atmosphere in this rustic old barnlike structure, complete with beamed ceilings and lanternlike light fixtures. Aged prime beef is grilled over an open oak fire, and the barbecue chicken is tender and flavorful. Don't be surprised to see your waiter or waitress get up onstage and belt out a couple of show tunes; when there's no live entertainment, a player piano fills the restaurant with its tinny renditions of old favorites. *2760 E. Butler Ave., tel. 602/ 779-3142. Reservations advised during summer months. Dress: informal. MC, V. Closed for lunch. Moderate.*

★ **Cottage Place.** Another unexpectedly elegant spot in a town known for hearty food and drive-through service, this restaurant is in a homey little cottage built more than 50 years ago. In addition to the cozy main dining room, there are two even more intimate ones; all are decorated in country French style. Service is friendly and professional. The menu focuses on classic Continental cuisine, with many innovative touches. Dishes range from Turkish-style braised lamb casserole with rice pilaf to grilled polenta layered with fresh vegetables and baked with Cheddar cheese. The mushrooms stuffed with herbed sausage and nuts make a wonderful starter, but dinners include both soup and salad, and you'll want to save room for the excellent desserts, made on the premises. *126 W. Cottage Ave., tel. 602/774-8431. Reservations advised. Dress: casual but neat. AE, MC, V. Dinner only, closed Mon. Moderate.*

Horsemen Lodge & Restaurant. In a ranch-style stone building decorated with hunting trophies (the furry kind that stare at you during dinner), this restaurant is very "Flagstaff," reflecting the blend of Native American and frontier cultures that shaped the area. The knotty-pine beams and huge stone fireplace make this a perfect place to spend a snowy evening. The menu features traditional American fare, prepared without pretense for the hearty appetite. *3 mi north of Flagstaff Mall on U.S. 89, tel. 602/ 526-2655. Reservations advised. Dress: casual but neat. MC, V. Dinner only, closed Sun. Moderate.*

★ **Sakura Restaurant.** The oddness of finding a good sushi bar in Flagstaff is compounded by the fact that the only other entrées available at Sakura are prepared *teppan* (Japanese grill) style. If your dining companion doesn't like raw fish, you'll be eating yours at a large table to the accompaniment of a grill chef's pyrotechnics. That said, the fish, flown in every other day from the West Coast, is excellent; the spicy sushi-style tuna salad will knock your socks off. And even if you haven't set foot in a Benihana's in years, you'll enjoy the well-seasoned, large portions of steak or seafood with vegetables being flipped around in front of you. *1175 W. Hwy. 66, tel. 602/773-9118. Reservations accepted. Dress: casual. No smoking. AE, D, DC, MC, V. Moderate.*

Buster's Restaurant. This deservedly popular restaurant, located in a strip shopping center close to the university, is built to handle volume efficiently. Students and families tend to frequent the comfortable booths and tables. The menu is varied—fresh seafood, homemade soups, salads, giant burgers, and mesquite-grilled steaks. Try the lahvosh appetizer—a giant cracker heaped with a choice of toppings ranging from smoked salmon to mushrooms—big enough for two to split as a meal. *1800 S. Milton Rd., tel. 602/774–5155. Reservations advised. Dress: informal. AE, D, DC, MC, V. Inexpensive–Moderate.*

Little America Coffee Shop. Part of the Little America motel, this is one of Flagstaff's busiest restaurants, offering both counter service and dining-room seating at tables or red vinyl booths in a room with huge wooden-and-brass chandeliers and beamed ceilings. As you might expect, the menu features American dishes, among them a tasty walnut-packed chicken salad. At breakfast the pancakes are light and fluffy, and are served with an efficiency that travelers who want to get an early start appreciate. A Sunday champagne brunch served in a ballroom down the hall offers a nice assortment of omelets, waffles, fruit, and salads. *2515 E. Butler Ave., tel. 602/779–2741. Reservations accepted. Dress: informal. AE, D, DC, MC, V. Open daily 24 hrs. Inexpensive–Moderate.*

Café Olé. Chili pepper strings, a neon cactus, and a pastel mural all add to the cheerful atmosphere at this tiny, family-run restaurant downtown, popular with local politicos and university professors. The Mexican fare includes freshly made burritos, tacos, and tostadas à la carte or in well-priced combinations. You can wash it all down with Cave Creek chili beer (but you'll need to drink something else to cool off). *119 S. San Francisco St., tel. 602/774–8272. No reservations. Dress: informal. No credit cards. Closed weekends in winter, Sun. in summer. Inexpensive.*

Kachina Restaurant. Tables in this family-style Mexican restaurant are Formica and chairs are vinyl, but the food is well prepared, spicy, and served in copious portions. The combination plates are a real bargain; you can get an enchilada, taco, and tostada with beans, rice, and a *sopapilla* (fried dough coated with powdered sugar), and coffee for $6. There are terrific breakfast specials too, and the selection of Mexican and American beers is unusually large. *2240 E. Santa Fe Ave., tel. 602/779–5790; and 522 E. Santa Fe Ave., tel. 602/779–1944. Reservations accepted. Dress: informal. MC, V. Inexpensive.*

Macy's. Students, skiers, nouveau and aging hippies, and just about everyone who likes good coffee jams into Macy's for the best cup in town. It's roasted on the premises in the huge red machine that dominates one wall of this bustling spot. Though coffee—including a variety of espressos and cappuccinos—is the focus, good fresh pastas, soups, and salads are also on offer for lunch and early dinner: Macy's opens at 6 AM every day, but the kitchen closes at 7 PM during the week. *14 S. Beaver St., tel. 602/774–2243. No reservations. Dress: informal. No smoking. No credit cards. Inexpensive.*

Lodging
Hotels and Motels

Best Western Woodlands Plaza Hotel. This upscale link in the Best Western chain is the glitziest accommodation in town—which isn't saying much in Flagstaff. The brass-and-marble lobby, although tasteful, is somewhat oddly eclectic in style. But the hotel is conveniently located near downtown and the main outbound roads; the rooms are large, comfortable, and nicely furnished in southwestern pastels; and there are two good restaurants on the premises, including Sakura (*see* Dining, *above*). *1175 W. Hwy. 66, 86001, tel. 602/773–8888 or 800/528–1234. 125 rooms with bath. Facilities: 2 restaurants, cocktail lounge, fitness center, outdoor pool, Jacuzzi, gift shop. AE, D, DC, MC, V. Expensive.*

Howard Johnson's. Just off I–40, this three-story motel is a convenient stop for travelers. It's a typical Howard Johnson's, with functional modern furniture. But the guest rooms are in an attractive ski lodge–style building, and some suites have fireplaces. A small heated indoor pool and 24-hour coffee shop are also pluses, and a courtesy van transports guests to the airport, train, or bus station. *2200 E. Butler Ave., 86004, tel. 602/779–6944 or 800/654–2000. 100 rooms with bath. Facilities: indoor pool, sauna, restaurant, lounge. AE, D, DC, MC, V. Expensive.*

★ **Little America of Flagstaff.** The biggest motel in town, with 248 rooms, this is a deservedly popular place. It's far enough from the tracks to allow visitors to sleep undisturbed as the trains roar through town; the grounds are surrounded by evergreen forests; and this is one of the few places in Flagstaff that offers room service. Rooms are surprisingly plush: All have brass chandeliers, comfortable sitting areas with French Provincial–style furniture, phones in the bathrooms, and large stereo TVs; king rooms have small refrigerators, too. *2515 E. Butler Ave. (Box 850), 86002, tel. 602/779–2741 or 800/352–4386. 248 rooms with bath. Facilities: pool, kitchenettes, restaurant, cocktail lounge, coffee shop, hiking trail, laundry service, gift shop, courtesy van, service station/garage. AE, D, DC, MC, V. Moderate.*

Monte Vista Hotel. Over the years since it was built in 1926, many Hollywood stars have stayed at this historic downtown hotel—the guest rooms come by the glamorous names attached to them honestly. The restored southwestern Deco lobby, with its shoeshine stand and curved archways, is appealing, and it'd be hard to find a less expensive lodging, or one with more character, in town. But rooms and hallways are somewhat dark, and the men buying lottery tickets and racing forms who hang out at the front desk make this an iffy choice for female travelers. *100 N. San Francisco St., 86001, tel. 602/779–6971. 45 rooms with bath. Facilities: restaurant, cocktail lounge, gift shop. AE, MC, V. Inexpensive.*

Bed-and-Breakfast

Inn at Four Ten. B&Bs are a nice alternative to the chain motels in Flagstaff, and this one offers a quiet but convenient downtown setting. Most of the accommodations in the beautifully restored 1907 structure are spacious suites, with private bath, private entrance, and minikitchen. The full breakfast might include crepes, blueberry pancakes, or quiche. There's no smoking inside. *410 N. Leroux St., 86001, tel. 602/774–0088 or 602/775–1424. 6 suites with bath, 1 disabled-accessible room with bath, 2 rooms share bath. No credit cards. Inexpensive–Moderate.*

Jerome

Dining **House of Joy.** Situated in a former bordello left over from Jerome's mining days more than 100 years ago, this now respectable restaurant attracts patrons from all over the region—perhaps as much for its legendary setting as for its food. The decor is just what you'd expect: lots of heavy, dark furniture, and even red lights. Book a table several weeks in advance as this popular restaurant is open only on weekends. Classic Continental dishes such as chicken Kiev and veal marsala are well prepared. The hot muffins are excellent, as are the desserts, which vary from one day to the next. *Hull Ave., just off Main St., tel. 602/634–5339. Reservations required. Dress: casual but neat. No credit cards; personal checks accepted. Closed weekdays; dinner only weekends. Expensive.*

Jerome Inn. A throwback to the days of Woodstock and tie-dye, this funky Main Street restaurant serves good burgers, soups, and salads. Seating is in plush booths or coffee shop–style tables, and the decor is eclectic, to say the least—old ads, silly posters, Tiffany-style lamps, and lots of plants. The 1920s-era jukebox doesn't work, but never mind; on any given day you might dine to the impromptu accompaniment of live folk music by a local duo. *Main St., tel. 602/634–5094. No reservations. Dress: casual. MC, V. Inexpensive.*

Lodging **The Cottage Inn.** Set in a 1917-era porch-fronted house off the main road (in a neighborhood known as Upper Hogback), this B&B offers beautiful views of Verde Valley. A pot of hot coffee greets early risers in a central sitting area, and a full breakfast is served upstairs in the dining room at 8 AM. The two bedrooms have a private bath and a private entrance; the sitting room, which can accommodate two on a pullout bed, is used when a party of six rents the entire house. Make your reservations in advance—the place is usually full. *747 East Ave., Box 823, 86331, tel. 602/634–0701. 2 rooms with bath. No credit cards; checks accepted. Moderate.*

Jerome Inn. The style is Victorian, and most of the rooms share baths in this creaky but characterful old hotel left over from Jerome's heyday almost 100 years ago. Reserve in advance, because it's one of only two hotels in town, and it's small (seven rooms). The bar and restaurant downstairs can be noisy, especially on Saturday night, and the walls in the rooms are thin. Try to book the Montana room—it's one of the hotel's largest, and it offers a lovely view of the mountains and downtown as well as a firm mattress. *Main St., Box 36, 86331, tel. 602/634–5094. 7 rooms, 1 with private bath. Facilities: library, restaurant. DC, MC, V. Moderate.*

Sedona–Oak Creek Canyon

Dining **L'Auberge de Sedona.** This highly regarded French restaurant has been playing musical chefs lately, but the current king of the kitchen has worked with Paul Bocuse and brings along a good deal of haute cuisine experience. One of the most romantic dining spots in Arizona, L'Auberge is done in country French style with Pierre Deux–type fabrics; ask for a table overlooking the stream, preferably in the smaller room near the entrance. The cuisine takes advantage of both classic and nouvelle styles, with light, subtle sauces, somewhat modest portions, and the freshest of ingredients. The six-course fixed-price menu ($55) might include smoked Scottish salmon, wild game consommé with duck ravioli, and filet mignon with foie gras, wild mushrooms, and truffle sauce. *L'Auberge La., tel. 602/282–1667. Reservations required. Jacket required. AE, D, DC, MC, V. Very Expensive.*

★ **Canyon Rose at Los Abrigados.** Canyon Rose brings together a lovely, intimate setting—plush booths or chairs upholstered in stylized floral patterns, rose-colored tablecloths, and dim lights from stylish brass wall sconces and chandeliers—and excellently prepared, beautifully presented food. This is the best of the Southwest, with local ingredients used in innovative combinations; the Oak Creek trout, for example, is sautéed in rolled oats and served with roasted corn relish and black-bean cakes. Service is impeccable, and the wine list is wide-ranging. *160 Portal La., tel. 602/282–ROSE. Reservations advised. Dress: casual but neat. AE, D, DC, MC, V. Expensive.*

Pietro's. A savvy entrepreneur from New York's garment district has managed to pull together the ingredients for a successful Sedona restaurant: good Northern Italian cuisine; a friendly, attentive staff, and a lively, casual atmosphere. Among the popular dishes are osso buco, veal rollatine, and duck ravioli; the eggplant and ricotta appetizer is a good starter. Such desserts as amaretto cheesecake, tiramisu, and zabaglione will destroy whatever's left of your diet. *2445 W. U.S. 89A, tel. 602/282–2525. Reservations advised. Dress: casual. AE, MC, V. Dinner only. Moderate–Expensive.*

Sedona Swiss. It's hard to go wrong with a chef who's used to pleasing Swiss embassy diplomats in Washington—and this very European restaurant doesn't. The breakfast pastry in the adjoining café is light and buttery, and such dinner specialties as *coquilles St. Jacques* (sea scallops poached in white wine) or rack of lamb with spaetzle are delicately seasoned and well prepared. The low-priced buffet lunch draws in the tour bus crowd (the restaurant sits on a street just off the main uptown drag), but in the evening the chalet-style dining room is suitably sedate. French, Italian, and German are all spoken here. *350 Jordan Rd., tel. 602/282-7959. Reservations advised. Dress: informal for breakfast and lunch, casual but neat at dinner. MC, V. No dinner Wed. Moderate–Expensive.*

★ **Heartline.** Attention to detail—fresh flowers on the tables, house salads without a leaf of iceberg, delicately spiced and endlessly refilled glasses of iced tea—makes this pretty café stand out in a town beginning to form a high Yuppie-restaurant profile. The menu is American with a south-western flavor: Dinner entrées might include oak-grilled salmon marinated in tequila and lime, or duck with pears and green peppercorns. A too-temptingly priced sampler for two allows you and your companion to try all the luscious desserts on the menu. Meals are served in a plant-filled, light wood-beamed dining room or, on fine days, on a rose-bush-lined terrace. *1610 W. U.S. 89A, tel. 602/282-0785. Reservations advised. Dress: casual but neat. AE, D, MC, V. No lunch Sun. Moderate.*

Rincon del Tlaquepaque. This lovely garden restaurant nestled in the upscale Spanish-style Tlaquepaque mall features Sonoran Mexican food and some Native American–inspired items such as Navajo tacos and pizzas. Towering sycamores shade the outdoor patio, where diners can watch shoppers stroll through the flower-filled and stone-sidewalked shopping area. Try the margaritas and *chimichangas*, deep-fried burritos filled with seasoned beef or chicken. *Tlaquepaque Arts and Crafts Village, AZ 179 at the bridge, tel. 602/282-4648. Reservations advised. Dress: informal. AE, MC, V. Closed Mon. Moderate.*

Cups. This fun and funky West Sedona café serves the best coffee and biscotti in town. There's probably not a matching piece of furniture in the three rooms where New Agers gather for freshly baked pastry in the morning, pasta at lunch, and poetry and live music in the evening. *1670 W. U.S. 89A, tel. 602/282-2531. No reservations. Dress: informal. MC, V. Inexpensive.*

Mandarin House. Its name notwithstanding, the Mandarin House serves everything from standard Cantonese to Szechuan fare, with dishes ranging from the exotic (shark fin salad) to the old standbys (egg foo young). Well-priced lunch specials include crispy egg rolls made on the premises. Dark green tablecloths, carved chairs, and dark wood furnishings lend this restaurant, just down the road from the Oak Creek Factory Stores, a certain elegance. *6486 Hwy. 179, Suite 114, tel. 602/284-9088. Reservations accepted but not required. Dress: casual. AE, MC, V. Inexpensive.*

Lodging **Enchantment Resort.** Designed as a tennis resort, En-
★ chantment has excellent sports facilities, but it's the stunning setting of Boynton Canyon that makes it unique. The

rooms, decorated in vibrant southwestern patterns, are set in 56 pueblo-style *casitas;* all have dazzling views, and many offer fireplaces and kitchenettes. Fresh-squeezed orange juice and a newspaper are delivered to the room each morning, and an upscale restaurant serves fine Continental cuisine. One drawback: Although flashlights are provided, it's difficult to find one's way around the largely unlit premises at night; less-than-intrepid guests can call the front desk for golf cart transport. *525 Boynton Canyon Rd., 86336, tel. 602/282–2900 or 800/826–4180. 162 rooms with bath. Facilities: 6 outdoor pools, 12 tennis courts, 6-hole golf course, fitness center, health center, aerobics, croquet, children's programs, guided hikes, bicycling, kitchenettes, restaurant, lounge, gift shop. AE, D, DC, MC, V. Very Expensive.*

Garland's Oak Creek Lodge. In the heart of Oak Creek Canyon, this lodge was built in the 1930s and bought by its current owners, Gary and Mary Garland, in the 1960s. Fifteen comfortably furnished cabins, some including fireplaces and some pullout beds for extra guests, share 17 acres of beautiful land (at an elevation of 5,000 feet) with an organic apple orchard. Accommodations look out over the canyon itself or the rugged cliffs surrounding it. The lodge is operated on a modified American plan, with excellent, copious breakfasts and dinners included in the room price. Garland's is usually booked solid months in advance–it's closed from November through April–but it's worth a phone call to check. *U.S. 89A, 8 mi north of Sedona (Box 152), 86336, tel. 602/282–3343. 15 cabins with bath. Facilities: restaurant, volleyball court, croquet, tennis court, swimming hole. MC, V. Very Expensive.*

★ **L'Auberge de Sedona Resort.** This resort consists of a central building and—the major attraction—a number of sweet, secluded cabins in a wooded setting along a stream. Phoenix couples flock to those romantic, country French hideaways and dine in the first-class French restaurant (*see* Dining, *above*). There's a small heated pool for summertime swimming. *L'Auberge La. (Box B), 86336, tel. 602/282–1661 or 800/272–6777. 96 rooms, 34 cottages, all with bath. Facilities: 2 restaurants, gift shop, pool, spa.AE, D, DC, MC, V. Very Expensive.*

★ **Los Abrigados.** This is one of those "I-would-happily-move-out-of-my-home-and-live-here" resorts—and indeed, some of the lovely, fully equipped units at Los Abrigados are available on a time-share basis. All the spacious suite accommodations, attractively decorated in shades of plum and teal or rust and salmon, have microwaves, minibars stocked with microwavable items, and coffee-making facilities, as well as two TVs and two phones; in addition, some have private spas and fireplaces. A state-of-the-art health club, offering such extras as massages and facials, will help burn off the calories picked up at the excellent Canyon Rose restaurant (*see* Dining, *above*). Guests can also picnic at Oak Creek, which runs through the grounds of this tree-lined property, built on the site of the oldest (1879) patented land in the area. *160 Portal La., 86336, tel. 602/282-1777 or 800/521-3131. 175 suites. Facilities: 2 restaurants; jazz lounge; health club with sauna, steam, whirlpool, tanning, and fitness classes; heated outdoor pool; 3 tennis courts; volleyball court. AE, D, DC, MC, V. Very Expensive.*

★ **Briar Patch Inn.** Set in a wonderfully verdant canyon with a rushing creek, this bed-and-breakfast has accommodations to match. All the hewn-wood cabins (in Native American and Mexican style) have kitchenettes; some offer decks overlooking Oak Creek, and many feature fireplaces. Summer mornings you can sit outside and enjoy home-baked breads and fresh egg dishes while listening to classical music performed live. New Age and crafts workshops are held on the premises at various times. *Star Rte. 3, off U.S. 89A 3 mi north of Sedona, Box 1002, 86336, tel. 602/282-2342. 10 cabins with bath, 5 rooms with bath. Facilities: fishing hole, library. MC, V. Expensive–Very Expensive.*

Poco Diablo Resort. One of Sedona's original resort properties, Poco Diablo sits on 22 green and beautifully landscaped acres south of town. All the accommodations and public areas underwent a major refurbishment in 1991. Some rooms have fireplaces and private whirlpools; all have private patios—some with spectacular red-rock views—and all are tastefully decorated and furnished in southwestern style. *1752 AZ 179 (Box 1709), 86336, tel. 602/282-7333 or 800/352-5710 in AZ, 800/528-4275 outside AZ. 104 rooms with bath. Facilities: 2 pools, 9-hole golf course, 4 tennis courts, 2 racquetball courts, restaurant, AE, D, DC, MC, V. Expensive–Very Expensive.*

Bell Rock Inn. Named after one of Sedona's red-rock landmarks, this motel in nearby Oak Creek Village is made of contemporary adobe, with well-furnished rooms in southwestern style. Many rooms have good views of Sedona's red rock spires. Bargain hunters take note: Right across the highway are the Oak Creek Factory Stores (*see* Exploring Sedona, *above*). *6246 AZ 179, 86336, tel. 602/282-4161. 47 rooms with bath. Facilities: restaurant, pool, Jacuzzi, tennis courts. AE, MC, V. Moderate.*

★ **Sky Ranch Lodge.** There may be no better vantage point in town from which to view Sedona's red-rock canyons than the private patios or balconies at Sky Ranch Lodge, perched near the top of Airport Mesa. Some rooms have stone fireplaces, some have kitchenettes; all are well decorated in dark blues and beiges with ceramic tile trim. Paths on the grounds wind around fountains and, in summer, through colorful flower gardens. This is an excellent value choice. *Airport Rd. (Box 2579), 86336, tel. 602/282-6400. 92 rooms, 2 cottages, all with bath, 20 rooms with kitchenette. Facilities: pool, whirlpool. Accepts pets. MC, V. Inexpensive–Moderate.*

The Arts and Nightlife

The Arts

Tourists who wish to visit the symphony, ballet, or theater must drive to Phoenix or Tucson. However, some excellent local events offer out-of-towners a chance to enjoy the unique cultural contributions of the area.

Flagstaff Perhaps the most exciting happening in town is the Flagstaff **All Indian Powwow,** held downtown during the weekend before the Fourth of July. Representatives of tribes from all over the world gather for three days every year to give exhibitions of native dances and to compete for performance awards in a variety of categories: men's, women's, boys', girls'—and even tiny tots'. Concurrently, at the **Native Arts Fair,** an international array of tribal crafts are displayed and sold. For details, contact the Flagstaff Visitors Center (*see* Important Addresses and Numbers in Essential Information, *above*).

Festival in the Pines, sponsored annually during the first weekend of August by the Mill Avenue Merchants' Association (tel. 602/967–4877), features an arts-and-crafts fair; 200 artists from all over the United States gather for this event in Flagstaff at Coconino County Fair Grounds at Fort Tuthill. Among the 20 categories of crafts shown here are watercolors, oil paintings, ceramics, and stained glass. In addition, food vendors compete with three entertainment stages—featuring musicians playing everything from country and western to rock—as well as carnival rides for the crowd's attention.

The **Coconino Center for the Arts** (2300 N. Fort Valley Rd., U.S. 180 N, tel. 602/779–6921) hosts a **Festival of Native American Arts** each summer from late June through early August. During this six-week period, artists from tribes of the Four Corners region are invited to exhibit jewelry, ceramics, weavings, and paintings. Special events include performances of Native American music and dance, crafts demonstrations, auctions, and a Native American banquet. Cowboy art is the featured attraction at the **Trappings of the American West** festival held here from mid-May to early June—everything from painting and sculpture to cowboy poetry readings.

Individual sales shows of artwork by Zuni, Hopi, and Navajo tribes are held at the **Museum of Northern Arizona** (3001 N. Fort Valley Rd., tel. 602/774–5211) a judged event that runs from late May through early August. Items collected at the reservations for this event by staff members include kachina dolls, jewelry, textiles, and ceramics. Native American dances and crafts demonstrations are also scheduled throughout the period.

From early June through the first week in August, the **Flagstaff Festival of the Arts** (403 N. Agassiz St., tel. 602/774–7750 or 800/266–7740) offers everything from art, films, plays, and dance to sunset jazz dinners and a Mexican fiesta.

Jerome The popular Jerome Music Festival will not be held in 1994 because Phelps Dodge is doing exploratory research at the town's old open mining pit, which was the event's venue. A number of smaller musical events have been planned, but as we go to press the schedule is not yet firm. For information, contact the **Jerome Chamber of Commerce** (Box K, 86331, tel. 602/634–2900).

Sedona The Sedona **Jazz on the Rocks Festival** (tel. 602/282–1985), held every September, always attracts a sellout crowd that fills the town to capacity; at jazz-festival time it's even more important than usual to book ahead for rooms. Call for particulars. The **Sedona Heritage Day Festival,** sponsored by the Sedona Historical Society (tel. 602/282–7508 weekdays 9–5), is celebrated in late June; it includes such activities as cake- and pie-baking contests and the reenactment of horseback mail delivery. Pie lovers should also take note of the **Sedona Apple Festival** (tel. 602/282–8766) in October; phone for specific dates and events. The **Sedona Arts Center** (tel. 602/282–3809) sponsors events ranging from classical concerts to plays; phone for information about upcoming programs.

Nightlife

A university town, **Flagstaff** has a number of places where the college crowd gathers after dark. The misleadingly named **Museum Club** (3404 E. Rte. 66, tel. 602/526–9434) is a tourist-friendly cowboy honky-tonk, housed in an old barnlike structure with a dance floor; there's usually a country-swing band. For live entertainment nightly— everything from bluegrass to jazz and rock—in a sociable atmosphere, try the **Main Street Bar and Grill** (4 S. San Francisco St., tel. 602/774–1519); the food's good, too, so come early for dinner. **Busters** (1800 S. Milton, tel. 602/774–5155) offers a large selection of domestic and imported beers, and **Fiddlestix** (702 S. Milton Rd., tel. 602/774–6620), though it's a meat market, hosts good reggae and rock bands.

The nightlife in Sedona, geared more toward a resort crowd, tends to be a bit less rowdy. **On the Rocks,** the lounge at Canyon Rose at Los Abrigados (160 Portal La., tel. 602/281–1777), hosts bands nightly, mostly of the swing and jazz variety. **Enchantment Resort** (525 Boynton Canyon Rd., tel. 602/282–2900) has an attractive bar where live piano and jazz keep the local and visiting beautiful people entertained. For a taste of old Sedona, try the **Oak Creek Tavern** (121 U.S. 89A, tel. 602/282–7921), an old western bar with a pool table, dark, private booths, and a giant stuffed polar bear. The **West 89th Street Night Club** (West U.S. 89A, tel. 602/282–1655) is the place to go if you feel like kicking up your heels on the dance floor.

6 Phoenix and Central Arizona

By Mark Hein

In central Arizona, one of the world's great deserts meets one of its great mountain ranges, providing a stunning variety of natural environments for the visitor to enjoy within easy touring distance. Central Arizona also combines some of the oldest human dwellings in the Western Hemisphere with the homes of contemporary Indian tribes and America's newest, fastest-growing major urban center, metropolitan Phoenix.

At the center of central Arizona lies the Valley of the Sun, named for its 330-plus days of sunshine each year. This 1,000-square-mile valley is the northern tip of the Sonoran Desert, a surprisingly fertile, rolling expanse of prehistoric seabed that stretches from central Arizona deep into northwestern Mexico.

The Valley, like the rest of the Sonora, is studded with cacti and creosote bushes, crusted with hard-baked clay and rock, and scorched by summer temperatures that can stay above 100° F for weeks at a time. But its dry skin responds magically to the touch of rainwater. Spring is a miracle of poppies strewn among the flower-crowned saguaros, of ruby, ivory, and gold blossoms bursting from the dry spikes of the ocotillo and the thorny beaver-tail pads of the nopal. And, as the Hohokam discovered, this miracle can be augmented by human hands. From 300 BC to AD 1450, their tilled, rowed, and irrigated fields yielded cotton, corn, and beans. Then, for reasons neither archaeology nor Indian lore has yet revealed, these skillful, energetic people suddenly abandoned their homes.

From the time the Hohokam left until the American Civil War, the once-fertile Salt River valley lay forgotten, used only by occasional small bands of Pima and Maricopa peoples. Then in 1865, the U.S. Army established Fort McDowell in the mountains to the east, where the Verde River flows into the Salt. To feed the men and the horses stationed there, Jack Swilling, a former Confederate army officer, had the idea of reopening the Hohokam canals in 1867. Within a year fields bright with barley and pumpkins earned the area the name of Punkinsville. But by 1870, when the town site was plotted, the 300 inhabitants had decided that their new city would rise "like a phoenix" from the ashes of a vanished civilization.

Phoenix indeed grew steadily. Within 20 years, it had become large enough—at about 3,000 people—to wrest the title of territorial capital from Prescott. It got a high school in 1895, and at statehood, in 1912, the area, irrigated by the brand-new Roosevelt Dam and Salt River Project, had a burgeoning cotton industry. Copper and cattle were mined and raised elsewhere but were banked and traded in Phoenix, and the cattle were slaughtered and packed here, in the largest stockyards outside Chicago.

Meanwhile climate, so long a crippling liability, became an asset. Desert air was the prescribed therapy for respiratory ills rampant in the sooty, factory-filled East; Scottsdale began in 1901 as "30-odd tents and a half-dozen adobe houses" put up by health seekers. By 1930, visitors seeking warm winter recreation rather than a cure were filling the elegant San Marcos hotel in Chandler and the new Arizona Biltmore, first of the many luxury resorts for which the area is known worldwide today.

When low-cost air-conditioning made its summer heat manageable, the Sun Belt boom began. From 1950 to 1990, the Phoenix urban area more than quadrupled in population, catapulting real estate and home building into two of the state's biggest industries. Cities planted around Phoenix have become its suburbs, and fields that for decades grew cotton and citrus now grow microchips and homes. Glendale and Peoria on the west side, Tempe, Mesa, and Chandler on the east, make up the nation's third-largest Silicon Valley.

The Valley of the Sun is ringed by mountains. In Phoenix itself are Squaw Peak to the north of downtown, and the Papago Peaks between Phoenix and Scottsdale. East of Phoenix, past Tempe and Mesa, stand the barren peaks of the Superstition Mountains, named for their eerie habit of seeming just a few miles away and luring unwary prospectors to a dusty death. Beyond the Superstitions, central Arizona is mountains all the way into New Mexico. South of Phoenix, easily visible from the airport, rise the much less lofty peaks of South Mountain Park. Not 5 miles from downtown, this 12-mile-wide chain of dry mountains divides the Valley from the rest of the Sonora Desert. West of Phoenix, past Glendale and Tolleson, the formidable, barren-seeming White Tank Mountains separate the Valley from the empty lands that slope steadily downward toward the Colorado River and the Mojave Desert of California on the other side.

But north of Phoenix, behind the dusty Hieroglyphic Mountains (misnamed for Hohokam petroglyphs found there), rises the gigantic Mogollon Rim. This shelf of land, almost as wide as Arizona, was thrust 2,000 to 5,000 feet into the air back in the Mesozoic age; it got its name for posing an overwhelming *mogollon* (obstruction) to Spanish-speaking explorers probing northward. Here, the slopes are green with pine trees, and the alpine meadows lush with grasses and aspens. Here, after gold was found in the early 1860s, President Lincoln sent the Arizona Territory's first governor to found the capital at Prescott and secure the mineral riches for the Union.

Today, the northern mountains serve as a cool, green refuge for Valley dwellers. The bumpy wagon roads up the Black Canyon toward Prescott and Flagstaff were key summer escape routes 100 years ago, and their dramatically engineered successor, the four-lane split-level I–17, leads tens of thousands on exodus every weekend from May to September.

Phoenix and central Arizona are places in which to take it easy, go slow, and dress informally. As the old desert hands say, you don't begin to see the desert until you've looked at it long enough to see the colors; and you aren't ready to get up and move until you've seen the sun go down.

Essential Information

Arriving and Departing

By Plane Most air travelers visiting Arizona fly into **Sky Harbor International Airport** (tel. 602/273–3300). Just 3 miles east of downtown Phoenix, it is surrounded by freeways linking it to almost every part of the metro area. Although it is one of the nation's half-dozen busiest airports, it is also one of the most compact.

Sky Harbor has four commercial terminals, each with rental luggage carts, taxi stands, car-rental booths, ATM banking, and courtesy telephones. Terminals 3 and 4—the latter completed in late 1990—also have extensive shops (from Godber's Jewelry to a Bloomingdale's boutique) and restaurants, and their car-rental booths are open 24 hours.

Answers & Apples passenger service desks at all four terminals (tel. 602/267–7964 or 602/267–7994) offer fax, currency exchange, and notary and insurance services; the airport chaplain's office (tel. 602/244–1346) aids travelers in distress.

Airlines Sky Harbor is the home airport of **America West** (tel. 800/247–5692) and a hub for **Southwest** (tel. 800/531–5601). Other airlines with frequent flights to Sky Harbor are **Alaska** (tel. 800/426–0333), **American** (tel. 800/433–7300), **Continental** (tel. 800/525–0280), **Delta** (tel. 800/221–1212), **TWA** (tel. 800/221–2000), **United** (tel. 800/241–6522), and **USAir** (tel. 800/428–4322).

For flights to the Grand Canyon, Page, Lake Powell, Lake Havasu, and other Arizona points, try **America West** (tel. 800/247–5692) and commuters' **Mesa Airlines** (tel. 800/637–2247) and **SkyWest** (tel. 800/453–9417).

Between the Airport and Downtown Its easy access to downtown Phoenix and Tempe (3 miles away to the west and east, respectively) is one of Sky Harbor's strong points. It's also only 15 minutes by freeway from Glendale (to the west) and Mesa (to the east).

Unfortunately, two favorite tourist areas, Scottsdale (to the northeast) and Sun City (to the northwest) are harder to reach—each takes 30 to 45 minutes by car and requires using surface roads for all or part of the trip.

Sky Harbor has limited bus service, ample taxi service, and very good shuttle service to points throughout the metro area. Very few hotels offer a complimentary limo or shuttle, but most resorts do. You will probably want to rent a car, either at the airport or from wherever you are staying (most rental firms will deliver).

These companies have airport booths or free pickup from nearby lots: **Alamo** (tel. 800/327–9633), **Avis** (tel. 800/331–1212), **Budget** (tel. 800/527–0700), **Hertz** (tel. 800/654–3131), **Thrifty** (tel. 800/367–2277), and, if you care more about your wallet than appearances, **Rent-A-Wreck** (tel. 602/254–1000).

By Bus **Phoenix Transit** buses (tel. 602/253–5000) will get you directly from Terminal 2, 3, or 4 to downtown Phoenix's outdoor bus terminal (1st and Washington Sts.) or downtown Tempe (Mill and University Aves.) in about 20 minutes for $1. Senior citizens and children ages 6–12 pay half fare; children 5 and under ride free.

The **Red Line** runs westbound to Phoenix every half hour from about 6 AM until after 9 PM weekdays (Saturday, you take the No. 13 bus and transfer at Central Avenue to the No. 0 north; there is no Sunday service). The Red Line runs eastbound to Tempe every half hour from 4 AM to 7 PM weekdays (no weekend service); in another 25 minutes, it takes you to downtown Mesa (Center and Main streets).

With free transfers, Phoenix Transit can take you from the airport to most other Valley cities (Glendale, Sun City, Scottsdale, etc.), but the trip is likely to be slow unless you manage to catch an express line.

By Taxi Only three firms—and one specializing in transporting handicapped travelers—are licensed to pick up at Sky Harbor's commercial terminals. All add a $1 surcharge for airport pickups, do not charge for luggage, and are available 24 hours a day. A trip to downtown Phoenix can range from $4 to $12, or $13.75 for a wheelchair-lift van. The fare to downtown Scottsdale averages around $13.

AAA Cab (tel. 602/253–8294), **Checker/Yellow Cab** (tel. 602/252–5252), and **Courier Cab** (tel. 602/232–2222) all charge around $2 for the first mile and $1.25 per mile thereafter. **American HTS** (tel. 602/272–7211) offers wheelchair and stretcher service, the former at a $15 pickup fee ($20 evenings and weekends) and $1.25 per mile. All expect tips.

The blue vans of **Supershuttle** (tel. 602/244–9000) also cruise Sky Harbor, each taking up to five passengers to their individual destinations, with no luggage fee or airport surcharge. Fares range from competitive with the cheapest taxi for a short run, such as downtown Phoenix or Tempe, to 25% or more below the best taxi fares on longer trips. You can reserve a Supershuttle back to the airport (call a day ahead and expect to be picked up two hours before your flight). Drivers expect tips.

By Limousine A few limousine firms are allowed to cruise Sky Harbor, and many more provide airport pickups by reservation. All of these are on 24-hour call. **La Limousine** (tel. 602/242-3094) can be hailed at the curb ($15 to $50, depending on distance) or reserved ($25 to $50). **Classic Limousine** (tel. 602/252-LIMO) will take up to five riders (by reservation only) for $30 to $50, depending on how far you're going. **Scottsdale Limousine** (tel. 602/946-8446) also requires reservations but offers a toll-free number (tel. 800/747-8234) and complimentary soft drinks; it costs from $55 to $85, plus tip.

By Car If you're coming to Phoenix from the west, you'll probably come on I-10—this transcontinental superhighway's last link was joined in 1990 in a tunnel under downtown Phoenix. The trip from the Los Angeles basin, via Palm Springs, takes five to eight hours, depending on where you start and how many rest stops you make. The older I-40 runs along old "Route 66," entering Arizona in the northwest, near Kingman; U.S. 93 traverses from there to Phoenix, for a total journey of 10 to 12 hours. From San Diego, I-8 slices across low desert to Yuma and on toward the Valley on what the Spanish called El Camino del Diablo (the Devil's Highway); at Gila Bend, take AZ 85 up to I-10. The trip takes a total of 8 to 10 hours.

From the east, **I-10** takes you from El Paso, across southern New Mexico, and through Chiricahua Apache country into Tucson, then north to Phoenix (a total of about 9 to 11 hours). The northeastern route, **I-40** from Albuquerque, crosses Hopi and Navajo historic lands to Flagstaff, where I-17 takes you south to Phoenix, also a 9- to 11-hour journey. For a scenic shortcut, take AZ 377 south at Holbrook, across Petrified Forest country to Heber, in the pines of the Mogollon Rim; then take AZ 260 down the 2,000-foot drop to Payson, and AZ 87 through saguaro cactus forests to Phoenix.

By Train **Amtrak** (tel. 800/USA-RAIL) has only one line, the former Southern Pacific line between New Orleans and Los Angeles, that passes through Phoenix; on Monday, Wednesday, and Saturday (8 AM eastbound, 11:30 PM westbound), it stops at the downtown terminal (4th Ave. and Harrison St., tel. 602/253-0121). It's in what is now the industrial part of town, and you may have to phone for a taxi. The much more heavily used former Santa Fe line between Los Angeles and Chicago runs through Flagstaff, 150 miles north of the Valley, stopping daily (8 AM eastbound, 10:30 PM westbound); it's a two- to three-hour ride by bus or car from there.

By Bus **Greyhound** (tel. 602/248-4040) has statewide and nationwide routes from its main terminal in the heart of downtown (525 E. Washington St.), sandwiched between the

Civic Plaza complex and the new America West Phoenix Suns Arena.

Important Addresses and Numbers

Tourist Information The **Phoenix and Valley of the Sun Convention and Visitors Bureau** (1 Arizona Center, Suite 600, tel. 602/254–6500) has a satellite office in the Hyatt Regency Phoenix (2nd and Adams Sts., tel. 602/254–6500). The **Phoenix Chamber of Commerce** (34 W. Monroe St., tel. 602/254–5521) is in the heart of downtown.

Emergencies **Police, fire,** or **ambulance** (tel. 911).
Highway emergencies (tel. 800/525–5555).

Hospitals **Samaritan Health Service** (tel. 602/230–CARE) has four Valley hospitals—Good Samaritan (downtown), Desert Samaritan (east), Maryvale Samaritan (southwest), and Thunderbird Samaritan (northwest)—and a Deer Valley (north) urgent-care clinic; all share a 24-hour hotline. **Scottsdale Memorial Hospital** (tel. 602/481–4411) has three campuses in the northeastern Valley. **Maricopa County Medical Center** (tel. 602/267–5011) has been rated one of the nation's best public hospitals.

Doctors The **Maricopa County Medical Society** (tel. 602/252–2844) and the **Arizona Osteopathic Medical Association** (tel. 602/840–0460) offer referrals during business hours on weekdays.

Dentists The **American Dental Association Valley** chapter (tel. 602/957–4864) has a 24-hour referral hotline.

Late-Night Pharmacies **Walgreen's** has eight 24-hour locations throughout the Valley—in east Phoenix (38th St. and Thomas Rd., tel. 602/275–7507), north Phoenix (7th St. and Bell Rd., tel. 602/375–0093), and west Phoenix (5127 W. Indian School Rd., tel. 602/247–1014); in the eastern suburbs of Tempe (1719 E. Southern Ave., Tempe, tel. 602/838–3642), Chandler (1986 N. Alma School Rd., Chandler, tel. 602/899–6713), and Mesa (330 E. Brown Rd., Mesa, tel. 602/898–8025; Main St. and Recker Rd., Mesa, tel. 602/985–0155); and in the western suburb of Peoria (6815 W. Peoria Rd., Peoria, tel. 602/878–7998). **Osco Drugs** has two 24-hour outlets, in central Phoenix (3320 N. 7th Ave., tel. 602/266–5501) and in Mesa (1836 W. Baseline Rd., tel. 602/831–0212).

Weather **Pressline** (tel. 602/271–5656, then press 3333) gives up-to-date Valley conditions and three-day forecasts, as does the **U.S. National Weather Service** (tel. 602/265–5550).

Getting Around

If you plan to see anything, *you will need a car.* The metro area developed in the automobile era, and only a few downtowns (Phoenix, Scottsdale, Tempe) are pedestrian-friendly. There is no mass transit beyond a bus system that does not even run seven days a week.

By Car Driving is easy in the Valley of the Sun: Rain is rare, fog makes headlines, and it never snows. Most metro-area streets are well marked and well lighted, and the freeway system (not funded until the late 1980s and still being built) has made dramatic strides in linking most of the Valley together. Arizona requires seat belts on front-seat passengers and children 16 and under. (For car-rental firms, *see* Between the Airport and Downtown, *above*.)

Around downtown Phoenix, AZ 202 (Papago Freeway), AZ 143 (Hohokam Freeway) and I–10 (Maricopa Freeway) make an elongated east–west loop, embracing the state capitol area on the west and the airport on the east. At midloop, AZ 51 (Squaw Peak Freeway) runs north into Paradise Valley. And from the loop's east end, I–10 runs south to Tucson, 100 miles away, while US 60 (Superstition Freeway) branches east to Tempe and Mesa.

Driving in the Valley presents one major challenge: Phoenix and all its suburbs are laid out on a single, 800-square-mile grid of horizontal and vertical streets. Even the freeways all run north–south and east–west. (Grand Avenue, running about 20 miles from downtown northwest to Sun City, is the *only* diagonal.) This makes places easy to find but means you must allow generous driving time to get from point A to point B, since you have to trace two legs of a right triangle to do it.

By Bus **Phoenix Transit** (tel. 602/253–5000) is a good rudimentary bus system, with 20 express lines and 42 regular routes that reach most of the Valley suburbs. But there are no 24-hour routes; only a skeletal few lines run between sundown and 10:30 PM or on Saturday; and there is no Sunday service. Fares are $1, with free transfers; senior citizens and children 6–18 pay half fare, and children 5 and under ride free. Phoenix Transit also runs a 25¢ **Downtown Area Shuttle** (DASH), with purple minibuses circling the area between the renovated east end of downtown and the state capitol, on the west end, at 10-minute intervals. The system also serves major thoroughfares in several suburbs—Glendale, Scottsdale, Tempe, and Mesa. In addition, **Dial-A-Ride** services (tel. 602/253–7755) are available throughout the Valley.

By Taxi Taxi fares are unregulated in Phoenix, except at the airport. (For a listing of leading firms and their fares, *see* Between the Airport and Downtown, *above*.) The 800-square-mile metro area is so large that one-way fares of $30–$50 are not uncommon; you might want to ask what the damages will be before you get in. Except within a compact area, such as central Phoenix, travel by taxi is not recommended.

Opening and Closing Times

Generally, banks are open Monday–Thursday 9–4, Friday 9–6. Selected banks have Saturday morning hours, and a few large grocery stores have bank windows that stay open until 9 PM.

Most enclosed shopping malls are open weekdays 10–9, Saturday 10–6, and Sunday noon–5; some of the major centers (*see* Shopping, *below*) are open later on weekends.

Many grocery stores are open 7 AM–9 PM, but several stores within major chains throughout the Valley are open 24 hours.

Radio Stations

AM **KTAR 620;** News, talk, sports; **KIDR 740;** Children; **KFYI 910;** News, talk; **KPHX 1480;** Spanish-language.

FM **KBAQ 89.5;** Classical; **KJZZ 91.5;** Jazz, National Public Radio; **KKFR 92.3;** Top 40; **KUPD 97.9;** Rock; **KNIX 102.5;** Country; **KVVA 107.1;** Spanish-language.

Guided Tours

Reservations for tours are a must all year, with seats often filling up quickly in the busy season, October–April. All tours provide pickup services at area resorts, but some offer lower prices if you drive to the tour's point of origin.

Orientation Tours **Gray Line Tours** (1646 E. University Dr., Phoenix 85034, tel. 602/437–3701) offers a daily three-hour narrated drive through Phoenix and Scottsdale for $27, touring downtown Phoenix, the Arizona Biltmore hotel, Camelback Mountain, mansions in Paradise Valley, Arizona State University, Papago Park, and Scottsdale's 5th Avenue. For $30, **Vaughan's Southwest Custom Tours** (Box 31312, Phoenix 85046, tel. 602/971–1381) offers a four-hour trip for 11 or fewer passengers in custom vans, stopping at the Heard Museum, the Arizona Biltmore, and the state capitol building. Vaughan's will also take visitors east of Phoenix on the Apache Trail, a scenic route that passes through old mining towns and includes a narrated boat ride on **Dolly's Steamboat Cruises** at Canyon Lake. The cost is $55, with the tour available September through May, weather permitting.

Special-Interest If you prefer to see the desert country from a four-wheel-
Tours drive vehicle, you'll find plenty of options. For example, **Carefree Jeep Adventures** (Box 5423, Carefree 85377, tel. 602/585–9755) travels into the Tonto National Forest on old stage and mining roads, where you can see petroglyphs and rock carvings, taste the fruit of cholla cactus, and hold target practice with tin cans and .22 rifles. That three-hour journey costs $50, as does a sunset tour; there's also a breakfast trip for $60. **Arizona Scenic Tours** (2948 E. Shangri-La Rd., Phoenix 85028, tel. 602/971–3601) heads

past Pinnacle Peak toward the Verde River on dirt desert roads. Two people can expect to pay $50 each (beverages included) for 3½ hours, but the price drops to $45 per person if more than two make the trip.

For a longer trip into the Bradshaw Mountains north of the Valley, **Explorer Desert Tours** (3310 W. Bell Rd., Phoenix 85023, tel. 602/938–1302 or 800/244–6689) takes 15-person vans to nature trails, gold mines, and a mountain steakhouse on the six-hour "Sundowner" tour, at $67 per person.

If you'd rather hike than ride, **The Open Road Tours** (1622 E. Gardenia Ave., Phoenix 85020, tel. 602/997–6474) takes hikers to the Squaw Peak Mountain Preserve or South Mountain Park for $35 per half day. Three- to five-day hikes can be arranged.

Cimarron Adventures and River Co. (7714 E. Catalina Dr., Scottsdale 85251, tel. 602/994–1199) arranges half-day float trips and moonlight dinner cruises down the Salt, Verde, and Gila rivers. Day trips cost about $55 per person, with the night cruise about $70. Special-occasion evening trips for two can be reserved for about $100 apiece.

Want to tour Phoenix from above? Check out the many hot-air-balloon ascents. **Pegasus Hot Air Balloon Co.** (Box 50893, Phoenix 85076, tel. 602/756–1161) sells typical flights valleywide at $110 per person. The cost includes champagne at the end of the one-hour ride and a souvenir photo. *See also* Hot-Air Ballooning in Sports and the Outdoors, *below.*

At the Estrella Sailport, **Arizona Soaring Inc.** (Box 858, Maricopa 85239, tel. 602/568–2318) offers sailplane rides in a basic trainer or high-performance plane for prices ranging from $48 to $90. The adventuresome can opt for a wild 15-minute acrobatic flight for $80.

If you prefer a less dizzying option, **Heritage Carriages** (7031 E. Camelback Rd., Suite 359, Scottsdale 85251, tel. 602/941–0369) leads 30-minute to four-hour horse-drawn-carriage tours around Old Scottsdale for $35–$160. Their desert-adventure tour for six heads out to the wilderness for a half- or full-day journey that includes a catered cookout. The cost starts at $250. They also offer horseback tours, from one hour to overnight, in the Tonto National Forest, for $20 to $150.

One of the most interesting guided tours in town explores **Taliesin West** (13201 N. 108th St., Scottsdale 85259, tel. 602/860–2700), winter headquarters of the Frank Lloyd Wright Foundation. With its redwood-and-rock design set at the base of the McDowell Mountains, Wright's winter home typifies his concept of blending function with nature. Hour-long guided tours cost $10; a weekly three-hour tour goes behind the scenes and talks with Wright associates working and studying at the site. The cost is $25.

Walking Tour A 45-minute self-guided walking tour of **Old Scottsdale** takes visitors to 14 historic sites in the area. Maps showing the route can be picked up in the **Scottsdale Chamber of Commerce** office (743 E. Scottsdale Mall, Scottsdale 85251, tel. 602/945–8481) weekdays 8:30–5, Saturdays 10–5, and Sundays 11–5.

Exploring

Highlights for First-time Visitors

Casa Grande (*see* Tour 4)
Downtown Scottsdale (*see* Tour 3)
Heard Museum (*see* Tour 2)
Heritage Square, The Mercado, and **Arizona Center** (*see* Tour 1)

Tour 1: A Walking Tour of Downtown Phoenix

Numbers in the margin correspond to points of interest on the Phoenix: Tours 1 and 2 map.

A stroll through the renovated east end of downtown gives you a look at Phoenix's past and present, as well as a peek at its future. In moderate weather, it's a pleasant walking day; from late May to mid-October, it's best to break it up over two days. And be sure to take advantage of the 25¢ DASH (Downtown Area Shuttle)—*see* By Bus in Getting Around in Essential Information, *above.*

You'll notice a number of Time Out options in this and the tours that follow—in the warm months, it's best to allow a half hour of sitting indoors, sipping a tall, cool drink (not alcohol; it speeds dehydration) for every hour of walking or shopping.

❶ Begin your tour at **Heritage Square,** from 6th to 7th streets between Monroe and Adams, a city-owned block of renovated turn-of-the-century homes in a parklike setting. (There's ample parking in adjacent lots, and it's free if you get your ticket stamped by a merchant along the walking tour.)

To the east, across 7th Street, you'll see the ornate brick bulk of Monroe School; built in 1914, it now houses part of the U.S. Department of Defense Analysis. Just south of it are the graceful modern copper-roofed condos of Renaissance Square, a pioneering urban project built on city-donated land.

The queen of Heritage Square itself is the **Rosson House,** an 1895 gingerbread Victorian in the Eastlake style (made famous in San Francisco). Built by a physician who served a

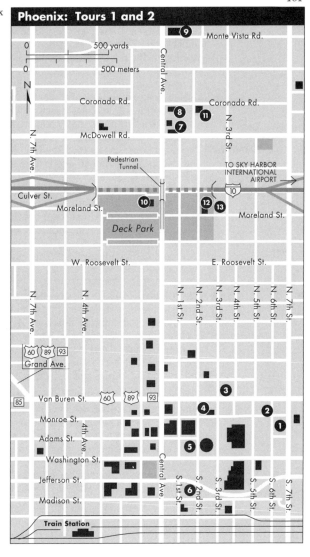

Phoenix: Tours 1 and 2

brief term as mayor, it is the sole survivor of the fewer than two dozen Victorians erected in Phoenix. It was bought and restored by the city in 1974. A 30-minute tour of this classic is worth the modest price. *6th and Monroe Sts., tel. 602/ 262–5071. Admission: $3 adults, $2 senior citizens and students, $1 children 6–12. Open Wed.–Sat. 10–3:30, Sun. noon–3:30.*

On the south side of the square, along Adams Street, stand four houses built between 1899 and 1901 on sites bought from the Rossons. The midwestern-style **Stevens House** holds the **Arizona Doll and Toy Museum** (602 E. Adams St., tel. 602/253–9337); next to it, in the California-style **Stevens-Haustgen House,** are the handworks of **Craftsmen's Gallery** (604 E. Adams St., tel. 602/253–7770). The fourth dwelling is the **Silva House,** a mail-order 1900 bungalow restored by the Salt River Project (one of the Valley's two major power companies and its largest irrigator) that includes a room devoted to Phoenix history and one with rotating displays on water and electricity in the Valley. Two houses on the south side of Adams Street are still being restored.

Time Out The third house in the row, the Bouvier-Teeter House, offers elegant refreshment—afternoon high teas at the **Heart in Hand Tea Room** (622 E. Adams St., tel. 602/256–7572), served Tuesday through Saturday from 10 to 6, Sunday from noon to 5. Or, for more casual fare in one of the square's two restored carriage houses, just north of the Heart in Hand Tea Room, **Jack and Jenny's Barn and Grill** (618 E. Adams St., tel. 602/255–0213) makes sandwiches to order and has a wide array of fruit, juices, soft drinks, and sweets.

❷ **The Mercado** (542 E. Monroe St., tel. 602/256–6322), a bright-colored, neo-Aztec fantasy built in 1990, occupies two blocks immediately north of Heritage Square, just across Monroe Street, from 5th to 7th streets. In it are shops with Latin American handicrafts, two fine local booteries, the Valley's only specialist in fine African handwork, and several boutiques and gift shops.

Before shopping, to attune your eye to Mexican art, spend some time at the **Museo Chicano** on the second story. It supports the work of modern Hispano-American artists in the United States and Mexico, and its exhibits portray the range of Hispanic culture, classic and modern. Its gift shop also offers some terrific bargains. *641 E. Van Buren St., tel. 602/257–5536. Admission: $2 adults, $1 senior citizens and students. Open Wed.–Sat. 10–5, Sun. noon–4.*

From The Mercado, cross 5th and Van Buren streets. On your right, you'll see the imposing buildings of old Phoenix Union High School, Greek Revival–style buildings that served as the city's first secondary school in 1900 and were abandoned three-quarters of a century later. With their shells preserved and their interiors remodeled, they are now home to several city and county offices.

On the northwest corner of the intersection, you'll see two glass-clad office towers with a lane of royal palms between ❸ them. Follow the palm trees: They lead to the **Arizona Center's** dramatic sunken garden and fountains (see how many giant bronze frogs you can find). Opened in 1991, this multiuse complex provides downtown's premier spot for cool, shaded outdoor sitting and wandering, even in the heat of summer.

On the other side of the ponds stands the curved, double-deck open structure of the city's newest downtown shopping mall. There are a variety of chain and specialty stores, from men's and women's clothing to southwestern art and '50s collectibles, and a host of clever cart merchants. And there's usually live music (including top Valley jazz artists) in the courtyard. In addition to hosting several good eateries, Arizona Center is the home of the state's biggest sports bar—would you believe eight restaurant-size spaces spread over two stories, indoors and out?

Time Out The most restful refreshment spot in the center is **Amalfi** (455 N. 3rd St., tel. 602/257–0605), a real Italian sidewalk café that does great Caesar salads, sandwiches, and desserts as well as Italian sodas and steamed coffees.

Leaving the Arizona Center at Amalfi, head south to 3rd and Van Buren streets. You can catch the 25¢ DASH shuttle here, or you can stroll a block south to Monroe, with the mission-style adobe of **St. Mary's Basilica** on your left, then a block west between the dramatic modern facades of the **Herberger Theater Center** (on your right) and **Symphony Hall** (on your left), facing each other across the fountain- and sculpture-dotted Phoenix Civic Plaza courtyard. One more block, south along 2nd Street past the Hyatt Regency Phoenix to Adams, takes you to the next stop.

Here, amid the splendor and dignity of downtown, is a building with children's paintings all over its windows. It's the **Arizona Museum of Science and Technology,** a hands-on exploratorium for children of every age. Permanent displays include exercises in gravity, centrifugal force, and optical illusions. *80 N. 2nd St., tel. 602/256–9388. Admission: $4.50 adults, $3.50 senior citizens and children 4–12. Open Mon.–Sat. 9–5, Sun. noon–5.*

Finally, if you're really an indefatigable walker and an avid sports fan, another two blocks down 2nd Street will take you to the site of the **America West Phoenix Suns Arena** (2nd and Jefferson Sts., tel. 602/222–5888). This multifacility sports palace is almost a mall in itself, with cafés and an athletic club and shops, in addition to the basketball-and-hockey stadium and team offices. It's an interesting tour even when there's no game on.

From the arena (or from Symphony Hall, across from the science museum, if you skip the arena), you can catch the DASH northbound for The Mercado and walk back to your car.

Tour 2: Cultural Center Walking Tour

The heart of Phoenix's new downtown cultural center is the rolling greensward of **Deck Park.** Begun in 1991 atop the I–10 tunnel under Central Avenue, it spreads a mile from 3rd

Avenue on the west to 3rd Street on the east, and a quarter mile from Portland Street north to Culver. Completed in 1993, it is the city's second-largest downtown park (the largest is half-century-old Encanto Park, 2 miles northwest).

Gathered around Deck Park, mostly to the north, are museums, theaters, an art center, and the central library. Seeing all of them makes a comfortable day tour in moderate weather; in the warm months, it is too much for one day. The No. 0 bus line runs up and down Central Avenue every 10 minutes on weekdays (at half fare from 9 to 3) and every 20 minutes on weekends.

7 Start at the **Phoenix Central Library** (12 E. McDowell Rd., tel. 602/262–4636), on the northeast corner of McDowell and Central. It's easy to find, and its palm-lined parking area has no time limit.

Immediately north of the library, in the same complex and **8** sharing a courtyard, is the **Phoenix Art Museum.** It is particularly noteworthy for its clothing and costume collection, fine Asian art, 19th-century European paintings and drawings, and the American West collection, featuring painters from Frederic Remington to Georgia O'Keeffe. *1625 N. Central Ave., tel. 602/257–1222. Admission: $4 adults, $3 senior citizens over 65, $1.50 students, children 5 and under free. Admission free on Wed. Tours free. Open Tues. and Thurs.–Sat. 10–5, Wed. 10–9, Sun. noon–5.*

Two blocks north, cross Monte Vista and turn right 100 **9** yards to the **Heard Museum.** In 1928 Dwight and Maie Heard donated their classic Arizona adobe home and their impressive southwestern art collection to found what has become the nation's leading museum of Native American art and culture. Orient yourself with the multimedia show, then see the award-winning "Native Peoples of the Southwest" exhibit; don't miss the kachina doll room (anchored by the Barry Goldwater collection). Modern Indian arts, interactive art-making displays for children, and live demonstrations by artisans are always on hand. In the spring, you may catch the annual Native American Arts & Crafts Show; call and ask, because its dates vary. *22 E. Monte Vista Rd., tel. 602/252–8840. Admission: $5 adults, $4 students and senior citizens, $3 juniors 6 to 18, $1 children, Native Americans free. Admission free Wed. after 5. Open Mon.–Sat. 10–5, Wed. 10–9, Sun. noon–5.*

If your day hasn't unaccountably disappeared in the museums, go back to Central, cross the street, and catch a No. 0 bus heading south. (Or walk, if it's below 90° F and you're hardy.)

At Culver Street, a long block south of McDowell, is the northern edge of Deck Park. The stately brick home with the gabled roof on the southwest corner is the **10** **Ellis-Shackelford House** (1242 N. Central Ave., tel. 602/

261–8699). One of Phoenix's first mansions, it was long the home of the Arizona Historical Society Museum (now in Papago Park, near the Phoenix Zoo). It houses the Phoenix Historic Preservation Office and, in back, the restored railcars of the **Phoenix Street Railway** (tel. 602/254–0307 to arrange a visit).

Time Out Halfway back to McDowell Road are two places that offer both rest and nourishment. At the **Spaghetti Company** (1418 N. Central Ave., tel. 602/257–0380) you can have lunch, spinach salad and wine, any of countless pasta dishes (try the house mizithra cheese on top), or other dinners, any day of the week. Across the street at **The Blue Fin** (1401 N. Central Ave., tel. 602/254–3171), the atmosphere is quick and informal, the Japanese fast food light and delightful.

Now you have a choice: You can head back to the library
⓫ complex, where you haven't yet seen the **Phoenix Little Theatre** (25 E. Coronado Rd., tel. 602/254–2151), just east of the museum and north of the library. Here the city's leading community theater group and its adjunct, the PLT Cookie Company, present plays and musicals for adults and children; you might end your day by catching a show.

If you're not ready to head back, you can go into Deck Park at the Ellis-Shackelford House, through the pedestrian tunnel under Central (with I–10 roaring beneath your feet), and walk 2½ blocks east to the **City Arts Center** (3rd
⓬ and Moreland Sts., tel. 602/262–6583). In the **Phoenix Visual Arts Building,** Valley professional and amateur artists do class and studio work in graphics, ceramics, sculpture, photography, and other media; check for current exhibits and
⓭ sales. Adjacent is the **Phoenix Performing Arts Building,** a venue for small, experimental dance and theater groups. A performance here is a fine way to spend an evening after a day spent walking the city's cultural paths.

Tour 3: Scottsdale Walking Tour

Numbers in the margin correspond to points of interest on the Scottsdale map.

Historic sites, nationally known art galleries, and lots of clever boutiques fill downtown Scottsdale, easily turning a walking tour into several hours if you browse. Historic Old Scottsdale features the look of the Old West, while fashionable 5th Avenue is known for its shopping. Cross onto Main Street and enter a world frequented by the international art set; discover more galleries and interior design shops on Marshall Way and Craftsman Court. Looming over the neighborhood is the new **Scottsdale Galleria** (4343 N. Scottsdale Rd., tel. 602/949–3222) with its 55 stores, 7 restaurants, and 8 theaters, including the giant-screen IMAX.

This tour offers an overview of the area; *see* the Shopping section, *below*, for some specific recommendations.

While your tour easily can be completed on foot, a trolley (cost: $2 in summer, free the rest of the year) runs through the 5th Avenue area; the Ollie Trolley tours all of Scottsdale and charges $2 for an all-day pass. For information for both, call 602/941–2957. Also look for the horse-drawn carriages that provide romantic transportation after dark on Heritage Carriages (tel. 602/941–0369), usually found where Brown Avenue intersects Main Street.

Begin your tour by parking in the free public lot on the northwest corner of 2nd Street and Wells Fargo Avenue east of Scottsdale Road. A portion of the garage is signed for a three-hour limit; go to upper levels that don't carry time restraints, as enforcement is strict.

Head north on the brick-paved sidewalks leading to ❶ **Scottsdale Mall.** This tree-shaded setting has plenty of benches and grassy areas for restful contemplation. To your right, walks lead to a sculpture- and fountain-filled plaza around Scottsdale's **city hall, public library,** and **Center for the Arts** (7383 E. Scottsdale Mall, tel. 602/994–2301). The center presents a full schedule of concerts, and exhibits are changed frequently. Its gift shop, **The Artspot,** has unusual jewelry as well as posters and art books.

After circling the plaza, head west to the redbrick ❷ **Scottsdale Chamber of Commerce** building (7343 Scottsdale Mall, tel. 602/945–8481), constructed in 1910 as Scottsdale's first schoolhouse. Inside, shopping maps and helpful tips are provided if you're looking for something special. Ask for the walking tour map of Old Scottsdale so you can note historic buildings as you go.

❸ Continue west into **Old Scottsdale** on Main Street. Billed as "The West's Most Western Town," this area features rustic storefronts and wooden sidewalks; it's touristy, but it's also the genuine item, giving visitors a taste of life here 80 years ago. Stores carry kitschy souvenirs, but you'll also find some nicer jewelry, pots, and Mexican imports.

Head north on Brown Avenue and turn left on 1st Avenue to continue sightseeing in Old Scottsdale.

Time Out The southeast corner of 1st Avenue and Scottsdale Road ❹ marks a landmark of sorts: the candy pink-and-white **Sugar Bowl Ice Cream Parlor** (4005 N. Scottsdale Rd., tel. 602/946–0051), run by a local family since 1958 and frequented from its beginning by Paradise Valley cartoonist Bil Keane (the menu carries his "Family Circus" work). Although sandwiches, soups, and salads are available, you're missing the point if you don't indulge in the gooey sundaes, floats, and parfaits.

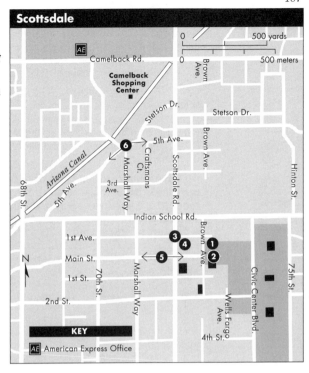

5 For an entirely different milieu, walk south on Scottsdale Road and turn right onto **Main Street.** This block is literally filled with art galleries on both sides of the street, featuring work that ranges from contemporary to western realism, Native American, and traditional. With very few exceptions, casual visitors are made welcome in the galleries, although children may be bored. Another option for viewing the galleries is the seasonal **Art Walk,** held from 7 to 9 PM each Thursday, October through May. The street takes on a party atmosphere during the evening hours when everyone is browsing.

Continue on Main Street across Marshall Way for several antiques shops, where specialties include elegant porcelains and china, fine antique jewelry, and Oriental rugs.

Time Out For a cool drink or light meal after gallery-hopping, two alternatives are close by. At **Bistro La Chaumière** (6910 E. Main St., tel. 602/946–5115), guests are served casual French fare in a solarium out front. Or head one block north on 70th Street to 1st Avenue and turn right to **Arcadia Farms** (7014 E. 1st Ave., tel. 602/941–5665), where such eclectic sandwiches as rosemary-seasoned *focaccia* with chicken, roasted eggplant, and feta cheese are brought out to diners on a tree-shaded patio. Desserts at both restaurants are exceptional, so leave room.

If you walk north on 70th Street and cross Indian School Road, you'll discover another niche of galleries, upscale gift and jewelry stores, and several specialty boutiques. Farther north on Marshall Way across 3rd Avenue, the street is filled with more art galleries and creative stores with a southwestern flair.

❻ When you reach the fountain with the prancing horses, you're on **5th Avenue,** a 40-year-old stretch that is a shopping tradition in Phoenix. Whether you're seeking cacti or casual clothing, fine art or handmade Indian jewelry, you'll find it here.

Off 5th Avenue, Stetson Drive has a few interesting stores carrying original Indian artifacts, as well as books on Arizona and the Southwest; here you'll find **O'Brien's Art Emporium** (7122 E. Stetson Dr., tel. 602/945–1082), the oldest art gallery in Scottsdale.

Tour 4: Casa Grande Ruins National Monument and Florence

Numbers in the margin correspond to points of interest on the Around Phoenix map.

An hour's drive south of Phoenix takes visitors back to prehistoric times and the site of Arizona's first known civilization, as well as one of its major pioneer western towns. The Casa Grande Ruins National Monument, 1 mile north of Coolidge, captures some vivid reminders of the Hohokam Indians, who began farming in this area more than 1,500 years ago. Florence, one of central Arizona's first cities, is rich in examples of Territorial architecture.

Start your tour by heading southeast on I–10 leaving Phoenix. You'll pass Exit 160, which leads to **Williams Air Force Base,** site of the largest pilot-training facility in NATO but recommended for closure soon. The same exit is the closest freeway access to **Compadre Stadium,** spring-training home of the Milwaukee Brewers each February and March.

❶ Soon you'll see a sign noting that you've entered the **Gila River Indian Reservation.** On the right, Exit 162A indicates **Firebird International Raceway** (20000 S. Maricopa Rd., tel. 602/268–0200), site of the Arizona National drag-racing finals each February and local Friday night races; **Firebird Lake** (20000 S. Maricopa Rd., tel. 602/268–0200), a boat-racing site where the World Hydroplane Finals are held each November; and **Compton Terrace** (20000 S. Maricopa Rd., tel. 602/796–0511), one of the Valley's largest outdoor concert venues.

The landscape changes to desert scrub, and the sun can become intense, so make use of sunscreen, hats, and drinking water. Large, strangely shaped saguaro cacti next begin to dominate the landscape, covering a hillside as you cross the

Around Phoenix

Prescott National Forest

ALT 89

Mingus Mountain

Prescott National Forest

Prescott Valley

ALT 89

Dewey **13**

Verde Valley

Prescott **14**

69

169

Humboldt

Mayer **12**

Skull Valley

89

Arcosanti

■

Cordes Junction **11**

Peeples Valley **15**

Bumblebee

Tonto National Forest

Hassayampa River

Horse Thief Basin

Sunset Point Rest Area **10**

Yarnell **16**

Bumblebee/ Horse Thief Basin **9**

Verde River

Black Canyon City **8**

Wickenburg **17**

89

Lake Pleasant

New River **7**

74

93

Paradise Valley

60

17

Sun City

Glendale

Scottsdale

Mesa

10

★ Phoenix

Tempe

60 89

Gila River

60

Gila River Indian Reservation **1**

10

89

Gila River **2**

GILA BEND INDIAN RESERVATION

Casa Grande Ruins National Monument

GILA RIVER INDIAN RESERVATION

387

3

287

Florence **5**

Coolidge

4

89

8

87

Tom Mix Monument **6**

10

N

TOHONÓ O'ODHAM INDIAN RESERVATION

0   20 miles

0   30 km

2 **Gila River**—usually dry, though it was swollen in early 1993 by one of its historic floods.

Time Out   Thirty-seven miles out of Phoenix off I–10 is a disabled-accessible **rest area** with covered picnic tables. It's the last available stop until you reach your destination 20 miles later.

Take Exit 185 east off I–10 and follow the signs a short way to AZ 387. It's a two-lane road flanked by saguaros, and the spring landscape features brilliant red-tipped ocotillo cacti and yellow and purple wildflowers. Halfway into this 7-mile stretch, you'll climb a rise and see the Gila River valley spread out below. Four miles later, turn right onto AZ 87 and head 7½ miles to the ruins.

3 The **Casa Grande Ruins National Monument,** established in 1918, provides a close look at a structure first seen by European explorers in the 17th century. Allow an hour to inspect the site, longer if park rangers are giving a talk at the interpretive ramada or leading a tour.

Start at the visitor center, where a small museum features artifacts and information on the Hohokam, who lived here and farmed irrigated cotton fields until they vanished mysteriously in about AD 1450. Step outside and begin your self-guided tour with an inspection of the 35-foot-tall Casa Grande (Big House), built around 1350 and still close to its original size. It's covered by a modern roof for protection from the sun and wind. Neighboring structures are much smaller, and only a bit of the 7-foot wall around the compound is still in evidence. The original purpose of Casa Grande still puzzles archaeologists; some think it was an ancient astronomical observatory.

Cross the parking lot by the covered picnic grounds and climb the platform for a view of an unexcavated ball court, said to date from the 1100s. Although only a few prehistoric sites can be viewed, more than 60 are included in the monument area.

A small gift shop in the lobby of the visitor center sells books about early Indian civilizations and other aspects of Arizona history. *1 mi north of Coolidge on AZ 87, tel. 602/723–3172. Admission: $1 adults, children under 16 and senior citizens over 62 free. Open daily 7–6.*

4 If traipsing among the ruins has given you an appetite, it's a short trip to **Coolidge,** 1 mile south on AZ 87, where you'll find fast-food hamburgers, chicken, and pizza. A public park with a children's playground is at 4th and Central avenues.

5 Take AZ 287 another 9 miles east from the monument to **Florence,** an old western town distinguished by an American Victorian courthouse and more than 125 other sites listed on the National Register of Historic Places. An annual walking tour of historic Florence is held on the first Saturday in February.

The **Pinal County Visitor Center** (912 N. Pinal St., tel. 602/868–4331) answers questions and provides brochures weekdays from 9 to 5 September through May and 10 to 2 June through August. Two attractions are the **Pinal County Historical Museum** (715 S. Main St., tel. 602/868–4382), which displays furnishings from early 1900s homes and Native American crafts and tools, and the **McFarland Historical State Park,** where the 1878-era Pinal County Courthouse (Main and Ruggles Sts., tel. 602/868–5216) houses memorabilia of former Governor and U.S. Senator Ernest W. McFarland.

Several attractive shops and restaurants are found on Florence's Main Street, including the turn-of-the-century **Florence General Store** (1218 N. Main St., tel. 602/868–5748) and **Old Pueblo Restaurant** (505 S. Main St., tel. 602/868–4784), serving good Mexican food.

Time Out At **Jim-Bob's Auld Tyme Ice Cream Parlor** (289 N. Main St., tel. 602/868–9392), ice cream and hard-packed frozen yogurt are made on the circa-1886 adobe-walled premises.

---

6 Fans of western-movie hero Tom Mix may want to drive 18 miles south on AZ 89 to the **Tom Mix Monument,** at the site of his fatal automobile accident in 1940. Pack some soft drinks; it's low desert (in fact, a showplace of dry-land vegetation), and no refreshments are on hand.

From Florence, retrace your route to Phoenix via AZ 287, 87, and 387 to link up with I–10 north and the 40-minute drive back to the Valley of the Sun.

Tour 5: Prescott and Wickenburg

Just over two hours north of Phoenix, after one of the most scenic drives in a state renowned for breathtaking vistas, you disappear into the tall pine country of Arizona's territorial capital. A slight westward jog on the way back leads you through legendary gold country and past modern dude ranches.

Start your tour by getting on I–17 (Black Canyon Freeway) and heading north. The sunken freeway is accessible from most major east–west arteries from Washington Street north. Between Van Buren Street and McDowell Road, it also connects with I–10 in a tall "stack" interchange.

Traveling north, you'll pass off ramps for **Metrocenter,** the western Valley's giant shopping-mall complex (*see* Shopping, *below*), and **Turf Paradise** (at Bell Road), the Valley's popular Thoroughbred horse track.

Abruptly, the developed areas thin out, and within 5 miles, as you pass the dark volcanic rubble of Adobe Mountain on your left, you are in open desert. Another half-dozen miles, just past Carefree Road (AZ 74), and you start climbing into foothills, where you'll see huge, spiky saguaro cacti; thick-leaved creosote bushes; and thin, spiny cholla cacti.

⑦ New River, spread out in the dry valley under which the Fria River's south fork flows, has service stations and several modest eating places.

Another 10 miles up the road is your last chance to be sure you're ready for the 2,000-foot ascent of the Mogollon Rim. On the way, the scenery shifts to classic desert mountainscape: exposed granite jutting up, covered with broken rock and scrappy vegetation; saguaros and creosote; and tall, lacy, green-limbed paloverde trees standing in the dry, flat washes. You may spot hawks or even eagles circling on the thermal currents, watching for prey.

⑧ At **Black Canyon City,** you enter Yavapai County and begin the climb up the rim. It's a beautifully graded modern highway, four lanes and completely divided, but it's a challenge—and an unfair one to an undercooled engine—so be sure to top out your car's fluids (and your own, if you don't want a half-hour wait).

Time Out   Almost out of town, Exit 244 offers you the choice of going west to the greyhound-racing track or east to the **Squaw Peak Buffalo Steakhouse** (Dog Track Rd., Black Canyon City, tel. 602/374–9247 or 602/395–9913). Choose the steak house: Besides big steaks, burgers, Maggie Mine sandwiches, and homemade pie, it has a family of live buffalo in a half-acre pen. Also on the site are a large gas station and a small souvenir shop.

As you make the dramatic climb up the Mogollon Rim, you can see the geologic strata of the upthrust earth neatly laid out in the roadside rock—rust and pink, black and purple—and feel the air temperature drop rapidly. And in 6 miles,
⑨ almost at the summit, you'll see the exit for **Bumblebee** and the **Horse Thief Basin.** The former, about 10 miles away, is a mining ghost town in the cleft of the Black Canyon to your left; the latter, some 20 miles farther along, is a beautiful wilderness area high in the Bradshaw Mountains on the other side. But go only if you've got good shoes and tires: 100 yards from the freeway, the paved road turns to dirt.

Three more miles and you suddenly reach the top—a wide, flat, grass-covered mesa, like a huge chunk of Nebraska pastureland stuck in the middle of purple mountaintops (and dotted with the clustered beaver-tails of nopal cacti). In fact, this semidesert plateau at about 4,000 feet *is* cattle-grazing land; you'll probably see some of the herds. At
⑩ **Sunset Point Rest Area,** you can also see the spectacular view off the mesa and across the Black Canyon; the rest area is on the southbound side, but you can switch back at the next exit, in about a mile.

In 10 more miles, you come to the edge of the plateau, and for a moment you see the breathtaking sweep of the Verde Valley from above; then you swoop down a steep incline, at the bottom of which is the **Cordes Junction** turnoff, AZ 69. Here, you leave I–17 and head northwest to Prescott.

But first, about a mile down a partly paved road northeast from the gas stations and cafés, is one of the world's architectural wonders—**Arcosanti.** This evolving community, masterminded by Italian architect Paolo Soleri, is being built by its residents as a totally energy-independent town. It looks almost like a huge playground or modern-art theme park, with its desert-rock retaining walls and festive forms in earth-cast concrete. But it's full of ideas for dramatic design and ecologically sensitive living; it's worth taking an hour out for a tour, eating at the café, and bringing home one of the hand-cast wind-bells. *I–17 at Cordes Junction, Mayer 86333, tel. 602/632–7135. Admission: $5. Open daily 9–5; tours hourly 10–4.*

Back on AZ 69, you're in the valley of Big Bug Creek (you can see its course by looking for the willows south of the road). In 7 miles, after crossing the Big Bug a couple of times, you'll reach **Mayer,** a provisioning center for the gold hunters who scoured the area in the last century. The tall stack of its long-silent smelter peers over a hill, and some enchanting historic buildings still stand on Main Street, a mile or so off the road.

Another 12 miles through the rolling chaparral hills (highlighted by white datura blossoms and fiery Indian paintbrush in the fall), past Mayer's sister mining town of Humboldt, is **Dewey.**

Time Out Right on the edge of town, take AZ 169 east toward the looming 7,000-foot shoulders of Mingus Mountain; after 100 yards, pull in at **Young's Farm** (AZ 169, tel. 602/632–7272). This family-run, 45-year-old farm with its 25-year-old store has become a beloved purveyor of potpies and pumpkins, sweet corn and cider, hayrides and honey, fresh bread, and wooden butterflies to folks from all over Arizona.

As you leave Dewey, the road widens to five lanes (the "Arizona lane" in the middle is for left turns only), and the landscape turns to scrub pines. In about 6 miles, you pass through **Prescott Valley,** a strip of mobile-home lots and fast-food stores that sprouted in the absence of zoning laws (watch your speed—they do have traffic laws), and then the pine trees and the hills suddenly grow taller.

Eight miles later, you enter **Prescott,** with the sandstone red Sheraton standing atop a butte in the foreground and Thumb Butte towering a few miles in the background. In a forested bowl at 5,300 feet above sea level, this lovely site was the first capital of the Arizona Territory and remains first choice for summer refuge among Phoenix-area desert dwellers.

As soon as you see the Sheraton, get into the left lane: For some reason, at the junction with U.S. 89, most lanes take you back out of town to the north. But the left lane becomes **Gurley Street,** the city's main drag. Immediately, you have a choice of motels, including the historic Mission Inn, now the **American Motel** (1211 E. Gurley St., 86301 tel. 602/778–0787), and the venerable **Senator Inn,** famous for its themed rooms (1117 E. Gurley St., 86301, tel. 602/445–1440).

Heading into town, you'll notice the many Victorian frame houses. Prescott was proclaimed capital by President Lincoln and settled by Yankees to ensure that gold-rich northern Arizona would be a Union resource—Tucson and southern Arizona were strongly pro-Confederacy. Despite a devastating downtown fire in July 1900, Prescott remains the Southwest's richest store of late-19th-century New England–style architecture (some wags say that long before Scottsdale declared itself "The West's Most Western Town," Prescott was "The West's Most Eastern Town").

About 1½ miles along Gurley is **Courthouse Plaza,** between Cortez and Montezuma streets. This is the heart of the city, where the old Yavapai County Courthouse stands, guarded by an equestrian bronze of turn-of-the-century journalist and lawmaker Bucky O'Neill, who died while charging San Juan Hill with Teddy Roosevelt. A block east of Courthouse Plaza, the historic **Hassayampa Inn** (122 E. Gurley St., 86301, tel. 602/778–9434) was recently restored to its classic 1927 splendor; it's priced like a Phoenix hotel but delivers memorable southwestern elegance for the money.

The quickest way to get oriented is to find the south end of the plaza. There, across from the courthouse's rear entrance, stands the **Chamber of Commerce** (117 W. Goodwin St., tel. 602/445–2000). Among the many maps and brochures here are two gems—"Historic Downtown Prescott: Walking Tour Guide" and "Prescott's Driving Tour Guide." Either of these will have you feeling like an old Prescott hand in a half-hour.

Flanking the plaza's west side, Montezuma Street, is **Whiskey Row,** named for a string of brawling pioneer taverns; some still stand, though the social activity there is much subdued. Upgrading one end of Whiskey Row is the mahogany-paneled **Hotel St. Michael** (205 W. Gurley St., tel. 602/776–1999), reopened in 1988 as a very modestly priced hostelry with a café and a row of underground shops. Near the middle is **Maude's** (146 S. Montezuma St., tel. 602/778–3080), an always full, fresh-scrubbed breakfast and lunch spot that would be at home in Mendocino or Santa Fe. And at the row's south end, the **Galloping Goose** (162 S. Montezuma St., tel. 602/778–7600) is a former gas station filled with lots of kitschy cowboy and Indian crafts alongside stunning collections of kachina dolls and jewelry by some of the Southwest's best working Native American artists.

Farther south on Montezuma is a good place to look for more lodging options. Four blocks from Whiskey Row is the **Prescott Country Inn** (503 S. Montezuma St., 86303, tel. 602/445–7991), a 1940s motor court transformed into a cozy bed-and-breakfast; about 2 miles farther, after Montezuma changes names (to White Spar and then Copper Basin Road), there is a mile-long stretch with seven hotels and motels in the pines, four restaurants strategically set among them.

Fun eating places are all over town. On the plaza's east side is the playful restored '50s experience of **Kendall's Burgers** (113 S. Cortez St., tel. 602/778–2472), complete with soda fountain; up the street a block or so is **Chris' New York Deli** (125 N. Cortez St., tel. 602/778–2472), a lively hole-in-the-wall with noshes that taste like Brooklyn's. Farther north is the classy fern-and-brass of **Murphy's** (201 N. Cortez St., tel. 602/445–4044), with a 60-beer pub and an award-winning kitchen that turns out prime rib and pasta, a dozen seafoods, and some sharp appetizers (how about bay shrimp nachos?). Back south to Gurley Street and west past Montezuma Street is **Nolaz** (216 W. Gurley St., tel. 602/445–3765), where Cajun dishes get tender treatment.

Time Out For unforgettable tortillas, go one block west of the plaza on Gurley Street, turn right on McCormick for half a block, and swing left into the curved driveway under the big apple tree. The little building beside the white house is **Angel's Food Products** (120½ S. McCormick, no phone). Try a tortilla hot from the oven.

Antiques and collectibles have become such an extensive part of the Prescott scene that the best bet is to stop at the first shop you see and ask for a brochure. The local dealers' group has put together a clear map of more than two dozen shops, noting their specialties and hours.

Lovers of the past also won't want to miss the **Sharlot Hall Museum,** a remarkable two-square-block re-creation of territorial Arizona, including the original log mansion of the governor, just two blocks west of Courthouse Square. Besides the mansion and museum, the parklike setting holds three other fully restored period homes, a working blacksmith shop, and the first territorial jail. It's easy to spend half or all of a day in this place. *415 W. Gurley St., tel. 602/445–3122. Admission free; donation requested. Open Apr.–Oct., Tues.–Sat. 10–5; Nov.–Mar., Tues.–Sat. 10–4, Sun. 1–5; closed Mon.*

Prescott also boasts the **Bead Museum** (140 S. Montezuma St., tel. 602/445–2431), an extensive historical collection; the respected **Phippen Museum of Western Art** (4701 Hwy. 89 N, about 5 mi north of the entrance to town, tel. 602/778–

1385); and the impressive **Smoki Museum** of Indian artifacts (100 N. Arizona, tel. 602/445-1230).

If you make Prescott a day trip, you'll probably find you've stayed a little longer than you expected. Your best bet is to end the day by retracing your route along Gurley Street, back onto AZ 69, and then south on I-17. The trip, from Courthouse Square to downtown Phoenix, can be done comfortably in 2½ hours, including a rest stop or two.

If you decide to spend a night or two in Prescott, you'll have some time to view another part of Arizona and its past on the way back to Phoenix. To do that, take Montezuma Street south out of town; in about 4 miles, it enters the **Prescott National Forest** and winds through the forested tops of the northern Bradshaw Mountain range (you saw the south end of these mountains across Black Canyon on the way up).

⑮ Then the road drops and winds about 15 miles to the lush meadows of **Peeples Valley,** named for the rancher who started a gold rush by finding nuggets in Antelope Creek. **⑯** Another 8 miles and you're at **Yarnell,** dropping below the timberline and into the desert.

Here you'll enter the watershed of the elusive Hassayampa River, whose furtive habits (traveling below the surface most of the year, then bursting into flood in winter or spring) gave the reputation of liars to locals who swore they lived on a river.

⑰ About 25 miles along the way is **Wickenburg,** home of dude ranches and tall tales. This city is named for Henry Wickenberg, whose nearby Vulture Mine was the richest gold strike in the Arizona Territory. On the main drag are the **Hassayampa Bridge,** the nearby **Jail Tree** (where prisoners were chained, not hanged, the desert heat sometimes finishing them off before their sentences were served), and the **Gold Nugget** (222 E. Wickenburg Way, tel. 602/684-2858), a western-style eating place where you can refresh yourself. Half a block north on Valentine Street is **Anita's Cocina** (62 N. Valentine St., tel. 602/684-5777), which offers creditable Mexican food. If you have time, the **Desert Caballeros** (21 N. Frontier St., tel. 602/684-7075), a local charitable equestrian group, maintains a fine museum of Hassayampa lore. If you opt for a longer stay in Wickenburg, there are plenty of dude ranches to accommodate you (*see* Lodging, *below*).

About 10 miles out of Wickenburg, you can save yourself considerable time by taking AZ 74 east (it's the Carefree Road you passed going north). In just 30 miles, it reaches I-17, leaving you with a 15-minute trip into downtown, whereas if you stay on U.S. 89, you angle into the urban area through every suburb on the west side before reaching downtown.

Tour 6: The White Mountains

Numbers in the margin correspond to points of interest on The White Mountains map.

The drive into eastern Arizona's White Mountains offers a representative tour of the state's many climatic regions and striking vistas. This trip can be completed as either of two loops, depending on which scenery proves most appealing. It's a demanding but possible day trip. But if you're going in the winter or early spring, you may need chains—and you'll probably want to take ski clothes and equipment as well, and make at least a weekend of it. During other seasons the beauty of the mountains and meadows makes at least an overnight stay all but irresistible.

From Phoenix, take I–10 and then U.S. 60 (the Superstition Freeway) east through the suburbs of Tempe, Mesa, and Apache Junction. The massive escarpment of the **① Superstition Mountains** heaves into view and slides by to the north, as the Phoenix metro area gives way to cactus- and creosote-dotted desert. The Superstitions are supposedly home to the legendary **Lost Dutchman Mine,** the location—not to mention the existence—of which has been hotly debated since pioneer days.

About 7 miles east of Apache Junction is King's Ranch Road, a bumpy 3-mile route to the Peralta Trail. The trail **②** winds up a small valley for a spectacular view of **Weaver's Needle,** a monolithic rock formation that is one of Arizona's more famous sights. This is about a two-hour side trip, including the medium-difficulty hike.

At Florence Junction, the four-lane freeway becomes a two-lane highway and starts rising steadily into the foothills of the Mescal Mountains.

Time Out Be sure to stop at the **Boyce Thompson Southwestern Arbo-③ retum,** about a dozen miles beyond Florence Junction. Its compact, informative walking tour takes in exhibits of Arizona's exotic desert flora, and it's a shady spot to break for a picnic lunch (*see* What To See and Do With Children, *below*).

Only a half-dozen miles farther on is **Superior,** the first of several modest mining towns and the launching point for a dramatic winding ascent through the Mescals to a 4,195-foot pass affording panoramic views of this copper-rich range and its huge, eerily dormant open-pit mines. Collectors will want to watch for antiques shops through these hills, but be forewarned: The quality varies considerably. The descent is just as quick into **Miami** and **Claypool,** once-thriving boom towns that have carried on quietly since major-corporation mining ground to a halt in the 1970s. The working-class buildings are dwarfed by the mountainous piles of copper tailings to the north.

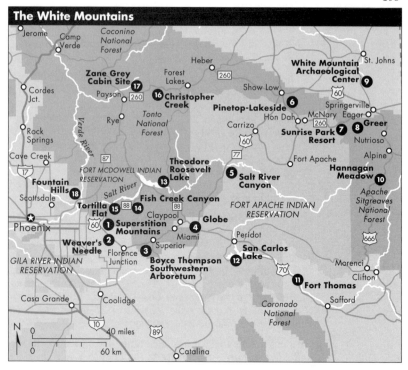

The White Mountains

④ Dotted with majestic cypress trees, **Globe,** in the southern reaches of Tonto National Forest, is the last and most cosmopolitan of these mining towns. This is a good place to eat and fill the gas tank if necessary, because it's the last appreciable town for about 90 miles of mostly mountainous country. **The Copper Manor** (637 E. Ash St., Globe, tel. 602/425–7124) is a humble café offering solid American and Mexican fare at reasonable prices. Look for its wall mural on the south side of U.S. 60 as you enter town.

After Globe, follow U.S. 60 north (don't continue east on U.S. 70), and the terrain immediately changes to the Tonto's ponderosa pine forests as the highway begins climbing through rolling hills. The highlight of this stretch **⑤** is the magnificent **Salt River Canyon,** about 40 miles past Globe. After entering the San Carlos Indian Reservation, U.S. 60 drops from the Natanes Plateau into a vast gorge, making a series of hairpin turns, to cross the Salt River and then climb out again along the canyon's northern cliffs. This is a truly spectacular chasm, unfairly overlooked in a state full of world-famous gorges.

Time Out Stop before crossing the bridge to stretch your legs and wander along the banks of the Salt, enjoying its rock-strewn rapids. On hot Arizona days you can slip your shoes off and dip your feet into the chilly water for a cool respite.

The road out of the Salt River Canyon offers several breath-taking overlooks worth stopping to enjoy. The highway continues to climb to the **Mogollon Rim**—a huge geologic upthrust that bisects Arizona from northwest to southeast—and its cool upland pine woods. **Show Low,** in the Sitgreaves National Forest, is a crossing point for east–west traffic along the rim and traffic headed for Holbrook and points north.

At Show Low, turn right onto AZ 260, and soon you'll find yourself in the newer tourist/retirement community of **Pinetop–Lakeside** (the two towns joined in 1984 but still have separate post offices). It's a lengthy succession of shopping malls, restaurants, and motels, more numerous than appealing. But the slowly curving highway through these twin towns is usually dotted on the weekends with fruit-and-vegetable stands, purveying modestly priced, wonderfully fresh Arizona produce.

If you plan to stay the night, there is an eclectic selection of hostelries worth considering, among them **Bartram's Bed and Breakfast** (Rte. 1, Box 1014, Lakeside 85929, tel. 800/257–0211); **Coldstream B&B** (Box 2616, Pinetop 85935, tel. 602/369–0115); and the cottages at **Spring Hill on Rainbow Lake** (Box 1040, Lakeside 85929, tel. 602/368–8688).

After Pinetop–Lakeside, the road dips into the Fort Apache Indian Reservation. At the tiny crossroads town of **Hon Dah,** AZ 260 swings east again. **McNary** is next, a ram-shackle Native American community built among the pines—but don't hurry through if you see a tent and a sign advertising Indian fry bread. Try this doughy fried dish with honey or other fillings for a taste of Indian cuisine.

Already more than a mile above sea level, the highway continues its gradual but steady climb after McNary into the White Mountains, leaving the reservation for the Apache National Forest. Get a breath of the thin, pine-scented air; it tends to be cool even in the middle of a summer day.

At AZ 273 winter and early spring visitors will want to turn right to **Sunrise Park Resort,** the state's largest ski area, with five day lodges, 11 lifts, and 65 trails on three mountains rising to 11,000 feet. Operated by the White Mountain Apache Indian Tribe, the resort is one of the most successful Native American business enterprises in the United States. The recently remodeled **Sunrise Ski Lodge** offers modern accommodations and solid American dining at reasonable prices. The tribe also operates a modest outdoor-sports center, which rents a variety of equipment, from cross-country skis to mountain bikes. *Sunrise Park Resort, Greer 85927, tel. 602/735–7676, for skiing reports, tel. 800/ 772–SNOW. Open year-round.*

Down AZ 260 another five minutes is the turnoff summer and fall tourists won't want to miss—AZ 373 for **Greer,** a tiny, charming community built around a meadow and trout ponds. Here are numerous lodges and resorts of varying quality and price. **Greer Lodge** offers a hearty and huge meal, with cozy overnight accommodations in a rustic log-cabin atmosphere; the friendly help keeps the fire in the stone fireplace stoked and roaring in the cool alpine evenings. *Greer Lodge, Box 244, Greer 85927, tel. 602/735–7515. Open year-round.*

This area of gently sloping national forest land is dotted with meadows, lakes, and small reservoirs and dominated by 11,590-foot Baldy Peak. It's a wonderland for outdoor activities: hunting, fishing, horseback riding, hiking, boating, camping. Much of it remains under the control of the Apache nation, so visitors must take care to respect the land as they do and to honor their wishes.

Another 10 minutes east on AZ 260 are the twin towns of **Springerville** and **Eagar,** in Round Valley. The region, hard against the New Mexico border, brims with Old West lore. This is where William Bonney (aka Billy the Kid) herded livestock before turning outlaw. Many of the towns were founded by Mormon pioneers and there is a big Mormon church between the two towns, but they are dominated by their high school's domed stadium, testament to the residents' love of sports and to the sometimes harsh winter weather.

9 For a pleasant stop and a step back 1,000 years, head north on AZ 666 about 12 miles from Springerville to the **White Mountain Archaeological Center.** At Raven Site Ruin, on a former cattle ranch, James and Carol Cunkle lead amateurs, students, and professionals in unearthing a pottery-making Indian culture that flourished from about AD 1000 to 1450. Half-day hikes visit nearby petroglyphs; day-long programs add hands-on training in ruin-sifting. Longer stays include accommodations at a restored 19th-century bunkhouse. The tiny museum is a marvel. *White Mountain Archaeological Center, HC 30, St. Johns 85936, tel. 602/333–5857. Admission: $3 adults, with guided 1-hour tour; children under 12 free. Open mid-Apr.–mid-Oct., daily 10–5.*

Springerville is a decision point: Should you head south or west on the return trip to Phoenix? At Springerville, AZ 260 joins U.S. 60, which continues east into New Mexico, and the so-called "Devil's Highway" (AZ 666), surely one of the world's curviest roads, coming down from the Painted Desert.

If you decide to head south from Springerville on AZ 666, this lonely highway passes through **Nutrioso** under 10,912-
10 foot Escudilla Mountain and eventually rises to **Hannagan Meadow,** one of Arizona's most splendid camping areas. Lush and isolated, it provides a home to elk, deer, and range cattle. Don't miss the splendid overlooks on the way.

Time Out Waiting by the roadside in the middle of the meadow is the log-built **Hannagan Meadow Lodge,** where you can enjoy a meal or a month in a setting of unparalleled peace and beauty, with people who have tuned in to life away from cities and towns, but not without amenities. *Hannagan Meadow Lodge, Box 335, Alpine 85920, tel. 602/339-4370. Open year-round.*

From Hannagan Meadow, the road south twists and turns as it descends into a huge wilderness devoid, for the most part, of humans, and passes under Rose and Mitchell peaks (there is camping near the latter).

Eventually passing through the mining towns of **Morenci** and **Clifton,** AZ 666 then swings back west, links up with U.S. 70, and provides a fairly straight shot through **Safford** and across rather uninteresting desert to Globe. As you ⑪ near **Fort Thomas,** keep your eyes peeled—$28,000 in gold pieces, meant to pay the soldiers there, was stolen back in May 1889 and still hasn't been found. About 12 miles farther along, on your left, you'll see towering 8,282-foot Mt. ⑫ Turnbull, then the spreading expanse of **San Carlos Lake,** a reservoir behind Coolidge Dam. (Dedicating it in 1927, Will Rogers observed, "If that was my lake, I'd mow it.") At Peridot, if you turn north on AZ 170, 4 miles brings you to the town of San Carlos: It used to be Rice, until the dam put the original San Carlos underwater.

Once you reach Globe, you can retrace your original route back along U.S. 60 to Phoenix. Or if you prefer, **The Apache Trail** (AZ 88) departs from Claypool to the north, passing ⑬ several ranches en route to the massive **Theodore Roosevelt Lake** reservoir, a favorite aquatic recreational area flanked by the desolate Mazatzal and Sierra Anchas mountain ranges. The Apache Trail eventually winds its way back to ⑭ Apache Junction via the bronze-hued **Fish Creek Canyon,** over a road that most survivors consider unforgettable.

Time Out Close to the end of the Apache Trail are the old-time restau-
⑮ rant, bar, and country store at **Tortilla Flat.** This is a fun place to stop for a well-earned rest and refreshment—miner- and cowboy-style grub, of course—before heading back the last 20 miles to civilization. *1678 W. Superstition Blvd., Apache Junction, tel. 602/984-1776. Open year-round weekdays 9-6, weekends 8-7.*

Back at Springerville, your other homeward option is to follow U.S. 60 west along the forested Mogollon Rim, enjoying its thrilling overlooks. From Show Low, take AZ 260 west along the Rim through a variety of small retirement and ranching communities. After **Forest Lakes,** the road dives off the Rim, hugging sheer cliffs for a 2,000-foot drop to the broad, verdant **Tonto Basin.**

Time Out Below the rim, in the Tonto Basin, is **Christopher Creek,** a
⑯ primitive community with a humble but decent restaurant,
the **Creekside** (HCR Box 146, Payson, tel. 602/478–4389).
The Christopher Creek Lodge (Star Route Box 119, Payson
85541, tel. 602/478–4300) offers no-frills log-cabin accommodations.

West of Christopher Creek a huge forest fire charred much
of the terrain several summers ago, destroying (along with
millions of trees) the antiques-filled **Zane Grey Cabin,** once
the home of the novelist whose popular tales, many made
into films, colorfully documented the rough-and-tumble life
of this corner of the Old West. Now his life and career are
recalled with photographs and new momentos, in the sim-
⑰ ple visitor center at the **Zane Grey Cabin Site.** *(Box 787,
Payson 85547, tel. 602/478–4243. Open year-round, daily
9–5).*

A dozen miles down the road and it's back to civilization in
Payson, a bustling vacation town with an interesting, unpretentious municipal golf course and a good supply of antiques shops. Turn south on U.S. 87 for the last hour-long
dash across the ridges of the Mazatzals.

Descending into a saguaro-studded basin, you reach the
Salt River again, this time on the Fort McDowell Mohave–
Apache Reservation, whose residents have outlasted the
fort where the U.S. Army based its northern campaign
against the Apaches. When you see the 140-foot spray of
⑱ the **Fountain Hills** fountain, get ready to turn right at Shea
Boulevard and head back, via Scottsdale, into Phoenix.

What to See and Do with Children

Aimed at children of elementary-school age, the **Arizona
Museum for Youth** displays fine arts in a manner attractive
to youngsters. Hands-on exhibits allow them to make crafts
or participate as they go through the museum. A tour takes
about 1–1½ hours. *35 N. Robson St., Mesa, tel. 602/644–
2468. Admission: $2. Open Tues.–Fri. 1–5, Sat. 10–5,
Sun. 1–5.*

Arizona Museum of Science and Technology (*see* Tour 1,
above).

About an hour east of Phoenix on U.S. 60, the **Boyce
Thompson Southwestern Arboretum** is one of the treasures
of the Sonoran desert. From the visitor center, well-
marked self-guided trails traverse 35 acres, winding
through all of the desert's varied habitats—from gravelly
open desert to lush creekside glades—rich with native flora
and wildlife. The **Smith Interpretive Center,** a National Historic Site, houses rotating displays on such topics as geology and mining plus two greenhouses with cacti and other
succulents. The arboretum is a wonderful place to stop for a
picnic on your way to the mining towns of Superior and Mi-

ami. *Box AB, Superior 85273, tel. 602/689–2811. Admission: $3 adults, $1.50 children 5–12. Open daily 8–5. Closed Christmas.*

Great Arizona Puppet Theatre (3302 N. 7th St., Phoenix 85011, tel. 602/277–1275) mounts a yearlong cycle of inventive puppet productions, mostly original, in a converted church; it also offers classes in puppet making and operation.

At the **Hall of Flame,** retired fire fighters lead tours past more than 100 restored fire engines and over 3,000 helmets, badges, and other fire-fighting-related articles. *6101 E. Van Buren St. (in Papago Park), tel. 602/275–3473. Admission: $4 adults, $1.50 children 6–17, children 6 and under free. Open Mon.–Sat. 9–5.*

Model-train displays, stores with railway memorabilia and items for the train hobbyist, and a restored Pullman car fill the popular **McCormick Railroad Park.** For 75¢, children can ride the miniature train or the 1929 merry-go-round. *7303 E. Indian Bend Rd., tel. 602/994–2408. Admission free. Open weekdays 10–7, weekends 11–7.*

At the foot of South Mountain, **Mystery Castle,** hand-built out of found desert rocks, is chock-full of oddities that will fascinate everyone in the family. There are 18 rooms with 13 fireplaces, 90 bottle-glass portholes, a downstairs grotto, and a rollaway bed with a mining railcar as its frame. *800 E. Mineral Rd. (at the south end of 7th St.) tel. 602/268–1581. Admission: $3 adults, $1 children 5–15. Open Tues.–Sun. 11–4.*

Phoenix Children's Theatre (1202 N. 3rd St., tel. 602/265–4142) stages a full season, usually adaptations of fairy tales and children's books, at the city's Performing Arts Building.

At the **Phoenix Zoo,** a new 21,000-square-foot Baboon Kingdom exhibit brings together more than 1,300 animals, grouped by continent of origin. Indian and African elephants (including one that produces artworks sold in galleries!) and a rare Sumatran tiger are among the attractions. A 30-minute narrated tour on the safari train costs $1 and gives a good overview of the park. *5810 E. Van Buren St. (in Papago Park), tel. 602/273–7771. Admission: $6 adults, $5 senior citizens over 62, $3 children 4–12. Open daily 9–5.*

Original and reconstructed buildings from all over Arizona set the stage for the **Pioneer Arizona Museum.** Guides in the blacksmith shop, print shop, schoolhouse, and homes demonstrate daily activities from the past. *Pioneer Rd. exit off I–17, tel. 602/993–0212. Admission: $5.75 adults, $5.25 senior citizens and students, $4 children 4–12, children 3 and under free. Open Wed.–Sun. 9–5, closed July 4–Oct. 1.*

The false fronts on **Rawhide's** dusty Main Street house "saloons," gift shops, old-time photo studios, and craftspeople as well as opportunities to take a stagecoach ride or to pan for gold. Hayrides travel a short distance into the desert for a cookout under the stars on weekends. *23023 N. Scottsdale Rd., Scottsdale, tel. 602/563–5111. Admission free; separate charges for shops, restaurants, attractions. Open weekdays 5–10 PM, weekends 11–10.*

Similar to Rawhide, but a better deal because the price of entry is all-inclusive, **Rockin' R Ranch** includes a petting zoo, a staged shoot-out, and—the main attraction—a nightly cookout and western stage show. Browse the shops until the chow—beef, beans, and biscuits—is served, followed by music and entertainment. Reservations are required. *6136 E. Baseline Rd., Mesa, tel. 602/832–1539. Admission (includes meal and show): $14.95 adults, $8.50 children 3–12. Open year-round; call for hours.*

The **Sunrise Preschool** (642 E. Monroe St., tel. 602/253–0381) at the east end of The Mercado (*see* Tour 1, *above*) offers high-quality child care at drop-in rates, 24 hours a day.

Shopping

Since its resorts began multiplying in the 1930s and 1940s, Phoenix has acquired a healthy share of high-style clothiers and leisure-wear boutiques. But well before that, western clothes were dominant here—jeans and boots, cotton shirts and dresses, 10-gallon hats and bola ties (the state's official neckwear). They still are. Plain or designer, cowboy or vaquero, with rivets or silver *conchos* or diamonds, western is always in style, and outfitters abound.

In the past decade, Sun Belt awareness has brought a tide of interest in southwestern furnishing styles as well, from the pastels of the desert mountains and skies to the handmade lodgepole furniture of the pueblo and rancho. These—as well as Mexican tiles and tinware, wrought iron and copper work, courtyard fountains and paper flowers—have never died out here. Always an essential part of the way southwesterners shape their homes, work spaces, and public places, these crafts have flourished in the current revival.

At the same time, the drivers of many a wagon train in the past century and many a U-Haul in this one have headed west and ended up unloading here. As a result, the shops and auctions of Phoenix and its suburbs contain an unexpectedly wide array of antiques and collectibles.

On the scene long before any of these, of course, were the fine and powerful arts of the Southwest's true natives—Navajo weavers, sand painters, and silversmiths; Hopi weavers and kachina-doll carvers; Pima and Papago basket makers and potters; and many more.

American Express offers Travelers Cheques built for two.

American Express® Cheques *for Two*. The first Travelers Cheques that allow either of you to use them because both of you have signed them. And only one of you needs to be present to purchase them.

Cheques *for Two* are accepted anywhere regular American Express Travelers Cheques are, which is just about everywhere. So stop by your bank, AAA* or any American Express Travel Service Office and ask for Cheques *for Two*.

Inspired by the region's rich cultural traditions, contemporary artists have flourished here as well, making Phoenix—and in particular, Scottsdale, a city with more art galleries than gas stations—one of the Southwest's two great art centers (alongside Santa Fe, New Mexico).

Most of the Valley's power shopping is concentrated in central Phoenix and downtown Scottsdale. But auctions and antiques shops cluster in odd places—and as treasure hunters know, you've always got to have an eye open.

Malls and Department Stores The open-air **Park Central Mall** (Central Ave. and Earll Dr., tel. 602/264–5575) is the oldest and closest to downtown, amid the high rises of Central Avenue. Anchored by a **Dillard's** department store (3033 N. 3rd Ave., tel. 602/277–0564), Park Central also has **Switzer's** (44 Park Central Mall, tel. 602/264–4361), a traditional Phoenix clothier; the ever-popular **Miracle Mile Deli** (9 Park Central Mall, tel. 602/277–4783); and **Leonard's Luggage** (Park Central Mall, tel. 602/264–3591), the Valley's oldest purveyor of luxury leather goods and accessories.

Metrocenter (I–17 and Peoria Ave., tel. 602/997–2641), on the west side of Phoenix, is an enclosed double-deck mall, the state's largest. The adjacent **Castles N Coasters** (9445 N. Metro Pkwy. E, tel. 602/997–7575), a miniature-golf park and video-game palace, and the in-mall **Metro Midway** (13615 N. 35th Ave., tel. 602/395–9915), an array of rides and games, make Metro the Valley's best mall for teens and younger children. Inside, its anchor department stores include **Robinson's** (9700 N. Metro Pkwy. E, tel. 602/943–2351). Metrocenter has nearly every store Park Central has (except the deli) and many more, but in a Muzak-filled, disinfected, deodorized environment that might as easily be in St. Louis or Seattle or Secaucus.

Fiesta Mall (AZ 360 and Alma School Rd., Mesa, tel. 602/833–5450) and the new **Superstition Springs Mall,** a dozen miles farther east (AZ 360 and Superstition Springs Rd., Mesa, tel. 602/832–0212), provide slightly smaller copies, without the youth attractions, for the eastern Valley—though the latter does boast a handsome indoor carousel and a pleasant outdoor cactus garden to stroll in. The somewhat older but just expanded **Paradise Valley Mall** (Cactus and Tatum Rds., tel. 602/996–8840) does likewise for northeastern Phoenix.

Scottsdale Fashion Square (Scottsdale and Camelback Rds., Scottsdale, tel. 602/990–7800) is a step upscale. Besides Robinson's and Dillard's, it is anchored by **Bullock's** (6900 E. Camelback Rd., Scottsdale, tel. 602/994–3111), and its mix of stores runs more to specialty shops; children will want everything in the **Disney Store** (7014 E. Camelback Rd., Scottsdale, tel. 602/423–5008).

Biltmore Fashion Park (24th St. and Camelback Rd., tel. 602/955–8400), about 8 miles west in Phoenix, is several more steps upscale. **I. Magnin** (2400 E. Camelback Rd., tel. 602/955–7200) and **Saks Fifth Avenue** (2500 E. Camelback Rd., tel. 602/955–8000) are its anchors, and designer boutiques are its stock-in-trade—**Banana Republic** (2582 E. Camelback Rd., tel. 602/955–9108), **Beaton's** (2480 E. Camelback Rd., tel. 602/955–5061), **Bruno Magli** (2542 E. Camelback Rd., tel. 602/956–6661), **Gucci** (2504 E. Camelback Rd., tel. 602/957–8710), and **Polo by Ralph Lauren** (2580 E. Camelback Rd., tel. 602/952–0155) are among them. Adult toy shops include **The Sharper Image** (2596 E. Camelback Rd., tel. 602/956–8077) and **Williams-Sonoma** (2450 E. Camelback Rd., tel. 602/957–0430). Biltmore Fashion Park also has more fine eating in a small compass than anywhere else in Arizona; *see* the reviews of **Roxsand, Steamers, Oscar Taylor's,** and **Christopher's** in the Dining section, *below.*

The Borgata (6166 N. Scottsdale Rd., tel. 602/998–1822), a re-creation of a medieval Italian walled village, may not quite challenge Biltmore Fashion Park for class, but it goes far beyond it in providing an amusing, theme-park approach to shopping. It has several good designer boutiques and interior-design shops and a handful of galleries of uneven quality.

Markets and Auctions **Guadalupe Farmer's Market** (9210 S. Avenida del Yaqui, Guadalupe, tel. 602/730–1945) has all the fresh ingredients of Mexican cuisine as you'd find them in a rural Mexican market—tomatillos, many varieties of chili peppers (fresh and dried), fresh-ground *masa* (cornmeal) for tortillas, cumin and cilantro, and on and on. **Mercado Mexico** (8212 S. Avenida del Yaqui, Guadalupe, tel. 602/831–5925), about six blocks north, sells childhood treats Mexican adults remember fondly, from *cajetas* (goat's milk candy) to cocoa blocks and sweet powders in paper tubes. But most of the shop consists of shelf after shelf of ceramic, paper, tin, and lacquer ware, at unbeatable prices.

John Brunk & Sons Auctions (4001 N. 7th St., tel. 602/264–3204) moves a barnful of cast-off furnishings, appliances, tools—and often several decent antiques or collectibles—twice each Wednesday, at 9 AM and from 7 PM until the last lot is gone. **Ron Brunk Inc. Auction** has a warehouse auction Sunday at noon in the western Valley, not far from Sun City (11001 N. 99th Ave., Peoria, tel. 602/933–7748). **Hudson & Associates** (3602 N. 35th Ave., tel. 602/269–8662) gavels off a diverse gathering of goods starting at 7 PM each Friday, as does **Ware's Auction** (38th Ave. at Indian School Rd., tel. 602/278–0489) at 7 PM Monday.

Barrett & Jackson Classic Car Auction (5530 E. Washington St., tel. 602/273–0791) is a nationally recognized dealer in rare and antique autos, and the annual mega-auction draws collectors from around the world.

Southwestern Arts and Crafts The **Heard Museum** (22 E. Monte Vista Rd., tel. 602/252–8848) sells the finest selection of southwestern Indian arts and crafts in the Valley—both traditional and modern—at its gift shop. The museum is also the ideal place for learning about whatever medium or art form interests you and to see Native American artists and artisans at work almost every day.

Herman Atkinson's Indian Trading Post (3957 N. Brown Ave., Scottsdale, tel. 602/949–9750) is another fine—but eclectic—source for Native American and especially Mexican work, from silver to lacquer goods to boots and paper flowers. Mixed in is a good deal of inexpensive (but often pretty good) tourist ware, and even an intriguing roomful of African carvings.

Godber's Jewelry (7542 E. Main St., Scottsdale, tel. 602/ 949–1133) is one of the oldest, most reliable Indian-jewelry outlets in central Arizona. Begun 60 years ago by a reservation trading-post family, it's a fine place for learning the many styles of southwestern jewelry and discovering your own preferences.

Gilbert Ortega (7229 E. Main St., Scottsdale, tel. 602/947– 2805) began as a reliable trader, then mushroomed into an industry with nine Scottsdale locations (including two at The Borgata), four in Phoenix, and one each in Tempe, Sun City, and Carefree. Only a fairly experienced Indian-jewelry buyer should shop here.

Folklórico (7216 E. Main St., Scottsdale, tel. 602/947–0758) is a fine purveyor of southwestern folk arts and crafts.

Finally, the shops at **The Mercado** (542 E. Monroe St., tel. 602/256–6322) include some delightful selections of gifts and art from Mexico and Latin America—and don't forget the gift shop at the **Museo Chicano** (641 E. Van Buren St., tel. 602/257–5536), on The Mercado's second floor.

Sports and the Outdoors

Participant Sports

When participating in outdoor sports in Phoenix, be aware that the desert heat imposes its particular restraints on activities. From May 1 to October 1, do not jog or hike from one hour after sunrise until a half hour before sunset. During those times, the air is so hot and dry that your body will lose moisture—and burn calories—at a dangerous, potentially lethal rate. Don't head out to desert areas at night, however, to jog or hike in the summer; that's when rattlesnakes and scorpions are out hunting. Hikers and bicyclists should wear light but opaque clothes, strong sunscreen (rated 15 or higher), high UV-rated sunglasses, and a hat or visor and should carry a water supply of one quart per person for each hour of activity, even in winter.

Bicycling Although its relatively level terrain is great, the desert makes special demands on cyclists: *See* the advice on hours and clothing, *above*. Be sure to have a helmet and a mirror when riding in the streets: There are few adequate bike lanes in the Valley.

Scottsdale's Indian Bend Wash (along Hayden Rd., from Shea Blvd. south to Indian School Rd.) has bikeable paths winding among its golf courses and ponds. **Pinnacle Peak,** about 25 miles northeast of downtown Phoenix, is a popular place to carry bikes to for the ride north to Carefree and Cave Creek, or east and south over the mountain pass and down to the Verde River, toward Fountain Hills. **Cave Creek** and **Carefree,** in the foothills about 30 miles northeast of Phoenix, offer pleasant riding with a wide range of stop-over options. **South Mountain Park** (*see* Hiking, below) is the prime site for mountain bikers, with its 40-plus miles of trails—some of them with challenging ascents, and all of them quiet and scenic.

For rentals, contact **Landis Cyclery** (712 W. Indian School Rd., tel. 602/264–5681; 2180 E. Southern Ave., Tempe, tel. 602/839–9383; 10417 N. Scottsdale Rd., Scottsdale, tel. 602/948–9280) or **Tempe Bicycle** (330 W. University Dr., Tempe, tel. 602/966–6896; 9180 E. Indian Bend Rd., Scottsdale, tel. 602/998–2219; 267 E. Bell Rd., tel. 602/375–1515).

To get in touch with fellow bike enthusiasts and find out about regular and special-event rides, contact the **Arizona Bicycle Club** (Gene or Sylvia Berlatsky, tel. 602/264–5478), the state's largest group, or the **Greater Arizona Bicycle Association** (Mike Gerads, tel. 602/496–0303).

Golf The Valley of the Sun is the valley of year-round golf par excellence. More than 100 courses, from par-3 to PGA championship links, are available (some lighted at night), and the PGA's Southwest section headquarters here. For a detailed listing, contact the **Arizona Golf Association** (*see* Chapter 1, Essential Information).

One of the newer, upscale courses, **Ahwatukee Country Club** (12432 S. 48th St., tel. 602/893–1161), set along the edge of South Mountain Park, is semiprivate but also has a public driving range. The **Arizona Biltmore** (24th St. and Missouri Ave., tel. 602/955–9655), the granddaddy of Phoenix golf courses, offers two 18-hole PGA championship courses, lessons, and clinics. Two low-price public courses, both in scenic city settings, are **Encanto Park** (2705 N. 15th Ave., tel. 602/253–3963) and **Papago Golf Course** (5595 E. Moreland St., tel. 602/275–8428). If you're in the Superstition Mountains area, try the desert course at **Gold Canyon Golf Club** (6100 S. Kings Ranch Rd., Apache Junction, tel. 602/982–9449). The best course in the Sun Cities, **Hillcrest Golf Club** (20002 N. Star Ridge, Sun City West, tel. 602/975–1000), is a PGA Senior Tour site. Take the children along to **PGA Tour Family Golf Center** (8111 E. McDonald

Dr., Scottsdale, tel. 602/991–0018), which combines goofy golf, a driving range, and lessons at all levels. For big, sweeping views of the city, **Thunderbird Country Club** (701 E. Thunderbird Trail, tel. 602/243–1262) has 18 holes of championship-rated play on the north slopes of South Mountain. **Tournament Players Club at Scottsdale** (17020 N. Hayden Rd., Scottsdale, tel. 602/585–3600), a 36-hole course created by Tom Weiskopf and Jay Morrish, is the site of the PGA Phoenix Open.

Health Clubs **The Arizona Athletic Club** (1425 W. 14th St., Tempe, tel. 602/894–2281), near the airport at the border between Tempe and Scottsdale, is the Valley's largest facility. It offers nonmember visitors a day rate of less than $15.

Jazzercise (tel. 602/420–1006) has 36 franchised sites in the Valley, where people who are already on a program can keep on course while on vacation.

Life Centers of Arizona (4041 N. Central Ave., tel. 602/265–5472), in central Phoenix, is geared to the working man and woman, so it offers nonmembers both reasonable day rates ($5–$15) and a variety of quick workout options.

Naturally Women (2827 W. Peoria Ave., tel. 602/678–4000; 3320 S. Price Rd., Tempe, tel. 602/838–8800; 7750 E. Mc-Dowell Rd., 602/947–8300) focuses on women, from its health profiles to its diet and exercise programs; it offers one free visitor's day, then a day rate of about $10 afterward.

Hiking The Valley boasts the best desert mountain hiking in the world—the **Phoenix Mountain Preserve System,** in the mountains ringing the city, even has its own park rangers, who can help you select and plan your hikes. For information and group hiking reservations, call the South Mountain Rangers' Office (tel. 602/495–0222).

Squaw Peak (2701 E. Squaw Peak Dr., just north of Lincoln) is a favorite two-hour hike that ascends the landmark mountain from a well-equipped park in the North Mountains Preserve. Children can handle this one if the adults take it slow. The rangers also lead a fine, easy hike through the park, introducing desert geology, flora, and fauna.

Camelback Mountain (north of Camelback Rd. on 48th St.), another landmark hike, has no park, and the trails are noticeably more difficult. This is for intermediate to experienced hikers.

The soft sandstone **Papago Peaks** (Van Buren St. and Galvin Pkwy.) were sacred sites for the Tohonó O'odham tribe and probably the Hohokam before them; now they provide accessible caves, some petroglyphs, and splendid views all around the Valley. This is another good spot for family hikes. The Phoenix Zoo, the Desert Botanical Garden, and the new Arizona Historical Society Museum are on the site.

South Mountain Park (10919 S. Central Ave.) is the jewel of the South Mountain Park Preserves. At 16,000 acres, it is the nation's largest city park, and its mountains and arroyos contain more than 40 miles of marked and maintained trails—all multiuse, for hiking, horseback riding, and mountain biking. It also has three auto-accessible lookout points, with 65-mile sightlines. The rangers can help you plan hikes to see some of the 200 petroglyph sites located so far.

Horseback Riding More than two dozen stables and equestrian tour outfitters in the Valley attest to the saddle's enduring importance in Arizona—even in this auto-dominated metropolis.

All Western Stables (10220 S. Central Ave., tel. 602/276–5862), one of several stables at the entrance to South Mountain Park, offers rentals, guided trail rides, steak fries, and hayrides.

The two **Hole-in-the-Wall Stables** (7677 N. 16th St., tel. 602/997–1466; 7777 Pointe Pkwy., tel. 602/431–0817) are both near large parts of the Phoenix Mountain Preserve System and have guided solo and group, hourly and overnight options.

Adjacent to the Phoenix North Mountains Preserve, **North Side Stables** (25251 N. 19th Ave., tel. 602/581–0103) offers everything from pony rides to pack trips—even stagecoach rentals.

Old MacDonald's Ranch (26540 N. Scottsdale Rd., Scottsdale, tel. 602/585–0239) provides guided trail rides, hayrides, and catered cookouts.

Superstition Stables (Windsong and Meridian Rds., Apache Junction, tel. 602/982–6353) is licensed to lead tours throughout the entire Superstition Mountains area for more experienced riders; easier rides are also available.

Hot-Air Ballooning Another unusual sport that has soared in the desert air is hot-air ballooning. The following are a few of the three dozen companies that offer uplifting experiences; all use FAA-certified pilots: **An Aeronautical Adventure** (tel. 602/991–4260) has daily flights and will sell you a balloon if the bug really bites. **Hot Air Promotions** (tel. 602/788–5555) features a champagne flight and free pickup and return at local resorts. **Naturally High** (tel. 602/252–6766) offers not only ascents with trained pilots but also training for aspiring crew members.

Jogging Phoenix's unique 200-mile network of canals provides a naturally cooled (and often landscaped) scenic track throughout the metro area. Two other popular jogging areas are Phoenix's **Encanto Park,** 3 miles northwest of Civic Plaza, and Scottsdale's **Indian Bend Wash,** which runs for more than 5 miles along Hayden Road—both have lagoons and tree-shaded greens.

Tennis At **Hole-in-the-Wall Racquet Club** (7677 N. 16th St., Pointe Hilton at Squaw Peak Resort, tel. 602/997–2543), eight paved courts are available for same-day reservation for $15/hour; at the affiliated **Watering Hole Racquet Club** (11111 N. 7th St., Pointe Hilton at Tapatio Cliffs Resort, tel. 602/997–7237) the 15 courts are hard and lighted for night games. **Mountain View Tennis Center** (1104 E. Grovers St., tel. 602/788–6088), just north of Bell Road, is a Phoenix city facility with 20 lighted courts that can be reserved for $2.50 for 90 minutes of singles. For the same price you can play at **Phoenix Tennis Center** (6330 N. 21st Ave., tel. 602/249–3712), another city facility with 22 lighted hard courts. **The Pointe Hilton at South Mountain Tennis Club** (7777 S. Pointe Pkwy., tel. 602/438–9000) has 10 lighted hard courts for $20/hour.

Tubing In a region not known for water, one indigenous aquatic sport has developed. Tubing—riding an inner tube down calm water and mild rapids—has become a very popular tradition on the Salt and Verde rivers. Outfitters that rent tubes include **Saguaro Lake Ranch Tube & Raft Rental** (13020 N. Bush Hwy., Mesa, tel. 602/984–2194), right on the way into the McDowell Mountains, where the river action is, from Phoenix, and **Salt River Recreation Tube Rental & Shuttle** (Bush St., Mesa, tel. 602/984–3305), conveniently located and offering transportation to and from your starting point.

Spectator Sports

Auto Racing **Phoenix International Raceway** (7602 S. 115th Ave., Tolleson, tel. 602/252–3833), the Valley's NASCAR track, is the site of a Winston Cup 500 each November and the Indy car Valvoline 200 each April.

Balloon Racing **The Thunderbird Hot-Air Balloon Classic** (tel. 602/978–7208) has grown into a schedule of festivities surrounding the national invitational balloon race, held each November.

Baseball *See* Chapter 1, Essential Information, for information on **Cactus League** spring training.

Basketball **The Phoenix Suns** (2nd and Jefferson Sts., tel. 602/379–SUNS) have been NBA playoff regulars for several years. Their new America West Phoenix Suns Arena is almost as exciting as their game.

Golf **The Phoenix Open** (tel. 602/585–4334), played each January at the Tournament Players Club in Scottsdale, is a $1 million event on the PGA Tour. In March, the women compete for the $550,000 purse in **Standard Register PING Tournament** (tel. 602/942–0000), held at the Moon Valley Country Club.

Rodeos **The Parada del Sol,** held each year by the Scottsdale Jaycees (3515 N. 75th St., Scottsdale, tel. 602/990–3179), includes a rodeo, a lavish parade famed for its silver-studded tack, and a 400-mile daredevil ride from Holbrook down the Mogollon Rim to Phoenix by the Hashknife Riders.

The Rodeo of Rodeos, sponsored by the Phoenix Jaycees (4133 N. 7th St., tel. 602/263–8671), boasts a parade and is one of the Southwest's oldest and best.

The World's Oldest Rodeo (117 W. Goodwin St., Prescott, tel. 602/445–2000), held each July as part of Frontier Days, gives the Phoenix rodeos a run for their money.

Dining

Phoenix's food traditions arose from a unique blend of Old West and New West cultures. In the mid-19th century, the north Mexican rancho cooking that had been in Arizona for 150 years was joined by the Anglo-European food of American settlers. Arizona Territory was also an outpost of the West's cattle-ranching boom, and railroads brought a significant early influx of Chinese settlers.

By the mid-20th century, the Valley was rich in Mexican food, mostly in the style of the adjoining Mexican state of Sonora; steak houses, from cowboy to fancy (Phoenix was a major stockyard center until the 1970s); and Chinese restaurants, mostly Cantonese. There was lots of good family eating, but not much haute cuisine; when Phoenicians wanted to get fancy, the men put on bola ties and the women donned silver-and-turquoise jewelry, and they paid someone to pour "Continental" sauces on their steaks.

Then, during the 1970s, things took off. Southeast Asian refugees brought peppery Oriental dishes that were instantly welcome in a city used to salsa and sweet-and-sour. Immigrants from Central America and the Middle East brought more variations on familiar themes, as well as new approaches. Soon, "southwestern international" was born—and by the late '80s, it had taken hold of America's culinary imagination. Today, as innovative chefs and restaurateurs create new offshoots, this lively, eclectic cuisine continues to thrive.

Few restaurants require men to wear a jacket and tie; in any of these, a bola tie (the official state ornament) will qualify. The *guayabera* (Mexican wedding shirt) is also an appropriate warm-weather option in all but the fanciest places. Similarly, slacks or a simple dress are welcome almost everywhere for women; the fanciest places expect a dress or pantsuit.

Restaurants are open daily, unless otherwise noted.

Highly recommended restaurants are indicated by a star ★.

Category	Cost
Very Expensive	over $40
Expensive	$20–$40
Moderate	$10–$20
Inexpensive	under $10

per person, excluding drinks, service, and sales tax (6%–7%)

American

Ruth's Chris Steakhouse. Most meat fanciers agree that steak seldom gets better handling than at this New Orleans–based chain. Amid brass, wood, and glass (and great views, in the Scottsdale location), you can get thick, juicy lamb or pork chops, but planks of beef are this restaurant's business. Calorie and cardiac watchers, beware: Portions are massive, and everything—even the broiled shrimp—comes swimming in the house butter bath. *2201 E. Camelback Rd., tel. 602/957-9600; 7001 N. Scottsdale Rd., Scottsdale, tel. 602/991-5988. Reservations required. Jacket suggested. AE, MC, V. Expensive.*

Steamers. Watching the chefs at work in the open kitchen is one of the main attractions of this spacious, brightly decorated seafood house. Another is the attentive, knowledgeable service staff; yet another is the wonderful array of New England–style standards, from chowders to halibut to lobster. (Don't stray into the fancy nouvelle part of the menu; simplicity is the strong point here.) *2576 E. Camelback Rd., tel. 602/956-3631. Reservations advised. Dress: informal. AE, MC, V. Expensive.*

★ **Top of the Market.** This smaller, slightly costlier annex upstairs from the larger, noisier Fish Market (itself a popular place) has captured the atmosphere of a San Francisco wharf restaurant. Its menu would stand up well in the City by the Bay, too. Everything from charbroiled orange roughy to whole Dungeness crab is skillfully handled and imaginatively seasoned; the handmade pastas are terrific, too. (But go someplace else for dessert.) *1720 E. Camelback Rd., tel. 602/277-3474. Reservations required. Dress: informal. AE, DC, MC, V. Expensive.*

American Grill. The decor is leather, brass, ferns, and etched glass; a large bar at the entry and a lounge with cozy tables and soft, live jazz add to the classic San Francisco pub ambience. But the action is in the glassed-in exhibition kitchen and the booths, where regional varieties of American cuisine (notably Cajun and southwestern) are prepared and consumed. The N'awlins Barbecued Shrimp is a fine appetizer; chowder in a bowl of sourdough bread can't be beat. Powerful desserts, too. *6113 N. Scottsdale Rd., Scottsdale, tel. 602/948-9907; 1233 S. Alma School Rd., Mesa, tel. 602/844-1918. Reservations advised. Dress: casual. AE, D, DC, MC, V. Moderate.*

Phoenix Dining

7th St.

Bell Rd.

Greenway Rd

17

Black Canyon Fwy.

Thunderbird Rd.

Peoria Rd.

Dunlap Ave.

35th Ave.

7th Ave.

Central Ave.

**PARADIS
VALLEY**

Glendale Ave.

19th Ave.

89

Grand Ave.

7th St.

16th St.

Squaw Peak Pkwy.

32nd St.

Camelbac

AE

Papago Fwy.

McDowell Rd.

Van Buren St.

10

202

24th St.

Buckeye Rd.

**Sky Harbor
International
Airport**

Lower Buckeye Rd.

19th Ave.

Salt River

Southern Ave.

Baseline Rd.

Dobbins Rd.

KEY

AE American Express Office

Durant's. This old downtown standby in black leather and red wallpaper hasn't changed since the '50s, and neither has its popularity (even its prices are charmingly out-of-date). It has a front door, but everyone enters through the kitchen from the parking lot. With its crowded bar and open booths, Durant's is one of Phoenix's prime see-and-be-seen places. On the menu, steaks and chops are prominent, of course, but check out the steamed clams or the chicken livers. *2611 N. Central Ave., tel. 602/264–5967. Reservations advised for dinner. Dress: informal. AE, D, DC, MC, V. Moderate.*

★ **Landmark.** After 50 years as a Mormon church and a brief turn as a college, this massive brick Victorian became a restaurant. It's done in lush carpeting, rose-patterned wallpaper, and wall-to-wall antiques; expect to wait a half-hour downstairs in the small lounge, surrounded by historical photos. Upstairs, you start at the huge salad bar of well-made Americana, from garden marinade to seafood salad and thick, rich soups. A sauerbraten-sauced pot roast with heavenly mashed potatoes leads the entrées; the Landmark pie is a must for fudge lovers. *809 W. Main St., Mesa, tel. 602/962–4652. No reservations. Dress: casual. AE, DC, MC, V. Moderate.*

Oscar Taylor's. Another favorite with the meat-and-potatoes crowd, this Chicago-style '20s steak house combines a cozy atmosphere, brisk service, and beautiful cuts of meat. The prime rib is a house specialty; the ribs are, too. But the best-kept secret is a huge, delicately simple veal chop. *2420 E. Camelback Rd., tel. 602/956–5705. Reservations advised. Dress: informal. AE, DC, MC, V. Moderate.*

Rose's. Comfortably elegant in blue and burgundy tones and conveniently located on the northern edge of downtown, the restaurant at the Best Western Executive Park hotel is a quiet, tony haven of American-Continental cuisine with some nice southwestern edges. Southwestern pasta dishes are a house specialty, as is the chicken quesadilla. *1100 N. Central Ave., tel. 602/252–2100. Reservations required. Dress: informal. AE, D, DC, MC, V. Moderate.*

★ **Rustler's Rooste.** The Johnny-come-lately among the Valley's western restaurants is the biggest and nearest to town—and the most fun. It's at the east end of South Mountain Park just off I–10 (take the Baseline exit west), in the theme-park atmosphere of The Pointe Hilton on South Mountain, Arizona's largest resort. Decorated in a playful miner-cowpoke style, complete with a slide from the bar down to the dining rooms, it offers excellent steaks, juicy barbecued pork ribs and chicken, hefty Mexican-style shrimp, and homemade ice cream. The Cowboy Stuff Platter ($16) puts a sample of almost everything the restaurant serves (except rattlesnake) on your plate. *7777 S. Pointe Pkwy., tel. 602/231–9111. Reservations advised. Dress: casual or western. AE, D, DC, MC, V. Moderate.*

★ **The Stockyards.** When Arizona had cattle barons, they cut their deals and steaks here. The feedlots and barons are gone, but the restaurant remains, a landmark just a half mile east of Sky Harbor Airport. Its ornate Victorian interior retains the original brass-trimmed bar and three salons—the black-leather Cattleman's Room, the gold-papered Gold Coast Room, and the mural-walled Rose Room. The menu features beef handled with respect, from massive prime rib and steaks to succulent calves' liver and calf fries (Rocky Mountain oysters). *5001 E. Washington St., tel. 602/273-7378. Reservations advised. Dress: informal. AE, DC, MC, V. Moderate.*

T-Bone Steakhouse. You drive south on 19th Avenue past the end of the pavement a ways, and there, on the slopes of South Mountain, is a big outdoor barbecue in a parking lot. Inside the rustic wooden building are wooden benches at oilcloth-covered tables; to the tables come steaks and chicken done to match the splendid, sweeping vistas of the desert sunset or the Valley lit up at night. Serve-yourself salad and beans, giant slices of toast, and fresh hot baked potatoes are always on hand, and sometimes an amateur western musician will take the microphone. *10037 S. 19th Ave., tel. 602/276-0945. No reservations. Dress: casual or western. AE, MC, V. Moderate.*

★ **Bev's Kitchen.** Some folks call it country, some call it soul food, and some just call it home. Whatever you call it, you may have to wait in line a bit to enjoy it, 'cause nobody does it better than Bev's. This unpretentious diner beside an auto lot on the south side contains gracious (but often very busy) staff and great food—hand-pounded chicken-fried steak, crumbling moist catfish, lively hot links, and potatoes and greens and corn and cabbage and yams done by people who love their vegetables (boiled down some, of course). Then there are those pies! *4220 S. 16th St., tel. 602/ 268-8569. No reservations. Dress: casual. No credit cards. Inexpensive.*

Ed Debevic's. This brash, noisy place adjacent to Marriott's Camelback Courtyard hotel is to restaurants what "Happy Days" was to TV—a nostalgic, half-accurate, but wholly entertaining revision of the '50s. It has red-leather dinettes, a working jukebox with Elvis and Tessy Brewer and dozens more, gum-snapping waitresses—and terrific burgers, malts, and fries. Blue plate specials, from chili to meatloaf and gravy, are a tasty hoot. With prodding, "Cookie" and the girls (and the waiters, led by a guest-kissing nerd) will provide tableside diversions. Forty-plus diners blush to remember, but children love it. *2102 E. Highland Ave., tel. 602/956-2760. Reservations advised on weekends. Dress: casual. MC, V. Inexpensive.*

The Eggery/The Good Egg. Cute decor (more airy and southwestern at Eggery outlets, more cluttered country at Good Eggs) and a lengthy menu mark this cheerful, comfy breakfast-brunch chain. Besides an array of cleverly named egg creations, from scrambler skillets to frittatas, as well as pancakes and waffles, there are welcome light options such as yogurt, granola, and fruit dishes. Service is brisk and friendly, children are welcome, and there's no rush despite the crowds. *5109 N. 44th St., tel. 602/840–5734; 4326 E. Cactus Rd. (at Paradise Valley Mall), tel. 602/953–2342; 2957 W. Bell Rd. (northwest), tel. 602/993–2797; 6149 N. Scottsdale Rd., Scottsdale, tel. 602/991–5416; 14046 N. Scottsdale Rd., Scottsdale, tel. 602/483–1090; 6990 E. Shea Blvd., Scottsdale, tel. 602/951–1123. No reservations. Dress: casual. AE, MC, V. Inexpensive.*

Lone Star Steak House. Tucked in an uptown corner mall, this noisy and crowded spot cluttered with Texas and country-western items does simple, effective things with steaks (including a classic chicken-fried) and serves up some of the best mashed potatoes you've had since you were a youngster. On the steaks, ask them to hold the lemon butter; the meat's better by itself. *6003 N. 16th St., tel. 602/248–STAR. Reservations accepted for groups of 5 or more. Dress: casual. AE, MC, V. Inexpensive.*

Mrs. White's Golden Rule Café. This little downtown, downhome lunch spot brings smiles to those who love liver and boiled cabbage, as well as to fanciers of such standard American fare as fried chicken and corn on the cob and yams. The food is cooked with a light, loving touch, service is friendly, prices are low, and the payin' is honor system. *808 E. Jefferson St., tel. 602/262–9256. No reservations. Dress: casual. No credit cards. Lunch only. Inexpensive.*

Unique Foods & Services. For snappy barbecue and soul classics done simply and with authority, this handsome little downtown café across the street from the restored Booker T. Washington School (now home of the *New Times* alternative newspaper) is the place to be. Hot links and ribs are memorable, and the delicate fried chicken reflects chef Wazir Karim's concern for healthful cooking. Greens and gumbo are cooked with love, and don't say you weren't warned about the bean pie. *1153 E. Jefferson St., tel. 602/257–0701. No reservations. Dress: casual. No credit cards. Inexpensive.*

Asian
Chinese
China Doll. The venerable ancestor of Valley Cantonese restaurants still is *the* place for family and association banquets and Chinese New Year's feasts. Its dinners—including ginger fish, for which you select your own tilapia swimming in the lobby tank—are reliably executed classics. And its dim sum, a cart of exotic afternoon snacks, is one of the best in town. Annie White is a gracious, witty hostess. *3336 N. 7th Ave., tel. 602/264–0538. Reservations advised. Dress: informal. AE, DC, MC, V. Moderate.*

★ **China Gate.** Seldom do chain restaurants rise so high or remain so consistent in quality—not to mention the breadth of cuisines, from Mongolian to Cantonese, Beijing to spicy Szechuan. Mandarin ribs are a special experience, as is the combination of shrimp and sea cucumber. Decor is striking, and layout emphasizes privacy amid open space. *3033 W. Peoria Ave., tel. 602/944–1982; 7820 E. McDowell Rd., Scottsdale, tel. 602/946–0720; 2050 W. Guadalupe Rd.,*

Mesa, tel. 602/897–0607. Reservations advised for dinner. Dress: casual. AE, D, DC, MC, V. Moderate.

Golden Moon Palace. A modest place in the somewhat seedy area just north of the state capitol mall, Golden Moon has been serving very fine food for a very long time. Half is simply decorated with red-leather booths and paper lanterns; half is a banquet room where local families celebrate and entertain guests. Service is gentle and attentive. The egg rolls are sweet and stuffed with fresh veggies, the garlic chicken is a masterpiece, and the fried rice is a meal in itself. *1408 W. Van Buren St., tel. 602/254–9229. Reservations advised for dinner. Dress: casual. AE, DC, MC, V. Closes 9 PM. Inexpensive.*

Gourmet of Hong Kong. Here are the bustling din and incomparable food of Hong Kong, in a tiny place near downtown. Staff and owners rush in and out of the narrow, steamy open kitchen to take your order and serve you; to-go diners stand between the tables, eagerly waiting. The house plate is a succulent, satisfying sampler; hot-sour chicken wings, Peking duck, lobster, and garlic pork are delightful. *1438 E. McDowell Rd., tel. 602/253–4859. Reservations advised. Dress: casual. MC, V. Inexpensive.*

Lucky Restaurant. Lucky you, if you look past the unpromising exterior, skip the buffet, and try something from the menu or the chalkboard. A little nerve and you'll have a rewarding adventure. If beef with bitter melons is available, don't miss it. The soft-shell crabs in black-bean sauce are unforgettable, too. *3317 N. 19th Ave., tel. 602/274–9477. No reservations. Dress: casual. No credit cards. Inexpensive.*

Indian **Indian Delhi Palace.** Midway between downtown and Tempe, right across from Motorola's semiconductor plant, you'll step through the door of a double storefront and into India. Attentive service and delightful flavors enhance the illusion. Sip tea and nibble home-baked *naan* and *kalcha* breads while perusing the long menu. The tandoori chicken and the yogurt lamb are two of many wonderful dishes, but the best bet is the inclusive dinner, a tour of the subcontinent's varied and subtle cuisine. The lunch buffet is another fun way to tour India's kitchens. *5050 E. McDowell Rd., tel. 602/244–8181. No reservations. Dress: informal. MC, V. Moderate.*

Japanese **Shogun.** In this small converted tavern, the cheerful staff
★ offers the best all-around Japanese experience in the Valley, starting with an outstanding sushi bar. At the tables, there are both finely turned standards such as teriyaki and tempura, and adventures into such unfamiliar areas as fish marinated in rice wine. Children are welcome here, too. *12615 N. Tatum Blvd., tel. 602/953–3264. Reservations advised. Dress: informal. DC, MC, V. Moderate.*

Yamakasa. Simple and serene in decor and service, this family-run restaurant offers excellent sushi and a menu that has been focused on the basics of tempura- and teriyaki-style cooking. No dazzle, but calm consistency makes this a refreshing place to enjoy an unhurried evening in the shadow of Fuji. *9301 E. Shea Blvd., Scottsdale, tel. 602/860–5605. Reservations advised. Dress: informal. AE, DC, MC, V. Moderate.*

Korean **Korean Garden.** Simple in decor and menu, this well-staffed, friendly place provides both familiar fare, such as *bulgoki* (grilled, marinated beef strips), and exotic treats such as *bibim bab* (a bowl of assorted vegetables and beef, with hot sauce, topped with a fried egg) and *jap chae* (panfried clear noodles with vegetables and beef). And the many kinds of *kimchi* (hot, marinated chopped cabbage) are a fiery treat. *1324 S. Rural Rd., Tempe, tel. 602/967–1133. No reservations. Dress: casual. MC, V. Inexpensive.*

Thai **Mint Thai.** A tiny, graceful place that started out remark-★ able and has never wavered, Mint Thai offers the broadest menu of the Valley's Thai restaurants—and if you find a dish not prepared with delicacy and power, it'll be a first. Soups range from the subtly simple *tom ka gai* (hot-sour in coconut milk) to the spectacular *Thai suki* (a beef-pork-chicken-squid-shrimp extravaganza); curries are gentler than those of north India, with deep flavors; the *rama* beef in peanut sauce is amazing. And you've never had sweet-and-sour like this before. Even the tea is unusually good. *1111 N. Gilbert Rd., Gilbert, tel. 602/497–5366. Reservations advised on weekends. Dress: casual. AE, MC, V. Moderate.*

Char's. This austerely simple restaurant gave birth to Phoenix's brood of Thai houses, and Grandpa Char still oversees things here. Meals are carefully prepared and courteously served, from the snappy skewered-chicken *satay* appetizer to the *tom yum gai* (hot-sour soup) and *yum yai* salad (chicken and shrimp salad with peanut dressing) to a noodle-rich *pad Thai* or a belly-warming curry. Tell your server if you want the pepper meter set on low; Thai like it hot. *927 E. University Dr., Tempe, tel. 602/967–6013. Reservations advised for large groups. Dress: casual. AE, MC, V. Inexpensive.*

Trans-Asian **Jasmine Café.** This bright eastern Valley spot, done in a California clutter of neon and ferns and collectibles, allows you to tour virtually all the Far East's cuisines at one sitting. The trans-Asian menu embraces Chinese, Japanese, Thai, Korean, and a little poetic license in a fun, endlessly varied array that's served in small portions—you can fill your table with experiments and share. The service is a bit uneven, but the food is worth it. *1805 E. Elliott Rd., Tempe, tel. 602/491–0797. No reservations. Dress: casual. DC, MC, V. Inexpensive.*

Deli **Tradition.** A north Phoenix corner not far from Paradise ★ Valley Mall hides a gem—a true New York deli. Pickles and other delicacies are flown in from Manhattan's finest purveyors; the brown, seed-rich Tradition mustard is concocted fresh, as is a host of wonderful meals and snacks, from creamy breakfast blintzes to a heavenly thick sweet-sour cabbage soup (chicken soup with the woiks will cure any ill) to heavenly chopped liver and piled wafers of corned beef on fresh marble rye, flaky sweet brisket, or fall-off-the-bone fricassee. And oh, the killer kugel and the double-chocolate pudding! You can't finish it all; take plenty home. *13637 N. Tatum Blvd., tel. 602/996-2202. No reservations. Dress: casual. AE, D, MC, V. Inexpensive.*

European French **Christopher's.** Christopher Gross, one of the Valley's leading chef-entrepreneurs, has re-created a bistro worthy of
★ the Champs-Elysées and, adjacent to it, an elegant, monogrammed linen-and-silver modern restaurant. They share an open kitchen (which competes with the bistro musicians for attention). Classic fish, veal, and chicken are flawlessly cooked, sauced, and presented—with delightful southwestern surprise touches. *2398 E. Camelback Rd., tel. 602/ 957-3214. Reservations required. Jacket and tie suggested. AE, DC, MC, V. Very Expensive.*

Voltaire. The Valley's most consistent classical French cuisine makes its home in a residential Scottsdale neighborhood. Nothing nouvelle here; there may not be a recipe that's less than 100 years old. But when you want to savor escargots, onion soup *gratinée*, and perfectly handled rack of lamb, this is the place. Then there's the hard work: crêpes suzette, cherries jubilee, or the exquisite crème caramel? *8340 E. McDonald Dr., Scottsdale, tel. 602/948-1005. Reservations required. Jacket and tie suggested. AE, MC, V. Closed Sun. and Mon. Expensive.*

German **Zur Kate.** Outside, you're in a corner mall on a busy Mesa thoroughfare; inside, you're in a friendly family inn in Bavaria. Steins and Tyrolean caps belonging to regulars line the walls; the soups are hearty and good, the sauerbraten, *kassler ripchen* (smoked pork loin), dumplings, and tiny *spätzle* noodles are wonderful. Not to mention the wursts. And the fresh apple strudel. Music and gemütlich service complete the pleasures. *4815 E. Main St., Mesa, tel. 602/ 830-1244. Reservations accepted. Dress: casual. MC, V. Closed Sun. Moderate.*

Greek **Greekfest.** Here, Greek cooking meets haute cuisine. In a
★ tasteful Athenian taverna, with painted vines and racked wines on the whitewashed walls, classic dishes are handled exquisitely. The feather-light *spanakopites* (spinach pie) appetizers; the sweet and succulent lamb; fresh, tart *dolmades* (grape leaves) stuffed to bursting and sour-light *avgolemono* as both soup and sauce—it's a quietly festive meal you won't soon forget. *1940 E. Camelback Rd., tel. 602/265-2990. Reservations advised. Dress: casual. DC, MC, V. Moderate.*

Greektown. At this warm family operation cheered by posters and murals, Papa greets, Mama cooks, and Son seats. The combo appetizer offers a tour of the Greek islands;

lamb stew and seafood are good bets. When it's time for dessert, there is honey, nuts, and filo dough aplenty—and Mama's rice pudding. Wash it down with good, thick coffee. *539 E. Glendale Ave., tel. 602/279–9677. Reservations advised. Dress: casual. AE, MC, V. Moderate.*

Italian **La Bruschetta.** In a tiny space between a comedy club and a
★ gas station, Gianni and Linda Scorza have tucked a tasty bit of Tuscany with 14 linen-draped tables, a mural of Florence, and palms in huge antique olive jars. The complimentary *bruschetta* (tangy bread topped with dried tomato and olive oil) comes first. For an appetizer, don't miss the colors and flavors of the marinated and cooked vegetables; for an entrée, consider light Gorgonzola-sauced pasta, roast Cornish hen dusted in herbs, or delicately tender squid. *4515 N. Scottsdale Rd., tel. 602/946–7236. Reservations required. Jacket suggested. AE, MC, V. Closed Sun. Expensive.*

Chianti. This charming little poster-hung restaurant stays crowded, but the unusually alert service neither forgets nor flusters you. The antipasto salad is a crisp overture of clear, tangy flavors, the pastas are well handled and sauced. Espresso or cappuccino, with perhaps a gelato or spumoni, ends a delightful meal. *3943 E. Camelback Rd., tel. 602/957–9840. Reservations advised. Dress: informal. AE, MC, V. Inexpensive.*

The Olive Garden. Plant-filled rooms, cleverly chopped into private nooks on varied levels, create a pleasing atmosphere. The food does more justice to the range of Italian cuisine than you would expect from a chain, from the garlicky bread sticks to a fine pesto and very creditable sauces (Alfredo and marinara are both consistently successful). A good place to explore beyond spaghetti and pizza, and a nonthreatening "grown-up" setting for the young. *10223 N. Metro Pkwy. E (at Metrocenter mall), tel. 602/943–4573; 9805 W. Bell Rd., Sun City, tel. 602/977–8378; 1261 W. Southern Ave. (at Fiesta Mall), Mesa, tel. 602/890–0440; 4868 E. Cactus Rd., Scottsdale, tel. 602/494–4327. No reservations. Dress: casual. DC, MC, V. Inexpensive.*

Spanish **Marquesa.** Two soft-hued, intimate rooms at the Scottsdale
★ Princess are accented with huge glass jars of jewellike vegetables and fruits and graceful giant clay olive-oil urns. Here, Catalan food gets an exciting southwestern interpretation. The stunning presentations match the flavors—duck-breast fillets in fruit sauce; pimientos stuffed with crab; a rich chowder of mussels, scallops, and spicy chorizo sausage; and huge shrimp in almond sauce, to name a few. Service is gracious, wines well chosen, desserts inspired. *7575 E. Princess Dr., Scottsdale, tel. 602/585–4848. Reservations required. Jacket and tie suggested. AE, DC, MC, V. Very Expensive.*

Tapas Papa Frita. Master chef Joseph Gutiérrez (the genius who created Marquesa) opened his own place here, in honor of his Spanish parents. The traditional *tapas* (tavern snacks of Madrid) are the basis of the menu—such exotic nibbles as fried squid in garlic mayonnaise, mushroom- and herb-stuffed little turnovers, countless escargot treatments. But magnificent Spanish entrées, such as sweet, spit-roasted pig and tender, heartily sauced oxtails, are not to be missed. Nor is the flamenco dancing, Thursday through Saturday evenings. *3213 E. Camelback Rd., tel. 602/381–0474. Reservations advised. Dress: informal. AE, DC, MC, V. Expensive.*

Mexican and Latin American ★ **La Hacienda.** About 20 miles northeast of downtown in the chichi Scottsdale Princess Resort, this tile-roofed hacienda filled with carved tables and chairs and huge clay *ollas* (water jars) shows what happens when Sonoran food goes haute cuisine. It ranges from a quesadilla stuffed with crab to the tableside drama of *cochinillo asado* (roast stuffed suckling pig), from a chili relleno filled with pork loin and nuts to the sea-sweet *cabrilla rellena de salpicón* (crab-stuffed bass in lime mayonnaise). It doesn't get any better, amigo! *7575 E. Princess Dr. (1 mi north of Bell Rd.), Scottsdale, tel. 602/585–4848. Reservations required. Dress: informal. AE, DC, MC, V. Expensive–Very Expensive.*

★ **Havana Café.** At this clean, cozy café in black and gray, you'll likely have to wait; try Arriba, the tapas bar upstairs, for Spanish-style snacks and sherry. Cuban cuisine is farther from Latin America's mainland than the island is, showing European influence. Pork becomes a moist, marinated, garlic-laden roast; tamales are moist and sweet, with meat mixed throughout the masa, not wrapped in it. Hot sauces are unheard of, and *papas fritas* (we call 'em french fries) are much in evidence. Talk about a sweet tooth—try the desserts, but have a cup of espresso at hand (don't put three teaspoons of sugar in that tiny cup, like Habaneros do). *4225 E. Camelback Rd., tel. 602/952–1991. No reservations. Dress: informal. AE, MC, V. Closed Sun. Moderate.*

Macayo. This family-run chain has been a Valley standby for half a century, and its six colorful outlets provide well-prepared Sonoran dishes in a romantic setting of folk-art decor: tacos, tostadas, tamales (especially the sweet green corn), chili relleno, *huevos rancheros* (fried eggs rancho style, atop corn tortillas and slathered with fresh salsa), refried beans—and creamy flan or honey-filled *sopapillas* (puffy tortillas) for dessert. It's a great place for introducing children to Mexican food. *4001 N. Central Ave., tel. 602/264–6141; 7829 W. Thomas Rd., tel. 602/873–0313; 1909 W. Thunderbird Rd., tel. 602/866–7034; 7005 E. Camelback Rd., Scottsdale, tel. 602/947–7641; 300 S. Ash Ave., Tempe, tel. 602/966–6677; 1920 S. Dobson Rd., Mesa, tel. 602/820–0237. Reservations advised for dinner. Dress: casual. AE, D, DC, MC, V. Moderate.*

La Tasca. Past this comfortable indoor-outdoor café that blends Mexican and Art Deco, shoppers stroll the cobbled lanes and pastel shop fronts of The Mercado center. *Canciones* play on the radio as black-vested waiters bring sherry or Mexican beer for you to sip while awaiting your meal in the unhurried air of Mexico City or Madrid. Appetizers include artfully presented *sopes* (hot minitortillas piled with shredded chicken, lettuce, Monterey Jack cheese, black beans, and a smart but gentle salsa). The soups, enchiladas, and especially the *barbacoa torta* (tender pork or chicken with light green barbecue sauce in fresh split rolls) make a lovely lunch or early dinner. *541 E. Van Buren St., tel. 602/340–8797. Reservations accepted. Dress: casual. AE, MC, V. Closed Sun. Moderate.*

Adrian's. This modest, creek-rock building with the wrought-iron grilles and tiny outdoor patio transports you in food and decor a little farther south than Sonora, to the coastal towns of Sinaloa on the Sea of Cortés (Anglos call it the Gulf of California). Many dishes are similar to Sonoran rancho fare, and Adrian does them well, especially pork with *nopalitos* (sliced cactus pads); but local Hispanic families keep coming for such treats as *Vuelve a la Vida* (Return to Life)—a cocktail of shrimp, abalone, oyster, and crab—or garlicky broiled whole pike over which you squeeze tiny, sweet Mexican limes. *2234 E. McDowell Rd., tel. 602/273–7957. No reservations. Dress: casual. No credit cards. Inexpensive.*

Bahía San Carlos. In the shadow of the Squaw Peak Parkway, just down the street from Adrian's, is its best competitor in the *mariscos* (seafood) category. This popular, noisy little place is hung with huge posters of Mexico's palm-shaded beaches and serves almost nothing but seafood. Tostadas piled with sweet-tangy *salpicón* (lime-soaked, seasoned, shredded crab) make a splendid appetizer; the *Caldo Siete Mares* (Seven Seas Soup) is a wonderful sampler of fish, squid, shrimp, crab, and more. *19th St. and McDowell Rd., tel. 602/340–0892. No reservations. Dress: casual. No credit cards. Inexpensive.*

★ **Los Dos Molinos.** One is an A-frame with a former life as a pseudo-Tyrolean hot dog outlet; another is a more standard storefront; and the third is a large white hostelry in south Phoenix. All three house pure, hot New Mexico–style cooking—Victoria Chávez and her daughters turn out delicious *barbacoa* (spicy rancho barbecue), multitextured *chilaquiles* (layered tortillas, cheeses, and homemade chili sauce), and other delights with a humor as lively as the seasonings. It keeps the handful of tables and booths full. Beware: The hot sauce can rip your lips off. *1156 W. Main St., Mesa, tel. 602/835–5356; 260 S. Alma School Rd., Mesa, tel. 602/835–5356, both closed Sun.; 8646 S. Central Ave., tel. 602/243–9113, closed Mon. No reservations. Dress: casual. No credit cards. Inexpensive.*

Eliana's. Salvadoran food is an interesting variation on the staple themes of Latin American fare, and this tiny converted pizzeria has plenty of heart and hearty food. You know tacos and burritos; now meet *papusas*, crisp crosses between tortillas and puffy pita pockets, stuffed with meat, cheese, and sauces. From tamales, it's a short but tasty leap to these veggie-filled varieties with their soft, creamy *masa* (cornmeal) wrappings. And the *sopas* (soups) are an adventure. *2401 N. 32nd St., tel. 602/957–9442. No reservations. Dress: casual. No credit cards. Inexpensive.*

Matador. This downtown tradition, across from the Hyatt Regency Phoenix in a tastefully Mayan-modern setting, is a fine way to meet Mexican food in general and Sonoran cuisine in particular. Dishes are reliable, authentic, and well spiced without burning and range from the familiar (tacos, enchiladas, quesadillas) to the adventurous (*menudo*, or tripe soup; *burros de lengua*, or beef-tongue burritos). It's also a perennially popular breakfast spot where civic leaders and groups gather before the workday hits high gear. *125 E. Adams St., tel. 602/254–7563. Reservations advised for large parties. Dress: casual. AE, D, DC, MC, V. Inexpensive.*

Toño's. Few Americans have tried goat or have drunk *horchata* (cinnamon-sugared rice water). But these are just two of the simple pleasures from rural Mexico awaiting you at this modest, clean storefront in south Phoenix. The service is so warm and personal that good-faith efforts at Spanish on your part and English on theirs somehow suffice. Toño handles goat the way Julia Child treats filet mignon; his *caldos* (soups) and *caldillos* (stews) are heartwarming. And there's nothing like a tall, cold glass of *horchata* on a warm desert evening. *24 E. Broadway Rd., tel. 602/243–9684. No reservations. Dress: casual. No credit cards. Inexpensive.*

Middle Eastern and North African
Chopandaz. Afghanistan's gift to the Valley is "The Horseman," where you can canter comfortably through crisp, moist shish kebabs, nutty rice, and a wonderful sweet-spicy mash of lentils. The atmosphere in this converted pizzeria is friendly (and the rug collection authentic); the owner-host takes pride in escorting guests through his homeland's hearty, often subtle cuisine. *1849 N. Scottsdale Rd., Tempe, tel. 602/947–4396. Reservations accepted. Dress: casual. MC, V. Closed Mon. Moderate.*

★ **The Moroccan.** Seated on tooled leather cushions, rinse your hands in warm rose water poured from a brass ewer, pull apart nutty hot pita and dip it in garbanzo-eggplant paste, then plow your way—fork free, if you dare—through a *fassi* (chicken in cilantro curry), a *m'rouzia* (honeyed lamb with raisins and almonds), or a good old couscous. Try some Moroccan red wine—and try ignoring the belly dancer. *4228 N. Scottsdale Rd., Scottsdale, tel. 602/947–9590. Reservations advised. Dress: informal. AE, MC, V. Moderate.*

Byblos. This Lebanese standby in Tempe is not heavy on ambience, but care is taken with the food, and the staff usually dines at one of the tables, inquiring regularly as to how you're doing. The appetizers are a good introduction, from the nutty *hummus* (garbanzo paste) to the complex flavors of *falafel* (herbed, deep-fried hummus in pita bread). But save room for the main courses, well sampled via the mixed grill, which includes three kinds of shish kebab. *3332 S. Mill Ave., Tempe, tel. 602/894–1945. No reservations. Dress: casual. AE, MC, V. Inexpensive.*

Southwestern International ★ **Vincent's on Camelback.** Vincent Guerithault is acknowledged to be among the West's master chefs extraordinaire; this is the place to experience his art. One of the handful of southwestern cuisine's originators, he joined his classical country-French training with Mexican traditions to create duck tacos, crab cakes in avocado salsa, lobster with smoky *chipotle* chili pasta, and so on. Racks of lamb and symphonic pâtés are here, too, as are a heart-smart menu and an intelligent wine list. Desserts aren't heart-smart, but they are luscious. *3930 E. Camelback Rd., tel. 602/224–0225. Reservations advised. Dress: casual but neat. AE, DC, MC, V. Very Expensive.*

★ **Compass Room.** Spectacular views have always made the Hyatt Regency Phoenix's rotating crown room an attraction. Since 1989, chef Mark Ching has given it food to match. In fact, it's become one of the most exciting galleries for southwestern culinary art. Consider this dinner: smoky eggplant soup, a salad of peppered lamb slivers and greens, a choice of fiery southwestern cioppino or beef tenderloin in jalapeño-jus reduction and cilantro-lime hollandaise. Whatever you have, try the "Cajun croutons," crusty fried oysters in a red-pepper mayonnaise, as a side or in the Caesar salad. After the room rotates another 90 degrees, try one of Ching's cobblers or his chocolate pâté. *122 N. 2nd St., tel. 602/252–1234. Reservations required. Jacket and tie suggested. AE, D, DC, MC, V. Expensive.*

★ **Eddie's Grill.** Its look and location are upscale—a modern office complex 4 miles north of downtown, black-trimmed art deco furniture, fine handmade ceramics on the tables. Its cuisine, as eclectic as the decor, makes this one of Phoenix's hottest half dozen. Chef-owner Eddie Matney's "Ameriterranean" is a playful, shifting blend of southwestern and North African. Try succulent Mo' Rockin' Shrimp in *chermoula* sauce (lime juice, olive oil, four kinds of pepper, coriander, cilantro, and mustard) or baked goat cheese with black beans and pita chips for starters. There's a Southwestern Tower (mixed greens and marjarita chicken with peppers and jack cheese dressing, layered in corn tortillas); and steak wrapped in herbed mashed potatoes—and Eddie loves to feed you. *4747 N. 7th St., tel. 602/241–1188. Reservations advised. Dress: informal. AE, MC, V. No dinner weekdays. Expensive.*

★ **Roxsand.** Chef-owners Roxsand and Spyros Scocos have woven together Greek, Asian, Continental, and Caribbean influences (among others) to create a unique trans-Continental cuisine. Eclectic is the word in this trendy but very friendly café-restaurant, where a solo snacker is as welcome as a hungry foursome. Be on the lookout for such surprises as sea-scallop salad, salmon with piroshki and cabbage roll, Jamaican jerked rabbit, and an ever-changing array of handmade desserts. This is a meal for adventurers. Roxsand shares Biltmore Fashion Park mall's casual elegance, adding its own lively energy. *2594 E. Camelback Rd., tel. 602/381-0444. Reservations advised. Dress: casual. AE, DC, MC, V. Expensive.*

Christo's. The sign says "Ristorante," and the northern Italian food is finely done. But Christo and Connie Panagiotakapoulos have reached throughout the Mediterranean for their cuisine, offering pastas, lamb dishes, calamari, and other regional specialties in a variety of accents. The decor and ambience are crisply contemporary, the service adroit. That's why everybody keeps coming back to this north-of-Camelback favorite. *6327 N. 7th St., tel. 602/264-1784. Reservations advised. Dress: informal. AE, MC, V. Closed Sun. Moderate-Expensive.*

Goldie's 1895 House. This charmingly restored downtown Victorian would fit right in on California's Mendocino coast. There's always soft music (live jazz, classical guitar) and an art gallery and museum that change shows regularly. Intimacy and understatement are the themes. Standards get subtle extra touches—a hot turkey sandwich on sourdough under a light dill sauce, or baked orange roughy in Parmesan-scallion butter—and there are surprises, such as roast duck in pomegranate sauce. Plan ahead: The hours are as compact as the rooms (lunch weekdays 11:30–2:30; brunch Sunday 11–3; dinner; 4:30–9; (dinner theater Thursday through Sunday). *362 N. 2nd Ave., tel. 602/254-0338. Reservations advised. Dress: casual. AE, DC, MC, V. Moderate.*

Timothy's. In this cozy cottage north of Camelback Road, chef-owner Tim Johnson offers a triple treat—Continental and Cajun cuisines and live jazz. He does jambalaya, steak au poivre, and veal Genovese; like the music, the food gets hottest when the voices blend, as in Cajun prime rib, or salmon in filo dough with chili hollandaise. It's not always quiet, but service is brisk and dinner is served until midnight. Grab a chair, cher! *6335 N. 16th St., tel. 602/277-7634. Reservations advised. Dress: casual. AE, D, DC, MC, V. Moderate.*

Lodging

Metro Phoenix has a considerable array of lodging options, from world-class resorts and dude ranches to roadside motels, from luxury and executive hotels to no-frills business suites and family-style operations where you can do your own cooking.

Resorts are usually far from the heart of town—too far to be convenient if your interests are in Phoenix proper. The exceptions: the historic Arizona Biltmore, unthinkably far out when it was built and now handily close in; the gigantic Pointe Hilton on South Mountain, less than 3 miles from the airport; and its two sister Pointe resorts, each within 7 miles of downtown. Most of the others are in Scottsdale, a self-contained, very tourist-friendly suburb; a few are scattered 20 to 30 miles out of town. And the dude ranches cluster around Wickenburg, 60 miles northwest.

Business and family hotels are closer to town—and to the average vacation budget. Until 20 years ago, families drove in from the west on Grand Avenue or from the east on Van Buren Street and pulled into any of dozens of courtyard motels with mission-style adobe facades. That is no longer a safe option, as the neighborhood is seedy; but aside from the airport, no single hotel district has emerged, so offerings are scattered throughout Phoenix and its suburbs.

Travelers flee snow and ice to bask in the Valley of the Sun. As a result, winter is the high season, peaking in January through March, and summer is giveaway time, when weekend packages at the fanciest resorts cost less than a winter night at a midrange hotel.

The rise of suite hotels in recent years—with kitchenettes for in-room meal preparation—is rapidly making room service obsolete in all but luxury or resort-class hotels. In its place, such complimentary services as a made-to-order breakfast, poolside or lounge happy hour, and a morning newspaper are becoming standard. Where room service is not noted below, expect some combination of these.

Highly recommended lodgings are indicated by a star ★.

Category	Cost*
Very Expensive	over $160
Expensive	$110–$160
Moderate	$60–$110
Inexpensive	under $60

All prices are for a standard double room, excluding 6½% state tax, 1% city tax, and 15% service charge.

Central Phoenix
Expensive

Embassy Suites. Just 5 miles from downtown, this 19-year-old, four-story open courtyard hotel was overhauled in 1990. Lush palms and olive trees hide bubbling fountains and a huge sunken pool, while four glass-walled elevators lift you to your floor. Free breakfast and evening social hour are shared in the spacious clubhouse at café tables, by a large sunken fireplace-conversation pit, and in front of a wide-screen TV off in a corner. Suites are compact but dramatic, with emerald carpets and drapes, Santa Fe geometric wallpaper and bedspreads. The tiny kitchenette has a microwave, sink, and bar refrigerator. The White Buffalo offers lunch and dinner with wonderful views. *2333 E. Thomas Rd., Phoenix 85016, tel. 602/957–1910 or 800/EM-*

BASSY, fax 602/955–2861. 183 suites. Facilities: pool, sauna, shop, restaurant, meeting rooms, free airport limo, parking. AE, D, DC, MC, V.

★ **Hilton Suites.** A model of excellent design within tight limits, this 11-story atrium opened in 1990. A more luxurious version of the frequent-traveler suites concept, it sits off Central Avenue, 2 miles north of downtown amid the Phoenix plaza cluster of office towers. The marble-floored, pillared lobby with giant urns opens into the atrium, with fountains, palms, and the lantern-lighted New Orleans-style restaurant. Modern fauvist art hangs on the walls; thematic colors are sand and bright teal blue, and Navajo-inspired motifs mark carpets and borders. Suites continue the bold design, with bleached wood furniture and rough-cut custom metal chandeliers. Each large bathroom opens to both living room and bedroom, which have two windows apiece (one that opens), and every couch is a sofa bed. Each room has a microwave (the gift shop provides snacks, as well as free VCR movies). This property is likely to become a classic. *10 E. Thomas Rd., Phoenix 85012, tel. 602/222–1111 or 800/HILTONS, fax 602/265–4841. 226 rooms. Facilities: pool, exercise room, sauna, shop, restaurant, bar, business center, covered parking. AE, D, DC, MC, V.*

Hyatt Regency Phoenix. This landmark faces Civic Plaza like a giant kachina figure, its disk-shaped rotating restaurant atop 24 floors of dark sandstone. Renovated in 1990, it has Hyatt's trademark atrium design and sky-view elevators. Desert- and Indian-style decor dominate; shops, meeting rooms, and an on-site branch of the visitors bureau attest to the focus on conventions, which crowd the hotel in spring. Rooms are comfortable, utilitarian, and modestly sized; there are balcony rooms on floors 3–7, poolside rooms on 3 (the atrium roof blocks east views on 8–10). The Theater Terrace Café's southwestern food and themed seasonal menus are a cut above standard hotel fare; the rooftop Compass Room's meals match its splendid views (*see* Southwestern International in Dining, *above*). *122 N. 2nd St., Phoenix 85004, tel. 602/252–1234 or 800/233–1234, fax 602/254–9472. 711 rooms. Facilities: pool, health club, shops, meeting rooms, 2 restaurants, bar-lounge, "gold passport" floors (6–8), concierge, covered parking. AE, D, DC, MC, V.*

OmniAdams. The city's oldest major hotel is its biggest disappointment. After a huge fire, total rebuilding, and a series of owners, the historic Adams Hotel is just a memory; in its place is a 19-story modern shell cleverly crafted for the desert, with sand-colored walls, arcaded sidewalks, and scooped arches shading each window. But inside is a worn-looking hostelry that scrapes by on overflow from the next-door Hyatt. Staff is willing, and the scale and services are those of a major hotel, but vacant shop spaces and deservedly empty restaurants give it away. Rooms are small and cheaply decorated—tiny desks, minibars that don't match the furniture, thin towels. Not worth the price. *111*

Ambassador Inn, **16**
Arizona Biltmore, **6**
Best Western
Executive Park, **20**
The Boulders, **13**
The Buttes, **28**
Camelback Courtyard
by Marriott, **9**
Comfort Inn
Airport, **24**
Crescent Hotel, **5**
Doubletree Suites, **26**
Embassy Suites, **18**
Flying E Ranch, **1**
Hilton Pavilion, **31**
Hilton Suites, **19**
Hotel Westcourt, **4**
Hyatt Regency
Phoenix, **23**
Hyatt Regency
Scottsdale at Gainey
Ranch, **11**
InnSuites
Phoenix/Central, **17**
Kay El Bar Ranch, **2**
Lexington Hotel, **7**
Marriott's Camelback
Inn, **10**
Mesa Travelodge, **30**
Motel 6 Scottsdale, **14**
Omni Adams, **21**
The Phoenician, **15**
The Pointe Hilton on
South Mountain, **29**
Quality Inn Desert
Sky, **25**
Radisson Tempe, **27**
Rancho de los
Caballeros, **3**
Ritz-Carlton, **8**
San Carlos, **22**
Scottsdale
Princess, **12**

230

Phoenix Lodging

e Reef Aqueduct

13

12

Scottsdale Rd.

Pima Rd.

0   4 miles

0   6 km

N

Scottsdale Municipal Airport

Thunderbird Rd.

Cactus Rd.

Shea Blvd.

SCOTTSDALE

Shea Blvd.

E

11

Scottsdale Rd.

Tatum Blvd.

Indian Bend Rd.

10

Lincoln Dr.

Mc Donald Dr.

ck Rd.

44th St.

AE **15** **14**

Indian School Rd.

Alma School Rd.

Beeline Hwy.

16

Thomas Rd.

Scottsdale Rd.

Hayden Rd.

McDowell Rd.

McKellips Rd.

Salt River

Country Club Rd.

Mesa Dr.

Brown Rd.

143

Priest Dr.

27

AE

University Dr.

MESA

Lindsay Rd.

Fwy.

Apache Blvd.

Dobson Rd.

60 89

Main St.

30

Broadway Rd.

28

10

TEMPE

360

31

Superstition Fwy.

McQueen Rd.

29

Price Rd.

Guadalupe Rd.

GILBERT

N. Central Ave., Phoenix 85004, tel. 602/257–1525 or 800/843–6664, fax 602/253–9755. 534 rooms. Facilities: pool, health club, sauna, outdoor jogging track, shops, meeting rooms, 2 restaurants, bar-lounge, concierge, limo-tour desk, covered parking. AE, D, DC, MC, V.

Moderate **Best Western Executive Park.** One of downtown's hidden
★ jewels, this small eight-story facility sits on Central Avenue at the new Deck Park (beneath which I–10 passes under the heart of the city). Finished in 1983 and renovated by new owners in early 1991, it's simply but elegantly decorated—peach and sand walls, prints by southwestern masters, unfinished antique reproductions. Moderate-size rooms have comfortable beds and large, well-lighted desks, compact brass-trimmed bathrooms with coffee makers, and (above the second floor) commanding city views. The eighth-floor suites are dramatic, with ample balconies and sitting rooms; off the drape-swathed bedroom is a vast dressing room with Roman tub, plus a standard bathroom with shower. Rose's restaurant does a nice array of American-Continental dishes, with southwestern accents. The Heard Museum, Phoenix Art Museum, and main library are within walking distance. This hotel has great charm, a great location—and great prices. *1100 N. Central Ave., Phoenix 85004, tel. 602/252–2100 or 800/528–1234, fax 602/340–1989. 107 rooms. Facilities: pool, health club, sauna, meeting rooms, restaurant, bar, parking. AE, D, DC, MC, V. Moderate.*

InnSuites Phoenix/Central. A mile east of the Embassy Suites is an older, cozier, and cheaper version of the open-courtyard suite hotel. Under its red tile roofs are apartment-style suites dating from the mid-1960s, with orange and brown outside trim and simple but stylish furnishings (rose carpet and a Japanese floral motif in wall art, drapes, and bedspreads) and half kitchen, complete with refrigerator, utensils, and dishes. Front suites hear 32nd Street's traffic; 24 second-story suites have balconies overlooking the pool and densely landscaped garden. An 8-by-10 nook serves daily breakfast, a second dispenses poolside happy hour, and a third houses the four-station exercise room. *3101 N. 32nd St., Phoenix 85018, tel. 602/956–4900 or 800/950–1688, fax 602/957–6122. 76 suites. Facilities: pool, exercise room, meeting rooms, free airport limo, parking. AE, D, DC, MC, V.*

Lexington Hotel. Only 3 miles from downtown, in a nest of midtown corporate-headquarters buildings, this is Phoenix's best bet for sports lovers. Carved out of the conference-poolside wing of the 25-year-old Del Webb TowneHouse (the old hotel became an office tower) in 1987, the Lexington now houses a sports bar (noisy and crowded), 11 racquetball courts (a national tournament site), an aerobics room, a 40-station machine workout center, a full indoor basketball court, and a large outdoor waterfall pool. The ambience is bright, modern, and informal.

Rooms range in size from moderate (in the cabana wing, where baths have bidets and first-floor rooms have poolside patios) to very small (tower wing) and were completely redecorated in early 1993. In the locker rooms, no amenity is spared. And the restaurant serves hefty, home-cooked meals. This is where visiting pro teams—and fans—like to stay. *100 W. Clarendon Ave., Phoenix 85013, tel. 602/279–9811 or 800/272–2439; fax 602/631–9358. 167 rooms. Facilities: pool, health club, sauna, shops, restaurant, 2 bars, covered parking. AE, D, DC, MC, V.*

San Carlos Hotel. Phoenix's second-oldest hotel is being reborn. Built in 1927, it was a popular downtown hub and landmark for decades; now, its seven stories are dwarfed by the Valley Bank Center and other skyscrapers. A 1990 refurbishment put deep blue carpeting in the halls and added new wallpaper, drapes, and spreads in the 120 snug rooms and suites (whose 3-inch concrete walls ensure quiet). Fixtures—from the pedestal sinks and old-fashioned toilets to Austrian crystal chandeliers in the lobby—echo '30s and '40s high style. *202 N. Central Ave., Phoenix 85004, tel. 602/253–4121 or 800/528–5446; fax 602/253–4121, ext. 209. 105 rooms. Facilities: pool, shops, restaurant, deli, pub, meeting rooms, covered parking. AE, D, DC, MC, V.*

Airport
Moderate–
Very Expensive
★

The Buttes. Two miles east of Sky Harbor, nestled in desert buttes at I–10 and AZ 360, is Phoenix's best hotel buy. Built in 1986, it joins dramatic architecture (the lobby's back wall is the volcanic rock itself), classic Southwest design (pine and saguaro-rib furniture, original works by major regional artists), and stunning Valley views. Rooms are moderate in size and comfortable, with a compact bath and half closet; decor includes desert colors and live cactus. "Radial" rooms are largest, with the widest views; inside rooms face the huge free-form pool in its rock amphitheater, with waterfall, Jacuzzis, and cantina. Concierge-floor amenities are well worth the nominal added fee. The elegant Top of the Rock restaurant, the adjacent lively Chuckawalla's lounge, and the quiet elegance of the dawn-to-midnight Market Café all are definite pluses. *2000 Westcourt Way, Tempe 85282, tel. 602/225–9000 or 800/843–1986, fax 602/438–8622. 353 rooms. Facilities: pool, health club, saunas, 5 tennis courts, jogging and hiking trails, shops, 2 restaurants, 3 bars, business center, meeting rooms, concierge floor, parking (with lot shuttle), AE, D, DC, MC, V.*

Doubletree Suites. In the Gateway Center, just a mile north of the airport, this striking hotel is the best of a dozen choices for the traveler who wants to get off the plane and into a comfortable room. Past the lobby full of modernist regional art lies a honeycomb of six-story towers, linked by mazes of walkways and richly landscaped gardens. The modest-size rooms are rose, blue-gray, and Navajo white with plain but comfy furniture. The kitchenettes have microwaves. Topper's, a pleasantly intimate restaurant, offers a relaxed wine bar. Business and sports facilities are extensive; the casual elegance and easy access attract visiting celebrities. *320 N. 44th St., Phoenix 85008, tel. 602/ 225–0500 or 800/528–0444, fax 602/225–0957. 242 suites. Facilities: pool, health club, sauna, 2 tennis courts, shops, restaurant, bar-lounge, meeting rooms, free airport shuttle, parking. AE, D, DC, MC, V.*

★ **The Pointe Hilton on South Mountain.** The Southwest's largest resort (950 suites on 1,000 acres), this Mexican-Mediterranean extravaganza opened in 1987 alongside the nation's largest city park (South Mountain, a 16,000-acre desert preserve). Of all the Valley's luxury resorts, this is the most convenient—3 miles from the airport, about 7 miles from downtown Phoenix or the eastern Valley. Three lavishly designed and decorated suite hotels (one set on winding hillside streets like a coastal village), a four-story sports center, and four separate restaurants are linked by landscaped walkways and roads; carts and drivers are on 24-hour call. Spacious, high-ceilinged suites combine undyed fabrics, whitewashed timbers, and lodge fireplaces with dark-wood accent furniture, cinnamon carpets, and Mexican handicrafts. Golf, tennis, riding, and several pools are among the amenities. *7777 S. Pointe Pkwy., Phoenix 85044, tel. 602/438–9000 or 800/876–4683, fax 602/431– 6535. 950 suites. Facilities: lake, 3 pools, health center, saunas, 100-horse stable, 10 tennis courts, 18-hole golf course, jogging and hiking trails, shops, 4 restaurants, 3 lounges, meeting rooms, parking. AE, D, DC, MC, V.*

Inexpensive **Ambassador Inn.** The scenic enclosed courtyard with flowers, fountain, and bubbling stream sets the tone for this 170-room property 4 miles north of Sky Harbor International Airport. The blue-and-brown traditionally styled rooms have refrigerators and electric stove tops. A small, newly added weight room with exercise bikes as well as a cheerful pink coffee shop and brass-trimmed bar are on the premises. Less than a mile away are shopping, golf, tennis, and an indoor ice rink. Rates are adjusted for room location, with those nearest the pool costing more than those on the street side, but all are bargains. *4727 E. Thomas Rd., Phoenix 85018, tel. 602/840–7500 or 800/624–6759, fax 602/840– 5078. 170 rooms. Facilities: exercise room, pool, whirlpool spa, restaurant, bar, banquet and meeting room, free airport shuttle, parking. AE, D, DC, MC, V. Inexpensive.*

Comfort Inn Airport. The location isn't scenic but it's convenient: This Spanish-style motel is 4 miles from downtown Phoenix and 2 miles north of Sky Harbor International Airport. A red-tile roof and Mexican-tile accents give character to the premises, where lush greenery surrounds the pool. The 49 traditional-style rooms are dark and small but include a table and two chairs. There's no restaurant, but Bill Johnson's Big Apple three blocks west has good biscuits, grits, and barbecue. *4120 E. Van Buren St., Phoenix*

85008, tel. 602/275–5746 or 800/228–5150. 49 rooms. Facilities: pool, parking. AE, D, DC, MC, V.

Quality Inn Desert Sky. Even though downtown Phoenix and the airport are only five minutes away, guests can retreat to a quiet garden at this modest two-story motel. Thick oleander hedges separate the parking lot from the well-tended courtyard and pool, which are surrounded on three sides by 90 rooms. First-floor accommodations open to the tropical greenery and flower beds from sliding patio doors. The orange-carpeted and dark-wood rooms are plain but large; the tiled bath has a separate dressing area. *3541 E. Van Buren St., Phoenix 85008, tel. 602/273–7121 or 800/ 221–2222, fax 602/231–0973. 90 rooms, 2 suites. Facilities: pool, coffee shop, lounge, parking. AE, D, DC, MC, V.*

Biltmore– Scottsdale *Very Expensive* **Arizona Biltmore.** After a summer '91 face-lift, the grande dame of Arizona resorts is as lively and lovely as ever. Designed by Frank Lloyd Wright's colleague Albert Chase McArthur, it has been a masterpiece among world-class resorts since it opened in 1929. The lobby has stained-glass skylights and wrought-iron pilasters. Rooms feature gold-foil ceilings, handmade teak furnishings, and brown-and-pink marble baths. Outdoors there are lush flower gardens and stunning views. Restaurants—all very good—range from casual to late-night elegant, with a soda fountain open till 10. *24th St. and Missouri Ave., Phoenix 85016, tel. 602/ 955–6600 or 800/950–0086, fax 602/381–7600. 502 rooms. Facilities: 3 pools, 12 lighted tennis courts, 2 PGA golf courses, health club, jogging paths, bike rental, 3 restaurants, 3 lounges, concierge, shopping limo, parking. AE, D, DC, MC, V.*

The Boulders. A dozen miles north of The Princess on Scottsdale Road, in the foothills town of Carefree, the Valley's most dramatic luxury resort hides among hill-size granite boulders. Opened in 1984, The Boulders offers adobe casitas (and patio homes for long-term rental) in a graceful desert landscape; golf courses stretch like carpeting between the giant stones, and a stunning main lodge by the architect Robert Bacon blends beautifully with its surroundings. Remodeled in the summer of 1992, the casitas are compact but comfortable, with curving, pueblo-style half-walls and shelves; each has a view patio, mini-kiva fireplace, stocked wet bar, and a spacious bath and dressing area with a deep tub and adobe vanity. The modified American plan features breakfast at The Latilla (the lodge's main restaurant) or at The Club on the green, and dinner at either The Latilla or the Palo Verde. The Latilla is Californian in style, the Palo Verde Southwest international. The nearby el Pedregal center, a dramatic twin to the resort, has shopping and more eating options; and Carefree multiplies these many times over. *34631 N. Tom Darlington Dr., Carefree 85377, tel. 602/488–9009 or 800/553–1717, fax 602/ 488–4118. 136 casitas, 22 patio homes. Facilities: fitness center, 2 pools, 6 tennis courts, 2 18-hole golf courses, jog-*

ging and hiking paths, horseback riding, Jeep and balloon rides, llama treks, room service, meeting rooms, parking. AE, D, DC, MC, V.

Marriott's Camelback Inn. Begun in the mid-'30s as a posh "by invitation only" resort, the Camelback Inn was bought and expanded in the late '60s by J. W. Marriott, who recouped his investment by selling the 423 casitas and suites as condos in 1970–72. (Owners are guaranteed four weeks a year.) The inn "Where Time Stands Still," as its adobe clock-tower entrance still proclaims, is an oasis of comfortable predictability in the gorgeous valley between Camelback and Mummy Mountains. The lobby, a classic of early southwestern design, is a high point; so is the young, helpful staff and the airy, calm, and clean 25,000-square-foot spa. The casita rooms are big on windows and amenities but small in size, and their architecture and decor are dull and embarrassingly motel-like. The Chaparral Room serves standard Continental fare, and the Navajo Room offers American and southwestern dishes; neither shows much imagination. The Camelback is content to rest on its laurels, and a steady stream of guests are, too. *5402 E. Lincoln Dr., Scottsdale 85253, tel. 602/948–1700 or 800/24CAMEL, fax 602/951–8469. 400 rooms, 23 suites. Facilities: spa, 3 pools, 10 tennis courts, 2 18-hole golf courses, hiking paths, horseback riding, Jeep and balloon rides, 5 restaurants, 2 lounges, room service, meeting rooms, parking. AE, D, DC, MC, V.*

The Phoenician. Before the Arizona financier Charles Keating was otherwise distracted, he and his wife devoted a lot of time to this resort, now Kuwaiti owned. You may question the suitability of the lobby's French provincial decor and its authentic Dutch master paintings to a desert locale, but there's no question that a great deal of attention was paid to details. It's the highest priced property in town, and you wouldn't want to stay here if you didn't have lots of money (or were not on an expense account)—for example, unless you shell out for valet parking each time, you have to wander around a labyrinthine underground garage to fetch your car. But if this type of petty concern never crosses your mind, relax and enjoy the superb service and luxurious facilities, which include a pool fully inlaid with mother-of-pearl. *6000 E. Camelback Rd., Scottsdale 85251, tel. 602/941–8200 or 800/888–8234. 442 rooms, 107 casitas, 31 suites. Facilities: 4 restaurants, boutiques, golf course, 11 tennis courts, 7 swimming pools, health club, sauna, steam room, beauty salon, barbershop, archery, badminton, croquet, volleyball, basketball, jogging trails, supervised children's programs. AE, D, DC, MC, V.*

★ **Scottsdale Princess.** The most tasteful of the Scottsdale resorts, the Princess can accommodate large groups—such as those who come to play in the PGA Tour Phoenix Open, held here every year—without seeming crowded. Rooms in the red-tile-roofed main building and the casitas, spread out over 450 beautifully landscaped acres, are furnished in

Spanish style, with large, carved pieces, but sand-colored rugs and bedspreads contribute to an overall airy effect; each has three telephones, an oversize tub, and such extras as an iron and an ironing board. The Marquesa Restaurant (*see* Dining, *above*) has been consistently rated one of the best in the state. *7575 E. Princess Dr., Scottsdale 85255, tel. 602/585–4848 or 800/344–4758, fax 602/585–0091. 400 rooms in main building, 125 casitas, 75 villas. Facilities: 5 restaurants, bar, nightclub, horseback riding, 2 18-hole golf courses, 9 tennis courts, 3 pools, health club, spa, racquetball, squash, steam bath, saunas, boutiques and pro shops, hairdresser. AE, D, DC, MC, V.*

Expensive–
Very Expensive
★

Hyatt Regency Scottsdale at Gainey Ranch. A fun place for families, with its complex of pools, fountains, waterslides, and lagoons plied by gondolas, this resort has a bit of a Disneyland ambience. At night the palm trees are lit up in bright shades of green and orange, and the public areas tend to be crowded. Rooms, which are comfortably if predictably furnished in contemporary style, offer all the expected amenities. A standout is The Golden Swan Restaurant, serving southwestern cooking at its best—light and wonderfully tasty. Three 9-hole courses offer golfers a choice of terrains—dunes, arroyo, or lakes—depending on whether you fancy sand or water traps. *7500 E. Doubletree Ranch Rd., Scottsdale 85258, tel. 602/991–3388 or 800/233–1234, fax 602/483–5550. 493 rooms. Facilities: 10 pools, lagoons, 9 tennis courts, 3 9-hole golf courses, health club, 3 restaurants, 2 lounges, concierge floor, parking. AE, D, DC, MC, V.*

★ **Ritz-Carlton.** Like an 11-story false front, this sand-colored neo-Federal mid-rise facing Biltmore Fashion Square mall hides a graceful, well-appointed luxury hotel that pampers the traveler. Built in 1988, it has large public rooms decorated with 18th- and 19th-century European paintings and handsomely displayed china collections. Rooms are moderately spacious with an armoire closeting a TV and refrigerator (stocked), a small closet with a safe, and a marble bath well supplied with amenities. Since the hotel is business-oriented, rates go down on the weekend. The compact, elegant health club and the daily high tea are highlights, and the modestly named The Restaurant is among the Valley's best at Southwest-flavored Continental. *2401 E. Camelback Rd., Phoenix 85016, tel. 602/468–0700 or 800/241–3333, fax 602/957–6076. 267 rooms, 14 suites. Facilities: health club, pool, 2 saunas, tennis court, concierge, concierge floor, business center, outdoor meeting pavilion, shop, covered valet parking, 2 restaurants, 2 bars. AE, D, DC, MC, V.*

Moderate **Camelback Courtyard by Marriott.** This four-story hostelry, which opened in 1990, delivers compact elegance in its public areas and no-frills comfort in its rooms and suites. A medium-size lap pool and whirlpool fill the courtyard, landscaped with granite boulders and palms. Standard doubles are handsomely carpeted and draped while suites are done in gray with rose accents. The considerable savings are achieved by dropping such "hotel" features as 24-hour room service (it's available from 5 to 10 PM) and relying on the attached Town and Country mall for gift and grooming shops, travel services, and the like. *2101 E. Camelback Rd., Phoenix 85016, tel. 602/955–5200 or 800/321–2211, fax 602/955–1101. 143 rooms, 12 suites. Facilities: health club, pool, whirlpool, spa, restaurant, bar, parking. AE, D, DC, MC, V.*

Inexpensive **Motel 6 Scottsdale.** The best bargain in Scottsdale lodging is easy to miss, but it's worth hunting for the sign along Camelback Road. Just steps away from the newly renovated Scottsdale Fashion Square and Camelview Plaza, this motel is also close to the specialty shops of 5th Avenue and Scottsdale's Civic Plaza. Amenities aren't a priority here, but the price is remarkable considering the stylish and much more expensive resorts found close by. Rooms are small and plain with brown carpets and print bedspreads, but the well-landscaped pool offers a pleasant outdoor respite under the palms. *6848 E. Camelback Rd., Scottsdale 85251, tel. 602/946–2280. 122 rooms. Facilities: pool, hot tub, parking. AE, D, DC, MC, V.*

East Valley **Hilton Pavilion.** This eight-floor atrium hotel, built in 1985
Moderate and redone in mid-1989, is in the heart of the East Valley, just off its main artery, the Superstition Freeway (AZ 360). The East Valley's largest shopping mall, Fiesta Mall, is almost next door, and downtown Phoenix is 18 miles away. The Pavilion's ambience is defined by etched glass and brass, tropical greenery, and Art Deco furniture; the staff is young and eager to help. Rooms are moderately spacious and darkly earth-toned, with small baths and closets and a large lighted table; corner suites and the top two floors have unstocked minibars and the best views. *1011 W. Holmes Ave., Mesa 85210, tel. 602/833–5555 or 800/544–5866, fax 602/649–1886. 263 rooms, 57 suites. Facilities: pool, whirlpool spa, weight room, restaurant, 2 bars, gift shop, parking. AE, D, DC, MC, V.*

Radisson Tempe. Set snugly between the Arizona State University campus and Old Town Tempe, this informal courtyard hotel is handy to the East Valley and downtown Phoenix. The tone is set by the spacious adobe-and-verdigris lobby and the young, polo-shirted staff. Many visitors come for ASU sports and the pro football Cardinals (the stadium is virtually next door); Tempe's Chamber of Commerce and visitor's bureau both headquarter here. Rooms are bright, simple southwestern and comfortable. The hotel has a pleasant, quiet sports bar, and a creditable restaurant (The Arches); guests also have Old Town Tempe's wide array of restaurants, shops, and clubs at their feet. *60 E. 5th St., Tempe 85281, tel. 602/894–1400 or 800/547–8705; fax 602/968–7677. 303 rooms. Facilities: pool, exercise* *club, sauna, 3 tennis courts, shops, 2 restaurants, bar-lounge, meeting rooms, parking. AE, D, DC, MC, V.*

Inexpensive **Mesa Travelodge.** Rooms are newly refurbished at this small, plain motel three blocks west of Mesa's downtown center: New blue carpet, cream wallpaper, and bedspreads and art prints in southwestern motifs brighten the 38 rooms overlooking a small pool. The motel's busy corner spot can mean continual street noise, but low prices help compensate. *22 S. Country Club Dr., Mesa 85210, tel. 602/964–5694 or 800/578–7878, fax 602/964–5697. 38 rooms. Facilities: pool, parking. AE, D, DC, MC, V.*

West Valley and **Crescent Hotel.** This eight-story, terraced white concrete
Metrocenter hostelry across I–17 from Metrocenter, the state's largest
Expensive shopping mall, was built in 1987 by financier Charles Keating. In 1989 it was taken over by the federal government, and it was purchased in 1991 by Kuwaiti investors. They appear to have made the Crescent a viable upper-end hotel. Mrs. Keating's "southwestern imperial" decor remains—vast public rooms with massive stone arches and concrete columns, terra-cotta tile floors and bleached-wood wall paneling, with rose carpets in the hallways. The sizable rooms continue the look with deep rose carpet, mauve bedspreads and drapes, and pale-toned furnishings. The full-size pool and tennis courts are well kept; the health club is small but well appointed. Charlie's restaurant is pricey and uneven, but there are ample eating options nearby. *2620 W. Dunlap Ave., Phoenix 85021, tel. 602/943–8200 or 800/423–4126, fax 602/371–2856. 332 rooms, 12 suites. Facilities: health club, pool, 2 saunas, whirlpool spa, tennis court, squash courts, putting green, volleyball court, concierge, concierge floor, business center, shop, restaurant, bar, parking. AE, D, DC, MC, V.*

Hotel Westcourt. This undistinguished-looking brown block sits on the outer circle of the huge Metrocenter shopping mall, but in a small space it packs 284 rooms around a large central pool. Modest-size rooms (identical to those in the stunning sister hotel, The Buttes) are done in muted southwestern colors, with bentwood chairs, minirefrigerators, and compact baths. The small concierge floor costs a minimal fee; lobby-suite sitting rooms overlook the atrium; poolside junior suites (carved from regular-size rooms) are like elegant little cabanas. Breakfast and luncheon buffets are available in Trumps Bar and Grill, as is menu service through the evening. Other dining options abound within a short walk. *10220 N. Metro Pkwy. E, Phoenix 85051, tel. 602/997–5900 or 800/858–1033, fax 602/997–1034. 269 rooms, 15 suites. Facilities: health club, pool, sauna, whirlpool spa, tennis court, concierge, concierge floor, business center, shop, 2 restaurants, bar, parking. AE, D, DC, MC, V.*

Wickenburg **Rancho de los Caballeros.** Now more of a luxury resort than
Very Expensive a dusty dude ranch, this 20,000-acre spread began with 320

acres in 1947 and gradually evolved to include an exclusive housing development, a championship golf course, and a 5,000-square-foot conference center. Trail rides are still a popular feature here, and the annual weeklong Los Caballeros Trail Ride, starting at the ranch, is a major event among southwestern horse folk. In the huge main lodge, the original *sala* (living room) has been remodeled; surrounding the copper fireplace now is bright, neo-Mexican decor, and adjacent are game rooms. The American Plan (15% tips included) meals are provided in the bright dining room (breakfast and dinner, restaurant style) and poolside from a half-dozen buffet carts. Rooms—from the original brick Sun Terrace duplexes to the recently built Bradshaw Suites (with optional kitchenette and sitting room)—are spacious and done in low-key southwestern decor; TVs are available on request only, and the baths do not have amenities. *1551 S. Vulture Mine Rd., Wickenburg 85390, tel. 602/684–5484, fax 602/684–2267. 73 rooms. Facilities: pool, horseback riding, cookouts, 4 tennis courts, 18-hole golf course, skeet and trap shooting range, parking. Closed June–Sept. No credit cards.*

Expensive **Flying E Ranch.** This spacious spread, on a breeze-swept rise with a 400-square-mile view, typifies the modern dude ranch. About 4 miles west of town to the site of the Wickenburg Massacre and then a mile back from the highway, the 21,000-acre ranch was built in 1946. Most of the rooms have wide views and the original knotty pine walls and whitewashed pine and leather furniture; bathrooms are clean and modern. Minirefrigerators and wet bars are unstocked, as is the lounge (which does have mixers for the sundown cocktail hour); bring your own spirits. But the staff's spirits are high and infectious; city slickers adore the morning, lunch, and evening cookout rides and the occasional "dudeos," in which Flying E greenhorns ride and rope against dudes from other spreads; and the weekly barn dance is not to be missed. American Plan meals are family style on gingham-checked oilcloth over trestle tables, with western music playing in the background. Rides cost extra. *Box EEE, Wickenburg 85358, tel. 602/684–2690 or 602/684–2173, fax 602/684–5304. 16 rooms. Facilities: pool and whirlpool, horseback riding, cookouts, weight room, tennis court, basketball court, outdoor chess, lounge, parking. Closed May–Oct. 31. No credit cards.*

Kay El Bar Ranch. Tucked into a hollow beside the Hassayampa River just 3 miles north of town, this is what dude ranches used to be—homey, comfy, and away from it all, with more horses than people, but not too many of either. This National Historic Site, opened as a dude ranch in 1925, was revived in 1980 by two sisters from the East, Jane Nash and Jan Martin. Immense old salt cedars tower over fat saguaros and some of the biggest mesquite trees in Arizona, all shading the 10-room adobe bunkhouse with its family-style lodge room; the two-bedroom, two-bath cottage (built in 1914); and the brightly decorated cookhouse, where eating is family style. Rooms are compact and clean, with small, modern bathrooms, and decor is down-home western. The American Plan rates include three hearty meals a day (some outdoors by the corral) and one two-hour ride. *Box 2480, Wickenburg 85358, tel. 602/684–7593. 10 rooms, 1 cottage. Facilities: pool, library, horseback riding, cookouts, volleyball, golf privileges, lodge room, parking. Closed May–mid-Oct. D, MC, V.*

The Arts and Nightlife

The Arts

Phoenix performing-arts groups have grown rapidly in number and sophistication, especially in the past two decades. Completion of the downtown **Symphony Hall** (225 E. Adams St., tel. 602/262–7272) and **Herberger Theater Center** (222 E. Monroe St., tel. 602/252–TIXS), which face each other across the Civic Plaza mall, has given many groups a state-of-the-art permanent home in elegant surroundings; the developing "cultural district" just 2 miles north, around Deck Park, houses several more.

The most comprehensive ticket agencies are **Dillard's** (13 locations including all Dillard's department stores and Phoenix Civic Plaza, tel. 602/678–2222) and the **Arizona State University ticket office** (Gammage Center, Tempe, tel. 602/965–3434).

Theater **Actors Theatre of Phoenix** (320 N. Central Ave., Suite 104, tel. 602/254–3475) is the resident theater troupe at the Herberger. Besides a full season of drama, comedy, and musical theater, it presents original one-act plays in its lunchtime Brown Bag series Tuesday through Thursday.

Arizona Theatre Company (Herberger Theater Center, 222 E. Monroe St., tel. 602/279–0534), Arizona's only full Equity company, splits its season between Tucson and Phoenix, where it performs at the Herberger. Its playbill usually includes four popular plays and two lesser-known works.

Black Theater Troupe (333 E. Portland St., tel. 602/258–8128) performs at the Herberger and at its own house, the Helen K. Mason Center, a half-block from the city's Performing Arts Building on Deck Park. It presents original and contemporary dramas and musical revues, as well as adventurous adaptations, such as its recent version of *Steel Magnolias*.

Mill Avenue Theatre (520 S. Mill Ave., Tempe, tel. 602/921–7777), a relative newcomer, established itself with *Guv: The Musical*, a long-running original satire (with constantly updated lyrics) on Arizona's politics. It regularly brings alternative-theater experiences to the Valley.

Dinner Theater **Copper State Players** (6727 N. 47th Ave., Glendale, tel. 602/
937–1671), the Valley's oldest dinner troupe, stages light
comedy at Max's, a West Valley sports bar and steak house.

Murder Ink (7000 E. Indian School Rd., Scottsdale, tel. 602/
423–8737) presents audience-participation whodunits at
the Impeccable Pig restaurant and antiques/crafts shop in
Scottsdale and other Valley locations.

Classical Music **Arizona Opera** (Symphony Hall, 225 E. Adams St., tel. 602/
266–7464), one of the nation's most highly respected re-
gional companies, stages a four-opera season, primarily
classical, in Tucson and Phoenix.

Phoenix Symphony Orchestra (3707 N. 7th St., tel. 602/
264–6363), the resident company at Symphony Hall, has
reached the first rank of American regional symphonies.
Its rich season includes orchestral works from the classical
and contemporary literature, a chamber series, composer
festivals, and outdoor pops concerts.

Dance **a ludwig co.** (tel. 602/965–3914), the Valley's foremost modern dance troupe, includes the choreography of founder-di-
rector Ann Ludwig of the Arizona State University faculty
in its repertoire of contemporary works.

Ballet Arizona (3645 E. Indian School Rd., tel. 602/381–
0184), the state's professional ballet company, presents full
seasons of classical and contemporary works (including
commissioned pieces for the company) in both Tucson and
Phoenix, where it is the resident dance company at the
Herberger Theater Center.

Film Harkins Theaters, a locally owned chain, is the only one in
the valley that shows anything but mass-market movies. Its
Cine Capri (2323 E. Camelback Rd., tel. 602/956–4200), a
classic wide-screen, superstereo theater from the '60s, occasionally offers a giant-screen revival such as *Dr. Zhivago*
or *Spartacus*. At **Camelview 5** (70th St. and Camelback Rd.,
tel. 602/864–0020), one screen usually shows a major foreign release or domestic art film.

Galleries The gallery scene in Phoenix and Scottsdale is so extensive that your best bet is to consult the Friday and Sunday
listings in *The Arizona Republic* or the Marquee section in
Saturday's *Phoenix Gazette*. Southwestern art—from traditional to avant-garde Native American, from the Cowboy
Artists of America to performance art—is varied and
abundant. Photography also enjoys a strong tradition in
Arizona.

Nightlife

Downtown Phoenix used to close up at sunset—until the
advent of The Mercado and the Arizona Center. The heart
of town at last has nightclubs, restaurants, and upscale
bars that compete with livelier resorts and clubs in

Scottsdale, along Camelback Road in north-central Phoenix, and elsewhere around the Valley.

Among music and dancing styles, country and western has the longest tradition here; jazz, surprisingly, runs a close second. Rock clubs also are numerous and varied, as are hotel lounges. At its major and minor venues, the Valley attracts a steady stream of pop and rock acts; for concert tickets, try **Dillard's** (13 Valley locations, including Phoenix Civic Plaza, tel. 602/267–1246).

The best listings and reviews are in the weekly *New Times* tabloid newspaper, distributed Wednesday; the Friday and Sunday Life & Leisure sections of *The Arizona Republic;* and the Marquee section of Saturday's *Phoenix Gazette.*

Bars and Lounges You can listen to the ivories tinkling at **The Plaza Bar** on the mezzanine of the Hyatt Regency Phoenix (122 N. 2nd St., tel. 602/252–1234), a quiet getaway with a sparkling downtown view.

A lively (during happy hour, noisy) upscale crowd takes advantage of the city's most spectacular view at **Chuckawalla's,** the lounge in Top of the Rock restaurant (2000 W. Westcourt Way, Tempe, tel. 602/225–9000) at The Buttes.

An elegant uptown spot, **Top of Central** (8525 N. Central Ave., tel. 602/861–2437) has soft music and room for larger groups.

Comedy **The Last Laugh** (8041 N. Black Canyon Hwy., tel. 602/995–5653) is the Valley's oldest successful comedy club.

The Improv (930 E. University Dr., Tempe, tel. 602/921–9877), part of a national chain, books better-known talent.

Country and **Cheyenne Cattle Co.** (455 N. 3rd St., tel. 602/253–6225), in
Western the Arizona Center downtown, is the newest country and western dance spot in town.

At **Mr. Lucky's** (3660 W. Grand Ave., tel. 602/246–0686), the granddaddy of Phoenix western clubs, you can dance the two-step all night (or learn it, if you haven't before).

Toolie's Country (4231 W. Thomas Rd., tel. 602/272–3100) books the best national acts, from Sweethearts of the Rodeo to Eddie Raven and Juice Newton.

Jazz **American Bar & Grill** (6113 N. Scottsdale Rd., Scottsdale, tel. 602/948–9907; 1233 S. Alma School Rd., Mesa, tel. 602/844–1918) books solo artists for long-term soft jazz gigs that fit its San Francisco–style lounges. (Good neo–New Orleans and southwestern food are featured, too.)

At **Unique Foods and Services** (1153 W. Jefferson St., tel. 602/257–0701), a fine jazz sextet accompanies the barbecue and greens Tuesday night.

Timothy's (6335 N. 16th St., tel. 602/277–7634) is yet one more venerated venue that joins top jazz performances with fine French-influenced Continental and Cajun cuisine.

Rock and Blues A small club, **Anderson's Fifth Estate** (6820 E. 5th Ave., Scottsdale, tel. 602/994–4168) mixes DJ nights, local bands, and occasional touring rock and country/folk acts.

Mason Jar (2303 E. Indian School Rd., tel. 602/956–6271) hosts regular alternative rock nights and occasional blues and rock oldies.

Warsaw Wally's (2547 E. Indian School Rd., tel. 602/955–0881) is the top Valley blues club, but its poolroom draws rough trade.

Singles With 36 TVs and five giant screens, as well as an outdoor volleyball court, **America's Original Sports Bar** (455 N. 3rd St., tel. 602/252–2112) in The Arizona Center is big and boisterous.

At the popular **Denim & Diamonds** (3905 E. Thomas Rd., tel. 602/225–0182), folks turn up in anything from jeans to glitzy jewelry for dancing and socializing.

In the Arizona Center, **Hooters** (455 N. 3rd St., tel. 602/257–0000) draws crowds with its T-shirted, short-shorted waitresses, its beer and burgers and potato skins menu, and its indoor-outdoor visibility.

Macayo's Depot Cantina (300 S. Ash Ave., Tempe, tel. 602/966–6677) combines a lively "meet market," frequented by students from the nearby ASU campus, with a very creditable Mexican restaurant.

Studebaker's (705 S. Rural Rd., Tempe, tel. 602/829–8495) joins bar, buffet, and dancing with live DJs for a noisy place to meet friends.

7 Tucson and Southern Arizona

By Trudy
Thompson Rice
and Edie Jarolim

A treasure of mountains, deserts, canyons, and dusty little cowboy towns, southern Arizona remains undiscovered, for the most part, by visitors; the vast majority of the state's tourists head north for the Grand Canyon, often neglecting the southern half of the state. But it would be a pity to miss southern Arizona. It's uncrowded, the weather is usually mild, and there is plenty to see and do. Among the area's myriad attractions are historic Tombstone, Yuma, and Bisbee, where you can indulge in Old West fantasies galore; the huge, oddly shaped cacti of Saguaro National Monument; the eerily towering rock formations of Chiricahua National Monument; the lively shops and restaurants in Nogales, across the Mexican border; and, of course, Tucson. A gateway to southern Arizona, Tucson offers the traveler everything from culture to sports, from ballet, symphony, and the University of Arizona's photography museum, boasting one of the largest modern collections in the country, to golf, tennis, and Hi-Corbett Field, where the Cleveland Indians compete with seven other major-league baseball teams during spring training.

Although it is Arizona's second-largest city, Tucson feels like a small town, albeit one enriched by its deep Hispanic and Old West roots. It is at once a bustling center of business and a kicked-back university and resort town. Metropolitan Tucson has some 665,000 year-round residents—making it second in population to the state's capital, Phoenix—but the population swells in the winter, when "snowbirds" come to the area to enjoy the warm sun that shines on the city more than 300 days every year. Winter temperatures hover around 65°F during the day and 38°F at night. Summers are unquestionably hot—with July averaging 101°F during the day and 73°F at night—but not as hot as in Phoenix: Although it is 100 miles to the south and both cities lie in desert valleys created by surrounding mountains, Tucson is cooler in the summer because it's higher in altitude (2,400 feet, compared with Phoenix's 1,100 feet). And because Tucson averages only 11 inches of rain a year (more than half of which falls from July to September), the low humidity makes even July's heat feel far more comfortable than one would expect.

In a part of the world where everything seems new and buildings more than 50 years old are known as historic places, Tucson is an exception. Historians have dated Tucson's earliest citizens to AD 100, when the Hohokam Indians made their home in the fertile farming valley. During the 1500s, Spanish explorers arrived to find Pima Indians enjoying the mild weather and growing crops.

The name Tucson came from the Indian word *stjukshon* (pronounced "STOOK-shahn"), meaning "spring at the foot of a black mountain." (The springs at the foot of Sentinel Peak, made of black volcanic rock, are now dry.) The name became Tucson (originally pronounced "TUK-son") in the mouths of the Spanish explorers who built the *presidio* (walled city) of San Augustin del Tuguison in 1776 to keep Native Americans from reclaiming the city. The walled city was affectionately called the Old Pueblo by its early settlers, and the nickname has stuck till this day.

Father Eusebio Francisco Kino, a Jesuit missionary, first visited the village in 1687 and returned a few years later to build missions in the area. His influence is still strongly felt throughout the region; especially noteworthy is the Mission San Xavier del Bac, just south of Tucson.

Four flags have flown over Tucson—those of Spain, Mexico, the U.S. Confederacy, and the Union. Arizona didn't become a state until 1912, so its colorful days as a territory are still very much a part of the area's lore. The Butterfield stage line was extended to Tucson in the 1850s, bringing in adventurers, a few settlers, and more than a handful of outlaws. Much of the city's growth was shaped by the University of Arizona, opened in 1891 on land "donated" by two gamblers and a saloon keeper (their benevolence was reputed to have been inspired by a bad hand of cards).

Tucson's growth really took off during World War II, thanks to Davis-Monthan Air Force Base. It was also around this time that air-conditioning made the desert hospitable to visitors and residents alike. Today the city's economy relies heavily on tourism, the university, and some high-tech industries. The resident population is now almost one-quarter Hispanic, and some of the best Mexican food north of the border can be found in restaurants here. The influence of Spanish and Mexican settlers is also strongly felt in the city's architecture and culture.

Tucson is a good jumping-off point for a visit to southern Arizona. Several day trips can be coordinated from the city, but for excursions to such towns as Bisbee, Douglas, and Nogales it's best to find lodging along the way. This isn't difficult, although it does take some advance planning: In some of the sparsely settled parts of southern Arizona, accommodations aren't always plentiful. As you might expect, the desert areas are popular in winter, and the cooler mountain areas are more heavily visited in summer months.

Check plane fares carefully when you're planning your trip. Though you may not want to spend time in Phoenix, sometimes it's cheaper to fly into that city and then take a scenic two-hour drive down the Pinal Pioneer Parkway (U.S. 89), or a speedier trip on I–10, to Tucson.

Essential Information

Arriving and Departing by Plane

Tucson International Airport (tel. 602/573–8000) is 8½ miles south of downtown, west of I–10 off the Valencia exit. Carriers include **Aero Mexico** (tel. 800/237–6639), **American** (tel. 800/433–7300), **America West** (tel. 800/247–5692), **Arizona Airways** (tel. 800/274–0662), **Continental** (tel. 800/525–0280), **Delta** (tel. 800/221–1212), **Morris Air** (tel. 800/444–5660), **Northwest** (tel. 800/225–2525), and **United** (tel. 800/241–6522).

Between the Airport and Downtown In addition to the modes of transportation listed below, many hotels provide courtesy airport shuttle service; inquire when making reservations.

By Car It makes sense to rent at the airport. Parking is not a problem, even downtown. Rental-car agencies at the airport include **Budget** (tel. 602/889–8800) and **National** (tel. 602/573–8050). The driving time from the airport to downtown varies, but it's usually less than half an hour, 20 minutes extra during rush hours (7:30–9 AM and 4:30–6 PM).

By Taxi Taxi rates vary widely; they are unregulated in Arizona. It's always wise to inquire about the cost of a trip before getting into a cab. You shouldn't pay much more than $16 from the airport to the heart of downtown. A few of the more reliable cab companies are **Yellow Cab** (tel. 602/624–6611), **Checker Cab** (tel. 602/623–1133; smoke-free cabs available on request), and **Fiesta Taxi** (tel. 602/622–7777), whose drivers speak both English and Spanish.

By Van or Bus **Arizona Stagecoach** (tel. 602/889–1000), with an office at the airport, takes groups and individuals to all parts of Tucson for $8.50 to $26, depending on the location.

If you're traveling light and aren't in a hurry, you can take a city **Sun Tran** (tel. 602/792–9222) bus to central Tucson for only 75¢. Bus 11, which leaves from a stop at the left of the lower level as you come out of the terminal, goes north on Alvernon Way, and you can transfer to most of the east–west bus lines from this main north–south road; ask the bus driver (they're all friendly and helpful) which one would take you closest to the location you need. You must have exact change, but transfers are free.

Arriving and Departing by Car, Bus, and Train

By Car From Phoenix, 111 miles northwest, I–10 east is the road that will take you to Tucson. Also the main traffic artery through town, I–10 has well-marked exits all along the route. At Casa Grande, 70 miles north of Tucson, I–8 connects with I–10, bringing travelers into the area from the west. From Nogales, 63 miles south on the Mexican border, take I–19 into Tucson.

By Bus Buses to Los Angeles, El Paso, Phoenix, Flagstaff, Douglas, and Nogales depart and arrive regularly from Tucson's **Greyhound** terminal (2 S. 4th Ave. at E. Broadway, tel. 602/792–0972). For information about travel from other cities, call the number listed for Greyhound/Trailways in your local yellow pages. For travel to Phoenix, **Arizona Shuttle Service, Inc.** (tel. 602/795–6771) runs express service from three locations in Tucson every hour on the hour, 4 AM–8 PM every day; the trip takes approximately 2 hours. One-way fares are $19 for adults, $10 for children under 12. Call 24 hours in advance for reservations.

By Train **Amtrak** serves the city with several westbound and eastbound trains weekly; the station is downtown at 400 East Toole Avenue (tel. 800/USA–RAIL).

Important Addresses and Numbers

Tourist Information The **Metropolitan Tucson Convention and Visitors Bureau** (130 S. Scott Ave., 85701, tel. 602/624–1817 or 800/638–8350), located downtown, is open weekdays 8–5 and weekends 9–4.

Emergencies For the **police, ambulance, fire department,** dial 911, a free call from public pay phones.

Doctors and Dentists **Community Information and Referral Services** (tel. 602/881–1794) will provide you with names of doctors or dentists who can assist you.

Hospitals **El Dorado Hospital and Medical Center** (1400 N. Wilmot Rd., tel. 602/886–6361), **Northwest Hospital** (6200 N. La Cholla Blvd., tel. 602/742–9000), **St. Joseph's Hospital** (350 N. Wilmot Rd., tel. 602/296–3211), **Tucson General Hospital** (3838 N. Campbell Ave., tel. 602/327–5431), **Tucson Medical Center** (5301 E. Grant Rd., tel. 602/327–5461), **University Medical Center** (1501 N. Campbell Ave., tel. 602/694–0111).

Late-Night Pharmacies Six **Walgreen** drugstores in the city have 24-hour prescription service; for the location nearest you, call 800/WALGREENS (800/925–4733). A number of Osco Drug stores also offer 24-hour prescription service; if you phone 800/654–OSCO and give the zip code of the place you're staying, you'll be referred to the closest open pharmacy.

Other Useful Numbers **Chamber of Commerce** (tel. 602/792–1212).
Local road conditions (tel. 602/573–7623).
State road report (tel. 602/573–7623).
Tucson Parks and Recreation Department (tel. 602/791–4873).
Weather (tel. 602/881–3333).

Getting Around

A car is almost a requirement if you're really going to explore Tucson and southern Arizona. You can get around downtown on foot and by bus or taxi, but getting to know the area requires a road trip or two.

By Car Most of the year, traffic in Tucson isn't especially heavy, but during the busiest winter months (December through February), streets in the central area of town can get congested. There's a seat-belt law in the state, as well as one that requires children under the age of four to ride in a secure child-restraint seat. Don't even think of drinking and driving; if you do, you'll spend your vacation in jail. Arizona's strict laws against driving under the influence are strongly enforced.

If you haven't rented a car at the airport (*see* Between the Airport and Downtown, *above*), you might try **U-Save Auto Rental** (tel. 602/790–8847 or 602/745–2119), **Enterprise** (tel. 602/747–9700 or 602/881–9400) or **Rent-A-Ride** (tel. 602/750–1900) in the city center. In addition, **Carefree Rent-A-Car** (tel. 602/790–2655) offers reliable used cars at good rates.

By Bus and Trolley Within the city limits, public transportation is available through **Sun Tran** (tel. 602/792–9222), Tucson's bus system. On weekdays, some buses run until 10 PM, but most run only until 7 PM, and service is more limited on weekends. A one-way ride costs 75¢ (transfers are free); those with valid Medicare cards can ride for 25¢. The **Sun Tran Trolley** runs between downtown and the University of Arizona, Monday–Saturday, for 25¢ each way. Call for information on Sun Tran bus and trolley routes and costs.

The city-run **Van Tran** (tel. 602/620–1234) offers transportation in specially outfitted vans for disabled riders. Call for information and reservations.

Opening and Closing Times

The majority of central city businesses, including shops and some restaurants, close at the end of the office workday, sometimes as early as 5:30 or 6. Malls have more extended hours; most stores are open weekdays 10–9, Saturday 10–6, and Sunday noon–5. Banking hours vary widely; most Tucson banks are open weekdays 9–4 (inside lobby services) and 9–5 (drive-in service); on Saturday some lobbies are open 8–2. Many banks have automated teller machines (ATMs), so customers with a banking network card can get cash when the banks are closed.

Radio Stations

AM KNST 790 News, talk

KTKT 990 Sports Entertainment Network

KJYK 1490 Top 40

KUAT 1550 National Public Radio, jazz

FM KUAT 89.1 National Public Radio, jazz

KUAZ 90.5 Classical

KXCI 91.3 Alternative rock, folk, blues, etc.

KLPX 96.1 Rock

KIIM 99.5 Country

Guided Tours

Orientation **Double K Excursions** (tel. 602/881–4734) and **Tucson Tour Company** (tel. 602/297–1911) take individuals and groups to such popular sights as Old Tucson, Sabino Canyon, and the Arizona–Sonora Desert Museum. Many tour operators are on limited schedules during the summer, but **Off the Beaten Path Tours** (tel. 602/296–0909) has excellent customized excursions year-round. **Mountain View Transportation & Jeep Tours** (tel. 602/622–4488), **Sunshine Jeep Tours** (tel. 602/742–1943), and **Trail Dust Jeep Tours** (602/747–0323) all offer trips to the Sonoran Desert in open-air four-wheel-drive vehicles.

Special-Interest Tours In the spring and fall, those interested in visiting the area's historic missions can contact **Kino Mission Tours** (tel. 602/628–1269), which has professional historians and bilingual guides on staff. If you've always wanted to star in a western and you're feeling flush, contact the folks at **Cowboy Movie Fantasy Camp** (tel. 602/750–8553): The day of filming is fun, and you'll end up with a video in which you appear to be doing dangerous cowboy stunts.

Walking Tours For an easy-to-follow self-guided tour of historic downtown Tucson, head for the **Visitors Bureau** (130 S. Scott Ave., tel. 602/624–1817 or 800/638–8350). If you want guidance, call to check whether the friendly and knowledgeable docents of the **Arizona Historical Society** (tel. 602/622–0956) are conducting any walking tours of the city during your stay; their schedule varies with the season and the day of the week.

Out-of-Town Tours Several tour companies offer bus or van excursions to points throughout southern Arizona. **Gray Line Tours** (Box 1991, Tucson 85702, tel. 602/622–8811) and **Great Western Tours** (Box 31831, Tucson 85751, tel. 602/721–0980) take groups or individuals to such destinations as Bisbee, Tubac, and Nogales. **Sonoran Desert Tours** (Box 10411, Phoenix 85064, tel. 602/840–9256) includes areas of Northern Mexico in its customized trips.

Exploring Tucson

Tucson covers more than 500 square miles in a valley ringed by mountains; for tours of the area it's necessary to have a car. The central part of town, where most of the shops, restaurants, and businesses are located, is roughly bounded by Wilmot Road on the east, Oracle Road on the west, River Road to the north, and 22nd Street to the south. The older downtown section, accessible just east of I–10 off the Broadway–Congress exit, is much smaller and easy to navigate on foot. (Streets there don't run true to any sort of grid, however, so it's best to get a good, detailed map.) If you're out walking in the hot weather, stop for frequent breaks to drink fluids: Tucson's dryness can dehydrate visitors quickly, especially if they are accustomed to living in a high-humidity area. Avoid alcohol because it aggravates dehydration, and wear sunscreen and a hat (even in the winter months if you're sun-sensitive).

Highlights for First-time Visitors

Arizona–Sonora Desert Museum (*see* Tour 3)
El Presidio District (*see* Tour 1)
Kitt Peak National Observatory (*see* Tour 5)
Mission San Xavier del Bac (*see* Tour 5)
Mt. Lemmon (*see* Tour 4)
Old Tucson Studios (*see* Tour 3)
Sabino Canyon (*see* Off the Beaten Track)
Saguaro National Monument (*see* Tour 3)
University of Arizona (*see* Tour 2)

Tour 1: El Presidio District

Numbers in the margin correspond to points of interest on the Tucson: Tours 1 and 2 map.

Originally the center of town, the downtown area is home to three historic districts: Barrio Historico, Armory Park, and El Presidio. The first two, somewhat spread out, are best toured by car; a map available from the Metropolitan Tucson Convention and Visitors Bureau (*see* Essential Information, *above*) marks a number of noteworthy sites. The El Presidio district, which has the greatest concentration of historical structures, can easily be explored on foot.

The area bounded by Franklin and Pennington streets on the north and south and by Church and Main avenues on the east and west encompasses more than 130 years of the city's architectural history, and dates from the original walled El Presidio del Tucson, a Spanish fortress built in 1776 when Arizona was still part of New Spain. The largest plaza in this historical area is now called **El Presidio Park**; it's bordered on the south side by several modern high-rise government buildings and on the east side by the mosaic-domed

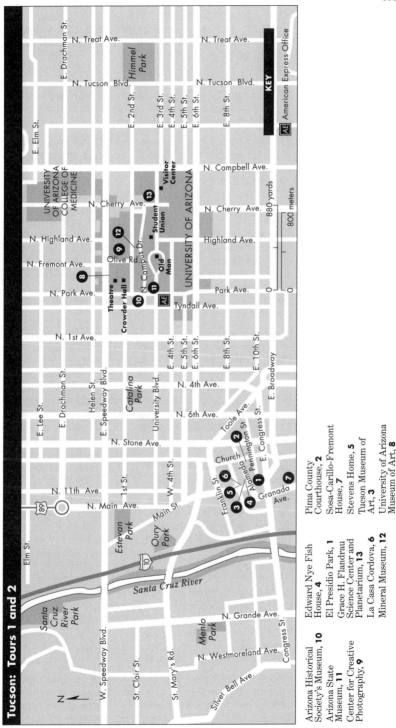

Tucson: Tours 1 and 2

N. Drachman St.
N. Treat Ave.
N. Treat Ave.
E. Drachman St.
N. Tucson Blvd.
N. Tucson Blvd.
Himmel Park
E. Elm St.
E. 2nd St.
E. 3rd St.
E. 4th St.
E. 5th St.
E. 6th St.
E. 8th St.

KEY
AE American Express Office

Visitor Center
N. Campbell Ave.
UNIVERSITY OF ARIZONA COLLEGE OF MEDICINE
N. Cherry Ave.
13
N. Cherry Ave.
Student Union
N. Highland Ave.
12
Highland Ave.
9
N. Fremont Ave.
Olive Rd.
Old Main
8
N. Campus Dr.
UNIVERSITY OF ARIZONA
N. Park Ave.
11
10
Park Ave.
Theatre
Crowder Hall
AE
Tyndall Ave.

880 yards
800 meters

N. 1st Ave.
E. 4th St.
E. 5th St.
E. 6th St.
E. 8th St.
E. 10th St.

E. Lee St.
E. Drachman St.
Helen St.
E. Speedway Blvd.
Catalina Park
University Blvd.
N. 4th Ave.
E. Broadway
N. 6th Ave.
N. Stone Ave.
Toole Ave.
2
Church
E. Congress St.
6
Alameda St.
N. 11th Ave.
89
Franklin St.
5
1
Pennington St.
3
4
Granada Ave.
7
N. Main Ave.
N. 1st St.
W. 4th St.
Main St.

Estevan Park
Oury Park
10
Elm St.
Santa Cruz River
Santa Cruz River Park
Menlo Park
N. Grande Ave.
St. Clair St.
N. Westmoreland Ave.
St. Mary's Rd.
Silver Bell Ave.
Congress St.
W. Speedway Blvd.

N

Arizona Historical Society's Museum, **10**
Arizona State Museum, **11**
Center for Creative Photography, **9**
Edward Nye Fish House, **4**
El Presidio Park, **1**
Grace H. Flandrau Science Center and Planetarium, **13**
La Casa Cordova, **6**
Mineral Museum, **12**
Pima County Courthouse, **2**
Sosa-Carillo-Fremont House, **7**
Stevens Home, **5**
Tucson Museum of Art, **3**
University of Arizona Museum of Art, **8**

② **Pima County Courthouse.** This Spanish Colonial-style structure, perhaps Tucson's most beautiful historical building, was built in 1927 on the site of the original single-story adobe court of 1869; a portion of the original Presidio wall can be seen on the courthouse's second floor, and another section of the fort was recently discovered in front of the building. The park itself, an attractive open area with a large modern sculpture in the center, is shared by a combination of city workers and homeless people.

Head north and cross Alameda Street to the Tucson Museum of Art and Historic Block. You can walk around the area on your own, but it's worth catching one of the free tours given by the museum every Wednesday and Thursday at 2 PM from October 1 through May 31. The five historic buildings on this block are listed in the National Register of Historic Places and include La Casa Cordoba, the Fish House, and the Stevens Home (*see below*). The other two residences, the **Romero House,** believed to incorporate another section of the Presidio wall, and the **Corbett House,** occupied for 56 years by the influential Tucson family for whom Hi-Corbett Field is named, are not open to the public. In the center of the museum complex is the **Plaza of the Pioneers,** honoring Tucson's early citizens.

③ If you're ready to go inside, the **Tucson Museum of Art** houses an impressive collection of pre-Columbian art. There is also a permanent display of 20th-century art depicting the West—some wonderful, some less than inspiring—and some interesting traveling shows. The museum's gift shop features a fine variety of works (jewelry, silk scarves, weavings, ceramics) by local artisans. *140 N. Main Ave., tel. 602/624–2333. Admission: $2 adults, $1 senior citizens and students, children under 12 free; Tues. free. Open Mon.–Sat. 10–4, Sun. noon–4. Free docent tours are available Oct.–May, Tues.–Fri. 11 AM and 2 PM, weekends 2 PM. Closed national holidays.*

When you leave the museum, walk down Main Avenue to the corner of Alameda (less than a block away) to the **④** **Edward Nye Fish House,** built in 1868 of adobe by the early Tucson merchant for whom it is named. Fish, a merchant, entrepreneur, and politician, and his wife, Maria Wakefield Fish, a prominent educator, shaped much of early Tucson history; they hosted such visitors as President and Mrs. Rutherford B. Hayes here. Their residence, notable for its 15-foot beamed ceilings and saguaro-cactus-rib supports, now houses the El Presidio art gallery, which sells contemporary and traditional Southwest oils, watercolors, bronzes, and ceramics. *120 N. Main Ave., tel. 602/884–7379. Admission free. Open Mon.–Sat. 10–5, Sun. 1–4.*

Also on Main Avenue, just north of the Fish House and architecturally similar, is the 1865 **Stevens Home.** Here wealthy politician and cattle rancher Hiram Stevens and his Mexican wife, Petra Santa Cruz, entertained many of

Tucson's leaders—including Edward and Maria Fish—during the 1800s. A drought brought the Stevenses' cattle ranching to a halt in 1893, and Stevens killed himself—having unsuccessfully attempted to kill his wife—in despair. The house was restored in 1980 and now hosts one of Tucson's best restaurants, Janos (*see* Dining, *below*).

For one of the best examples of simple but elegant adobe architecture, head across the Plaza of the Pioneers to **La Casa Cordova.** One of the oldest buildings in Tucson, with the original part built in about 1848, it is now home to the Mexican Heritage Museum. When you enter La Casa Cordova through the double doors on Meyer Avenue, the room on your right has an exhibit of the history of the Presidio; three rooms off the patio display furnishings of the Indian and pioneer settlers of the period. If you are lucky enough to be here from November through March, don't miss the Naciemento, a traditional Christmas display filling an entire room with miniatures arranged in elaborate scenes from the Old and New Testaments and from Mexican rural life. When you visit the museum, you'll understand why adobe—brick made of mud and straw, cured in the hot sun—was so widely used in early Tucson. It offers a natural insulation from the heat and cold, and it is durable in Tuscon's dry climate. In some cases the woody cactus ribs built into the walls and ceilings for extra support poke through the hard-packed adobe. *175 N. Meyer Ave., tel. 602/624–2333. Admission free. Open Mon.–Sat. 10–4, Sun. noon–4. Closed national holidays.*

Time Out Old Town Artisans, across Meyer Avenue from Casa Cordova, is a 13-room marketplace set in a 19th-century adobe building. If the quality of the southwestern crafts sold here is not as high as it was in the past, the pretty **Courtyard Café** (186 N. Meyer Ave., tel. 602/622–0351) on the patio is still a fine place to enjoy a salad or a sandwich.

Not, strictly speaking, in the Presidio district, the nearby **Sosa-Carillo-Fremont House** is worth a short detour south. The only building spared when the surrounding barrio was torn down to build the Tucson Convention Center, this is one of Tucson's oldest adobe residences. Originally purchased by José Maria Sosa in 1860, it was owned by the Carillo family for 80 years; Arizona's Territorial Governor, John C. Fremont, may have spent a night or two here when the place was briefly rented out to his daughter in 1880. The restored house, now a branch of the Arizona Historical Society, is furnished in 1880s fashion and features rotating displays of territorial life. *151 S. Granada Ave., tel. 602/ 622–0956. Admission free. Open Wed.–Sat. 10–4. Walking tours of the Presidio and Tucson Historic District are given Oct.–Apr., Sat. at 10: $3.25 adults, children under 7 free.*

Tour 2: University of Arizona Neighborhood

A university—especially in the Southwest—might not seem to be the most likely spot for a vacation visit, but this one is unusual. Not only is the institution itself of historical importance, but it also hosts museums for special interests ranging from photography to mineralogy. Parking in the university area is a hassle, so it's best either to leave your car elsewhere or take extra care to park it legally in a university lot. Although there are several lots throughout the campus, they're often crowded, so it's a good idea to park in the first legal spot you find. Read and heed all the signs: They mean business.

The U of A, as the University of Arizona is known locally (versus ASU, its rival state university in Phoenix), covers 325 acres and is a major economic influence for the city. More than 35,000 students attend graduate and undergraduate classes here. The original land for the university was "donated" by a couple of gamblers and a saloon owner in 1891, and $25,000 of territorial money was used to build Old Main (the original building) and hire six faculty members. The money ran out before the Old Main's roof was placed, but a few enlightened local citizens pitched in with the funds to finish it. Most of the city's populace was less enthusiastic about the institution: They were disgruntled when the 13th Territorial Legislature granted the University of Arizona to Tucson and awarded rival Phoenix with what they considered to be the real prize—an insane asylum and a prison.

Note: For all of the university's institutions, it's best to call ahead and verify opening and closing hours; continuing budget cuts have caused schedule changes in a number of cases.

Start your tour on the northwestern corner of campus, at the junction of Speedway and Olive roads. Here you'll find
8 the **University of Arizona Museum of Art,** with a wide-ranging collection of European paintings from the Renaissance through the 17th century. A collection of bronze and plaster sculptures by Jacques Lipschitz is a highlight of the museum. *Tel. 602/621–7567. Admission free. Open Sept.–mid-May, weekdays 9–5, Sun. noon–4; mid-May–Aug., weekdays 10–3:30, Sun. noon–4. Closed Sat., national and state holidays. Call ahead to verify hours.*

Those interested in a more contemporary art form should
9 head for the **Center for Creative Photography,** just southeast of and across Olive Road from the University of Arizona Museum of Art. Set up to house the university's extensive Ansel Adams holdings, this is one of the world's largest collections of 20th-century photography, including works by such artists as Paul Strand, W. Eugene Smith, and Edward Weston. Changing exhibits in the main gallery highlight various holdings of the collection, but if you'd like

to spend an hour looking at the pictures of a particular photographer in the center's archives, call to arrange an appointment. *1030 N. Olive Rd., tel. 602/621–7968. Admission free. Open Sun.–Fri. noon–5. Closed Sat., national and state holidays.*

Head directly south one block on Park Avenue to the ⑩ **Arizona Historical Society's Museum.** If you're driving and this is your first stop, park your car in the lot at the corner of 2nd and Euclid streets and then inquire at the museum about the token system. Well-displayed exhibits transport the visitor through Arizona history, starting with the Hohokam Indians and Spanish explorers and highlighting important influences such as mining and cattle ranching. Children are welcome, and several exhibits are geared to the interests of older young people. The museum's gift shop focuses on items from the late 1800s; many are reproductions, but there are a number of antiques as well. Unusual souvenirs are also available at the library, which houses an extensive collection of historical Arizona photographs and sells reprints of most of them for a small fee. *949 E. 2nd St., tel. 602/628–5774. Admission free. Open Mon.–Sat. 10–4, Sun. noon–4. Closed national and state holidays.*

If you're interested in learning more about the original inhabitants of the state, head farther south for about three blocks, staying on Park Avenue. On University Boulevard, ⑪ just inside the main gate of the university, is the **Arizona State Museum,** the oldest in the state, dating from territorial days (1893). Dioramas highlight wildlife native to the area, and extensive displays contrast the different lifestyles of Arizona's Native American tribes. One of the more unlikely exhibits is the world's largest collection of tree rings. *Park Ave. (at University Blvd., just inside the main gate), tel. 602/621–6302. Admission free. Open Mon.–Sat. 9–4, Sun. noon–4. Closed national holidays.*

Time Out   Just outside the campus gate, University Boulevard is lined with student-oriented eateries. You won't find sophisticated fare, but portions tend to be hearty and prices low. **Geronimoz** (800 E. University Blvd., tel. 602/623–1711) stands out for its good burgers and large selection of beers.

Walk directly east from the Arizona State Museum about three blocks to Old Main and head straight north (left) for three blocks to the Geology, Mines, and Metallurgy Build-⑫ ing. Here you'll find the **Mineral Museum,** which houses an extensive, well-displayed collection of fossils and minerals. Children will enjoy the huge dinosaur footprint and the fossil that shows the flying reptile from millions of years ago. *Old Geology Bldg., N. Campus Dr. (2nd bldg. west of parking garage at 2nd St. and Mountain Ave.), tel. 602/621–4227. Admission free. Open weekdays 8–3 (unstaffed noon–3). Closed university holidays.*

From the Mineral Museum, head directly east two blocks to
❸ the **Grace H. Flandrau Science Center and Planetarium** on
Cherry Avenue at the Mall, an open grassy area. Tucson is
a major center for astronomy; lighting ordinances have
been designed here to allow viewing of the usually clear desert skies at night, even in the center city. Planetarium attractions include a 16-inch public telescope, the impressive
Star Theatre, where a multimedia show brings astronomy
to life, and an interactive meteor exhibit. Laser light shows
are held here at night. Take your camera; special adapters
allow you to take pictures through the telescopes. *Cherry
Ave. and University Blvd., tel. 602/621-4515. Theater admission: $4.50 adults, $4 senior citizens, $2.50 students
and children 3–13, children under 3 not admitted; laser
light shows: $5. Open Mon. 9–5, Tues.–Thurs. 9–5 and 7–
9:30, Fri. 9–5 and 7–midnight, Sat. 1–5 and 7–midnight,
Sun. 1–5. Showtimes vary; call 602/621-7827 for recorded
message. Telescope hours during the summer are Tues.–
Sat. 8–10 PM; in winter, Tues.–Sat. 7–10 PM.*

Tour 3: Tucson Mountain Park
and Saguaro National Monument West

*Numbers in the margin correspond to points of interest on
the Tucson: Tours 3–5 map.*

If you have a car at your disposal and are interested in getting to know the flora and fauna of the Sonora Desert—as
well as some of its depictions in the cinema—this is an ideal
trip for you. If you don't drive, at least consider taking one
of the many tours to the Arizona–Sonora Desert Museum
(*see* Guided Tours in Essential Information, *above*) in the
17,000-acre **Tucson Mountain Park.** Also within the boundaries of the park, which is just south of Saguaro National
Monument West, is the Old Tucson theme park. Your best
plan is to head out early in the morning to Saguaro National
Monument, the farthest of the three and the one without
shaded areas for you to duck into. Then spend the rest of the
morning at the Arizona–Sonora Desert Museum, and at
lunchtime go over to Old Tucson, which offers the best
choice of eateries. Most of the shows featured in Old Tucson
don't start until noon, in any case. If you're not going to visit Old Tucson, consider bringing lunch along; there are lots
of picnic and barbecue areas in Saguaro National Monument. Or plan to eat at the Desert Museum cafeteria, which
has unusually good food.

From Tucson, take Speedway Boulevard west to where it
joins Anklam Road and becomes Gates Pass Road; here you
will see signs for Old Tucson Studios. At this juncture
Gates Pass Road becomes Kinney Road; continue on for
about 12 miles (passing signs for the Arizona–Sonora De-
❹ sert Museum) until you come to **Saguaro National Monument West.** The two portions of the Saguaro National
Monument are separated by the city of Tucson: The eastern

259

Tucson: Tours 3–5

N

2 miles

3 km

CORONADO NATIONAL FOREST

Summerhaven

Mt. Bigelow

Catalina Hwy.

17 Bear Wallow

18 Mt. Lemmon Ski Valley

CORONADO NATIONAL FOREST

Saguaro National Monument (East)

CORONADO NATIONAL FOREST

Old Spanish Tr.

Tanque Verde Rd.

Tanque Verde Creek

22nd St.

Escalante Rd.

Houghton Rd.

Mountain View

Sabino Canyon

Pantano Rd.

Speedway

Broadway

Wilmot Rd.

TUCSON

10

89

Oro Valley

Ina Rd.

Orange Grove Rd.

Roger Rd.

River Rd.

Grant Rd.

Campbell Ave.

University of Arizona

6th Ave.

10

South Tucson

Tucson International Airport

Tangerine Rd.

El Camino de Cerro

Gates Pass Rd.

Tucson Mountain Park

Kinney Rd.

Mission Rd.

19

89

19 Mission San Xavier Del Bac

Rillito

Santa Cruz River

Marana

10

Avra Valley Rd.

Sandario Rd.

Manville Rd.

14 Saguaro National Monument (West)

15 Arizona-Sonora Desert Museum

16 Old Tucson Studios

Hill Rd.

Valencia Rd.

86

Ajo Highway

SAN XAVIER INDIAN RESERVATION

Trico Rd.

Brawley Wash

Three Points

Sasabe Rd.

86

Silverbell Rd.

Avra Valley Rd.

Silverbell Rd.

Silver Bell

TOHONO O'ODHAM INDIAN RESERVATION (PAPAGO)

20 Kitt Peak National Observatory

portion covers more than 62,000 acres and climbs through five climate zones; the smaller western portion, the one explored on this tour, has more than 21,000 acres, all approximately at the same elevation. Both sections of the park are forested by the huge saguaro (pronounced "suh-WAR-oh") cactus, which is native to the Sonora Desert and known for its towering height (often 50 feet) and arms that reach out in weird configurations. The cactus is ribbed vertically with accordion-like pleats that expand to store water gathered through its shallow roots during the infrequent desert rain showers. In the springtime (usually April or May), the giant succulent sports a tiny party hat of white blooms. At any time of year, the sight of these kings of the desert ruling over their quiet domain is awe-inspiring.

The slow-growing cacti (they can take up to 15 years to grow 1 foot) are protected by state and federal laws, so enjoy but don't disturb them. In recent years, they have suffered a decline because a decrease in the coyote population has led to an abundant rabbit population. Rabbits and other small animals nibble at the base of the young saguaro, gathering nutrients and water for survival and thereby hindering or halting the cactus's slow growth.

You'll see the most wildlife if you go through the park early in the morning, when the animals are at their liveliest. Desert critters such as snakes and scorpions aren't necessarily hostile unless you crowd them, so just watch your step and respect their habitat.

The visitor center at the Saguaro National Monument West is worth a stop in to peruse the assortment of books and brochures on desert flora and fauna. In addition, there's often an exhibit showcasing photography of the area, and you can get information here on the various hiking trails in the park. Ask here how to get to Signal Hill, where visitors can explore petroglyphs (rock drawings) left by the Hohokam Indians centuries ago. Rangers are knowledgeable and friendly and can also advise you on the best places to see a sunrise or, in season, desert flowers. *Tel. 602/883–6366. Admission free. Open daily 8–5.*

About another half-mile south of the visitor center, on
⑮ Kinney Road, the **Arizona–Sonora Desert Museum** is not to be missed; it's the second most popular tourist attraction—after the Grand Canyon—in the state. The name "museum" is misleading for this site, which is more like a beautifully planned zoo. In this microcosm of a desert environment, hummingbirds, cactus wrens, rattlesnakes, scorpions, bighorn sheep, and even beavers all busy themselves in a natural habitat ingeniously planned to allow the visitor to look on without disturbing them. Besides the wildlife exhibits, there is also the Earth Sciences Center, which features a damp limestone cave and meteor and mineral displays that encourage visitors to feel the texture of the stones and inspect them under magnifying glasses. Exhibits and inter-

active programs change with the season. For example, during the spring visitors are invited to help identify local wildflowers.

Allow at least two hours for your visit to the museum, longer if you have some real nature lovers with you. You'll be outdoors most of the time, so take a jacket if you're visiting in winter and take frequent water breaks if you're visiting in summer; it can get really hot and dry here. Wheelchairs and strollers are available; pets aren't allowed. *2021 N. Kinney Rd., tel. 602/883-2702. Admission: $7.95 adults, $1.50 children 6–12, children 5 and under free. Open Mar.– Sept., daily 7:30–6; Oct.–Feb., daily 8:30–5. Ticket sales stop 1 hr before closing time.*

16 Go another 2 miles south on Kinney Road to get to **Old Tucson Studios.** Signs all along the way from town will direct you to this film set cum theme park, which will look familiar to you if you've seen even one old western flick. More than 250 westerns have been shot here during the last 50 years, including *Gunfight at the OK Corral, Rio Lobo,* and *The Last Outpost,* starring Ronald Reagan. The TV series "High Chaparral," "Little House on the Prairie," and, more recently, "The Young Riders" have all used the set of frontier and adobe buildings of Old Tucson as a backdrop.

Time Out Enjoy Ruby's Red Garter Revue, a corny but fun honky-tonk show, while having a burger or ribs at the **Red Dog Palace Saloon** at Old Tucson. There are also a half-dozen other places in the complex where you can have a snack or a drink.

Young children may be frightened by the loud gunfights staged in the streets, but the older ones will love them. Sheriff's deputies constantly run after bad guys (all local actors), and willing visitors are enlisted to take part in the chase through the park. Less energetic guests can sit down to view some of the films shot on location here. Other attractions include magic shows, stunt shows, a petting farm, stagecoach rides—and, as you might imagine, souvenir shops galore. Snacks can be purchased at food shops, and the Royal Oak Saloon offers full meals. *201 S. Kinney Rd. (inside Tucson Mountain Park), tel. 602/883-6457. Admission: $10.95 adults, $6.95 children 4–11, children 3 and under free; after 5 PM $6.95 adults, $6.20 children. Open daily 9–9.*

Tour 4: Mt. Lemmon

This tour takes you to the southernmost ski slope of the continental United States, but you don't have to be a skier to visit; during the warm months, you can enjoy hiking and picnicking in this lovely area. In summertime the mountain's 9,157-foot elevation brings welcome relief from the heat, and in the winter, the craggy old mountain often sports a cap of snow that draws all levels of enthusiasts.

Mt. Lemmon is one of the Santa Catalina Mountains, which stand guard at the northern rim of the valley that is Tucson. Every 1,000 feet of elevation in these mountains is equivalent to traveling 300 miles north—thus the vegetation at the top of Mt. Lemmon is similar to that found in southern Canada. Standing in a forest of pines blanketed by snow, you might have trouble remembering that there's a desert with cacti and wildflowers less than 35 miles away.

If you're making the trip in the winter, check road conditions with the **Pima County Sheriff's Department** (tel. 602/741–4900). For temperate days, consider packing a picnic lunch. Wear layers of clothing so you can cool or warm yourself as you change elevation. And be sure to fill up the tank before you leave town because there are no gas stations on Mt. Lemmon Highway.

If all's clear, take I–10, Speedway Road exit, and head east 10 miles to Pantano Road; then turn north, drive 1½ miles, and turn east onto Tanque Verde Road. Go another 1½ miles and turn north onto Catalina Highway, which becomes Mt. Lemmon Highway. Drive this road for 30 twisting, climbing miles until you come to Mt. Lemmon Ski Valley—unless the heat inspires you to turn off a little side road to the cool, charming village of Summerhaven. It's not a good idea to take trailers and recreational vehicles on this mountain road, and it's best for all drivers to travel during daylight hours. Safety aside, it would be a pity to miss seeing the rock formations along the way; they look as though they were carefully balanced against one another by architects from another planet.

Hikers can take any number of side trips on this tour; information on routes and weather conditions is available from the Pima County Sheriff's Department. There are some 150 miles of well-marked and well-maintained trails in the Mt. Lemmon area, for all levels of expertise. Of the several trails around Rose Canyon Lake, a good one for beginners is the **Green Mountain Trail,** which starts a half mile past the Rose Canyon turnoff from Mt. Lemmon Highway. The route takes you 4 miles (one-way) from San Pedro Vista— with lovely mountain views to the east—to General Hitchcock Campground. More experienced hikers will enjoy the half-mile trek, ascending more than 600 feet, to the top of **Mt. Bigelow** from the Palisades ranger station. It's coming down that's the hard part. For more information, *see* Hiking, *below*.

⑰ If you've brought your lunch, watch for **Bear Wallow** just after milepost 22 on Mt. Lemmon Highway. There are picnic areas and plenty of room to stretch out under a tree for a siesta. You probably won't see any bears, but the variety of birds is astounding. Watch for electric-blue Steller's jays and hummingbirds of many varieties.

⑱ Mt. Lemmon Highway ends at **Mt. Lemmon Ski Valley** (tel. 602/576–1321, or 602/576–1400 for a recorded snow report). Skiing here depends on natural conditions—that is, there's no artificial snow—so call ahead for information; some winters there's plenty of powder, and others it's rather scarce. There are 16 runs, open daily, ranging from beginner to advanced. Lift tickets cost $25 for an all-day pass and $20 for a half day (starting at 1 PM); children 12 and under ski for $10. Ski equipment can be rented, and private instructions start at $16 an hour. Summertime (late May through September) visitors will enjoy a ride on the double-chair lift that whisks them to the top of the slope—some 9,100 feet. The cost is $4.50 for adults and $2 for children under 12. Many hikers ride the lift and then head out on one of several trails that crisscross the summit.

Time Out   The **Iron Door** (tel. 602/576–1321) in Mt. Lemmon Ski Valley is open weekends 9:30–5:30, weekdays 10–5. During the winter, the focus is on burgers, chili, corn bread, and soups; in warmer weather, lots of salads turn up on the menu. This place is popular on the weekends, and parking is limited.

Tour 5: Mission San Xavier del Bac and Kitt Peak National Observatory

Head to the second-largest Indian reservation in the country, that of the Tohonó O'odham tribe, for a mountain drive and a tour of a national observatory, with a stop at a historic mission. It's at least 10°F cooler on Kitt Peak than it is in Tucson, so in winter take along a jacket. There are few stations along the road, so fill the car before you leave town.

Drive southwest of Tucson about 9 miles on I–19, and get off on San Xavier Road; about three-quarters of a mile to the west, you'll come to the shining White Dove of the Desert, or **Mission San Xavier del Bac** (tel. 602/294–2624) which you can see miles before you actually reach the turnoff road. San Xavier del Bac, the oldest Catholic church in the United States still serving the community for which it was built, was founded in 1692 by the Jesuits and built of native materials by Franciscan missionaries between 1777 and 1797. Today it is owned by the Tohonó O'odham Indian tribe (the name means "Desert People Who Have Come from the Earth"). Legends surround the mission. The bell tower remains unfinished, it is said, because a workman fell to his death from there; no one dared to go up afterward because his ghost haunted it. (In fact, the unfinished bell tower was probably a ploy to fool the Spanish IRS, which could not levy its heavy taxes on buildings until they were completed.) Mass is celebrated daily at 8:30 AM, with an additional mass at 5:30 PM Saturday; on Sunday, services are held

8, 9:30, 11, and 12:30. On Sundays and religious holidays, there's often a mariachi band—one of the many Mexican influences in evidence here. Call for information about special celebrations.

The beauty of the mission, with elements of Spanish, Baroque, and *mudejar* (Spanish Islamic) architectural styles, is highlighted by the stark desert landscape against which it is set. Among the ornate carvings above the entrance is one of a cat chasing a mouse. Legend has it that the church will belong to the people for whom it was built, the Tohonó O'odham Indians, until the cat catches the mouse; another holds that the capture of the mouse will mark the end of the world. Inside, there's a wealth of painted statues, carvings, and frescoes; the mission has been called the Sistine Chapel of the United States by Paul Schwartzbaum, who worked on restoring Michelangelo's masterwork in Rome and is helping to supervise the restoration of the mission's artwork that began in 1992. A visitor center in the front part of San Xavier del Bac offers displays of the history and architecture of the church; it's adjoined by a gift shop, open from 9 to 5.

Across the parking lot from the mission, San Xavier Plaza has a number of shops that sell fine Native American crafts. Much of the work is by the Tohonó O'odham Indians (look especially for jewelry, pottery, and baskets featuring the man-in-the-maze designs, and for friendship bowls, both particular to the tribe), but works of the northern Arizona Hopi and Navajo are also represented.

Time Out   For wonderful Indian fry bread—large, round pieces of dough brought up fresh from the hot oil and topped with all sorts of delicious possibilities—stop in **The Wa:k Snack Shop** (tel. 602/573–9191) at the back of the plaza. You can also have breakfast or a Mexican lunch here.

When you leave the mission, go back on San Xavier Road to I–19 and head north for 14 miles to Exit 99 (Ajo Way); take this west onto AZ 86, then drive 36 miles to the junction with AZ 386. Turn left and start your 13-mile ascent up the winding road to Kitt Peak (elevation 6,882 feet), part of the Quinlan Mountain range.

A visitor center museum features exhibits on astronomy and information about the telescopes at the facility; tapes, mostly about the cosmos, run continuously in a minitheater. Free guided tours, which take about an hour, depart from the center weekdays at 11, 1, and 2:30; on weekends, an additional tour is given at 9:30 AM. Complimentary brochures enable you to take self-guided tours. A gift shop sells excellent examples of Tohonó O'odham handiwork as well as astronomy-related items.

Funded by the National Science Foundation and managed by **20** a group of more than 20 universities, **Kitt Peak National Ob-**

servatory is part of the Tohonó O'odham reservation. After much discussion back in the late 1950s, tribal leaders agreed to share their 4,400 square miles—only the Navajo have more land—with the observatory's 19 telescopes. Among these is the McMath, the world's largest solar telescope, which is cooled by piped-in coolant. From a visitors' gallery, you can see into the telescope's light-path tunnel, which goes down hundreds of feet into the mountain. In addition to the vital research into aspects of the sun carried out here, Kitt Peak scientists have also observed distant galaxies. The scientists and staff are friendly and knowledgeable and keen to share their enthusiasm for astronomy; you never get the sense here, as you do at other serious scientific installations, that you are intruding. A picnic area is about 1½ miles below the observatory; aside from vending machines in the observatory buildings, there is no place to get food within 20 miles of Kitt Peak. *National Optical Astronomy Observatories (Kitt Peak), tel. 602/322–3426 or 602/322–3350 for recorded message. Suggested donation: $2. Open daily 9–3:45. Closed Thanksgiving, Christmas Eve and Day, New Year's Day; museum and gift shop closed Mon. during summer.*

What to See and Do With Children

There are plenty of things to occupy children in Tucson and southern Arizona. Besides the activities listed here, a number are cited in Participant Sports, *below.* (Remember, however, that when you take children outdoors, their skin is especially prone to sunburn and windburn. Protect them with hats and sunscreen, and offer liquids frequently to prevent dehydration.) Many resorts also have activities designed to entertain children while their parents sightsee without them. Inquire when you make reservations.

Arizona–Sonora Desert Museum (*see* Tour 3, *above*).

Biosphere 2. This is a trip for school-age children; little ones will enjoy being outdoors but won't really appreciate the tour. (*See* Off the Beaten Track, *below.*)

The dry limestone **Colossal Cave,** 20 miles east of Tucson and 6 miles north of I-10, is filled with stalagmites and stalactites. The cave has never been fully explored, and legend has it that gold is hidden in the dark recesses. *Old Spanish Trail Rd., tel. 602/647–7275. Admission: $6.50 adults, $5 children 11–16, $3.50 children 6–10, children 5 and under free. Open Oct.–Mar., Mon.–Sat. 9–5, Sun. and holidays 9–6; Apr.–Sept., Mon.–Sat. 8–6, Sun. and holidays 8–7.*

Children love the old-fashioned melodramas at the **Gaslight Theatre** (7010 E. Broadway, tel. 602/886–9428), where hissing the villain and cheering the hero are part of the audience's duty. Tickets are $12 for adults, $10 for students and senior citizens, and $6 for children 12 and under. There is free popcorn, and beer, wine, and soft drinks are available.

At **Golf'n'Stuff Family Fun Centers,** children can play video games and miniature golf, ride bumper boats, and drive little race cars. *6503 E. Tanque Verde Rd., tel. 602/296–2366. No admission fee; each attraction priced separately. Open Sun.–Thurs. 10 AM–10 PM, Fri.–Sat. 10 AM–1 AM.*

International Wildlife Museum allows youngsters to touch and feel different animal skins, and teaches them many other things about more than 200 species of birds and mammals from all over the world. There's a theater that shows wildlife films, a gift shop, and a small restaurant that features buffalo burgers. *4800 W. Gates Pass Rd., tel. 602/624–4024. Admission: $4.50 adults, $3.75 senior citizens, students, and military, $1.50 children 6–12, children under 6 free. Open daily 9–5:30. Closed Thanksgiving, Christmas, and New Year's Day.*

Kids interested in aerospace technology will enjoy the walk through U.S. aviation history at the **Pima Air Museum.** Among the more than 180 models on display are a full-scale replica of the Wright brothers' 1903 Wright Flyer and a mock-up of the X-15, the world's fastest aircraft. *6000 E. Valencia Rd., tel. 602/574–9658. Admission: $5 adults, $4 senior citizens over 62 and military personnel, $3 children 10–17, children 9 and under free. Open daily 9–5. Closed Christmas.*

The small but well-designed **Reid Park Zoo** won't tax the children's—or your—patience. If you're visiting in the summertime, go early while the animals are active. *1100 S. Randolph Way, tel. 602/881–4753. Admission: $3 adults, $2 senior citizens over 62, 75¢ children 5–14, children 4 and under free. Open Sept. 15–Mar. 14, daily 9:30–4:30; Mar. 15–Sept. 14, weekdays 8:30–3:30, weekends and holidays 8:30–5:30.*

At **Tucson Children's Museum,** kids are encouraged to touch and explore the exhibits, which are oriented toward science, language, and history. There are fun things to do—and learn—for children of all ages. *200 S. 6th Ave., tel. 602/884–7511. Admission: $3 adults, $1.50 senior citizens and children 3–14. Open Tues.–Fri. 9–2, Sat. 10–5, Sun. 1–5.*

Off the Beaten Track

It sounds a bit like the stuff of science fiction: In order to study how human beings can live in harmony with their environment, eight persons set up housekeeping for two years in an enclosed three-acre environment. But this exercise in recycling on a grand scale is going on now at **Biosphere 2.** As we go to press, the first group of Biosphereans was scheduled to leave the dome in September 1993, with a new group entering shortly thereafter.

To get to Biosphere 2, drive north on Oracle Road (U.S. 89), a major north–south road through Tucson, to Oracle Junction, where the road turns into AZ 77. Drive 5½ miles northeast to milepost 96.5, follow the signs for a half mile to SunSpace Ranch Conference Center Road, make a right turn, and drive 2 miles to the guard gate. You'll be required to check in here before you proceed the final half mile to Biosphere 2. No pets, tape recorders, or cameras are allowed inside, and no picnicking is permitted on the site.

The miniature world created within Biosphere includes tropical rain forest, savanna, desert, thorn scrub, marsh, ocean, and agricultural area as well as a living area for the humans who inhabit the sphere—along with 3,800 plant and animal species. The privately funded project is being watched with interest—as well as some skepticism—by scientists all over the world; there has been a good deal of controversy regarding the credentials of the project's participants and certain equipment being used to help control the environment. Walking tours—given continually and lasting about two hours—don't enter the sphere, of course, which is sealed, but a film explains the project, and visitors are able to look at the human and animal residents through observation areas. Much of the tour is outdoors: Wear a hat, walking shoes, and sunscreen. The Biosphere Café, overlooking the Santa Catalina Mountains, offers meals and snacks. Attractive, reasonably priced hotel rooms, also with excellent views, are available on Biosphere's premises. *Hwy. 77, mile marker 96.5, tel. 602/825–6200 or 800/ 828–2462. Admission: $12.95 adults, $10.95 senior citizens, $10 students 18 or over with ID, $6 children 5–16, children 4 and under free. Open daily 8–6; tours given 8:30–4. Closed Christmas.*

On the way back into town from Biosphere, you might want to stop off at **Tohono Chul Park,** which is making its own effort to preserve our environment—specifically the desert region. On its 35 acres, a demonstration garden, greenhouse, geology wall, and other exhibits educate visitors about the unique area, while shady nooks and nature trails allow for leisurely sitting or strolling. Two gift shops, a small art gallery, a tearoom (*see* Dining, *below*), and the Haunted Bookshop (*see* Shopping, *below*) are additional reasons to visit this lovely landscaped setting. *7366 Paseo del Norte, tel. 602/742–6455. Admission: $2 donation suggested. Park open daily 7 AM–sunset; building open Mon.– Sat. 9:30–5, Sun. 11–5.*

All year round, but especially during summer, locals flock to **Sabino Canyon** in the northeast corner of town. Part of the Coronado National Forest but filled with saguaros and other desert flora and fauna, this is a good spot for hiking, picnicking, or enjoying the waterfalls, streams, natural swimming holes, and shade trees that provide a respite from the heat. No cars are allowed; a narrated tram ride (45 minutes round-trip) takes you to the top of the canyon and another takes you to adjacent Bear Canyon. When there's a full moon, nighttime tram tours are offered. *Sabino Canyon Rd. in the Santa Catalina foothills, tel. 602/749–2861 or 602/749–8700. Tram fare: $5 adults, $2 children 3–12, children 2 and under free; Bear Canyon tram fare: $3 adults, $1.25 children. Call for tram schedules, which change throughout the year. Visitor center open weekdays 8–4:30, weekends 8:30–4:30.*

The site of the first European settlement in Arizona, **Tubac** lies 45 miles south of Tucson (take I–19 to exit 34). Parts of the original fort established by the Spanish in 1751 may be seen at the Tubac Presidio State Park and Museum (tel. 602/398–9346). The town itself is home to many craftspeople and artists (*see* Shopping, *below*). Three miles south of Tubac, at **Tumacacori National Monument** (tel. 602/398–2341), you can visit one of the mission churches that Jesuit missionary Father Eusebio Francisco Kino founded in Arizona and northern Mexico.

Wineries   Wyatt Earp might've been hooted out of town if he'd swaggered up to a bar and ordered a glass of cabernet, but wine is in these days in cowboy country. Connoisseurs debate the merits of the various wineries that have sprung up in this area since 1974, but if you want to decide for yourself, you might start a tour with **R.W. Webb** (13605 E. Benson Hwy., tel. 602/762–5777); take I–10 east about 12 miles, and get off at Vail, exit 279. Most of the other growers are in the area where Routes 82 and 83 intersect: Get back on I–10 for two more exits, then drive south on Route 83 for 24 miles to Sonoita. Growers in the scenic ranching region nearby include the kosher **Santa Cruz Winery** (lower Elgin Rd., Elgin, tel. 602/455–5375), **Sonoita Vineyards** (3 mi southeast of Elgin, tel. 602/455–5893), and **Arizona Vineyards** (2301 Patagonia Hwy., 3 mi north of Nogales on Rte. 82, tel. 602/287–7972). Most of them give tours and tastings Thursday through Sunday; call for hours. **Karen's Wine Country Café** in Elgin (tel. 602/455–5282) is an excellent place to begin or end a tour.

Tucson for Free

De Grazia's Gallery in the Sun is the museum, gallery, workshop, former home, and gravesite of the Arizonan artist Ted DeGrazia, who depicted Southwest Indian and Mexican life. Built by the artist himself with the help of Native American friends, the sprawling, spacious single-story museum utilizes only natural material from the surrounding desert. None of DeGrazia's original oil paintings, sculptures, or watercolors are for sale, but the museum's gift shop offers a wide selection of cards, prints, lithographs, ceramics, and books by and about the colorful artist. *6300*

N. Swan Rd., tel. 602/299-9191. Admission free. Open daily 10-4.

Fort Lowell Park and Museum, now a city park, was once the site of a Hohokam Indian village and, many centuries later, a fort. At a small museum run by the Arizona Historical Society, a reconstructed commanding officers' quarters gives visitors a glimpse of military life in territorial days. There are also rotating exhibits of photographs and frontier artifacts. *2900 N. Craycroft Rd., tel. 602/885-3832. Admission free. Open Wed.-Sat. 10-4.*

Shopping

There are a lot of special gifts and souvenirs to be found in the Tucson area. **Native American crafts** range from exquisite jewelry and basketry to the more pedestrian (but still authentic) tourist items. You'll see an abundance of both varieties in shops and even in some department stores. **Locally produced food items** can be fun to give to friends at home: orange-blossom honey, cactus honey, cactus candy, and pepper salsa are a few treats to consider. Desert Rose Salsa is a popular item among both natives and visitors. If you call many of Tucson's Mexican restaurants a couple of days ahead, they will freeze some fresh tamales for you to transport in a special package with dry ice. (If you plan to try this, call your airline to make arrangements.) And if you're in Tucson during citrus season, consider stopping at one of the many roadside stands whose signs proclaim "We ship!" and investigate sending a box of grapefruit or oranges back home.

Hard-core bargain hunters usually head for **Nogales,** the Mexican border town south of Tucson. To get there, drive south on I-19 for 63 miles. Prices are low (be sure to bargain for the best deal), and you'll find some well-crafted items as well as plenty of schlock (Nogales probably has the most onyx chess sets east of Tijuana).

Those looking for work by regional artists might drive down to **Tubac,** an artist's community 45 miles south of Tucson, just off I-19 at Exit 34 (*see* Off the Beaten Track, *above*). The more than 70 shops—mostly staffed by the artists who make the goods sold in them—range from carved wooden furniture and hand-thrown pottery to delicately painted tiles and silk-screened fabrics. The annual Tubac Festival of the Arts has been held in February for more than 30 years; for exact dates, contact the Tubac Chamber of Commerce (tel. 602/398-2704).

In Tucson itself, much of the retail activity is focused around malls, but you'll find shops with more character in two areas. The **downtown** district hosts a number of art galleries, antiques shops, and crafts stores; Congress Street is a particularly good block to browse, and the Old Town Artisans complex (186 N. Meyer Ave., tel. 602/623–6024), near the Tucson Museum of Art, has a large selection of southwestern wares. The adjoining **4th Avenue** neighborhood, near the University of Arizona, is also fertile ground for unusual items. The Fourth Avenue Merchants Association (509½ 4th Ave., tel. 602/624–5004) represents the many artsy boutiques and restaurants that line 4th Avenue between 2nd and 9th streets.

Malls   **Tucson Mall** (4500 N. Oracle Rd. at Wetmore Rd., tel. 602/293–7330) is probably the most heavily shopped mall in town, serving both the sophisticated and the family shopper with two floors of stores, including Dillard's, Broadway Southwest, Sears, J C Penney, and almost 200 other smaller specialty shops. For tasteful southwestern T-shirts, belts, jewelry, and posters, try Señor Coyote, on the second floor of the mall.

El Con Mall (3601 E. Broadway at Alvernon Way, tel. 602/327–8767) is Tucson's oldest mall and has more than 130 stores, including J C Penney, Foley's, and Montgomery Ward. Possibly its most popular store is a huge House of Fabrics, headquarters for crafters as well as needleworkers of all persuasions. Quilters, home garment sewers, and decoupage artists all come here for supplies and inspiration.

Park Mall (5870 E. Broadway at Wilmot Rd., tel. 602/748–1222) is an east side family shopping mecca, one of those utilitarian places where you can get all that practical stuff checked off your list in one trip. It has more than 120 stores, including Sears, Dillard's, and Broadway Southwest.

Foothills Mall (7401 N. La Cholla Blvd. at Ina Rd., tel. 602/742–7191), the most upscale of the malls, isn't usually very crowded. In addition to such department stores as Dillard's and Foley's, it features a variety of tony boutiques. If you're experiencing shopper's fatigue, a cup of the good coffee at the Java House might perk you up.

Specialty Shops   Check the **Cabat Studio** (627 N. 4th Ave., tel. 602/622–6362)
Art Galleries   for exceptional southwestern paintings and ceramics by Erni and Rose Cabat. **Impressions II, Ltd.** (2990 N. Swan Rd., tel. 602/323–3320) features work by R. C. Gorman and many other internationally known artists, as well as art by several talented but well-kept local secrets. Downtown, **Etherton/Stern Gallery** (135 S. 6th Ave., tel. 602/624–7370), which specializes in contemporary art, carries some fine vintage photographs.

Books   **Tohono Chul Park** (*see* Off the Beaten Track, *above*) is home to the **Haunted Bookshop** (tel. 602/297–4843), with its outstanding selection for bibliophiles of all ages. There's a coffeepot on the porch in the wintertime, plenty of nooks for a quiet read, and a tunnel for children to crawl through.

In the downtown area, **Book Arts Gallery** (49 N. Scott St., tel. 602/884–5501) features beautiful handmade books as well as rare editions of more conventionally published work. Near the University of Arizona, the **Audubon Nature Shop** (300 E. University Blvd., tel. 602/629–0510) carries hiking maps, field guides, and binoculars, along with a wide range of natural history books. Also in the neighborhood is **Books West Southwest** (2452 N. Campbell Ave., tel. 602/326–6661), focusing on regional works, and **Settlers West Books & Prints** (6420 N. Campbell Ave., tel. 602/577–8749), which has a large collection of Western and wildlife prints, some of them limited editions.

Cacti   You won't need to stick a cactus in your suitcase if you want to take back a spiny souvenir: **B&B Cactus Farm** (11550 E. Speedway Blvd., tel. 602/721–4687), on the far eastern side of town, has a huge selection of desert plants and ships all over the country.

Gifts   **Desert House Crafts** (2837 N. Campbell Ave., tel. 602/323–2132) has been part of the Tucson art scene for more than 40 years. Designs are inspired, and execution is flawless.

Sangin (300 N. 6th Ave., tel. 602/882–9334) is set in a historic warehouse filled with baskets, home furnishings, dried flower arrangements, and jewelry—some imported, some made by local artists. The one-way street system downtown makes the store a bit hard to find, but the chilipepper baskets and twined-branch cacti are worth searching for.

Native American Arts and Crafts   **Bahti Indian Arts** (St. Philip's Plaza, 4300 N. Campbell Ave., tel. 602/577–0290) specializes in Native American art, including high-quality jewelry, pottery, baskets, and more. **Huntington Trading Co.** (111 E. Congress, tel. 602/628–8578) carries masks and pottery made by the Yaqui and Tarahumara Indians. The **Kaibab Shops** (2841 N. Campbell Ave., tel. 602/795–6905) have been selling a wide variety of Native American crafts in Tucson for more than 40 years.

Needlework Supplies   Needle artists will enjoy **The West** (5615 E. River Rd., tel. 602/299–1044). Staffed by volunteers who donate profits to local charities, this shop has one of the best selections of needlework supplies in the area.

Western Wear   **Corral Western Wear** (5870 E. Broadway Blvd., tel. 602/747–2117), with a large array of shirts, hats, belts, jewelry, and boots, caters to both urban and authentic cowboys and girls. **The Bootery** (2511 S. Craycroft Rd., tel. 602/790–1212) has the largest selection of western footwear in town.

Sports and the Outdoors

Participant Sports

Ballooning What better way to take advantage of Arizona's mild winter months than to take a quiet balloon ride in the early morning hours and get a bird's-eye view of the frisky desert wildlife down below? Many operators offer balloon rides over the Tucson area. Two reputable companies in the region are **Balloon America** (Box 31255, Tucson 85751, tel. 602/299–7744; Oct.–June only) and **A Southern Arizona Balloon Excursion** (Box 5265, Tucson 85703, tel. 602/624–3599). Both welcome individuals and groups and offer champagne celebrations and daily flights by FAA-licensed pilots. Prices range from $115 to $250 per person, depending on the company, season, and length of the flight.

Bicycling Tucson has designated bikeways, routes, lanes, and paths for bikers all over the city. You can cycle through rugged terrain, up and down winding roads, or even along frequently used byways in the Tucson area. There are many sights to see while pedaling on the outskirts of Tucson, where you will be likely to encounter less traffic. If you want even more isolated and scenic locations, try some of the mapped biking tours for the southern part of Arizona; contact the **Metropolitan Tucson Convention and Visitors Bureau** (130 S. Scott Ave., tel. 602/624–1817 or 800/638–8350) for additional information.

Reliable and centrally located places for bike rentals include **The Bike Shack** (835 N. Park Ave., tel. 602/624–3663) and **Full Cycle** (3232 E. Speedway Blvd., tel. 602/327–3232). **Sunrise Bicycle** (4772 E. Sunrise Dr., tel. 602/577–2292) will deliver and pick up bikes without charge, and includes a helmet in the price of the rental.

There are a number of cyclists' clubs in Tucson, and many of them offer tours throughout southern Arizona. Write ahead to **La Touristas** (3450 N. Stone Ave., No. 171, Tucson 85705) and **Tucson Wheelmen** (1016 Chauncey St., Tucson 85719)—neither has an official telephone number—for information about upcoming tours. Or call the **Greater Arizona Bicycling Association**'s (Box 43273, Tucson 85733, tel. 602/885–8807) week-by-week recorded newsline of rides in the Tucson area; they're for all ages and levels, and visiting bicyclists are welcome to participate.

Bird-watching Birders consider **Ramsey Canyon,** in the Huachuca Mountains directly south of Tucson, one of the best places in the country to sight a variety of unusual species. Even closer to Tucson, in the nearby Santa Rita Mountains, **Madera Canyon** is another bird lovers' haven.

Camping There are at least 100 camping areas scattered throughout the southern region of Arizona; the weather's usually good enough year-round—though it can get very chilly at night in the desert—to make sleeping out under the vast, starry night sky an appealing option. Summertime is the time to camp in the state's cooler higher-altitude campgrounds.

The closest public campground to Tucson is probably at **Catalina State Park,** about 9 miles north of town on U.S. 89 (11570 N. Oracle Rd., tel. 602/628–5798). Located in the desert foothills of the Santa Catalinas, the campground accommodates tenters as well as recreational vehiclers. It fills up quickly in good weather because it's close to town; unfortunately, there is no reservation system.

Recreational vehicles can park in any number of facilities around town; the **Metropolitan Tucson Convention and Visitors Bureau** (130 S. Scott Ave., tel. 602/624–1889 or 800/638–8350) can provide information about specific locations.

The *Arizona Campground Directory* lists all the campgrounds in the state. For a copy—and for additional information on camping in southern Arizona—contact the Arizona Office of Tourism (1100 W. Washington, Phoenix 85007, tel. 602/542–8687).

Golf You can easily dedicate a vacation to golf in Tucson, which has some of the best desert courses in the country and 300 days of sunshine in which to play them. *The Tucson & Southern Arizona Golf Guide,* published by Tucson Guide Quarterly, Inc. (Box 42915, Tucson 85733, tel. 602/322–0895), describes and rates all the local courses; send $1 for a copy. For a golf package based on your budget, interests, and experience, you might contact **Tee Time Arrangers** (tel. 800/742–9939). If you're planning to stay a week or more, **Tucson's Resort Golf Card,** offering year-round discounts at seven of the area's best courses, is a good deal; write 6286 E. Grant Rd., Tucson 85712 or call 602/886–8800 for information.

Resorts Many avid golfers check into one of the tony local resorts (described in more detail in Lodging, *below*) and do nothing but tee off for a week. Those specializing in golf vacations include **Tucson National Golf & Conference Resort** (2727 W. Club Drive, tel. 602/297–2271), home of the Northern Telecom Open, with 27 holes; **Westin La Paloma,** which has a 27-hole layout designed by Jack Nicklaus (rated among the top 75 resort courses by *Golf Digest*); **Sheraton El Conquistador,** its 45 holes in the Santa Catalina foothills affording 360° views of the city; and the 36-hole Tom Fazio–designed **Loews Ventana Canyon** course. Those who don't mind getting up early to beat the heat will find some excellent golf packages at these places in the summer. In high season (Jan. 15–Apr. 15) only guests can play the courses, but the rest of the year all but Westin's La Paloma Country Club are open to the public.

Municipal Courses The flagship of the five low-priced municipal golf courses within the city of Tucson (Randolph North, Randolph

South, El Rio, Fred Enke, and Silverbell) is **Randolph North,** which hosted the PGA and LPGA Tour for many years. For details about these city-operated courses, contact the Tucson Parks and Recreation Department (tel. 602/791–4873); for weekday reservations at any one of them, call 602/791–4336 one week in advance.

Public Courses In Tucson the Arnold Palmer–managed **Starr Pass Golf Club** (3645 W. 22nd St., tel. 602/622–6060) was developed as a Tournament Player's Course; a cohost of the Northern Telecom Open with Tucson National (*see* Resorts, *above*), it offers 18 highly rated holes. Two executive courses, **Cliff Valley** (5910 N. Oracle Rd., tel. 602/887–6161) and **Dorado Country Club** (6601 E. Speedway, tel. 602/885–6751), are good for those who just want to play a few short rounds.

South of Tucson, near Nogales, **Rio Rico Golf & Racquet Club** (1550 Camino a la Posada, tel. 602/281–8567) was designed by Robert Trent Jones, Jr.; an excellent 18-hole course, it's one of Arizona's biggest sleepers. In Green Valley **San Ignacio Golf Club** (4201 S. Camino del Sol, tel. 602/648–3468), designed by Arthur Hills, is a challenging desert course in a beautiful setting; nearby **Canoa Hills** (1401 Calle Urbano, tel. 602/791–2049) is a good choice for the average golfer.

Hiking Tucson is a wonderful place for hiking; there are many desert trails to explore in the winter, and in summer the nearby mountain ranges offer cooler trekking options. The Exploring section (*see* Tours 3, 4, and 5, *above*) offers some options for day trips that include good hiking opportunities: **Tucson Mountain Park, Mt. Lemmon,** and **Kitt Peak. Sabino Canyon** (*see* Off the Beaten Track, *above*) has a variety of trails closer to town. In addition, for hiking inside Tucson city limits, you might test your skills climbing trails up Sentinel Peak, generally called **"A" Mountain** (it sports a huge *A* first painted on it by fans of a victorious university football team in 1915). State and city parks in the area also offer a variety of hiking experiences; there are literally hundreds of trails within the immediate Tucson area. **Catalina State Park** (11570 N. Oracle Rd. [U.S. 89], tel. 602/628–5798), less than 10 miles north of town, is crisscrossed by hiking trails.

If you want to go a bit farther afield, head south past the Huachuca Mountain range, where you can wander in and out of old **ghost towns** such as Fort Duquesne, Pearce, and Washington Camp in the Patagonia Mountains. To the east of Tucson, beyond the Rincons and the Whetstone Mountains, the Dragoon Mountains are both beautiful and of historical interest; located here is **Cochise's Stronghold,** where the Apache chief hid out with his people during 11 years of battle with U. S. troops. Farther east, **Chiricahua National Monument** (*see* Southeastern Arizona, *below*) offers a number of well-marked trails in a striking setting.

The local chapter of the **Sierra Club** (735 N. 5th Ave., Suite 212, Tucson 85705, tel. 602/620–6401) welcomes out-of-town visitors to their weekend hikes around the area; there's no fee, even for nonmembers. For hiking on your own, a good source of information is **Summit Hut** (5045 E. Speedway, tel. 602/325–2554), which has an excellent collection of hiking reference materials and a friendly staff who will help you plan and outfit your trip; packs, tents, bags, shoes, and skis can be rented here.

Horseback Riding What's a trip to the Southwest without at least one bout on the back of a horse? **Desert-High Country Stables** (6501 W. Ina Rd., tel. 602/744–3789) offers a variety of trail rides; haywagon rides and cookouts are available, too. **Pantano Stables** (4450 S. Houghton Rd., tel. 602/298–9076) features special holiday and birthday rides—and even western weddings—in addition to regular trail rides. **Pusch Ridge Stables** (11220 N. Oracle Rd., tel. 602/297–6908) is adjacent to Catalina State Park, and its riders may even see bighorn sheep in the Santa Catalina foothills.

Rockhounding If rockhounding interests you, before you plan your trip write to the Arizona Office of Tourism (1100 W. Washington, Phoenix 85007, tel. 602/542–8687) and ask for brochure RG/150M/8-89, which offers information about the best places in the area to visit. Amateur traders and buyers might consider joining the thousands of professionals who come to town in February for the huge **Tucson Gem and Mineral Show** (Box 42543, Tucson 85733, tel. 602/322–5773), the largest of its kind in the world. Many precious stones as well as affordable samples are displayed and sold here, and even if you don't buy a thing, it's fun to look at all the fascinating rocks and gems. If you do plan to attend, make reservations far in advance; in 1994 every hotel and car-rental agency in town is likely to be booked up from February 10 through February 13.

When you're in the Huachuca City area, you might stop by the **Opal Art Gallery** (junction AZ 82 and Evans Rd., Huachuca City 85616, tel. 602/456–9202), run by Mike Anderson and Cheri Saunders. They discovered Arizona's precious blue opal in the area about 15 years ago and still mine for the pale-blue-and-white stones used in the lovely jewelry they sell in their shop.

Spectator Sports

Cactus League Baseball In 1993 Tucson's **Hi-Corbett Field** (900 S. Randolph Way, tel. 602/791–4266 or 602/791–4873) welcomed the Colorado Rockies to their inaugural season of Cactus League practice games (*see* Chapter 1, Essential Information). For information about the team schedule and about tickets, call 602/327–9467.

Located adjacent to Randolph Park, Hi-Corbett Field is home to the Tucson Toros, a minor-league team (tel. 602/

325–2621 for information), as well as spring-training home to the Rockies. Many picnickers and squirrels sit side by side in the nearby park to enjoy the games. Inside the stadium, during the training games, beer is sold behind first and third bases. Parking isn't as easy to come by in the area, so park in any of the Randolph Park lots west of Hi-Corbett Field and take a short, pleasant walk through the park to get to the stadium.

Greyhound Racing It's fun to watch the sleek racing dogs compete at **Tucson Greyhound Park** (2601 S. 3rd Ave., corner of S. 4th Ave. and 36th St., tel. 602/884–7576), but parimutuel wagering is the real attraction. There are two betting areas, the concession and bar area on the main floor and the clubhouse restaurant and bar upstairs. From January through April, doors open nightly (except Monday) at 6 PM, and the first race starts promptly at 7:30 PM; doors open at 12:30 PM for matinees on Wednesday, Saturday, and Sunday, and the first race starts at 2 PM. From May to December, there's no race on Tuesday night. Admission to the clubhouse is $3, $1.25 for the concession area. Only persons 18 or older can bet.

Dining

Tucson's culinary reputation is growing, and there are restaurants in town to satisfy every appetite. Southwestern cuisine, naturally featured here, ranges from barbecue and cowboy steaks to light nouvelle recipes that use such innovative ingredients as cactus and blue corn.

Tucson's residents have long boasted about their city's Mexican food, some rather grandly proclaiming their town "Mexican Food Capital of the U. S." (a title regularly challenged by San Antonians and Phoenicians). Most of the Mexican food in Tucson is Sonoran style—that is, derived from the cooking native to the adjoining Mexican state of Sonora. It's the type that's familiar to most Americans, featuring cheese, mild peppers, corn tortillas, and beef or chicken. Although Sonoran Mexican food has a well-earned reputation for being high in calories and saturated fats, many restaurants in Tucson now feature authentically prepared *pescado* (fish) or *pollo* (chicken) dishes that are flavorful yet lower in cholesterol. (Note that the salsa, or hot sauce, served with baskets of tortilla chips may be spicier than what you are used to. Proceed with caution. Similarly, when you ask waiters whether a dish is "hot," remember that their definition may be quite different from yours.)

Dress is more casual in Tucson than in many cities its size. A few restaurants request that men wear jackets to dinner. The issue of whether to wear a tie takes on a new slant here—there's at least one cowboy steak house where anyone caught wearing such formal neckwear will have it snipped off and added to the restaurant's collection of city-slicker garb.

Fall, winter, and spring make up the high season for travel here; it's a good idea to call ahead for reservations during these busy months. Some restaurants close for a portion of the summer, taking advantage of the slow time to make repairs or give staff vacations. Again, it's wise to call ahead, this time to ensure that your intended destination is open and hasn't altered its hours. Don't assume, incidentally, that you'll have to dine indoors in summer—many Tucson restaurants cool their outdoor patios with a system in which the temperature is lowered by a very fine mist emitted from unobtrusive pipes overhead, allowing patrons to dine comfortably.

While Tucson's variety of restaurants is akin to that of its big-city cousins, the city doesn't offer much in the way of late-night dining; most restaurants in town are shuttered by 10 PM. Some spots that keep later hours are noted below. If you're just looking for a quick bite, you might head for I–10— an array of all-night fast-food places and coffee shops can be found near the exits—or for the University of Arizona neighborhood, where students pulling all-nighters can always find some brain food; **Coffee, Etc.** (2830 N. Campbell Ave., tel. 602/881–8070), which has great coffee and a varied menu, is now open 24 hours.

Category	Cost*
Very Expensive	over $35
Expensive	$25–$35
Moderate	$15–$25
Inexpensive	under $15

per person, excluding drinks, service, and 7% sales tax (5% state plus 2% city)

Highly recommended restaurants are indicated by a star ★.

American **Solarium.** This striking, plant-filled restaurant was cre-
Expensive ated by artists with an eye to the environment: The dining room, with its inlaid tile mosaics, abundant wood and glass, and metal sculptured door, blends in well with its sylvan surroundings. The food is not really the main draw, though the heart-healthy entrées, which range from a charbroiled halibut fillet to poached sea scallops to pasta primavera, are tasty. The wine list is impressive, offering a full range of California bottles, and the fresh-ground coffee is great. *6444 E. Tanque Verde Rd., tel. 602/886–8186. Reservations advised. Dress: casual. AE, DC, MC, V. No lunch weekends.*

Moderate **Rancher's Club.** The two wood grills on which most of the
★ foods are prepared are the key to the success of this upscale western-style restaurant—with lots of dark wood, mounted animal heads, and sidesaddles—but you have to

Tucson Dining and Lodging

Dining

Anthony's, **8**

Arizona Inn
Restaurant, **34**

Boccata, **11**

Café Poca Cosa, **27**

Café Terra Cotta, **12**

Caruso's, **29**

Daniel's, **13**

El Charro Café, **23**

El Minuto Cafe, **25**

Frank's, **36**

The Gold Room, **5**

Govinda, **14**

Jack's Original
Bar-B-Q, **40**

Janos, **26**

Jerome's, **48**

Le Bistro, **15**

Li'l Abner's, **3**

Millie's Pancake
Haus, **44**

New Delhi Palace, **41**

Olson's, **32**

Olive Tree, **46**

Pinnacle Peak
Steakhouse, **45**

Presidio Grill, **35**

Rancher's Club, **37**

Seri Melaka, **39**

Solarium, **43**

South Tucson/
4th Avenue, **22**

The Tack Room, **49**

Tanque Verde
Ranch, **51**

Tohono Chul Tea
Room, **4**

Ventana Room, **7**

Yamato, **16**

279

KEY

AE American Express Office

Lodging

Arizona Inn, **34**

Best Western Royal
Sun Inn and Suites, **20**

Canyon Ranch, **50**

Casa Tierra, **18**

Doubletree Hotel, **31**

El Presidio Bed and
Breakfast Inn, **24**

Embassy Suites
Tucson-Broadway, **38**

Frontier Motel, **19**

Holiday Inn Tucson
Airport Hotel and
Convention Center, **30**

Hotel Congress, **28**

Lazy K Bar Guest
Ranch, **1**

The Lodge on the
Desert, **33**

Loews Ventana
Canyon Resort, **7**

Park Inn/ Santa
Rita, **27**

Peppertrees, **21**

Ramada Inn
Foothills, **47**

Rodeway Inn Tucson
North, **17**

Sheraton Tucson El
Conquistador, **9**

Tanque Verde
Ranch, **51**

Triangle L Ranch Bed
& Breakfast, **6**

Tucson Hilton
East, **42**

Westin La Paloma, **10**

Westward Look
Resort, **5**

White Stallion
Ranch, **2**

come here ready to make some decisions. As the friendly staff explains, different woods impart different flavors to foods, so diners are offered a choice of grills. The lobster is especially good, and the steaks are excellent, too (a note on the menu advises "Our steaks are copious and we encourage you to share"). An array of sauces, butters, and condiments provides diners with interesting ways to flavor their food. And—yet another choice to make—there's an incredible variety of beer. *5151 E. Grant Rd., tel. 602/321–7621. Reservations advised. Dress: casual. AE, DC, MC, V. Closed Sun. No lunch Sat.*

Inexpensive **Frank's.** Weekend mornings, locals line up outside this Tucson institution (open 25 years) for hearty, inexpensive breakfasts like huevos rancheros or scrambled eggs with chorizo. Don't worry—the wait is never long; Candace, voted the rudest waitress in town, keeps things moving along briskly inside. You'll have more time at lunch—when such fare as liver and onions or meatloaf is available for under $5—to peruse the postcards, corny posters, and sketches covering the walls. *3843 E. Pima St., tel. 602/881–2710. No reservations. Dress: casual. No credit cards. No dinner.*

Millie's Pancake Haus. Millie's place looks like a little European café, with lace curtains and cheerful waitresses in frilly aprons. Pancakes and waffles are the specialty here, with varieties ranging from Russian blintzes and rolled French pancakes with Cointreau sauce to buttermilk or potato pancakes. Lunch includes a nice array of sandwiches, blue plate specials, and, on Sunday, chicken and dumplings. Reservations are accepted every day except Sunday, when you can expect to wait for a table on the comfortable patio. *6530 E. Tanque Verde Rd., tel. 602/298–4250. Reservations advised for 6 or more; no reservations on Sun. Dress: casual. No credit cards. No dinner; closed Mon.*

Cajun **Jerome's.** It may seem strange to think of New Orleans spe-
Moderate cialties in the desert, but at Jerome's the menu goes beyond the usual jambalaya and etouffé. This casual, comfortable eatery serves some of the best fresh fish in town. There's a raw bar complete with chilled Gulf oysters, cherrystone clams, Gulf shrimp cocktail, and calamari ceviche. Buttermilk biscuits and bread pudding with bourbon sauce supply any calories saved by eating the excellent mesquite-grilled mahimahi. Sunday champagne brunch is a well-priced indulgence. *6958 E. Tanque Verde Rd., tel. 602/721–0311. Reservations advised. Dress: casual. AE, D, DC, MC, V. No lunch Sat.*

Continental **Ventana Room.** This lovely dining room in the Loews
Very Expensive Ventana Canyon Resort is a triumph of understated ele-
★ gance. Muted colors and low ceilings don't compete with the spectacular views, either of the lights of Tucson or the towering waterfall on the resort property. The contemporary Continental menu, which changes seasonally, has a Califor-

nia-inspired emphasis on lower-fat, lower-cholesterol preparation and beautiful presentation. Daily specials might include mesquite-grilled New Zealand rack of lamb with oyster mushrooms and mustard sauce or seared sea scallops on herbed vegetables and coulis of red pepper. The wine list meets the high standards of the menu, and service is impeccable without being overbearing. *7000 N. Resort Dr., tel. 602/299–2020. Reservations advised. Jacket and tie advised. AE, D, DC, MC, V. Dinner only.*

Expensive **Anthony's.** This is an elegant yet comfortable place for a tasty meal and a lovely view of the city. Pink linen, stemmed crystal, and pink-rimmed china lend a light, festive look to the dining room. On a nice day, ask for a patio table. Lamb Wellington, Norwegian salmon sautéed lightly in a tomato-basil sauce, and bananas Foster are all good dinnertime choices; for lunch you might try the crisp-baked lemon chicken with potato pancakes. The wine list is extensive. *6440 N. Campbell Ave., tel. 602/299–1771. Reservations advised. Dress: casual but neat. AE, DC, MC, V. Closed Sun. lunch.*

Arizona Inn Restaurant. This confident, friendly establishment, a Tucson classic, welcomes old friends and new visitors alike. Sit out on the patio for a lovely view of the grounds of this 60-year-old adobe inn, or enjoy the view through huge windows in the dining room, a light, airy place with many 1930s southwestern details. On chilly evenings there's a fire. Steamed fish of the day served with ginger and leeks is a specialty, and the excellent venison curry is also popular. For dessert, try a slice of the terrific apple or pecan pie. Breakfast here is also a treat. *2200 E. Elm St., tel. 602/325–1541. Reservations advised. Jacket suggested for dinner. AE, MC, V.*

The Gold Room. Located at the beautiful Westward Look Resort in the Santa Catalina foothills north of town, this rather upscale restaurant offers a panoramic view of Tucson sparkling in the sun (or twinkling at night) through its glassed-in dining room—as well as excellent food. The restaurant has gone through a number of chefs in the last two years, but 1993 started out with David Lalli from the Tack Room (*see below*)—a promising development. Popular Continental dishes such as chateaubriand for two and veal scaloppine remain staples of the menu. *245 E. Ina Rd., tel. 602/297–1151. Reservations advised. Jacket advised at dinner. AE, D, DC, MC, V.*

French **Le Bistro.** Set in a nondescript building on a busy road near
Moderate-Expensive the university, Le Bistro is one of the prettiest restaurants
★ in town: Towering palms preside over pink lace—covered tables, burgundy chairs, and Art Nouveau–style etched mirrors. The setting is matched by the creations of young chef/owner Laurent Reux; born in Brittany, he offers many fish and shellfish dishes inspired by the seascape of his native region, such as supreme of salmon in a ginger crust with lime butter. Another popular specialty is Long Island

duck in a raspberry vinaigrette. A revolving glass dessert display at the entrance will leave you pondering throughout the meal whether to opt for the triple chocolate mousse cake, say, or the Key-lime tart. You can't hope for a more reasonably priced French lunch, and seasonal dinner specials for $12.95 include soup or salad, a choice of two entrées, and dessert. *2574 N. Campbell, tel. 502/327–3086. Reservations advised on weekends. Dress: casual but neat. D, MC, V. No lunch on weekends.*

Greek
Moderate

Olive Tree. Located in an appealing Santa Fe–style building, the Olive Tree serves up fine versions of such Greek standards as moussaka, shish kebab, and stuffed grape leaves, but also includes more unusual dishes on its menu. The Lamb Bandit is baked in foil with two types of cheese, potatoes, and vegetables; the daily fresh fish specials are broiled in garlic, oregano, and olive oil, and served with a well-prepared orzo. This is not light cuisine. If you don't have room for the super-sweet baklava, a cup of strong Greek coffee makes for a satisfying finish. *7000 E. Tanque Verde Rd., tel. 602/298–1845. Reservations advised. Dress: casual but neat. AE, MC, V. No lunch Sun.*

Indian
Inexpensive-Moderate

New Delhi Palace. Vegetarians, carnivores, and seafood lovers will all find something to enjoy at this elegant Indian restaurant. The congenial staff is helpful in explaining the menu, which features a wide variety of tandoori dishes, curries, rice, and breads. The "heat" of each dish can be adjusted to individual preference by the chef. If you're undecided, a lunch buffet and complete dinners offer nice samplings of several dishes. The atmosphere is quiet, with Indian music played softly, and tasteful displays of Indian objets d'art. *6751 E. Broadway, tel. 602/296–8585. Reservations advised. Dress: casual. DC, MC, V.*

Italian
Expensive
★

Daniel's. A fine Northern Italian menu, an excellent wine and beer list, the largest selection of single-malt Scotches in town, and service that is attentive but not overbearing draw a sophisticated crowd to this chic art deco-style restaurant. The grilled eggplant and mushroom appetizer, *fusilli* pasta with sun-dried tomatoes and pine nuts, and *bistecca alla fiorentina* (a tender rib-eye steak marinated in olive oil and herbs) are among the many recommended dishes; for dessert, a heavenly rum tiramisu somehow manages to be light and rich at the same time. *St. Phillips Plaza, 4340 N. Campbell Ave., tel. 602/742–3200. Reservations advised. Jacket advised. AE, DC, MC, V. Dinner only.*

Moderate-Expensive

Boccata. Set in a tasteful mall in the foothills of the Santa Catalina Mountains, this pretty restaurant serves excellent northern Italian cuisine, with some southern French dishes for good measure. The flowered tablecloths match the delicate aubergine and Tuscan yellow walls, and the artwork ranges from contemporary to Victorian whimsy. A good wine list complements such pasta entrées as penne *ciao bel-*

la (with grilled chicken and a delicate white-wine and Gorgonzola sauce) and veal ravioli; the steamed mussel appetizer is plentiful. Save some room for the rich cheesecake served with a cranberry coulis. *5605 E. River Rd., tel. 602/577–9309. Reservations advised. Dress: casual but neat. AE, DC, MC, V. Lunch served Fri. only. Open for Sun. brunch.*

Moderate **Olson's.** Although the name and the southwestern decor suggest otherwise, this is an Italian restaurant, owned by University of Arizona men's basketball coach Lute Olson and his son, Greg. Don't worry—the original owner, Joe Scordato, a bona fide Italian, still expertly oversees operations. There are a few American and Continental dishes on the menu, but the focus is southern Italian, with such specialties as *pesce alla griglia* (salmon or swordfish grilled in a lemon-and-white-wine butter) and *braciole con fettuccine* (beefsteak with stuffing served over pasta with tomato sauce). *3048 E. Broadway, tel. 602/323–3701. Reservations advised. Dress: casual. AE, D, DC, MC, V. Closed Sun.*

Inexpensive **Caruso's.** The crowds that sometimes gather outside this huge but homey Italian restaurant might lead you to think they were giving something away inside—and you wouldn't be entirely wrong. Portions of the tasty lasagna, eggplant parmigiana, shrimp marinara, and other southern Italian standards are so large that it's the rare person who doesn't leave here with a free lunch for the next day. Prices are reasonable and combination dishes are available, so for once you won't have to covet whatever your dining companion has ordered; you can have it all. Haute cuisine this ain't, but if you need a pasta fix in a cheerful environment, you can't go wrong at Caruso's. *434 N. 4th Ave., tel. 602/624–5765. Reservations accepted for 6 or more. Dress: casual. AE, MC, V. Dinner only.*

Japanese **Yamato.** Colorful paper lanterns line the walls of this mod-
Moderate est eatery, tucked away in a strip mall near the university. A sushi bar serves fish flown in daily from California, and a number of combination dinners such as shrimp tempura and teriyaki chicken are available. *Yaki soba* (beef and vegetables heaped on wheat noodles) makes a tasty, hearty meal. Many of Yamato's Japanese patrons gather on Saturday night for laser karaoke sing-alongs. *857 E. Grant Rd., tel. 602/624–3377. Reservations advised for groups of 5 or more. Dress: casual. AE, MC, V. Closed Sun.*

Malaysian **Seri Melaka.** Malaysian food, like Thai, uses plenty of cur-
Inexpensive ry, coconut, and other tasty condiments in its sauces. This popular restaurant on the east side of town is an excellent place to try the cuisine, and to indulge in good versions of such dishes as *satay* (grilled meat on a skewer with peanut sauce) and *lemak* (shrimp or chicken with vegetables in a sweet curry sauce). An extensive selection of well-prepared Chinese dishes is also on the menu. *6133 E. Broadway, tel.*

602/747–7811. Reservations accepted. Dress: casual. MC, V.

Mexican   **Café Poca Cosa.** This is a marvelously colorful (hot pink,
Inexpensive bright green, and tropical orange) and lively restaurant in
★   an unlikely spot: the downtown Park Inn. Locals caught on
to this hip, friendly place before the tourists did. Though
portions are generous, the Mexican dishes are not prepared
in the usual cheese-saturated Sonoran style. The menu,
which changes daily, might include *pollo á mole* (chicken in
a spicy chocolate-based sauce) or pork *pibil* (made with a
tangy Yucatan barbecue seasoning). Consider a breakfast
of green chili tamales on the outdoor patio when the weather is fine. The tiny original restaurant across the street (20
S. Scott Ave.), also a lively treat, is open for breakfast and
lunch during the week. *88 E. Broadway, tel. 602/622–6400.
Reservations advised for large parties. Dress: informal.
MC, V. No dinner Sun.*

El Charro Café. Started by Monica Flin in 1922, and run by
her grandniece and her grandniece's husband today, El
Charro still serves excellent versions of the American-Mex-
ican staples Flin claims to have originated—chimichangas
(flour tortillas rolled around seasoned beef or chicken and
deep-fried) and cheese crisps, most notably. Daily "fitness-
fare" specials such as seafood enchiladas are delicious as
well as healthful. You can dine outside on the front porch or
inside in one of the bright, cheerful dining rooms. A gift
shop next door sells mementos of this Tucson classic. *311 N.
Court Ave., tel. 602/622–1922. Reservations advised.
Dress: casual (but no tank tops). AE, DC, MC, V.*

El Minuto Café. This brightly decorated, bustling restaurant in Tucson's historic barrio is a good bet for those seeking a late meal downtown; it's open until 2 AM weekends, 11
during the week. In business for more than 50 years and recently expanded, El Minuto serves up crispy chimichangas,
huge burritos, and green corn tamales (in season) made just
right. All the ingredients are fresh and the Mexican beer selection is large. *354 S. Main Ave., tel. 602/882–4145. Reservations not required. Dress: informal. AE, MC, V.*

South Tucson/4th Avenue. Every Tucsonian you meet will
argue the merits of a favorite "real" Mexican restaurant,
but invariably it's on or near 4th Avenue in South Tucson.
Technically a separate city, South Tucson has a large Mexi-
can-American population and thus many authentic and inexpensive places to find good south-of-the-border cuisine.
Among the most popular: **Crossroads** (2602 S. 4th Ave., tel.
602/624–0395); **Gran Guadalajara** (2527 S. 4th Ave., tel.
602/620–1321); **Guillermo's Double L** (1830 S. 4th Ave., tel.
602/792–1585); **La Hacienda** (4207 6th Ave., tel. 602/889–
6613); **Micha's** (2908 S. 4th Ave., tel. 602/623–5307); **Mi
Nidito** (1813 S. 4th Ave., tel. 602/622–5081); and
Xochomilcho (2702 S. 4th Ave., tel. 602/882–5636). You'd
be hard pressed to have a bad meal—or a bad time—at any

of these friendly, informal places. Many have mariachi bands on the weekends. MC and V are accepted at most.

Southwestern **Janos.** Comfortably situated in the Hiram Stevens House,
Expensive-Very an adobe home built in 1855, this downtown restaurant—in
Expensive the El Presidio neighborhood, adjacent to the Tucson Mu-
★ seum of Art—offers innovative and eclectic Southwest menus that will please nouvelle cuisine fans (if not less adventurous and heartier eaters). A series of small, flower-filled dining rooms create an intimate, elegant atmosphere. Typical offerings include black-bean-and-sweet-corn chowder, and grilled ahi with green chili pasta and roasted tomato coulis. The summer and fall $12.95 dinner specials allow the less well-heeled to indulge in a meal here. *150 N. Main Ave., tel. 602/884-9426. Reservations advised. Dress: casual but neat. AE, D, MC, V. Closed Sun. Nov.-mid-May; Sun. and Mon. late May-Oct.*

The Tack Room. This restaurant has won many awards for its food, and the setting—in a rustic but elegant old adobe—is romantic, but the service is a tad over-fussy and the menu is safer than that at other first-rate restaurants in town. That said, it's still worth coming here for a splurge. Dark wood beams and furnishings and a blue-and-maroon color scheme are complemented by the lighter dusty-rose linen; walls are hung with southwestern landscapes by local artists. Arizona steak flavored with four types of mild peppercorns is a favorite, as is the rack of lamb, prepared with mesquite honey, cilantro, and southwestern limes. *2800 N. Sabino Canyon Rd., tel. 602/722-2800. Reservations advised. Jacket suggested. AE, D, DC, MC, V. Closed Mon. mid-May-mid-Dec., closed first 2 weeks of July.*

Moderate-Expensive **Café Terra Cotta.** Everything about this restaurant says
★ Southwest—from the decor, with its bright pastels and bleached woods, to the food, which features such contemporary Southwest specialties as prawns stuffed with herbed goat cheese, pork tenderloin with black beans, and pizzas with sun-dried tomatoes; the garlic custard appetizer is superb. The place for native yupsters as well as their out-of-town guests, Café Terra Cotta offers an impressive by-the-glass California wine list. Come here, too, for a tasty Sunday brunch. *4310 N. Campbell Ave. (at St. Philip's Plaza, southeastern corner of River and Campbell), tel. 602/577-8100. Reservations strongly advised for dinner. Dress: casual. AE, D, DC, MC, V.*

Presidio Grill. If it weren't for the saguaro cactus flanking the cash register, you might at first think you were in one of New York's chic SoHo haunts: This large, noisy room has beamed tinwork ceilings, trompe l'oeil pillars, and plush booths. But the food is southwestern all the way. Bluecorn pancakes with prickly-pear syrup appear on the breakfast menu; lunch and dinner entrées include chicken Santa Fe, served with black beans, flour tortillas, grilled scallions, and two types of salsa; and an eggplant, onion, sun-dried tomato, and mozzarella pizza. In the University of Arizona area, this place is open unusually late (for Tucson) on weekends and attracts a mix of students, professionals, and out-of-towners. *3352 E. Speedway Blvd., tel. 602/327–4667. Reservations advised for 5 or more. Dress: casual. MC, V.*

Moderate **Li'l Abner's.** Located in the old Butterfield Express stagecoach rest stop, dating from the early 1800s, this Old West institution draws locals, who go straight for the mesquite-broiled 2-pound porterhouse steaks. There's nothing here for vegetarians, except for the unlimited salad, beans, and salsa that come with all the entrées. On weekends, you can chow down to the sounds of a live country band. It's about a 20-minute drive from downtown. *8500 N. Silverbell Rd., tel. 602/744–2800. Reservations advised. Dress: informal. MC, V. Dinner only.*

Pinnacle Peak Steakhouse. No nouvelle-cuisine fans welcome here: Anybody caught eating fish tacos or cactus jelly would probably be hanged from the rafters—along with all the ties snipped from loco city slickers. This is a cowboy steak house that the tourists love. It's fun, it's Tucson, and the food ain't half bad, either, pardner. The excellent mesquite-broiled steaks come with salad, baked potatoes, and pinto beans; if you can handle it after all that, try the hot apple cobbler with vanilla ice cream. The restaurant is part of Trail Dust Town, a re-creation of a turn-of-the-century town, complete with an "opera" house featuring cancan girls and a barbershop quartet, souvenir shops, and an old-time photographer's studio, where you can have your picture taken in western garb. *6541 E. Tanque Verde Rd., tel. 602/296–0911. No reservations. Dress: casual. D, DC, MC, V.*

Tanque Verde Ranch. For the total southwestern experience, drive 12 miles east of Tucson into the foothills of the Rincon Mountains to this dude ranch that caters to tourists and locals alike. Call ahead to find out what's on the menu, which changes daily: Entrées range from roast duck à l'orange to lobster sautéed with guacamole sauce. Meals are followed by such entertainment as square dancing or informative slide shows on the area's wildlife. Sometimes the dining room is abandoned in favor of Cottonwood Grove, where there's a steak fry or a barbecue. *14301 E. Speedway Blvd., tel. 602/296–6275. Reservations required. Dress: informal. AE, D, MC, V.*

★ **Tohono Chul Tea Room.** This is a good choice for anybody seeking a quiet cup of tea or glass of wine, a satisfying sandwich, a crunchy salad, or a particularly toothsome dessert. The setting is unique—the tearoom is nestled in a wildlife sanctuary and surrounded by a fantastic cactus garden. Although the tearoom is typically southwestern, with lots of light wood and glass, the menu covers southwestern, Mexican, and American dishes. House favorites include chicken enchiladas made with Monterey Jack cheese, corn, and green chilies, and a sliced-tomato-and-basil sandwich served on French sourdough bread. Sunday brunch is especially good. *7366 N. Paseo del Norte, tel. 602/797–1711. Reservations accepted for 8 or more. Dress: informal. AE, MC, V. Breakfast and lunch only.*

Inexpensive **Jack's Original Bar-B-Q.** For those who like their Southwest cuisine messy and in big portions, this is the place to come. Jack's ribs are smoky, meaty, and without equal in these parts; the sauce is rich and subtly flavored. The beans are also a real treat. Jack's impresses through good, honest food, not atmosphere—the floor is linoleum; the chairs and flowers are plastic. *5250 E. 22nd St., tel. 602/750–1280. No reservations. Dress: informal. No credit cards.*

Vegetarian **Govinda.** The only place in town with a strictly nonmeat
Inexpensive menu, this Hare Krishna–run restaurant offers reasonably priced all-you-can-eat lunch and dinner buffets that include vegan options. Selections of hot and cold dishes vary daily, but ingredients are consistently fresh and the food is tasty if not particularly spicy. The atmosphere in the pretty, light wood dining room is somewhat subdued—perhaps because no alcohol is served or permitted. *711 E. Blacklidge Dr., tel. 602/792–0630. Reservations not required. Dress: casual. MC, V. Closed Sun.–Tues.*

Lodging

In Tucson you can enjoy the luxury of a desert resort or the more basic accommodations offered by small motels. A number of guest ranches, some of them from the 1800s when they were real working cattle ranches, can be found on the outskirts of town. The mountains surrounding Tucson host a bountiful array of campsites and parks for recreational vehicles, offering a cool respite from the desert heat in summer (*see* Camping in Participant Sports, *above*).

There is also a variety of bed-and-breakfast establishments in the area, ranging from bedrooms in modest homes to private cottages nestled on wildlife preserves. The **Arizona Association of Bed and Breakfast Inns** (3101 N. Central Ave., Suite 560, Phoenix 85712, tel. 602/277–0775) can provide referrals to member inns in the area. Seven of the larger, more professionally run inns in town have formed **Premier Bed & Breakfast Inns of Tucson** (3661 N. Campbell Ave., 85719, tel. 602/628–1800); write or call for a brochure. **Old Pueblo HomeStays** (Box 13603, Tucson 85732, tel. 602/790–2399 or 800/333–9776) specializes in smaller, more casual B&Bs in Southern Arizona and northern Mexico.

Prices vary widely between seasons. Room rates in summer—generally defined as April 15 through October 1—are much lower than those in the winter, and visitors who don't mind warm weather can get some real deals at resorts that are quite pricey during the busy time. Locals often take advantage of weekend packages offered during summer months, spending the weekends resort hopping and enjoying their town in a way usually reserved for visitors.

Unless otherwise indicated, rates for guest ranches include meals and most activities.

Category	Cost*
Very Expensive	over $150
Expensive	$100–$150
Moderate	$60–$100
Inexpensive	under $60

All prices are for a standard double room, excluding room tax (9.5% in Tucson and 6.5% in Pima County). Prices given here are winter, or high-season, rates.

Highly recommended hotels are indicated by a star ★.

Hotels

Expensive
★
Arizona Inn. Although this landmark '30s-era inn is close to the university and downtown, you feel as though you're away from it all on its 14 acress of lushly landscaped grounds. All rooms have patios and lovely period furnishings; many have fireplaces. Service is excellent—friendly but unobtrusive. The staff hosts small conferences beautifully, attending to the details without fuss. Locals as well as guests frequent the hotel's restaurant (*see* Dining, *above*). *2200 E. Elm St., 85719, tel. 602/325–1541. 80 rooms with bath. Facilities: pool, 2 tennis courts, library, gift shop, cocktail lounge, restaurant. AE, MC, V.*

Best Western Royal Sun Inn and Suites. Convenient to both the University of Arizona and downtown, this tan-brick motel is decorated in pleasing southwestern-style pastels. All the rooms have hair dryers, small refrigerators, and VCRs; suites also have whirlpool baths. Don't expect the unexpected, but if you're looking for spacious, clean lodging and efficient service, this is a reasonable choice. *1015 N. Stone Ave., 85705, tel. 602/622–8871 or 800/545–8858. 58 rooms, 20 suites, all with bath. Facilities: pool, exercise room, dry saunas, spa, dining room, cocktail lounge. AE, D, DC, MC, V.*

Doubletree Hotel. Convenient to the airport and to the center of town, this comfortable, contemporary-style property is also across the road from the municipal golf course at Randolph Park, which hosts the LPGA tournament every year; most of the participants stay at the Doubletree. Rooms are large, and done in salmon or turquoise with southwestern-style furnishings. The pretty Cactus Rose Restaurant serves excellent nouvelle southwestern cuisine and the Javelina Cantina in the lobby is a fun place in which to have a beer. *445 S. Alvernon Way, tel. 602/881–4200 or*

800/528–0444. 295 rooms with bath. Facilities: restaurant, bar, pool, Jacuzzi, tennis courts. AE, D, DC, MC, V.

Tucson Hilton East. Recently in the news because of the previous owner's financial difficulties, this east side property is now under new management. It's convenient to Sabino Canyon and Saguaro National Monument East as well as to Davis–Monthan Air Force Base. An airy glass-atrium lobby takes full advantage of the view of the Santa Catalina Mountains. Rooms are nicely furnished, with modern light wood fittings, pastel carpeting, and subtly patterned pastel bedspreads. The Wine Bar features one of the most extensive selections in town. The VIP level offers extra service and luxuries such as complimentary hors d'oeuvres, deluxe Continental breakfast, and a library. *7600 E. Broadway, 85710, tel. 602/721–5600. 225 rooms with bath. Facilities: pool, exercise room (VIP level only), restaurant, bar. AE, D, DC, MC, V.*

Moderate **Embassy Suites Tucson-Broadway.** This centrally located hotel is 10 miles from Tucson International Airport, 5 miles from downtown, and a bit less than 5 miles from the University of Arizona. Accommodations are two-room suites (with a kitchenette) opening onto an atrium full of plants. Furnishings are tasteful if not exciting. Among the extras are a free cooked-to-order breakfast every morning and complimentary happy hour every evening; transportation to the airport and parking are also on the house. *5335 E. Broadway, 85711, tel. 602/745–2700 or 800/363–2779. 142 suites with bath. Facilities: outdoor heated pool, whirlpool, microwaves in rooms, washer and dryer for guest use on premises. AE, D, DC, MC, V.*

Holiday Inn Tucson Airport Hotel and Convention Center. Favored by businesspeople, this property is five minutes from the airport and adjacent to I-10. The decor is a mix of Mexican and Spanish, with the usual dark print bedspreads and carpets throughout. In contrast, the light, cheerful lobby has a plant-filled atrium with a waterfall; *saltillo*-tiled floors and white stucco walls give it an open, southwestern feel. There are free shuttles to the airport and to the large El Con shopping center. *4550 S. Palo Verde Blvd., 85714, tel. 602/746–1161 or 800–HOLIDAY. 299 rooms with bath. Facilities: pool, sauna, whirlpool, tennis court, exercise room, 2 restaurants, cocktail lounge. AE, D, DC, MC, V.*

The Lodge on the Desert. Although the ambience is that of an exclusive inn, prices at this little hotel, established in 1936, are reasonable. The place has retained the old-fashioned feel of a Mexican hacienda: The adobe architecture is accented with hand-painted Mexican tile and open-beamed ceilings; fireplaces warm many of the rooms in the winter; and lush gardens make the patios feel cool and private. The property is convenient to the university, near two major shopping malls, and within a mile of golf, racquetball, and tennis facilities. Note: with charm, as is often the case, comes old plumbing. And service here seems to have slipped in recent years. *306 N. Alvernon Way, Box 42500, 85733, tel. 602/325–3366 or 800/456–5634. 40 rooms with bath. Facilities: library, pool, shuffleboard, ping-pong, croquet, restaurant, cocktail lounge. AE, D, DC, MC, V.*

Ramada Inn Foothills. Families as well as business travelers stay in this Ramada Inn on the northeastern side of town, close to restaurants, Sabino Canyon, and mall shopping. This property has a fresh, clean feel about it: A light stucco building with rounded corners, it has an updated adobe look. Furnishings are standard motel style, but they're fairly new and more than serviceable. There's a complimentary cold breakfast buffet and complimentary cocktails in the evening. Free passes to a local health club are available, and golf and tennis facilities are nearby. *6944 E. Tanque Verde Rd., 85715, tel. 602/886–9595 or 800/228–2828. 113 rooms with bath. Facilities: pool and sauna, restaurant, cocktail lounge. AE, D, DC, MC, V.*

Rodeway Inn Tucson North. Located in the university area, this hotel caters to business as well as leisure travelers. The basic boxy motel architecture has been adapted to local style—a stucco exterior is accented with tasteful, low-key stripes of turquoise and pink. The pool is in a nicely landscaped courtyard studded with umbrella-shaded tables. Rooms are nothing fancy, but they are adequate, and there's a handy laundry facility on the premises. *1365 W. Grant Rd., 85745, tel. 602/622–7791 or 800/228–2000. 146 rooms with bath. Facilities: pool, restaurant, cocktail lounge, coin-operated laundry. AE, D, DC, MC, V.*

Inexpensive **Frontier Motel.** You can recognize this small motel between the university and downtown by its red-tile roofs and brick facade. It's nothing fancy, but it's clean and comfortable, and convenient to public transportation. Fourteen of the rooms have fully equipped kitchenettes; there is also a barbecue grill out by the pool and a restaurant next door. Weekly and monthly rates are available. *227 W. Drachman, 85705, tel. 602/798–3005. 20 rooms with bath. Facilities: pool, guest laundry, covered parking. AE, D, MC, V.*

★ **Hotel Congress.** Loved by many for its idiosyncratic charm, this downtown hotel is not for those who want the bland comforts of chain lodgings. Built in 1919, this property has been restored to its original western version of Art Deco style. The rooms, which vary in size, are individually furnished: All have black-and-white tiled baths and the original iron beds; some have desks and tables. Near the Greyhound and Amtrak stations and the main Sun Tran terminal, and close to downtown art galleries and restaurants, this is an excellent choice for those who don't have a car. The downside of this convenient location is noise, which is compounded on weekend nights when music from the popular Club Congress filters up to some of the rooms. Still, if you're young at heart and looking for an inexpensive and memorable establishment, you can't beat this Tucson landmark. *311 E. Congress St., 85701, tel. 602/622–8848. 40* *rooms with bath. Facilities: restaurant, bar, nightclub. AE, MC, V.*

Park Inn/Santa Rita. When this hotel became a Park Inn in 1991 (it had been a Days Inn during the late 1980s), it also reclaimed the name by which it had been known in Tucson for years—the Santa Rita. The property was spiffed up during the past decade—modern furnishings, hand-painted Mexican tile, and adobe walls brighten the lobby—but rooms are rather dark and drably furnished, and the place sometimes shows its age in the plumbing. Still, the hotel is conveniently located near the downtown arts district and across the street from the visitor center, and it's home to Café Poca Cosa, one of the most popular Mexican restaurants in town (*see* Dining, *above*). There's a complimentary cold breakfast buffet and a free happy hour in the afternoon. *88 E. Broadway, 85701, tel. 602/622–4000 or 800/437–7275. 165 rooms with bath. Facilities: beauty parlor, pool, Jacuzzi, sauna, restaurant. AE, D, DC, MC, V.*

Bed-and-Breakfasts

Moderate-Expensive   **El Presidio Bed and Breakfast Inn.** This B&B in the historic El Presidio district offers four charming accommodations, two in a Victorian adobe home built more than 100 years ago, and two in separate guest houses. The Carriage House, furnished with Eastlake antiques dating from the 1880s, and the Gatehouse, done in French country style, both have private entrances off a beautiful old courtyard, and both have kitchenettes. Guest rooms come well stocked with fruits and bottled water, and all have phones, TVs, and robes. Co-owner Patti Tocci is a caterer, and guests enjoy her excellent, copious breakfasts. Smoking is not allowed. *297 N. Main Ave., 85701, tel. 602/623–6151. 3 suites, 1 room, all with bath. No credit cards.*

Moderate   **Casa Tierra.** For a real desert experience, head out to this
★   bed-and-breakfast on 5 acres of land near the Arizona-Sonora Desert Museum and Saguaro National Monument; for the last 1½ miles you'll be driving along a dirt road. An adobe house built by Lyle Hymer-Thompson in 1989 expressly to serve as a B&B has three guest rooms, all with private bath and kitchenettes; all look out onto a lovely central courtyard with a palo verde tree and other desert foliage and also have their own private entrances from individual back patios. The southwestern-style furnishings include Mexican *equipales* (chairs with pigskin seats), tiled floors, and viga-beamed ceilings. The delicious breakfasts prepared by Karen Hymer-Thompson might include blue-corn pancakes, breakfast burritos, or oatmeal apple waffles; there's always lots of fresh fruit and baked goods to accompany them. *11155 W. Calle Pima, 85743, tel. 602/578–3058. 3 rooms with bath. Facilities: hot tub. No credit cards. Closed June–Aug.*

Peppertrees. Set in a restored Victorian just off the University of Arizona campus, Peppertrees allows guests their privacy along with the usual B&B camaraderie. Two lovely southwestern-style guest houses in the back of the tree-shaded main house have full kitchens, washers and dryers, and individual patios; 1½ baths are shared by two bedrooms in each unit (a room in the main house has a bath across the hall). Host Marjorie Martin, the author of a recently published cookbook, prepares elaborate morning repasts for her visitors; her buttery shortbread, served at afternoon tea, is sold at local markets. *724 E. University Blvd., 85719, tel. 602/622–7167. 5 rooms. Facilities: landscaped patio. MC, V.*

The Triangle L Ranch Bed & Breakfast. Out near Biosphere 2, a 45-minute drive northeast of Tucson at an elevation of 4,500 feet, Triangle L offers four private cottages—all at least 75 years old and furnished with antiques—scattered about the property's 80 acres. Buffalo Bill was among the regular visitors to the ranch, which was built in the 1880s. Hiking and sitting on the porch are activities equally favored by visitors. A ranch breakfast of eggs, homemade breads, fresh fruit, and plenty of coffee is served daily. Smoking outdoors only. *2805 N. Triangle L Ranch Rd., Box 900, Oracle 85623, tel. 602/896–2804 or 800/266–2804. 2 private cottages with bath, 2 with bath and kitchen. D, MC, V.*

Guest Ranches

Moderate-Expensive   **Tanque Verde Ranch.** One of the country's oldest guest ranches, Tanque Verde sits on more than 600 beautiful acres in the Rincon Mountains between Coronado National Forest and Saguaro National Monument. There's plenty to do, from guided nature walks and trail rides to tennis and swimming. Rooms in the main ranch house or in private casitas are all furnished in tasteful southwestern style; most have patios and some have fireplaces. Service is relaxed but very attentive. Cookouts and indoor meals are delicious (*see* Dining, *above*). Many of the guests have been coming here for years; it's not unusual for more than two generations of a family to visit together. *14301 E. Speedway Blvd., 85748, tel. 602/296–6275. 65 rooms with bath. Facilities: indoor and outdoor pools, 5 tennis courts (1 lighted for night use), spa, exercise room, basketball, volleyball, horseshoes, fishing, horseback riding. AE, D, MC, V.*

Moderate   **Lazy K Bar Guest Ranch.** In the Tucson Mountains, 16 miles northwest of town at an altitude of 2,300 feet, this family-oriented guest ranch will please children as well as adults. Steak cookouts are held every Saturday night, and the daily fare in the community dining room is hearty and good. As you might expect, horseback riding is a focus, with mounts available for greenhorns as well as those with experience. Riders are entertained with tales of the Old West as they explore the Saguaro National Monument on horseback. There are 23 rooms, all with private bath, situated in eight *casitas*, or cottages. The older buildings are made of Mexican Indian stucco and contain rooms with fireplaces and wood-beam ceilings. Rooms in the newer, adobe-brick buildings are larger and more modern. Rates for children 17 and under are very reasonable. There's a three-day minimum stay. *8401 N. Scenic Dr., 85743, tel. 602/744–3050. 23 rooms with bath. Facilities: pool, library, large-screen TV in the main lodge, BYOB bar. AE, MC, V. Closed June 15– Sept. 1.*

★ **White Stallion Ranch.** If you feel as if this place is right out of the film *High Chaparral*, you won't be imagining things. Many scenes from the movie were shot on the ranch, which sits on 3,000 acres of desert mountain land. The True family—Cynthia, Russell, and Michael—has run the White Stallion for almost 30 years, and it feels like a family place, where children are welcome and large groups are easily accommodated. There are no phones or TVs in the spare but comfortable rooms. Horseback rides, a weekend rodeo, and hikes along mountain trails are just a few of the activities offered. A herd of longhorn cattle and a wide variety of birds, desert cottontail rabbits, and peacocks make their home on the grounds. Children will enjoy the petting zoo, where sheep and tiny goats gently nuzzle their visitors. *9251 W. Twin Peaks Rd., 85743, tel. 602/297–0252 or 800/ 782–5546. 29 rooms with bath. Facilities: bar, ping-pong, 2 pool tables, TV/VCR room with video library, pool, hot tub, 2 tennis courts, shuffleboard, basketball, volleyball, horseback riding. No credit cards. Closed May–Sept.*

Resorts

Very Expensive **Canyon Ranch.** Mel and Enid Zuckerman opened Canyon Ranch in 1979 on the site of the old Double U Guest Ranch, set on 70 acres in the desert foothills north of Tucson. Two activity centers include a 62,000-square-foot spa complex and an 8,000-square-foot Health and Healing Center, where dietitians, exercise physiologists, behavioral-health professionals, and medical staff counsel guests on everything from kicking the smoking habit to losing weight. Guests are pampered while they're being shaped up. The food is unobtrusively healthful, satisfying—within reason—even big appetites. Rooms are luxuriously furnished in muted southwestern tones. Be aware, however, that unless you're seriously rich, the benefits of the stress reduction programs may be wiped out when you get the bill: Almost all of the ranch's special services cost extra. *8600 E. Rockcliff Rd., 85715, tel. 602/749–9000 or 800/742–9000. 67 standard rooms, 45 deluxe rooms, 41 luxury suites, all with bath. Facilities: 1 indoor and 3 outdoor pools, 8 tennis courts, basketball, squash, racquetball, handball, extensive workout equipment. D, MC, V.*

Loews Ventana Canyon Resort. One of the newer desert resorts, Ventana Canyon is unquestionably luxurious, but also snootier than most Tucson properties. The setting is spectacular: Expect to see desert cottontails around the 93 acres of grounds, along with hummingbirds, quail, and other birds; don't be surprised if you find yourself sharing the golf course with a cottontail or two. Rooms are modern and chic, furnished in soft pastels and light woods; each bath has a miniature TV. The center of this open, airy property is an 80-foot waterfall that cascades down the Catalina Mountains into a little lake. Four restaurants offer guests a choice of casual poolside snacks and elegant dining; the upscale Ventana Room (*see* Dining, *above*) serves first-rate Continental cuisine. *7000 N. Resort Dr., 85715, tel. 602/ 299–2020 or 800/234–5117. 398 rooms with bath. Facilities: 2 pools, golf course, 10 tennis courts, spa, health club, gift shops, hairdresser, cocktail lounge, disco, 4 restaurants. AE, D, DC, MC, V.*

★ **Sheraton Tucson El Conquistador.** You'll know you're in the Southwest when you step into the cathedral-ceilinged lobby of this golf and tennis resort: It has a huge copper mural filled with cowboys and cacti, as well as a wide-window view of one of the pools set against a backdrop of the rugged Santa Catalina Mountains. This friendly, relaxing place draws families and out-of-town conventioneers as well as locals, who take advantage of summer rates for the Sheraton's excellent sports facilities. Rooms, either in private casitas or the main hotel building, feature stylish light-wood furniture with tin work and pastel-toned spreads and curtains, as well as balconies or patios; some of the suites have kiva-shaped fireplaces. With its wide selection of Mexican beers and live mariachi music, The Dos Locos Cantina keeps guests from heading south of the border. Biosphere 2 is just about a 10-minute drive up the road from here. *10000 N. Oracle Rd., 85737, tel. 602/742–7000 or 800/325–7832. 438 rooms with bath. Facilities: 45 holes of golf, 31 lighted tennis courts, 11 indoor racquetball courts, riding stables, 3 outdoor pools, 2 fitness centers, sauna and Jacuzzi, bicycle rentals, volleyball, basketball, 5 restaurants, gift shops. AE, D, DC, MC, V.*

Westin La Paloma. Vying with the Sheraton and Loews Ventana for convention business, this sprawling pink resort offers lots of options for individual and family relaxation. The resort's golf, fitness, and beauty centers are top-notch; a huge pool has the only swim-up bar in Tucson; and reasonably priced child care at a special play lounge helps both parents and kids enjoy their stay. Accommodations make tasteful use of southwestern colors and copper tones; views from private balconies are of the city lights, golf course, or grounds. The casual Desert Garden restaurant affords wonderful views of the Santa Catalina Mountains, while the more upscale La Villa specializes in freshly imported seafood. *3800 E. Sunrise, 85718, tel. 602/742–6000 or 800/876– 3683. 487 rooms with bath. Facilities: golf course, 12 lighted tennis courts, volleyball, croquet, racquetball, pool, 3* *spas, aerobics, exercise and weight rooms, beauty center, jogging and cycling trails, bike rentals, 5 restaurants, 2 bars, shopping arcade, business center. AE, D, DC, MC, V.*

★ **Westward Look Resort.** Set on 80 acres in the Santa Catalina foothills north of town, Westward Look is 45 years old but is being completely refurbished. Either a city or a mountain view is available from the 244 well-appointed rooms spread across the landscaped grounds, traversed by golf carts driven by hotel staff to transport guests. The resort is dimly but beautifully lit at night, the better for guests to stargaze. In-room hot-beverage makers, irons and ironing boards, and refrigerators are among the many special touches. The resort's Gold Room restaurant is excellent (*see* Dining, *above*), and the lobby lounge features live entertainment every night but Monday. While offering the full range of facilities, Westward Look is more intimate than the other Tucson resorts. It draws many repeat visitors. *245 E. Ina Rd., 85704, tel. 602/297–1151 or 800/722–2500. 244 rooms with bath. Facilities: 3 heated pools, 3 spas, 8 tennis courts (5 lit for night playing), cocktail lounge, 2 restaurants. AE, D, DC, MC, V.*

The Arts and Nightlife

The Arts

Tucson, known as the most cultured of Arizona's cities, is one of only 14 cities in the United States that is home to a symphony as well as to opera, theater, and ballet companies. Winter is the high season for most of Tucson's cultural activities because that's when most of the visitors come, but there's something going on all the time.

Summer is when **Downtown Saturday Night,** a year-round event, comes alive. On the first and third Saturday nights of each month (around 7–10 PM), Tucson's downtown arts district opens up its galleries, studios, and cafés. There's dancing in the street—everything from calypso to square dancing—and musical performances ranging from jazz to gospel. Most of the activity takes place along Congress Street and Broadway (from 4th Avenue to Stone Street) and along 5th and 6th avenues, but the action radiates in all directions. For information about this event and about festivals, free workshops and classes, and performances in the downtown arts district, contact **The Tucson Partnership, Inc.** (tel. 602/624–9977); this organization also offers material on self-guided gallery and historic district walking tours.

The cost of attending any cultural event in Tucson will be a pleasant surprise to anyone who's accustomed to paying East or West Coast prices—symphony tickets can be purchased for as little as $5 for some concerts, and tickets to a touring Broadway musical can often be had for as little as $22. Parking is frequently free. Most of the city's cultural activity takes place either downtown in the arts district, where the Tucson Convention Center complex and the old El Presidio neighborhood are, or at the University of Arizona. For information about events at the **Tucson Convention Center** (260 S. Church St.), call 602/791–4266. Tickets to Tucson arts and entertainment events can often be purchased through **Dillard's Box Office** (tel. 602/678–2222 [information] or 800/638–4253 [phone orders with credit cards]).

The free *Tucson Weekly,* found in most supermarkets and convenience stores, and the Friday edition of *The Arizona Daily Star* both have complete listings of what's on in town.

Dance Tucson shares its professional ballet company, **Ballet Arizona** (tel. 602/882–5022), with Phoenix; performances, which range from classical to contemporary, are held at the Music Hall in the Tucson Convention Center (*see above*). The most established of the modern companies, **Orts Theatre of Dance** (930 N. Stone Ave., tel. 602/624–3799), gives three indoor and four outdoor performances a year.

Music The **Tucson Symphony Orchestra** (443 S. Stone Ave., tel. 602/882–8585 [box office] or 602/792–9155 [main office]), part of Tucson's cultural scene for more than 60 years, holds concerts in the newly refurbished Music Hall (260 S. Church St., tel. 602/791–4836) in the Tucson Convention Center complex. A variety of concerts and recitals, many of them free, are offered by the **University of Arizona's School of Music** (tel. 602/621–3065); a chamber music series is hosted by the **Arizona Friends of Music** (tel. 602/298–5806) at the Leo Rich Theater in the Tucson Convention Center from October through April. The **Arizona Opera Company** (3501 N. Mountain Ave., tel. 602/293–4336), headquartered in Tucson, puts on four major productions each year at the Tucson Convention Center's Music Hall.

From late February through late June, the Tucson Parks and Recreation Department hosts a series of **free concerts,** most of them held on the weekend at the De Meester Outdoor Performance Center in Reid Park. The Tucson Pops Orchestra and the Arizona Symphonic Winds alternate performances much of the time, but there are also special events, such as the Old Time Fiddlers concert and Jazz Sundae. It's smart to arrive at least an hour before the music starts (usually at 7:30) so that you can position your blanket exactly where you want it. Call 602/791–4079 for the schedule.

The **Southern Arizona Light Opera Co.** (1202 N. Main Ave., tel. 602/323–7888 [east side ticket office] or 602/884–1212 [west side ticket office]) is becoming increasingly popular.

Tucson's jazz scene encompasses everything from afternoon jam sessions in the park to Sunday jazz brunches at the resorts in the foothills. The **Tucson Jazz Society** (Box

44163, 85733, tel. 602/743–3399) offers information about the many events around town.

Poetry The **Tucson Poetry Festival** is held in early spring. A large range of poets, some internationally acclaimed—Allen Ginsberg and Amiri Baraka have been participants—come to town for three days of readings and related events. Call 602/321–2163 or 602/322–0895 for details.

The **University of Arizona Poetry Center** (1216 N. Cherry Ave., tel. 602/321–7760) runs a free series open to the public. Phone during fall and spring semesters for information on scheduled readers.

Theater Theater groups in town include Arizona's state theater, the **Arizona Theatre Company** (tel. 602/884–8210), which performs everything from classical to contemporary drama at the Temple of Music and Art (330 S. Scott Ave., tel. 602/622–2823 [tickets]) from November through May; it's worth coming just to see the beautiful, newly restored Spanish Colonial/Moorish–style theater. The drama department at the University of Arizona (tel. 602/621–1162) also offers productions of all styles and periods through the **Studio Theatre Series** and through the **University Theatre.** The **a.k.a. theatre** (125 E. Congress St., tel. 602/623–7852) specializes in avant-garde productions, and **Invisible Theatre** (1400 N. 1st Ave., tel. 602/882–9721) presents contemporary plays and musicals.

Nightlife

If Tucson doesn't have the huge selection of bars and clubs available in some major cities, there's something here to suit nearly every taste. Even if you can't two-step, it's worth stopping into one of the many local country-and-western bars; a number of the clubs offer free dance lessons, and the crowd is friendly to city slickers and cowpokes alike. Most of the major resorts have night spots that offer late-night drinks and sometimes dancing.

Rock/Variety **Club Congress** (311 E. Congress St., tel. 602/622–8848) is the main venue in town for cutting-edge rock bands. At the **Cushing Street Bar and Restaurant** (343 S. Meyer Ave., tel. 602/622–7984) the focus is on blues, though live jazz and rock acts are also booked. The **Chicago Bar** (5954 E. Speedway Blvd., tel. 602/748–8169) features reggae on Wednesday and Thursday nights, rocking blues on Friday and Saturday nights. Nearby **Berky's** (5769 E. Speedway Blvd., tel. 602/296–1981) has live music—Motown, R&B, and blues—six nights a week. During the school year, cars line the drive of the Loews Ventana Canyon resort, where the **Flying V Bar & Grill** (tel. 602/299–2020, ext. 5280) packs the collegiate crowd into its disco.

Jazz Of the various clubs around town, **Cafe Sweetwater** (340 E. 6th St., tel. 622/6464) is the most consistent in the quality of its jazz acts—and the food's pretty good, too.

Country and Western An excellent house band gets the crowd two-stepping nightly at the **Maverick** (4702 E. 22nd St., tel. 602/748–0456). On Sunday night the **Cactus Moon Cafe** (5470 E. Broadway Blvd., tel. 602/748–0049) has a terrific all-you-can-eat buffet for $2 and free dance lessons. It's worth a drive to the **Wild Wild West** (4385 W. Ina Rd., tel. 602/744–7744), the Southwest's largest country-and-western nightclub, with a rotating bar, two dance floors, pool tables, and video games.

Southeastern Arizona

The southeastern corner of Arizona is a mix of ghost towns, rugged rock formations, dense, deep forests, and mountain mining towns. It's the site of Chiricahua National Monument, one of Arizona's best-kept secrets, and a paradise for birders, hikers, and antiquers—and anyone who has an interest in frontier history. Many consider this to be Arizona's most scenic region.

Much of this area is part of **Cochise County,** named in 1881 in honor of the chief of the Chiricahua Apache. Cochise waged war against troops and settlers for 11 years, but he was respected by Indian and non-Indian alike for his integrity and leadership skills. Today Cochise County is dotted by small towns, many of them much smaller—and all much tamer—than they were in their heyday. It's hard to imagine now, but Tombstone, headquarters for most of the area's gamblers and gunfighters, was once bigger than San Francisco. These days it derives most of its revenue from tourism, and the wildest visitor is usually a six-year-old traveling with Granny and Gramps on a winter vacation from North Dakota.

The area's terrain ranges from the rugged forests of its mountains to the desert grasslands of Sierra Vista. Cochise County is home to six and part of the seventh—including the Huachucas, Mustangs, Whetstones, and Rincons—of the 12 mountain ranges that compose the 1.7-million-acre Coronado National Forest.

Essential Information

Getting There By Car From I–10, an east–west road, take U.S. 80 south (turn off at Benson) to reach Tombstone, Bisbee, and Douglas.

By Bus **Greyhound** (tel. 602/792–0972) has service from Tucson to Douglas and Bisbee; you'll need to book a tour if you want to take the bus to Tombstone.

Tourist Information **Bisbee Chamber of Commerce** (7 Naco Rd., tel. 602/432–5421)

Douglas Chamber of Commerce (1125 Pan American, tel. 602/364–2477)

Tombstone Tourist Association (Allen and 4th Sts., tel. 602/457–3939)

Guided Tours   For an in-depth look at historic sights in Tombstone and the surrounding areas, contact **Tombstone Western Tours** (Box 362, Tombstone 85638, tel. 602/457–3256 or 800/228–1228).

Exploring

The loop tour suggested below covers the highlights of the region and should take at least two days; three days would offer a more leisurely trip, perhaps with some hiking and an excursion across the border from Douglas to the pleasant town of Agua Prieta in Mexico. If your time is more limited, consider taking a day trip through Texas Canyon to Tombstone and Bisbee, or one via Willcox to Chiricahua National Monument.

Numbers in the margin correspond to points of interest on the Southeastern Arizona map.

From Tucson, head east on I-10 for approximately 63 miles, where you'll see signs telling you that you're entering **Texas Canyon.** The rock formations here are exceptional—the huge boulders appear to be delicately balanced against one another.

Texas Canyon is also the home of the **Amerind Foundation** (the name is derived from the contraction of the words "American" and "Indian"), founded by the amateur archaeologist William Fulton in 1937 to learn about Native American cultures. Take Exit 318 off I–10 and continue southeast for 1 mile until you reach the turnoff to the Amerind Foundation, a research facility and museum housed in a beautiful Spanish-style structure built between 1930 and 1959.

Visitors to the museum are given an overview of Native American cultures of the Southwest and Mexico through well-designed rotating displays of archaeological materials, crafts, and photographs. The museum store is well stocked with books on history and Native American cultures, as well as items created by Native American craftspeople. The adjacent Fulton-Hayden Memorial Art Gallery offers an eclectic but interesting assortment of art (mostly from the Southwest) collected by William Fulton. The beautiful natural setting and the quality of the exhibits at the foundation make a visit here a delightful as well as an educational experience. *Dragoon, tel. 602/586–3666. Admission: $3 adults, $2 senior citizens and children 12–18, children under 12 free. Open Sept.–May, daily 10–4; June–Aug., Wed.–Sun. 10–4. Closed national holidays.*

From the Amerind Foundation, return to I–10 and backtrack 12 miles to **Benson,** once the hub of the Southern Pa-

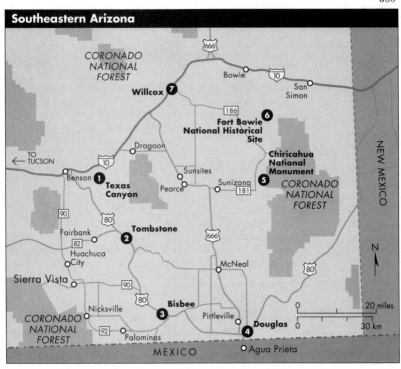

Southeastern Arizona

cific Railroad and a stop on the Butterfield Stagecoach route, but now a fairly sleepy little town. As you go through Benson on I–10, watch for Ocotillo Road, Exit 304. It's worth a detour for the **Singing Wind Bookshop** (Ocotillo Rd., tel. 602/586–2425), located about 3 miles out of town on a ranch. It's a good idea to call before you drive out here because the shop's proprietor runs it in her spare time (she runs the ranch, too) and doesn't always keep regular hours. The unlikely location houses an excellent collection of books on Arizona wildlife, history, and geology.

Time Out   For a good green-chili burrito or a patty melt, stop in at the **Horseshoe Cafe** (154 E. 4th St., tel. 602/586–3303), which has occupied its current site on Benson's main street for more than 50 years. The neon horseshoe on the ceiling, the macramés of local cattle brands, and the large Wurlitzer jukebox all give this casual restaurant and lounge a unique western character.

At Benson you'll pick up U.S. 80. Drive 24 miles south, through some rolling hills, to **Tombstone.** Headquarters of many of the West's rowdies in the late 1800s, Tombstone grew on the site of a wildly successful silver mine, which was discovered in 1877 by prospector Ed Schieffelin, who had been cautioned that "all you'll find there is your tombstone"—the area, originally called Goose Flats, was prone to Apache attack. He struck one of the West's richest veins of silver in the tough old hills and gave the town its name as an ironic "I told you so" to his detractors. The mine itself he called the Lucky Cuss, figuring that, indeed, he was one.

The promise of riches attracted all types of folks, including the outlaw type. Soon gambling halls, saloons, and houses of prostitution sprang up all along Allen Street. In 1881 the Earp family and Doc Holliday battled to the death with the Clanton boys at the famous shoot-out at the OK Corral. Over the past 100 years or so, scriptwriters and storytellers have done much to rewrite the exact details of the confrontation, but it's a fact that the town was indeed the scene of several gunfights in the 1880s. On Sundays, visitors are treated to replays of some of these on Allen Street.

Tombstone's rough-and-ready heyday was popularized by Hollywood in the 1930s and capitalized on by the local tourist industry in the decades that followed, but there's more to the town than the OK Corral, the souvenir shops on Allen Street, and the staged shoot-outs. "The town too tough to die" (it survived two major fires, an earthquake, the closing of the mines, and the removal of the county seat to Bisbee) was also a cultural center, and many of its original buildings remain intact. Check with the **Tombstone Tourist Association** (Allen and 4th Sts., tel. 602/457–3939) for a walking tour that includes several of the town's currently unmarked sights.

As you enter Tombstone, stop at **Boot Hill Graveyard,** where the victims of the OK Corral shoot-out are buried; it's on the northwestern corner of town, facing U.S. 80. The commercialism of the place may turn you off (you enter through a gift shop that sells novelty items in the shape of tombstones), but the site itself is interesting. Chinese names in one section bear testament to the laundry and restaurant workers who came from San Francisco during the height of Tombstone's mining fever. About a third of the more than 350 graves dug here from 1879 to 1974 are unmarked.

Once you've bought your tombstone-shaped yard sign, drive into town (less than 3 miles) on U.S. 80, which turns into Fremont Street. When you reach 3rd Street, head two blocks south to Toughnut Street, where the **Tombstone Courthouse State Historic Park** offers an excellent introduction to the town's past. The largest settlement between San Francisco and St. Louis in 1881, Tombstone was chosen as the seat of the newly established Cochise County; the courthouse built the next year was an expensive, stylish affair. Displays include a reconstruction of the original courtroom; numerous photographs of prominent—and notorious—town figures; and such area artifacts as the dozens of types of barbed wire used by local cattle ranchers.

Toughnut and 3rd Sts., tel. 602/457–3311. Admission: $2 adults, $1 children 12–17, children under 12 free. Open daily 8–5. Closed Christmas.

Go one block east on Toughnut and turn right onto 4th Street for the **Rose Tree Inn Museum.** Originally a boarding house for the Vizina Mining Company and later a popular hotel, this museum, with its 1880s period rooms and huge rose bush on the patio (listed in the Guinness Book of Records as the largest in the world), displays the gentler side of life in Tombstone. *Toughnut and 4th Sts., tel. 602/457–3326. Admission: $1.50 adults, $1.25 senior citizens, children under 14 free. Open daily 9–5. Closed Christmas.*

You'll get a more dramatic version of the town's history, narrated by Vincent Price, in the **Historama** on Allen Street, a block to the north. At the adjoining **OK Corral,** a recorded voice-over details the town's most famous event, while life-size figures of the gunfight's participants stand poised to shoot. Photographer C.S. Fly, whose studio was next door to the corral, didn't record this bit of history, but Geronimo and his pursuers were among the historical figures he did capture with his camera. Many of his fascinating Old West images may be viewed at the **Fly Exhibition Gallery.** *Allen St. bet. 3rd and 4th Sts., tel. 602/457–3456. Admission: Historama $1.50, OK Corral and Fly Exhibition Gallery $1.50; children under 6 free. Open daily 8:30–5; Historama shows every hour on the hour 9–4.*

Allen Street, the town's main drag, is lined with restaurants and curio shops. Many of the street's buildings still bear bullet holes from their livelier days, and some of the remaining artifacts are interesting—including the **original printing presses** for the town's newspaper, the *Tombstone Epitaph* (9 S. 5th St., tel. 602/457–2211), founded in 1880 and still publishing. (If the town's other newspaper, *The Nugget,* had survived instead, the Clanton boys might be mourned as martyrs today, but it was the Earp-supporting *Epitaph* and its version of history that endured.)

Two dollars will admit you to **The Bird Cage Theater** (6th and Allen Sts., tel. 602/457–3421). The displays in this former music hall, where Caruso, Sarah Bernhardt, and Lillian Russell—among others—performed, are dusty and chaotic. If you poke around, however, you can find such treasures as the 1881 Black Maria hearse that brought all the victims of the OK Corral shoot-out—and everyone else who died in Tombstone—to the Boot Hill cemetery.

Time Out Sightseeing is thirsty work, and what better place to wet your whistle than one of Tombstone's saloons? The **Crystal Palace** (Allen and 5th Sts., tel. 602/457–3611) sports a beautiful mirrored mahogany bar, wrought-iron chandeliers, and tinwork ceilings; locals come here to dance to the live country and western music. Those seeking solid refreshment in a historic setting might stop in for a burger at **Nellie**

Cashman's (5th and Toughnut Sts., tel. 602/457–2212), a restored 1879 building.

From Tombstone, take U.S. 80 for 24 miles south to Bisbee.
The drive here is a scenic one, climbing another 1,000 feet
to a final elevation of more than a mile (5,490 feet).

❸ Like Tombstone, **Bisbee** was a mining boomtown, but its
wealth was in copper, not silver, and its success much long-
er-lived. It wasn't until 1975 that the last mine closed and
the city went into decline. However, it was rediscovered in
the early 1980s by burned-out city dwellers and revived as a
kind of Woodstock West. The permanent population is a mix
of retired miners and their families, aging hippie jewelry
makers, and enterprising young restaurateurs and antiques dealers. The three rather disparate groups seem to
get along fine—Bisbee is that kind of place.

When you drive through Mule Mountain Tunnel on U.S. 80,
you'll be getting close. You'll see the pretty, compact town
hugging the steep mountainside on your left. If you want to
head straight into town, get off at Brewery Gulch interchange. You can park here and cross under the highway,
taking Main or Commerce or Brewery Gulch streets, all of
which meet here.

Another option is to continue driving on U.S. 80 about a
quarter of a mile to where it intersects with AZ 92. Pull off
the highway on the right into a gravel parking lot, where a
short, typewritten history of the **Lavender Pit Mine** can be
found attached to the hurricane fence surrounding the area
(Bisbee isn't big on formal exhibits). The hole left by the
copper miners is huge, with piles of lavender-hued "tailings," or waste, creating mountains around it. Arizona's
largest pit mine yielded some 94 million tons of copper ore
out of more than 280 million tons of raw materials before the
town's mining activity came to a halt. If you're interested in
buying jewelry made from Bisbee Blue, the pretty turquoise stone still extracted from Lavender Pit, walk across
the parking area toward the mountains to the right of the
Bisbee Blue shop.

For a real lesson in mining history, however, you need to
take the **Copper Queen mine tour.** The mine is less than a
half-mile to the east of the Lavender Pit, across U.S. 80
from downtown at the Brewery Gulch interchange. (If
you're claustrophobic, sit this one out at one of Bisbee's
many restaurants. Although there is plenty of ventilation
in the mine, it's dark and close in here. Note, too, that
the tour might be scary for very small children.) Tours
are led by one of Bisbee's several retired copper miners,
who are wont to embellish their official spiel with tales
from their mining days. They're also very capable, safety-
minded people (any miner who survives to lead tours in
his older years would have to be), so don't be concerned
about the precautionary dog tags (literally—they're

donated by a local veterinarian) issued to each person on the tour.

The tours, which depart daily at 9, 10:30, noon, 2, and 3:30 (you can't enter the mine at any other time), last anywhere from 1 to 1½ hours, and visitors go into the shaft via a little open train, like those the miners rode when the mine was active. Before you climb aboard, you're outfitted in miner garb—a yellow slicker and a hard hat that runs off a battery pack strapped to your waist. You may want to wear a sweater or light coat under your slicker because the temperature in the mine is a brisk 47°F on the average. You'll travel by train thousands of feet into the mine, up a grade of 30 feet (not down, as many visitors expect). The slicker will keep you protected from the occasional drips and sprinkles—natural seepage from the ground. *1 Dart Rd., tel. 602/432–2071. Admission: $8 adults, $3.50 children 7–11, $2 children 3–6, children under 3 free. Open daily. Closed Thanksgiving and Christmas.*

Right across the street from the mine, in Queens Plaza, is the **Mining and Historical Museum,** housed in the old redbrick Phelps Dodge general office (Phelps Dodge was the operator of the town's copper mines). The museum is filled with old photographs and artifacts from the town's mining days, and explores other aspects of the first 40 years of Bisbee's history, from 1887 to 1920. It's fun to walk out of the museum and view those same buildings you've just seen depicted inside. *Queens Plaza, tel. 602/432–7071. Admission: $3 adults, $2 senior citizens, children under 18 free. Open daily 10–5. Closed Christmas and New Year's Day.*

Behind the museum is the venerable old **Copper Queen Hotel** (*see* Lodging, *below*), built a century ago. It has housed the famous as well as the infamous: "Black Jack" Pershing, John Wayne, Teddy Roosevelt, and mining executives from all over the world made this their home away from home. The walls are hung with historic photographs and framed mementos such as checks for lodging, stock transfers, and correspondence relating to other business transactions that took place more than a hundred years ago (check out the ones by the public telephones in the lobby).

The Copper Queen is adjacent to **Brewery Gulch,** today a short street running north and south (walk out the front door of the Copper Queen, make a left, and you'll be there within about 20 paces) that's largely abandoned and lined with boarded-up storefronts. In the old days, the brewery housed there allowed the dregs of the beer that was being brewed to flow down the street and into the gutter.

Time Out **Café Maxie** (tel. 602/432–7063), in –2 Copper Queen Plaza, once the Phelps Dodge General Mercantile Store and now the town's convention center, is a good place for homemade soups and sandwiches. The eclectic menu reflects the background of the owners, Steve and Ida Jensen—he's German, she's Italian. Brightly colored parachutes are suspended from the ceiling, creating a festive, airy atmosphere. Take a trip upstairs to the rest rooms for a view of the lobby down below, with its rich copper (what else?) light fixtures and handrails.

There are no boarded-up storefronts on Bisbee's **Main Street,** which is very much alive and retailing. This hilly commercial thoroughfare is lined with appealing crafts shops, boutiques, and restaurants, many of them in well-preserved turn-of-the-century brick buildings.

From Bisbee, continue southeast on U.S. 80 until you reach **Douglas,** on the U.S.–Mexico border. The town was founded in 1902 by James Douglas to serve as the copper-smelting center for the mines in Bisbee. Before then, the site was the annual roundup ground for local ranchers, Mexican and American—among them John Slaughter, who was the sheriff of Cochise County after Wyatt Earp. Douglas's house, now owned by the Arizona Historical Society, is open to the public as the **Douglas/Williams House Museum** (1001 D Ave., tel. 602/364–7370), and the 300-acre **Slaughter Ranch/San Bernardino Land Grant** (17 mi east of Douglas, tel. 602/558–2474) is a National Historic Landmark. Both are worth a visit, but the must-see in town is the **Gadsden Hotel** (*see* Lodging, *below*), built in 1907. The lobby boasts a solid white Italian marble staircase, two authentic Tiffany vaulted skylights, and a 42-foot stained-glass mural; 1,000 ounces of 14-karat gold leaf were used to decorate the capitals. When you leave the hotel and walk out onto G Street, Douglas's main thoroughfare, you'll be taking a stroll back through time; a film company shooting here recently had to do very little to make the restaurants and shopfronts fit its 1940s plot line.

Neither Douglas nor Agua Prieta across the way in Mexico, fit the stereotype of border towns—both are clean, pleasant places. **Agua Prieta** offers well-priced Mexican goods, and shopping here involves neither haggling nor hassling. But it's easy to imagine you're far from the States when you sit in the leafy plaza at the center of town.

After touring Douglas, get back on U.S. 80 in the direction of Bisbee. It's less than a half-mile to the turnoff for U.S. 666; go north on this road for about 41 miles until you reach the intersection with AZ 181, where signs will direct you to Chiricahua National Monument, approximately 10 miles away.

The vast fields of desert grass you've passed during most of the drive are suddenly transformed into a landscape of forest, mountains, and striking rock formations as you enter the 12,000-acre **Chiricahua National Monument.** Dubbed the "Land of the Standing-Up Rocks" by the Chiricahua Apache, who lived in the mountains for centuries—and, led by Cochise and Geronimo, tried for 25 years to prevent white pioneers from settling here—this is an unusual site for a variety of reasons. The vast outcroppings of volcanic rock worn by erosion into strange pinnacles and spires are set in a forest where autumn and spring occur at the same time; because of the particular balance of sunshine and rain in the area, in April and May visitors will see brown, yellow, and red leaves co-existing with new green foliage. Summer in Chiricahua National Monument is exceptionally wet: From July through September, there are thunderstorms nearly every afternoon. In addition, few other areas in the United States have such a variety of plant, bird, and animal life; along with the plants and animals of the Southwest, the Chiracahua Mountains also host a number of Mexican species. Deer, coatimundis, peccaries, and lizards live among the aspen, ponderosa pine, Douglas fir, oak, and cyprus trees—to name just a few. This is a natural mecca for bird-watchers, and hikers have more than 17 miles of scenic trails, ranging from a half-mile to 13 miles long. At the visitor center, you can purchase a brochure describing the trails for 10¢; free lists of the mammals, snakes, and birds in the region are also available, and in spring and summer rangers give interpretive talks at the visitor center or at the campground amphitheater. *Chiricahua National Monument, Dos Cabezas Route, Box 6500, Willcox, AZ 85643, tel. 602/824–3560. Entry fee: $4 per car. Visitor center open daily 8–5.*

In Chiricahua National Monument, AZ 181 turns into AZ 186. Continue north on this road for about 5 miles; you'll see signs directing you to the well-maintained gravel road leading to Bowie and the **Fort Bowie National Historical Site,** in the Dos Cabezas (Two-Headed) Mountains. A ranger station here (tel. 602/847–2500) is open daily from 8 AM until 5 PM. Admission to the site is free.

The fort and the nearby **Butterfield stage stop** played important parts in Arizona's history. The stage stop, in the heart of Chiricahua Apache land, was a crucial link in the journey from East to West in the mid-19th century. Chief Cochise and the stagecoach operators ignored one another until sometime in 1861, when hostilities broke out between U.S. Cavalry troops and the Apache. After an ambush by the chief's warriors at Apache Pass in 1862, U.S. troops decided a fort was desperately needed in the area, and Fort Bowie was built within weeks. There were skirmishes for the next 10 years, followed by a peaceful decade; then renewed fighting broke out in 1881. Geronimo, the new leader of the Indian warriors, finally surrendered in 1886. The fort was abandoned eight years later and fell into disrepair.

In order to get to the fort from the ranger station, you must take a 1½-mile unpaved footpath. Today the site is virtually in ruins, and there is no showcase museum or visitor center (though there are picnic grounds and rest rooms). Instead, there is an eerie silence in this place, where the last of

Arizona's battles between Native Americans and U.S. troops was fought.

When you get back to the gravel road, take it another 6 miles north until you reach Bowie, where you'll pick up I–10. If you take it west for 15 miles, you'll arrive at the turn-off for the town of **Willcox.** With fewer than 4,000 residents, Willcox is a major cattle-shipping center; its downtown looks like an Old West movie set. An elevation of 4,167 feet renders the climate here moderate in summer and a bit chilly in winter. Apple pie fans from all over Arizona know this little town, located in an apple-growing area, as headquarters; enterprising Willcox cooks bake pies for customers as far away as Phoenix.

Stay on the I–10 frontage road and follow the signs to the historical district. Here you'll find the **Rex Allen Arizona Cowboy Museum,** set up as a tribute to Willcox's most famous native son, cowboy singer Rex Allen. He starred in several rather average cowboy movies during the '40s and '50s for Republic Pictures, but he's probably most famous as the friendly voice that narrated Walt Disney nature films. *155 N. Railroad Ave., tel. 602/384-4583. Suggested donation: $2 single, $3 couple, $5 family. Open daily 10–4. Closed Thanksgiving, Christmas, and New Year's Day.*

Less than a block down the street is the **Willcox Commercial Store.** Established in 1881, it's the oldest retail establishment in Arizona that's still operating in its original location; locals like to boast that Geronimo used to shop here. Today it's a clothing store, with a large selection of western wear.

As you leave town, stop at **Stout's Cider Mill** (it's on the frontage road to I–10—roll down your windows and follow the aroma of apples and nutmeg). Adjacent to Stout's, the **Museum of the Southwest** focuses on the life of the cowboy and the Native American in the late 1800s and early 1900s; the Cowboy Hall of Fame salutes the Arizona cattlemen. *1500 N. Circle I Rd., tel. 602/384-2272. Admission free. Open Mon.–Sat. 9–5, Sun. 1–5.*

To return to Tucson from Willcox, take I–10 west for 78 miles. It's an easy drive, unless you're doing it in the summertime toward the end of the day. You're best off waiting until the sun has gone down and out of your eyes.

Dining and Lodging

Bisbee **Roka.** Opened in early 1993 by the chef who drew diners to
Dining The Wine Gallery Bistro (*see below*), Roka is already the
★ darling of the hip Bisbee crowd. The constantly changing Northern Italian–style evening menu is small, but you can count on whatever you order—chicken with ricotta and basil cannelloni, sea scallops with spinach pasta—to be wonderful. Portions are generous, and the entrée price

($9.50–$14) includes soup, salad, and a pasta-based main course preceded by a sorbet. Lunch is a more casual, mostly vegetarian affair. The dining room, with exposed brick walls and the original 1906 tinwork ceiling, looks onto a central bar, which offers a nice selection of wines and cognacs. *35 Main St., tel. 602/432–5153. Reservations advised. Dress: casual but neat. No smoking. MC, V. Closed Sun. and Mon. Moderate.*

Stenzel's. Although this small, attractive restaurant, set in a wooden cabin off the side of the road, is touted by locals for its seafood specialties, they're not really Stenzel's strongest suit. The barbecued ribs and grilled chicken breast are fine, however, and the fettuccine Alfredo is outstanding. There's a decent wine list, and this is a good place to try the excellent Electric ale brewed locally. *207 Tombstone Canyon, tel. 602/432–7611. Reservations advised for dinner. Dress: casual. No credit cards; personal checks accepted. Closed Tues.; dinner only weekends. Moderate.*

The Wine Gallery Bistro. A favorite of many of the Yuppie residents in town, this cozy little place, located on three levels of another of Bisbee's venerable old buildings, features an excellent wine list, focusing on California bottles. Tasty homemade soups are served at lunch; the contemporary southwestern menu changes constantly, but there's always a good range of seafood, poultry, and vegetarian entrées for dinner. Dishes might include *crêpes Provençale* with a spicy vegetable filling, or Athenian shrimp broiled with feta cheese. *41 Main St., 602/432–3447. Reservations accepted. Dress: informal. No credit cards. Closed Sun. and Mon. Moderate.*

Lodging
★ **Copper Queen Hotel.** Built by the Copper Queen Mining Company (which later became the Phelps Dodge Corporation) at a time when Bisbee was the biggest copper-mining town in the world, this hotel in the heart of downtown Bisbee was built in 1902. Some of the rooms are tiny and the walls are thin, but there's a Victorian charm about the place. Guests over the years have included a host of wild and crazy prospectors as well as more respectable types. Today's visitors are also a varied lot, as likely to include a film producer scouting locations as a retired snowbird from Minnesota or a family from Phoenix. *11 Howell Ave., Drawer CQ, 85603, tel. 602/432–2216 or 800/247–5829. 43 rooms with bath. Facilities: pool, dining room, saloon, gift shop. AE, MC, V. Moderate.*

The Bisbee Grand Hotel. Restored to Victorian excess in 1986, this 1906 structure on Main Street has 11 elaborately decorated accommodations. Some feature huge brass beds, others beds with lush red-velvet canopies; one suite even has a fountain with running water in its sitting room. The lodging section is adjoined by a western saloon and "ladies parlor." In keeping with the general melodrama of the place, the Bisbee Grand runs themed murder mystery weekends. *61 Main St., Box 825, 85603, tel. 602/432–5900* *or 800/421–1909. 4 rooms and 3 suites with bath, 4 rooms share 3 baths. Facilities: bar, meeting rooms, complimentary breakfast. AE, MC, V. Inexpensive–Moderate.*

Clawson B&B. Terrific views of the town from the sun porch, a light-filled kitchen, and generous but health-conscious breakfasts are among the reasons to seek out this B&B on Old Bisbee's Castle Rock. The owners' art and antiques collections grace a beautifully restored former residence, built in 1895 for the manager of the Copper Queen Mine. *116 Clawson Ave., Box 454, 85603, tel. 602/432–5237. 1 room with bath, 2 rooms share bath. MC, V. Inexpensive–Moderate.*

Douglas
Lodging

The Gadsden Hotel. Although recently refurbished, the rooms at this hotel—declared a National Historic Monument in 1976—are rather strangely decorated: Some fine antique pieces are thrown in among mismatched rugs, bedspreads, and drapes; the shower curtains are discordantly modern. But the accommodations, which include suites and apartments with kitchenettes, are clean, comfortable, and very reasonably priced, and the art-deco–style public areas are beautifully maintained. The hotel bar, with its array of local brands and local characters, looks to be straight out of *The Life and Times of Judge Roy Bean*, which was filmed here. *1046 G Ave., 85607, tel. 602/364–4481. 160 rooms with bath. Facilities: restaurant, coffee shop, bar, dress shop, beauty salon. AE, D, MC, V. Inexpensive.*

Pearce
Dining and
Lodging
★

Grapevine Canyon Ranch. This guest ranch in the Dragoon Mountains, approximately 80 miles southeast of Tucson, adjoins a working cattle ranch. Visitors get the chance to watch—and, in some cases, participate in—real day-to-day cowboy activities. Horses for all levels of experience are on hand, and there are lots of trails for hiking this quintessentially Western terrain. Grapevine is also a good base from which to explore towns such as Douglas, Tombstone, and Bisbee, and nearby Chiricahua National Monument. Accommodations, either in adjacent cabins or private casitas, vary—some are rather plain, while others have striking southwestern-style furnishings—but all have spacious decks and porches. There's a four-night minimum stay during peak season, two-night minimum off-season. *Box 302, 85625, tel. 602/826–3185, fax 602/826–3636. 12 rooms with bath. Facilities: pool, hot tub, riding, game room, TV/video room, gift shop. AE, D, MC, V. Expensive.*

Tombstone
Dining

Bella Union. A good spot for a leisurely dinner—service is none too swift here—the Bella Union offers well-priced American standards such as steaks and chops in a nice setting. The 1881 building, off the main commercial drag, has a tastefully restored front saloon with a piano and low-key dining room decor. An olde-gazette–style menu highlights breakfast combinations, blue-plate lunch specials, and a wide range of dinner entrées; live dinner shows are presented on weekends. *401 E. Fremont St., tel. 602/457–3656.*

Reservations advised for dinner shows. Dress: casual. AE, D, MC, V. Moderate.

Longhorn Restaurant. Like most of the places in town, this one has been rigged up for the city slickers, so they'll get an idea of what it was like to grab some grub about 100 years ago in these here parts. Done in dark woods, the Longhorn is decorated with posters and artifacts from Tombstone's wilder days. Burgers, sandwiches, steaks, and Mexican dishes are available here. Service is very efficient. *Allen and 5th Sts., tel. 602/457–3405. No reservations. Dress: informal. MC, V. Inexpensive.*

Lodging **The Best Western Look-Out Lodge.** Set off U.S. 80 on the way into town, this motel has a lot of character. The rooms, refurbished in 1992, feature western-print bedspreads, Victorian-style lamps, and locally made wood-hewn clocks; all have views of the Dragoon Mountains and desert valley. A Continental breakfast is included in the rate. The front desk closes at 10 PM, so you'll need to check in and make your phone calls before then. *Hwy. 80 West, Box 787, 85638, tel. 602/457–2223 or 800/528–1234. 40 rooms with bath. AE, D, DC, MC, V. Facilities: heated outdoor pool. Inexpensive–Moderate.*

Buford House B&B. Built as a boarding house in 1880, this Territorial-style adobe structure looks modest from the outside but boasts four very attractively decorated theme rooms. The downstairs walls are lined with historical photographs. One of the former owners, Cid Wilson, was the last stagecoach driver in Arizona and repaired coaches for Hollywood westerns in the 1930s and '40s. Breakfasts include homemade breads and a house-special potato, egg, and cheese casserole. Ask about the murder mystery weekends and the chuck wagon cookout packages. *113 E. Safford St., Box 38, 85638, tel. 602/457–3168 or 800/355–1880. 1 room with bath, 3 rooms share bath. Facilities: hot tub, barbecue area. No credit cards. Inexpensive–Moderate.*

Southwestern Arizona

Many folks just speed through Southwestern Arizona on their way to California, but the area has much to offer travelers willing to slow down for a closer look. The turbulent history of the west is writ large in this now-sleepy part of the state. It's home to the Tohonó O'odham Indian reservation (largest in the country after the Navajo Nation's) and site of such towns as Ajo, created—and almost undone—by the copper-mining industry. Yuma, abutting the California border, was a major crossing point of the Colorado River as far back as the time of the Conquistadors.

Natural history is also a lure in this starkly scenic region: Organ Pipe Cactus National Monument provides a number of trails for desert hikers, while birders and other nature watchers will revel in the many unusual species to be observed at the little-visited Imperial National Wildlife Refuge on the lower Colorado.

Essential Information

Getting There Running north–south, AZ 85 to **Ajo** connects with the east–
By Car west I–8 at Gila Bend and with I–10 at Buckeye. For a scenic route west from Tucson, take AZ 86, which hooks up with AZ 85 at Why.

From the east, I–10 intersects with I–8 to **Yuma** near the town of Casa Grande; it's then a direct drive along I–8 west to San Diego. U.S. 95 is the route to take south from Las Vegas; it continues on past Yuma into Mexico.

By Bus You can get to Yuma via **Greyhound;** call your local office for information.

The **Ajo Stage Line** (tel. 800/242–9483) has twice-weekly bus service from Tucson to Ajo.

By Train **Amtrak** (tel. 800/872–7245) runs trains to Yuma from Tucson and Los Angeles three times a week.

By Plane Both **Delta Airlines** (tel. 800/453–9417) and **America West** (tel. 800/247–5692) have frequent direct flights to Yuma from Phoenix. Delta also flies nonstop from Los Angeles, while America West offers nonstops from Las Vegas.

Tourist **Ajo Chamber of Commerce** (Hwy. 85, just south of the pla-
Information za, tel. 602/387–7742). Open Mon.–Sat. 8:30–4:30.

Yuma Convention and Visitors Bureau (377 Main St., tel. 602/783–0071). Open weekdays 9–5.

Exploring

Numbers in the margin correspond to points of interest on the Southwestern Arizona map.

On warm weekends and especially during semester breaks, the 130-mile route from Tucson to Ajo is well traveled by cars headed southwest to Puerto Penasco (Rocky Point), Mexico, the closest outlet to the sea for Arizonans. Much of the time, however, one can go for long stretches west on AZ 86 without seeing another vehicle. A great part of the way the landscape is flat, abundant with low-lying scrub and cactus as well as mesquite, ironwood, palo verde, and other desert trees.

About 36 miles out of Tucson, you'll come to the turnoff for Kitt Peak (*see* Tour 5, *above*); to the south is the 7,730-foot Baboquivari Peak, considered sacred by the Tohonó O'odham as the home of their deity, I'itoi or "elder brother." Baboquivari sits on the eastern boundary of the Tohonó O'odham reservation, which covers some 4,400 square miles between Tucson and Ajo, stretching south to the Mexican border and north almost to the city of Casa Grande.

A little less than halfway between Tucson and Ajo, **Sells,** the tribal capital of the Tohonó O'odham, is a good place to stop for gas or a soft drink. Much of the time there's little to see or do here, but in March an annual rodeo and fair attract thousands of visitors; for details, call 602/383–2978.

At **Why,** approximately 60 miles from Sells, AZ 86 forks off into the north and south sections of AZ 85. Originally the name of the community at this Y-shaped intersection was spelled, simply and descriptively, "Y"; but in 1950 the town was told that it had to have a three-letter name in order to be assigned a postal code. Hence the querying appellation that has kept travelers wondering ever since.

❶ Take AZ 85 north for 10 miles to reach **Ajo,** another town with a curious name. "Ajo" (AH-ho) is Spanish for garlic, and some say the town got its name from the wild garlic that grows in the area. Others claim the word is a bastardization of the Indian word "au-auho," referring to red paint derived from a local pigment.

For many years Ajo, like Bisbee to the east, was a thriving Phelps Dodge company town. Copper mining had been attempted in the area in the late 19th century, but it wasn't until the arrival of John Greenway, general manager of the Calumet & Arizona Mining Company, in 1911 that the region began to be developed profitably. Calumet and Phelps Dodge merged in 1935, and the huge New Cornelia pit mine produced millions of tons of copper until the mine finally closed in 1985. With the town's main source of revenue gone, Ajo looked for a time as though it might shut down, but many retirees are now being lured here by the warm climate and low-cost housing.

Ajo, set in a desert valley flanked by low mountain ranges to the north, south, and west, is indeed a very pretty place to live. At the center of town and of community activities is a sparkling white Spanish-style **plaza,** designed in 1917 by Isabella Greenway, wife of the Calumet mine manager and an important figure in her own right: In the 1930s she opened the Arizona Inn in Tucson, and she was friends with such dignitaries as Eleanor Roosevelt. The shops and restaurants that line the plaza's covered arcade today are rather modest; unlike Bisbee, Ajo hasn't yet drawn an artistic crowd—or the upscale boutiques and eateries that tend to follow.

On Indian Village Road at the outskirts of town, the **New Cornelia Open Pit Mine Lookout Point** provides a panoramic view of the town's huge open pit mine, almost 2 miles wide. Some of the abandoned equipment remains in the pit, and various stages of mining operations are diagrammed at the visitors' ramada, which doubles as a real estate office. The number of buildings listed for sale—including the town

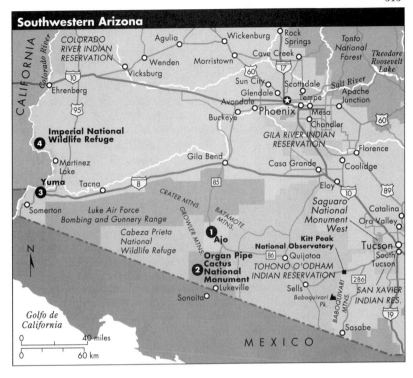

Southwestern Arizona

hospital—comment poignantly on the gaping hole that was once the town's source of revenue.

Nearby, the **Ajo Historical Society Museum** has collected a melange of articles related to Ajo's past from local townspeople. The displays are rather disorganized, but some of the historical photographs and artifacts are fascinating, and the museum is set in the Territorial-style St. Catherine's Indian Mission, built around 1916. *160 Mission St., tel. 602/387–7105. Admission free. Open daily 1–4.*

Twenty minutes from Ajo, the 860,000-acre **Cabeza Prieta National Wildlife Refuge** was established in 1939 as a preserve for endangered bighorn sheep and other Sonoran desert wildlife. A permit is required to enter, and a 4-wheel-drive vehicle recommended to traverse the rugged terrain. For additional information or for an entry permit, contact the refuge office (1611 N. 2nd Ave., Ajo 85321, tel. 602/387–6483).

Anyone interested in exploring the flora and fauna of the Sonoran desert should head for **Organ Pipe Cactus National Monument,** abutting Cabeza Prieta but much more accessible to visitors; from Ajo, backtrack to Why and take AZ 85 south for 22 miles to reach the visitor center. The monument is the largest gathering spot north of the border for organ pipe cacti. These multiarmed cousins of the saguaro are fairly common in Mexico but rare in the States. Because they tend to grow on south-facing slopes, you won't be able to see many of them unless you take one of the two scenic loop drives, the 21-mile Ajo Mountain Drive or the 53-mile Puerto Blanco Drive, both on winding, graded dirt roads. The latter trail, which takes half a day to traverse, brings you to Quitobaquito, a desert oasis with a flowing spring. *Rte. 1, Box 100, Ajo 85321, tel. 602/387–6849. Admission: $4 per vehicle. Visitor center open daily 8–5.*

The drive from Ajo to Yuma is quick if not very picturesque: Take AZ 85 north for 40 miles to Gila Bend to pick up I–8 west. You'll come to three freeway exits for Yuma just before the California border.

❸ Many people tend to think of **Yuma** as a convenient en route stop—these days, between San Diego and Phoenix or Tucson—and this was equally true in the past. It's difficult to imagine the lower Colorado River, now dammed and bridged, as either a barrier or a means of transportation, but up until the early part of the century, this section of the great waterway was a force to contend with. Records show that since at least 1540 the Spanish were using Yuma (then the site of a Quechan Indian village) as a ford across a relatively shallow juncture of the Colorado.

Some three centuries later, the advent of the shallow draft steamboat made the settlement a point of entry for fortune seekers heading up through the Gulf of California for mining sites in eastern Arizona. Fort Yuma was established in 1850 to guard against Indian attacks, and by 1873 the town was a county seat, U.S. Port of Entry, and an army quartermaster depot. The building of the Yuma Territorial Prison in 1876 helped stabilize the economy.

The steamboat shipping business, undermined by the completion of the Southern Pacific Railroad line in 1877, was finished off by the building of Laguna Dam in 1909, which controlled the overflow of the Colorado River and made agricultural development in the area possible. In World War II Yuma Proving Ground was used to train bomber pilots, and General Patton readied some of his desert war forces for battle at a number of classified areas near the city. Many people who served here during the war returned to Yuma to retire, and the city's economy now relies largely on tourism. According to weather statistics, the sun shines more on Yuma than on any other U.S. city.

Most of the interesting sights in Yuma are at the north end of town. Stop in at the Convention and Visitors Bureau (*see* Tourist Information, *above*) and pick up a walking tour guide to the **historic downtown area.** Highlights include the Century House, which now hosts the **Arizona Historical Society Museum.** This adobe structure, built around 1870 and once owned by prominent businessman E.F. Sanguinetti, exhibits artifacts from Yuma's territorial days and details the military presence in the area. It's in a pretty complex with rose gardens, an aviary, small shops, and a restaurant. *240 S. Madison Ave., tel. 602/782–1841. Admission free. Open Oct.–Apr., Tues.–Sat. 10–4, Sun. noon–4. Closed May–Sept.*

If you cross the railroad tracks at the northernmost part of town, you'll come to **Yuma Crossing National Historic Landmark,** which consists of the Quartermaster Depot, the Territorial Prison, and Fort Yuma to the north. The mess hall of the former fort, later used as a school for Indian children, now serves as the **Fort Yuma Quechan Indian Museum.** Historical photographs, archaeological items, and Quechan arts and crafts, including beautiful beadwork, are on display here. *On CA 24, 1 mi north of town, tel. 619/572–0661. Admission 50¢. Open weekdays 8–noon and 1–5. Closed holidays.*

On the other side of the river from Fort Yuma, the **Quartermaster Depot,** created toward the end of the Civil War period, was responsible for resupplying army posts to the north and east. Freight brought upriver by steamboat was unloaded here and distributed by wagon overland to Arizona forts; the depot's earliest building (1853) originally served as the home of riverboat captain G.A. Johnson. Dubbed "the Williamsburg of the West" by *Arizona Highways* magazine, the site has costumed interpreters explaining the displays, with reenactments of historical events on weekends. The quartermaster's office now houses a museum, and other structures are being furnished with period pieces. *Tel. 602/329–0404. Admission: $2 adults, $1.50 senior citizens 55 and over, $1 children 6–15, children 5 and under free. Open daily 10–5.*

Head a few blocks east under the I–8 overpass to get to the most notorious—and fascinating—tourist sight in town, **Yuma Territorial Prison.** Built largely by the convicts themselves, the prison operated from 1876 until 1909, when it outgrew its usefulness. The hilly site on the Colorado River, chosen for security purposes, precluded further expansion.

Visitors gazing today at the tiny cells that held six inmates each, often in 115°F heat, are likely to be appalled, but the prison was once considered a model of enlightenment: In an era when beatings were common, the only punishments meted out were solitary confinement and assignment to a dark cell. The complex housed a hospital as well as the only library in Yuma, open to the public; the 25¢ fee charged townspeople for a prison tour financed the acquisition of new books. The inmates' food was sufficiently varied and plentiful to inspire locals to dub the place the "Country Club of the Colorado."

The 3,069 people who served time at this penal institution, the only one in Arizona territory during its tenure, included men and women from 21 different countries. They came from all social classes and were sent up for everything from armed robbery and murder to violation of the Mexican Neutrality Act and polygamy. R.L. McDonald, incarcerated for forgery, had been the superintendent of the Phoenix public school system; chosen as the prison bookkeeper, he absconded with $130 of the inmates' money when he left. Pearl Hart, convicted of stagecoach robbery, gained such notoriety for her crime that she attempted a career in vaudeville after her release.

Different groups continued to come, more or less voluntarily, after the prison closed. When the local high school burned down, classes were held for four years (1910–14) in the former hospital. In the 1920s rail-riders took a break from the freights to sleep in the unsupervised buildings, and during the Depression the abandoned cells provided shelter for many homeless people. A number of films, including *Red River Valley*, were shot here in the 1930s and '40s. The site of the former mess hall opened as a museum in 1940, and the entire prison complex was designated a State Historic Park in 1961. *Near Exit 1 off I–8, Box 10792, Yuma 85366, tel. 602/783–4771. Admission: $3 adults, $2 juniors 12–17, children 11 and under free. Open daily 8–5; free tours at 9, 11, 2, and 3:30.*

A drive to the far southern end of town will take you past citrus orchards and ranches to the 40-acre **Saihati Camel Farm.** The landscape near Yuma inspired Saudi Arabia native Abdul-Wahed Saihati to raise and breed his favorite animals here, along with Arabian horses and more exotic desert-loving breeds such as oryx and wild cats. It's fun to help feed the well-groomed, friendly dromedaries—not a biter or spitter among 'em—and to see some rare animal species, many of them purchased from the San Diego Zoo, at close range. *15672 S. Ave. 1 E (between County 15th and County 16th Sts.), tel. 602/627–2553. Guided tours $3, daily at 10 and 3. Reservations advised.*

Although shallow river steamers are no longer in operation, you can still take a boat ride up the Colorado with **Yuma River Tours** (1920 Arizona Ave., Yuma 85364, tel. 602/783–4400). Twelve-person jet-boat excursions run by Smokey Knowlton, who has been exploring the area for more than 35 years, offer a unique look at the formerly active life of the river; you glide past Indian petroglyphs as well as abandoned steamboat landings and mining camps. Tours range from one-hour trips ($12.50 per person), which leave from the Quartermaster Depot, to full-day excursions ($49, including lunch) departing from Fisher's Landing at Martinez Lake, 23 miles north of Yuma.

❹ These full-day tours are the best way to visit the 25,765-acre **Imperial National Wildlife Refuge,** created by backwaters formed when the Imperial Dam was built. Something of an anomaly, the refuge is home both to species indigenous to marshy rivers and to creatures which inhabit the Sonoran desert that lines its banks here—desert tortoises, coyotes, bobcats, and bighorn sheep. Most of all, though, this is bird lovers' heaven. Thousands of waterfowl and shorebirds live here year-round, and migrating flocks of swallows pass through in the spring and fall. Expect to see everything from pelicans and cormorants to Canadian geese, snowy egrets, and a variety of rarer species. Canoes can be rented at Martinez Lake Marina, 3½ miles southeast of the refuge headquarters. It's best to visit from mid-October through May, when temperatures are lowest and the ever-present mosquitoes least active. *40 mi north of Yuma off U.S. 95, tel. 602/783-3371. Admission free. Visitor center open mid-May–mid-Oct. weekdays 7–3, weekends 10–2; mid-Oct.–mid-Mar. weekdays 8–4, weekends 10–2; mid-Mar.–mid-May weekdays 7–3, closed weekends.*

Dining and Lodging

Ajo **Guest House Inn.** Built in 1925 to accommodate visiting
Lodging Phelps Dodge VIPs, this lodging is one of six southwest "Bird 'n' Breakfast Fly-Inns": Guests can head out early to nearby Organ Pipe National Monument or just sit on the patio and watch the quail, cactus wrens, and other warblers that visit the Sonora desert. Rooms are furnished in a range of southwestern styles, from light Santa Fe to rich Spanish colonial. *3 Guest House Rd., 85321, tel. 602/387-6133. 4 rooms with bath. DC, MC, V. Inexpensive–Moderate.*

Yuma **Chretin's Mexican Food.** A Yuma institution, Chretin's
Dining opened as a dance hall in the 1930s before it became one of the first Mexican restaurants in town in 1946. Customers enter through the back, passing the kitchen and cashier's stand, into three substantial dining areas decorated with murals and Native American designs. The food is all made on the premises, right down to the chips and tortillas. Popular dishes include the chile rellenos and the beef and chicken machaca burritos; the margaritas are super. *485 S. 15th Ave., tel. 602/782-1291. Reservations accepted except Jan.–Mar. Dress: informal. MC, V. Inexpensive.*

Lutes Casino. Almost always packed with locals at lunchtime, Lutes Casino at the historic North End of town lays claim to be the oldest pool hall and domino parlor in Arizona. This large, funky restaurant and bar, decorated with photos of the bad old days, is the place for a brew and a burger. Try the potato tacos or the "Especial" hot dog/ cheeseburger combo, which tastes a lot better than it sounds. *221 S. Main St., tel. 602/782-2192. No reservations. Dress: informal. No credit cards. Inexpensive.*

Lodging **Holiday Inn Express.** Rooms in this motel, located near a large shopping center, are generic but comfortable. Many complimentary extras are included in the rate: breakfast, cocktail hour, airport shuttle, newspaper, and passes to a nearby health club. All rooms have coffee makers and refrigerators, and a number offer microwaves. *3181 4th Ave., 85364, tel. 602/344–1420 or 800/HOLIDAY, fax 602/341–0158. 120 rooms. Facilities: pool, Jacuzzi, barbecue area, nonsmoking rooms. AE, D, DC, MC, V. Moderate.*

★ **Best Western Coronado Motor Hotel.** This Spanish tile-roofed lodging, convenient to both the freeway and downtown historical sights, was built in 1938 and is run by the son of the original owner. Bob Hope used to stay here during World War II, when he entertained the gunnery troops training in Yuma. Photos of Yuma's territorial days line the walls of the hotel's restaurant, where guests enjoy a free Continental breakfast. The rooms, recently remodeled, have such extras as VCRs (with two free films each night), refrigerators, hair dryers, and modem phone jacks; some have Jacuzzis and microwaves. Family suites with full kitchens are available. *233 4th Ave., 85364, tel. 602/783–4453 or 800/528–1234. 49 rooms, including 20 family suites. Facilities: restaurant, lounge, pool, Jacuzzi, laundromat, video library, 3 gift shops. AE, D, DC, MC, V. Inexpensive–Moderate.*

Index

Personal Itinerary

Departure *Date*

Time

Transportation

Arrival *Date*   *Time*

Departure *Date*   *Time*

Transportation

Accommodations

Arrival *Date*   *Time*

Departure *Date*   *Time*

Transportation

Accommodations

Arrival *Date*   *Time*

Departure *Date*   *Time*

Transportation

Accommodations

Personal Itinerary

Arrival *Date*   *Time*

Departure *Date*   *Time*

Transportation

Accommodations

Arrival *Date*   *Time*

Departure *Date*   *Time*

Transportation

Accommodations

Arrival *Date*   *Time*

Departure *Date*   *Time*

Transportation

Accommodations

Arrival *Date*   *Time*

Departure *Date*   *Time*

Transportation

Accommodations

Personal Itinerary

Arrival *Date* *Time*

Departure *Date* *Time*

Transportation

Accommodations

Arrival *Date* *Time*

Departure *Date* *Time*

Transportation

Accommodations

Arrival *Date* *Time*

Departure *Date* *Time*

Transportation

Accommodations

Arrival *Date* *Time*

Departure *Date* *Time*

Transportation

Accommodations

Addresses

Name	*Name*
Address	*Address*
Telephone	*Telephone*
Name	*Name*
Address	*Address*
Telephone	*Telephone*
Name	*Name*
Address	*Address*
Telephone	*Telephone*
Name	*Name*
Address	*Address*
Telephone	*Telephone*
Name	*Name*
Address	*Address*
Telephone	*Telephone*
Name	*Name*
Address	*Address*
Telephone	*Telephone*
Name	*Name*
Address	*Address*
Telephone	*Telephone*
Name	*Name*
Address	*Address*
Telephone	*Telephone*

Fodor's Travel Guides

Available at bookstores everywhere, or call 1–800–533–6478, 24 hours a day.

U.S. Guides

Alaska

Arizona

Boston

California

Cape Cod, Martha's Vineyard, Nantucket

The Carolinas & the Georgia Coast

Chicago

Colorado

Florida

Hawaii

Las Vegas, Reno, Tahoe

Los Angeles

Maine, Vermont, New Hampshire

Maui

Miami & the Keys

New England

New Orleans

New York City

Pacific North Coast

Philadelphia & the Pennsylvania Dutch Country

The Rockies

San Diego

San Francisco

Santa Fe, Taos, Albuquerque

Seattle & Vancouver

The South

The U.S. & British Virgin Islands

The Upper Great Lakes Region

USA

Vacations in New York State

Vacations on the Jersey Shore

Virginia & Maryland

Waikiki

Walt Disney World and the Orlando Area

Washington, D.C.

Foreign Guides

Acapulco, Ixtapa, Zihuatanejo

Australia & New Zealand

Austria

The Bahamas

Baja & Mexico's Pacific Coast Resorts

Barbados

Berlin

Bermuda

Brazil

Brittany & Normandy

Budapest

Canada

Cancun, Cozumel, Yucatan Peninsula

Caribbean

China

Costa Rica, Belize, Guatemala

The Czech Republic & Slovakia

Eastern Europe

Egypt

Euro Disney

Europe

Europe's Great Cities

Florence & Tuscany

France

Germany

Great Britain

Greece

The Himalayan Countries

Hong Kong

India

Ireland

Israel

Italy

Japan

Kenya & Tanzania

Korea

London

Madrid & Barcelona

Mexico

Montreal & Quebec City

Morocco

Moscow & St. Petersburg

The Netherlands, Belgium & Luxembourg

New Zealand

Norway

Nova Scotia, Prince Edward Island & New Brunswick

Paris

Portugal

Provence & the Riviera

Rome

Russia & the Baltic Countries

Scandinavia

Scotland

Singapore

South America

Southeast Asia

Spain

Sweden

Switzerland

Thailand

Tokyo

Toronto

Turkey

Vienna & the Danube Valley

Yugoslavia

Special Series

Fodor's Affordables

Caribbean

Europe

Florida

France

Germany

Great Britain

London

Italy

Paris

**Fodor's Bed &
Breakfast and
Country Inns Guides**

Canada's Great
Country Inns

California

Cottages, B&Bs and
Country Inns of
England and Wales

Mid-Atlantic Region

New England

The Pacific
Northwest

The South

The Southwest

The Upper Great
Lakes Region

The West Coast

The Berkeley Guides

California

Central America

Eastern Europe

France

Germany

Great Britain &
Ireland

Mexico

Pacific Northwest &
Alaska

San Francisco

**Fodor's Exploring
Guides**

Australia

Britain

California

The Caribbean

Florida

France

Germany

Ireland

Italy

London

New York City

Paris

Rome

Singapore & Malaysia

Spain

Thailand

Fodor's Flashmaps

New York

Washington, D.C.

Fodor's Pocket Guides

Bahamas

Barbados

Jamaica

London

New York City

Paris

Puerto Rico

San Francisco

Washington, D.C.

Fodor's Sports

Cycling

Hiking

Running

Sailing

The Insider's Guide
to the Best Canadian
Skiing

Skiing in the USA
& Canada

**Fodor's Three-In-Ones
(guidebook, language
cassette, and phrase
book)**

France

Germany

Italy

Mexico

Spain

**Fodor's
Special-Interest
Guides**

Accessible USA

Cruises and Ports
of Call

Euro Disney

Halliday's New
England Food
Explorer

Healthy Escapes

London Companion

Shadow Traffic's New
York Shortcuts and
Traffic Tips

Sunday in New York

Walt Disney World
and the Orlando Area

Walt Disney World
for Adults

**Fodor's Touring
Guides**

Touring Europe

Touring USA:
Eastern Edition

**Fodor's Vacation
Planners**

Great American
Vacations

National Parks
of the East

National Parks
of the West

**The Wall Street
Journal Guides to
Business Travel**

Europe

International Cities

Pacific Rim

USA & Canada

INTRODUCING

Fodor's WORLDVIEW
TRAVEL UPDATE

AT LAST, YOUR OWN PERSONALIZED LIST OF WHAT'S GOING ON IN THE CITIES YOU'RE VISITING.

KEYED TO THE DAYS WHEN YOU'RE THERE, CUSTOMIZED FOR YOUR INTERESTS, AND SENT TO YOU BEFORE YOU LEAVE HOME.

EXCLUSIVE FOR PURCHASERS OF FODOR'S GUIDES...

Fodor's WORLDVIEW
TRAVEL UPDATE

Introducing a revolutionary way to get customized, time-sensitive travel information just before your trip.

Now you can obtain detailed information about what's going on in each city you'll be visiting <u>before</u> you leave home—up-to-the-minute, objective information about the events and activities that interest you most.

This is a special offer for purchasers of Fodor's guides – a customized Travel Update to fit your specific interests and your itinerary.

Travel Updates contain the kind of time-sensitive insider information you can get only from local contacts – or from city magazines and newspapers once you arrive. But now you can have the same information before you leave for your trip.

The choice is yours: current art exhibits, theater, music festivals and special concerts, sporting events, antiques and flower shows, shopping, fitness, and more.

The information comes from hundreds of correspondents and thousands of sources worldwide. Updated continuously, it's like having your own personal concierge or friend in the city.

You specify the cities and when you'll be there. We'll do the rest — personalizing the information for you the way no guidebook can.

It's the perfect extension to your Fodor's guide and the best way to make the most of your valuable travel time.

Your Itinerary:
Customized reports available for 160 destinations

9-1
Rege
The
in this
domain
tion as Jo
worthwhile
the perfoma
Tickets are us
venue. Altern
mances are cance
given. For more in
Open-Air Theatre, In
NW1 4NP Open Air
Tel: 935-5756. Ends: 9-1
International Air Tattoo
Held biennially, the world's
military air display incl
demostra-
tions, militar
bands a

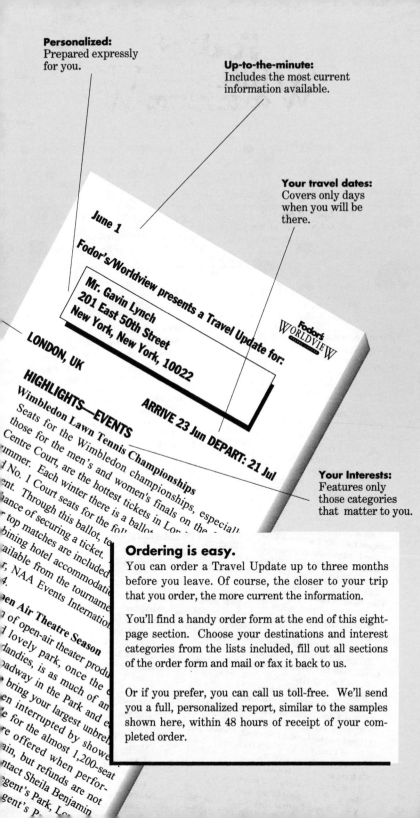

Personalized:
Prepared expressly for you.

Up-to-the-minute:
Includes the most current information available.

Your travel dates:
Covers only days when you will be there.

June 1

Fodor's/Worldview presents a Travel Update for:

Mr. Gavin Lynch
201 East 50th Street
New York, New York, 10022

Fodor's
WORLDVIEW

LONDON, UK

ARRIVE 23 Jun DEPART: 21 Jul

HIGHLIGHTS—EVENTS

Wimbledon Lawn Tennis Championships
Seats for the Wimbledon championships, especial
those for the men's and women's finals on the
Centre Court, are the hottest tickets in Lon
ummer. Each winter there is a ballo
No. 1 Court seats for the fol
ent. Through this ballot, te
ance of securing a ticket.
bining hotel accommodati
top matches are included.
ailable from the tourname
, NAA Events Internatio
4.

Your Interests:
Features only those categories that matter to you.

en Air Theatre Season
of open-air theater produ
lovely park, once the
dandies, is as much of an
adway in the Park and e
bring your largest unbre
en interrupted by showe
e for the almost 1,200-seat
e offered when perfor-
ain, but refunds are not
ntact Sheila Benjamin
gent's Park, Lo
gent's P

Ordering is easy.

You can order a Travel Update up to three months before you leave. Of course, the closer to your trip that you order, the more current the information.

You'll find a handy order form at the end of this eight-page section. Choose your destinations and interest categories from the lists included, fill out all sections of the order form and mail or fax it back to us.

Or if you prefer, you can call us toll-free. We'll send you a full, personalized report, similar to the samples shown here, within 48 hours of receipt of your completed order.

Fodor's
WORLDVIEW
TRAVEL UPDATE

Special concerts—
who's performing
what and where

One-of-a-kind,
one-time-only events

Special interest,
in-depth listings

Children — Events

Angel Canal Festival
The festivities include a children's funfair, entertainers, a boat rally and displays on the water. Regent's Canal. Islington. N1. Tube: Angel. Tel: 267 9100. 11:30am-5:30pm. 7/04.

Blackheath Summer Kite Festival
Stunt kite displays with parachuting teddy bears and trade stands. Free admission. SE3. BR: Blackheath. 10am. 6/27.

Megabugs
Children will delight in this infestation of giant robotic insects, including a praying mantic 60 times life size. Mon-Sat 10am-6pm; Sun 11am-6pm. Admission 4.50 pounds. Natural History Museum, Cromwell Road. SW7. Tube: South Kensington. Tel: 938 9123. Ends 10/01.

Childminders
This establishment employs only women, providing nurses and qualified nannies to

Music — Jazz & Blues

Tito Puente's Golden Men of Latin Jazz
The father of mambo and Cuban rumba king comes to town. Royal Festival Hall. South Bank. SE1. Tube: Waterloo. Tel: 928 8800. 8pm. 7/15.

Georgie Fame and The New York Band
Riding a popular tide with his latest album, the smoky-voiced Fame and his keyboard are on a tour yet again. The Grand. Clapham Junction. SW11. BR: Clapham Junction. Tel: 738 9000 7:30pm. 7/07.

Jacques Loussier Play Bach Trio
The French jazz classicist and colleagues. Kenwood Lakeside. Hampstead Lane. Kenwood. NW3. Tube: Golders Green, then bus 210. Tel: 413 1443. 7pm. 7/10.

Tony Bennett and Ronnie Scott
Royal Festival Hall. South Bank. SE1. Tube: Waterloo. Tel: 928 8800. 8pm. 7/11.

Santana
Royal Festival Hall. South Bank. SE1. Tube: Waterloo. Tel: 928 8800. 8pm. 7/12.

Count Basie Orchestra and Nancy Wilson Trio
Royal Festival Hall. South Bank. SE1. Tube Waterloo. Tel: 928 8800. 8pm. 7/14.

King Pleasure and the Biscuit Boys
Royal Festival Hall. South Bank. SE1. Tube Waterloo. Tel: 928 8800. 6:30 and 9pm. 7/16.

Al Green and the London Community Gospel Choir
Royal Festival Hall. South Bank. SE1. Tube Waterloo. Tel: 928 8800. 8pm. 7/13.

BB King and Linda Hopkins
Mother of the blues and successor to Bessi Smith, Hopkins meets up with "Blues Boy King. Royal Festival Hall. South Bank. SE 928 8800. 6:30 and 9pr

Music — Classical

Marylebone Sinfonia
Kenneth Gowen conducts music by Puc and Rossini. Queen Elizabeth Hall. S Bank. SE1. Tube: Waterloo. Tel: 928 8 7:45pm. 7/16.

London Philharmonic
Franz Welser-Moest and George Benj conduct selections by Alexander G Messiaen, and some of Benjamin's own positions. Queen Elizabeth Hall. South SE1. Tube: Waterloo. Tel: 928 8800. 8p

London Pro Arte Orchestra and Forest C
Murray Stewart conducts selectio Rossini, Haydn and Jonathan Willcocks Queen Elizabeth Hall. South Bank. Tube: Waterloo. Tel: 928 8800. 7:45pm

Kensington Symphony Orchestra
Russell Keable conducts Dvorak's Elizabeth Hall. South Bank

Here's what you get . . .

Detailed information about what's going on — precisely when you'll be there.

Show openings
during your visit

Reviews by
local critics

Exhibitions & Shows—Antique & Flower

Westminster Antiques Fair

Over 50 stands with pre-1830 furniture and other Victorian and earlier items. Thu-Fri 11am-8pm; Sat-Sun 11am-6pm. Admission 4 pounds, children free. Old Royal Horticultural Hall. Vincent Square. SW1. Tel: 0444/48 25 14. 6-24 thru 6/27.

Royal Horticultural Society Flower Show

The show includes displays of carnations, summer fruit and vegetables. Tue 11am-7pm; Wed 10am-5pm. Admission Tue 4 pounds, Wed 2 pounds. Royal Horticultural Halls. Greycoat Street and Vincent Square. SW1. Tube: Victoria. 7/20 thru 7/21.

Hampton Court Palace International Flower Show

Major international garden and flower show taking place in conjunction with the British

eater — Musical

Sunset Boulevard

In June, the four Andrew Lloyd Webber musicals which dominated London's stages in the 1980s (Cats, Starlight Express, Phantom of the Opera and Aspects of Love) are joined by the composer's latest work, a show rumored to have his best music to date. The 1950 Billy Wilder film about a helpless young writer who is drawn into the world of a possessive, aging silent screen star offers rich opportunities for Webber's evolving style. Soaring, aching melodies, lush technical effects and psychological thrills are all expected. Patti Lupone stars. Mon-Sat at 8pm; matinee Thu-Sat at 3pm. In-person sales only at the box office; credit card bookings, Tel: 344 0055. Admission 15-32.50 pounds. Adelphi Theatre. The Strand. WC2. Tube: Charing Cross. Tel: 836 7611. Starts: 6/21

Leonardo A Portrait of Love

A new musical about the great Renaissance arti and inventor comes in for a London premier tested by a brief run at Oxford's Old Fire Stati utumn. The work explores the relations Vinci and the woman

Alberquerque • Atlanta • Atlantic City • Ne
Baltimore • Boston • Chicago • Cincinnati
Cleveland • Dallas/Ft.Worth • Denver • De
• Houston • Kansas City • Las Vegas • Los
Angeles • Memphis • Miami • Milwaukee •
New Orleans • New York City • Orlando •
Springs • Philadelphia • Phoenix • Pittsburg
Portland • Salt Lake • San Antonio • San Di
• San Franc • Seattle • St Louis • Tamp
Oslo • Was lu • Island •
Hawaii • Kauai • Maui • Abacos • Bimini
Ex Countryside • Hamilton • uilla
Ber
Antigua & B
Gorda • Barbados • Dominica • Gren
cia • St. Vincent • Trinidad &Tobago
ymans • Puerto Plata • Santo Doming
Aruba • Bonaire • Curacao • St. Ma
ec City • Montreal • Ottawa • Toron
Vancouver • Guadeloupe • Martiniqu
elemy • St. Martin • Kingston • Ixta
o Bay • Negril • Ocho Rios • Ponce
• Grand Turk • Providenciales • S
St. John • St. Thomas • Acapulco •
& Isla Mujeres • Cozumel • Guadal
a • Los Cabos • Manzinillo • Mazatl
City • Monterrey • Oaxaca • Puerto
do • Puerto Vallarta • Veracruz • Ix
am • Athens • Barcelona •

Fodor's WORLDVIEW
TRAVEL UPDATE

Spectator Sports — Other Sports

Greyhound Racing: Wembley Stadium

This dog track offers good views of greyhound racing held on Mon, Wed and Fri. No credit cards. Stadium Way. Wembley. HA9. Tube: Wembley Park. Tel: 902 8833.

Benson & Hedges Cricket Cup Final

Lord's Cricket Ground. St. John's Wood Road. NW8. Tube: St. John's Wood. Tel: 289 1611. 11am. 7/10.

siness-Fax & Overnight Mail

Post Office, Trafalgar Square Branch

Offers a network of fax services, the Intelpost system, throughout the country and abroad. Mon-Sat 8am-8pm, Sun 9am-5pm. William IV Street. WC2. Tube: Charing Cross. Tel: 930 9580

Interest Categories

For your personalized Travel Update, choose the categories you're most interested in from this list. Every Travel Update automatically provides you with *Event Highlights* – the best of what's happening during the dates of your trip.

1.	**Business Services**	Fax & Overnight Mail, Computer Rentals, Photocopying, Secretarial , Messenger, Translation Services

Dining

2.	**All Day Dining**	Breakfast & Brunch, Cafes & Tea Rooms, Late-Night Dining
3.	**Local Cuisine**	In Every Price Range—from Budget Restaurants to the Special Splurge
4.	**European Cuisine**	Continental, French, Italian
5.	**Asian Cuisine**	Chinese, Far Eastern, Japanese, Indian
6.	**Americas Cuisine**	American, Mexican & Latin
7.	**Nightlife**	Bars, Dance Clubs, Comedy Clubs, Pubs & Beer Halls
8.	**Entertainment**	Theater—Drama, Musicals, Dance, Ticket Agencies
9.	**Music**	Classical, Traditional & Ethnic, Jazz & Blues, Pop, Rock
10.	**Children's Activities**	Events, Attractions
11.	**Tours**	Local Tours, Day Trips, Overnight Excursions, Cruises
12.	**Exhibitions, Festivals & Shows**	Antiques & Flower, History & Cultural, Art Exhibitions, Fairs & Craft Shows, Music & Art Festivals
13.	**Shopping**	Districts & Malls, Markets, Regional Specialities
14.	**Fitness**	Bicycling, Health Clubs, Hiking, Jogging
15.	**Recreational Sports**	Boating/Sailing, Fishing, Ice Skating, Skiing, Snorkeling/Scuba, Swimming
16.	**Spectator Sports**	Auto Racing, Baseball, Basketball, Football, Horse Racing, Ice Hockey, Soccer

Please note that interest category content will vary by season, destination, and length of stay.

Destinations

The Fodor's/Worldview Travel Update covers more than 160 destinations world-wide. Choose the destinations that match your itinerary from this list. (Choose bulleted destinations only.)

United States (Mainland)
- Albuquerque
- Atlanta
- Atlantic City
- Baltimore
- Boston
- Chicago
- Cincinnati
- Cleveland
- Dallas/Ft. Worth
- Denver
- Detroit
- Houston
- Kansas City
- Las Vegas
- Los Angeles
- Memphis
- Miami
- Milwaukee
- Minneapolis/ St. Paul
- New Orleans
- New York City
- Orlando
- Palm Springs
- Philadelphia
- Phoenix
- Pittsburgh
- Portland
- St. Louis
- Salt Lake City
- San Antonio
- San Diego
- San Francisco
- Seattle
- Tampa
- Washington, DC

Alaska
- Alaskan Destinations

Hawaii
- Honolulu
- Island of Hawaii
- Kauai
- Maui

Canada
- Quebec City
- Montreal
- Ottawa
- Toronto
- Vancouver

Bahamas
- Abacos
- Eleuthera/ Harbour Island
- Exumas
- Freeport
- Nassau & Paradise Island

Bermuda
- Bermuda Countryside
- Hamilton

British Leeward Islands
- Anguilla
- Antigua & Barbuda
- Montserrat
- St. Kitts & Nevis

British Virgin Islands
- Tortola & Virgin Gorda

British Windward Islands
- Barbados
- Dominica
- Grenada
- St. Lucia
- St. Vincent
- Trinidad & Tobago

Cayman Islands
- The Caymans

Dominican Republic
- Puerto Plata
- Santo Domingo

Dutch Leeward Islands
- Aruba
- Bonaire
- Curacao

Dutch Windward Island
- St. Maarten/ St. Martin

French West Indies
- Guadeloupe
- Martinique
- St. Barthelemy

Jamaica
- Kingston
- Montego Bay
- Negril
- Ocho Rios

Puerto Rico
- Ponce
- San Juan

Turks & Caicos
- Grand Turk
- Providenciales

U.S. Virgin Islands
- St. Croix
- St. John
- St. Thomas

Mexico
- Acapulco
- Cancun & Isla Mujeres
- Cozumel
- Guadalajara
- Ixtapa & Zihuatanejo
- Los Cabos
- Manzanillo
- Mazatlan
- Mexico City
- Monterrey
- Oaxaca
- Puerto Escondido
- Puerto Vallarta
- Veracruz

Europe
- Amsterdam
- Athens
- Barcelona
- Berlin
- Brussels
- Budapest
- Copenhagen
- Dublin
- Edinburgh
- Florence
- Frankfurt
- French Riviera
- Geneva
- Glasgow
- Interlaken
- Istanbul
- Lausanne
- Lisbon
- London
- Madrid
- Milan
- Moscow
- Munich
- Oslo
- Paris
- Prague
- Provence
- Rome
- Salzburg
- St. Petersburg
- Stockholm
- Venice
- Vienna
- Zurich

Pacific Rim Australia & New Zealand
- Auckland
- Melbourne
- Sydney

China
- Beijing
- Guangzhou
- Shanghai

Japan
- Kyoto
- Nagoya
- Osaka
- Tokyo
- Yokohama

Other
- Bangkok
- Hong Kong & Macau
- Manila
- Seoul
- Singapore
- Taipei

Fodor's WORLDVIEW Travel Update **Order Form**

THIS TRAVEL UPDATE IS FOR (Please print):

Name

Address

City	**State**	**ZIP**

Country	**Tel #** ( ) -

Title of this Fodor's guide:

Store and location where guide was purchased:

INDICATE YOUR DESTINATIONS/DATES: Write in below the destinations you want to order. Then fill in your arrival and departure dates for each destination.

		Month	Day		Month	Day
(Sample) LONDON	From:	6 /	21	To:	6 /	30
1	From:	/		To:	/	
2	From:	/		To:	/	
3	From:	/		To:	/	

You can order up to three destinations per Travel Update. Only destinations listed on the previous page are applicable. Maximum amount of time covered by a Travel Update cannot exceed 30 days.

CHOOSE YOUR INTERESTS: Select up to eight categories from the list of interest categories shown on the previous page and circle the numbers below:

1   2   3   4   5   6   7   8   9   10   11   12   13   14   15   16

CHOOSE HOW YOU WANT YOUR TRAVEL UPDATE DELIVERED (Check one):

❏ Please mail my Travel Update to the address above **OR**

❏ Fax it to me at **Fax #** ( ) -

DELIVERY CHARGE (Check one)

	Within U.S. & Canada	Outside U.S. & Canada
First Class Mail	❏ $2.50	❏ $5.00
Fax	❏ $5.00	❏ $10.00
Priority Delivery	❏ $15.00	❏ $27.00

All orders will be sent within 48 hours of receipt of a completed order form.

ADD UP YOUR ORDER HERE. *SPECIAL OFFER FOR FODOR'S PURCHASERS ONLY!*

	Suggested Retail Price	Your Price	This Order
First destination ordered	~~$13.95~~	$ 7.95	$ 7.95
Second destination (if applicable)	~~$ 9.95~~	$ 4.95	+
Third destination (if applicable)	~~$ 9.95~~	$ 4.95	+
Plus delivery charge from above			+
		TOTAL:	$

METHOD OF PAYMENT (Check one): ❏ AmEx   ❏ MC   ❏ Visa   ❏ Discover
❏ Personal Check   ❏ Money Order

Make check or money order payable to: Fodor's Worldview Travel Update

Credit Card # **Expiration Date:**

Authorized Signature

SEND THIS COMPLETED FORM TO:
Fodor's Worldview Travel Update, 114 Sansome Street, Suite 700, San Francisco, CA 94104

OR CALL OR FAX US 24-HOURS A DAY
Telephone **1-800-799-9609** • Fax **1-800-799-9619** (From within the U.S. & Canada)
(Outside the U.S. & Canada: Telephone 415-616-9988 • Fax 415-616-9989)

(Please have this guide in front of you when you call so we can verify purchase.)

Offer valid until 12/31/94.